The Essays of
Virginia Woolf

The Essays of Virginia Woolf

VOLUME I

1904–1912

EDITED BY

ANDREW McNEILLIE

HARCOURT BRACE JOVANOVICH, PUBLISHERS

SAN DIEGO   NEW YORK   LONDON

Library of Congress Cataloging-in-Publication Data
Woolf, Virginia, 1882–1941.
The essays of Virginia Woolf.
Bibliography: p.
Includes index.
Contents: v.1. 1904–1912.
I. McNeillie, Andrew.   II. Title.
PR6045.072A6 1987   824′.912   86-29520
ISBN 0-15-129055-5 (v.1)

Printed in the United States of America
First American edition
B C D E

Contents

Introduction

Virginia Woolf was arguably the last of the great English essayists. In the course of a career of almost forty years as a literary journalist, much of it passed in anonymity in the columns of the *Times Literary Supplement*, she made of the personal essay, the review, the biographical study, the commemorative article, an art of her own. That art is characteristically brilliant and robust. (Virginia Woolf's was emphatically not 'a small talent sedulously cultivated'.)[1] If it is also an art tending to presuppose an acquaintance with literature that the majority could not begin to have had time to acquire, it is none the less democratic in spirit: uncanonical, inquisitive, open, and unacademic. It is quite antithetical, it should be said, both to the 'great traditionalism' of F. R. Leavis, that dire scourge of literary journalism, and to the quest for the higher culture of T. S. Eliot, with whom in other important respects Virginia Woolf has much in common. What is more, it is an art expressed in a fluent, witty and unwaveringly demotic prose.[2] By it, we are forcibly reminded of the traditional nature of so much of Virginia Woolf's achievement, and of her unique position among modernist writers as a woman of letters.

From beginning to end, the essays, which together exceed a million words in length, form an invaluable record of their author's intellectual and professional life, from the years of her apprenticeship to those of her maturity, when she stood recognised as one of the most important writers of her generation.

To date, the most compendious edition of the essays[3] has been that collected by Leonard Woolf and published by The Hogarth Press in 1966 and 1967. Many readers of this introduction will be acquainted with those four volumes. They gathered the essays which Virginia Woolf had herself prepared for publication in book form (in the two series of

The Common Reader, 1925 and 1932) and a similar number of others selected by Leonard Woolf upon the criterion that none 'seemed ... to fall below the standard which Virginia Woolf set for herself in *The Common Reader*'. The essays were divided into two groups – one roughly 'literary and critical', the other 'biographical' – and then further arranged according to a literary-historical chronology, so that 'a critical essay on a writer born in, say, 1659 precedes one on a writer born in, say, 1672, and a biographical essay on Chaucer precedes one on Sir Walter Raleigh'. Leonard Woolf's *Collected Essays* was thus a kind of extended *Common Reader*, presenting us with the essays themselves, or a large selection of them, in a companionable arrangement.

To the reader interested in the author's development and the context in which her professional life was lived, how it began, and how she regarded it, Leonard Woolf's approach offered no assistance. In the twenty years since the *Collected Essays* first appeared, several notable advances in the study and elucidation of Virginia Woolf's life and work have served to underline this inadequacy. We now have Virginia Woolf's complete diary[4] and her correspondence at our disposal, and together these do much to document their author's journalistic career. We have, too, her memoirs, published as *Moments of Being*, and her *Complete Shorter Fiction*; and we have Quentin Bell's masterful biography. A third edition of B. J. Kirkpatrick's bibliography of Virginia Woolf's writings, itemising many newly identified contributions to journals, appeared in 1980; and in 1983 were published two works that are invaluable to students of the essays: *Virginia Woolf's Reading Notebooks* by Brenda R. Silver and *Virginia Woolf's Literary Sources and Allusions: A Guide to the Essays* by Elizabeth Steele. The time, therefore, could hardly be better chosen for the preparation of a new and definitive collection of her essays, of which the present work, reproducing with annotations the articles Virginia Stephen published in the period from 1904 until her marriage in 1912 to Leonard Woolf, is the first of six projected volumes.

At the time when she embarked on her journalistic career, the personal essay, the essay upon a topic, still had its practitioners. (Among these we should mention Max Beerbohm, 'our solitary essayist', as Virginia Woolf later called him.)[5] She herself wrote and published what might be described as personal or occasional essays, upon such subjects as 'Haworth, November, 1904', 'On a Faithful Friend', 'The Decay of Essay-writing', 'Street Music', 'An Andalusian Inn', 'A Priory Church',

'The Value of Laughter', 'A Walk by Night', 'The Opera', 'Impressions at Bayreuth' – all of which appear in this volume. Her gifts were so substantial, and so rehearsed, that she might have written nothing but essays of this sort. Her 'precious Ms book' contained 'hints for dozens of articles';[6] she could write 3000 words 'twice as easily'[7] as she could write 1500; indeed she could not help writing.[8] But, whatever her predilections, a young writer apprenticing herself in earnest as a literary journalist could best expect, in the early 1900s, to fulfil her 'old ambition' to 'make a little money'[9] by writing reviews. As Arnold Bennett – the archetypal 'tradesman of letters'[10] – had already cautioned, '. . . editors have little use for essays'.[11] (That was in *Journalism for Women: A Practical Guide*, 1898 – a book one only regrets Virginia Woolf had not the opportunity to review.)

She began in November 1904, at the suggestion of Violet Dickinson, to send examples of her work to Margaret Lyttelton, a friend of Violet who edited the women's pages of the *Guardian*, a weekly newspaper for the clergy. Virginia was twenty-two. Her father, Sir Leslie Stephen, a man of great eminence in the world of letters to which his daughter now sought entry, had died in February. By November his children were established at 46 Gordon Square; Bloomsbury was in its infancy; and, as her letters of this period reveal, Virginia was extremely excited about her writing, and very determined to make money. She was also, initially, somewhat careless in her dealings, as the opening of this informative extract from a letter written on 11 November to Violet Dickinson suggests:

I dont in the least expect Mrs Lyttelton to take that article [on Manorbier] – I stupidly didn't typewrite it – indeed wrote it myself rather hurriedly and illegibly as I hate copying – and forgot to give my address, or to enclose a stamped envelope for return. So I dont think my chances are good. I dont in the least want Mrs L's candid criticism; I want her cheque![12] I know all about my merits and failings better than she can from the sight of one article, but it would be a great relief to know that I could make a few pence easily in this way – as our passbooks came last night, and they are greatly overdrawn. It is all the result of this idiotic illness, and I should be glad to write something which would pay for small extras. I honestly think I can write better stuff than that wretched article you sent me. Why on earth does she take such trash? – But there is a knack of writing for newspapers which has to be learnt, and is quite independent of literary merits.[13]

From the next letter to Violet Dickinson we learn that Mrs Lyttelton has read the article on Manorbier (which does not survive) and written to Violet about it; and now, far from scorning her opinion, Virginia welcomes it. Mrs Lyttelton has become 'a very sensible woman' whose criticisms 'however stringent will be worth attending to'.[14] In fact, Mrs Lyttelton now invited Virginia to contribute an article of 1500 words 'on any subject' to her part of the paper. The article she finally submitted at this generous invitation was 'Haworth, November, 1904', about a visit to the Brontë parsonage which she had made while a guest of Margaret and Will Vaughan at Giggleswick. This was to be Virginia's second publication and it appeared anonymously, as did all her contributions to the *Guardian*, in the issue for 21 December. Her first published article had come out in the previous week's issue – a modest review of a novel, *The Son of Royal Langbrith*, by the American writer W. D. Howells. It shared a page with, among other things, an unsigned review of *Whosoever Shall Offend*, a novel by F. Marion Crawford; criticism by J. E. T. of a performance of *Everyman*, a work by the composer Dr Walford Davies; and by E. S. Day, under the heading 'A Christmas Mystery', an account of a dramatisation of 'Miss Buckton's poem *Eager Heart*', which had startled London into 'sudden reverent admiration'; a note on 'Glasgow Co-operation of Trained Nurses' and letters to the editor on 'Training Midwives' and the 'Association of Trained Charwomen'. This was hardly inspiring company for Virginia, but fairly typical of that which she kept in the next two years.

Her last contributions to the *Guardian* were a review of *The Private Papers of Henry Ryecroft*, published in February 1907; and an obituary of her Quaker aunt, Caroline Emelia Stephen, which appeared in the main part of the paper in April 1909.

A few words should also be said here about the *Guardian* proper. Anglo-Catholic in outlook, it set itself to establish in the public mind 'a clear view of the ground taken by the High Church on matters religious and political'.[15] It did not neglect the arts. Readers of the review 'The Son of Royal Langbrith' might also read, in the main part of the same issue of the paper, about the 'Autumn Exhibition of the New English Art Club' and have their attention drawn to 'Mr Roger Fry's charming drawing of St John's College, Oxford'. But, none the less, it was a pretty dull clerical newspaper, replete with articles on such subjects as 'Episcopal Visitations', 'Church Schools', 'The Position of the Unbeneficed Clergy', and fusty advertisements for church organs, patent medicines, and, very regularly, for Vino Sacro, a wine which 'does not permanently stain altar linen'. It would be difficult to imagine a more unlikely outlet for even an anonymous daughter of Sir Leslie Stephen.[16] In the case of one who was also a denizen of emergent Bloomsbury ('Whenever I take up my pen for the Guardian Saxon comes behind and suggests all sorts of proprieties')[17] the unlikelihood comes spiced with additional irony. Even Virginia, whose powers of imagination and fancy knew few bounds, could not quite conceive 'how they got such a black little goat into their fold'.[18]

Among the books – the novels perhaps especially – that Mrs Lyttelton invited Virginia to review, for the diversion of what the latter referred to as the 'parsonesses',[19] were many that were also very dull. The most significant exception was *The Golden Bowl*. Virginia wrote 'a very hardworking review' of this, 'Mr Henry James's Latest Novel', for the *Guardian*. But then the 'official eye' fell upon it and she had to cut it by 'quite half', rendering it now, in her view, 'worthless'.[20] (Her several brushes with officialdom of this kind and of a less tolerable unilateral variety are documented below in the notes to the articles concerned.) James too was a special case. Virginia, it should be remembered, knew him at first hand; he was one of those 'great figures', friends of her parents, who 'stood in the background' of her childhood and youth; and she could recall 'the hesitations and adumbrations with which Henry James made the drawing room rich and dusty'.[21] Moreover, his influence upon the young men at Cambridge who were to form the nucleus of Bloomsbury had been considerable. 'I have just finished *The Golden Bowl* & am astounded. Did he invent us or we him? He uses *all* our words in their most technical sense & we cant have got them all from him,' Leonard Woolf wrote to Lytton Strachey from Ceylon on 23 July 1905.[22] All of which makes the loss of so much as half of what Virginia had to say about James at this time, even in the straitened circumstances of a review, nothing less than exasperating. (Her copious notes on *The Golden Bowl* are reproduced as Appendix III; readers should also turn to the essay 'Portraits of Places'.)

Inevitably, perhaps, those of her contributions to the *Guardian* that stand out are the more imaginative pieces such as 'Haworth, November, 1904', 'On a Faithful Friend' (an obituary of the Stephen family's dog 'Shag' – albeit 'rather cobbled'[23] by Mrs Lyttelton), 'An Andalusian Inn' (recording a visit to the Iberian Peninsula in 1905), 'The Value of Laughter', and 'A Walk by Night' (with its anticipations of *To the Lighthouse*). Another such piece is her remarkable improvisation 'Street Music' which Leopold Maxse published in the *National Review* in December 1905 (see Appendix IV for the background to this and to the other periodicals to which Virginia Woolf occasionally contributed). Articles such as these freed her pen from the domination of facts, of which she was never over fond, and were of a kind she had rehearsed in her journals. But, as has already been suggested, they did not represent the way ahead.

This was to be largely determined by the *Times Literary Supplement*, for which she began to write in 1905 (her first review in its pages being 'Literary Geography' in the issue for 10 March). The *TLS* offered no escape from books and facts and its trade was strictly in reviews as far as Virginia was concerned in these early years. Bruce Richmond, who edited the paper from 1902 to 1938,[24] sent her books as miscellaneous as those which she received from Mrs Lyttelton: works of fiction, biography, history, travel. He became Virginia's most important journalistic mentor (after her father) and his paper 'the Major Journal'[25] in her life, a fact she acknowledged in her diary on the occasion of Richmond's retirement. 'I learnt a lot of my craft writing for him,' she wrote, paying as she did so what is an extraordinary compliment: 'how to compress; how to enliven; & also was made to read with a pen & notebook, seriously'.[26] (A fairly extreme example of Richmond's editorial schooling of Virginia was his rejection, in April 1905, of her review of Edith Sichel's *Catherine de' Medici and the French Revolution*. This he turned down on the grounds that it was not written in the academic spirit, but promptly made up for it by sending her 'a peace offering' of '3 fat books about Spain'.)[27] By such discipline she was, in time, to gain great freedom as a writer of *TLS* leaders. These were articles so polished that she could incorporate them with little or no revision into her *Common Reader* volumes.

Her other significant opportunity in this early period was provided by Reginald Smith, the editor of the *Cornhill Magazine* (the journal Leslie Stephen edited from 1871 to 1882 – the year of Virginia's birth). In 1905 Smith had made Virginia 'crosser than ever'[28] by rejecting without explanation an unsolicited article she had submitted to him on the letters of Boswell. And, indeed, Smith does appear generally to have lacked tact and to have been at times more than a little condescending. Certainly, he did not enjoy Richmond's degree of success in dealings with Virginia. But he did have a commodity that Richmond could not, at this time at least, consistently offer her: he had abundant space. This he invited Virginia and Lady Robert (Nelly) Cecil to share, as contributors to a column entitled 'The Book on the Table', in which, in alternate issues, they were each to review books of their choice. (In practice, the 'choice' seems largely to have been Smith's.) This was in 1908.

During that year, Virginia wrote for the *Cornhill* on the memoirs of Sarah Bernhardt and those of Lady Dorothy Nevill, on the biography of John Delane, editor of *The Times*, on Theodore Roosevelt, on Louise de La Vallière and on the journal of Lady Holland. (Of these, 'John Delane' and '*The Journal of Elizabeth Lady Holland*' served to introduce her to an American readership for the first time, being reprinted in July 1908 and January 1909 respectively in the *Living Age*, Boston.) Her articles were signed and the whole episode was undoubtedly exciting and moderately prestigious, with pleasant family associations. But it was only an episode, and quite a brief one. Smith, for his part, proved eager to encourage. 'I really believe, dear Miss Stephen,' he wrote to her at one point, 'that if you will put heart and head into it, you will make a mark in reviewing.'[29] But he also liked to instruct, in considerable detail, and what is more he would, without consultation, add words to her sentences and cut out others – until she threatened to resign.[30] She did not resign but when, in 1909, Smith declined to publish her 'Memoirs of a Novelist'[31] – the first in a planned series of fictional portraits – her association with the *Cornhill* ceased.

In the years 1909–12 she contributed exclusively to the *TLS* (with the exception of her obituary of Caroline Emelia Stephen in the *Guardian*; and 'The Opera' and 'Impressions at Bayreuth' in *The Times*). It was a period in which she produced essays that announced very clearly the end of her apprenticeship as a reviewer. In such pieces as 'The Genius of Boswell', 'A Friend of Johnson', 'Sterne', 'Oliver Wendell Holmes', 'Sheridan', 'Lady Hester Stanhope', 'Emerson's Journals' and 'The Novels of George Gissing' her command of her medium is complete. Her allusions and references confine themselves less to the works ostensibly under review than once they did and, ranging freely, reveal a wider and more fertile familiarity with her subjects, their works and lives. As in her first published review, '*Royal Langbrith*', she took no account of W. D. Howells's other novels, his status as a critic, or, for that matter, the incidentally interesting facts that he was Abraham Lincoln's official biographer and Mark Twain's friend, so, at the opposite extreme, in her last review in this volume, on 'The Novels of George Gissing', she celebrates her subject at length and in depth but with the barest passing reference to only one of the works listed at the head of her article. This would seem to amount to a declaration of the reviewer's liberty to write as she pleases.

But journalism could never quite afford that freedom to the satisfaction of Virginia Woolf, or perhaps to any writer of imaginative literature. Writing for an editor, writing for payment, under the pressure of deadlines, entailed, even at its freest, compromises and courtesies of a kind not exacted in writing fiction, or diaries, or letters. To the reviewer, suavity, politeness and the sidelong approach were, it seemed, inescapable.[32] For the hard fact remained, as she noted while 'sobbing in misery' over Vernon Lee's *The Sentimental Traveller* (reviewed in the *TLS*, 9 January 1908), that 'though this is true as truth, as the Sage said in the fairy tale, still it can't be said in print . . . '[33] There were subterfuges – such as she believed she employed in 'A Week in the White House' (*Cornhill Magazine*, August 1908). Here, she claimed, the 'sublety [*sic*] of the insinuations is so serpentine that no Smith in Europe will see how I jeer the president to derision, seeming to approve the while'.[34] But if editors could be duped, surely readers might also miss the point? Abandon all subterfuge and the editor would cut and tame such 'truth' as print was not permitted to accommodate. This was the fate of her attempt 'to scourge that Fine Lady the Baroness', Elizabeth von Arnim, whose novel *Fräulein Schmidt and Mr Anstruther* (reviewed in the *TLS*, 10 May 1907) she privately condemned as 'chatter and trash'.[35] These examples underline how important her correspondence is in revealing the sharp (and usually amusing) clashes that could arise between her 'true' or private opinions about a book and those she published. (For the most part, she proved a generous reviewer. Distrusting, as she once said, 'the critical attitude of mind',[36] she almost always contrived to say something encouraging about even the most transparently unsuccessful productions.)

By 1909 her letters begin to be less preoccupied with the subject of reviewing. Now 'Melymbrosia', her first novel (begun in 1907 and eventually published as *The Voyage Out*, in 1915), concerns her increasingly, reminding us of the main course of her ambition. We should remind ourselves too, at this point, of the wider passage of her life. In 1904, as we know, her father had died; had he lived there would perhaps have been 'No writing, no books'.[37] In 1905, as her career as a journalist was just beginning, she branched out to give weekly classes in history to working women at Morley College. In November 1906 her brother Thoby Stephen died tragically; and in that same month F. W.

Maitland's *Life* of her father was published. (To this she contributed her 'Impressions', reprinted here.) Her life was laden with tragedy. Now Bloomsbury, in coping with its collective grief at Thoby's death, became more intimate (and, in the eyes of those stuffily in league with respectability, increasingly outrageous). Her sister Vanessa, upon whom Virginia was emotionally profoundly dependent, married Clive Bell in 1907 and, in the following year, their son Julian was born. Virginia and Clive now embarked on their legendary flirtation, the most significant aspect of which was the opportunity it afforded them to discuss Virginia's novel. In 1909, Caroline Emelia Stephen, who had never wanted her niece to become a pot-boiling journalist, died, leaving Virginia a legacy of £2500. In the same year, Virginia was momentarily engaged to Lytton Strachey. In 1910 she volunteered to work for Women's Suffrage and took part in the *Dreadnought* hoax. Roger Fry that year organised the First Post-Impressionist Exhibition and became a part of Bloomsbury. In 1911 Leonard Woolf of the Colonial Service returned home on leave from Ceylon; and in August 1912 he and Virginia were married.

But this was far removed from 'my room at this moment', in December 1904, 'on a dark winter's evening – all my beloved leather backed books standing up so handsome in their shelves, and a nice fire, and the electric light burning and a huge mass of manuscripts and letters and proof-sheets and pens and inks over the floor and everywhere'.[38] Which is where we must now begin.

1 – *IV VW Diary*, 19 May 1931 (VW on Max Beerbohm and Lytton Strachey).
2 – See Quentin Bell on the virtues of Bloomsbury's prose in 'Bloomsbury and "the Vulgar Passions"', *Critical Inquiry*, vol. 6, no. 2, Winter 1979.
3 – See Abbreviations and Bibliography below for details concerning this and the other publications referred to in this introduction.
4 – An edition of her early journals is currently in preparation.
5 – 'Addison', *IV VW Essays* and *CR1*
6 – *I VW Letters*, no. 192, to Violet Dickinson, 1 December 1904.
7 – *Ibid.*
8 – *Ibid.*, no. 198, to Madge Vaughan, 1 December 1904.
9 – *Ibid.*, no. 195, to Emma Vaughan, 27 November 1904.
10 – *III VW Diary*, 8 September 1930.
11 – According to Bennett, at that time himself an editor (of *Woman*), 'Fleet Street at this moment' was 'simply running with women who are writing fanciful essays and not selling them . . .'

12 – For nine of her contributions to the *Guardian* (*'Lone Marie'*, *'The Devil's Due'*, *'The House of Mirth'*, 'A Description of the Desert', *'The Brown House and Cordelia'*, '"Delta"', 'A Walk by Night', *'The Tower of Siloam'*, *'After His Kind'* – some 5100 words) she earned, according to her Reading Notebook (MHP, B 1a), £3 9s. 0d. On this basis her total earnings from the women's pages, to which she contributed approximately 26,000 words, may be calculated to have been about £17 10s. 0d.

13 – *I VW Letters*, no. 191, to Violet Dickinson, 11 November 1904.

14 – *Ibid.*, no. 192, 14 November 1904.

15 – *Newspaper Press Directory*, 1904.

16 – As his obituary in the *Guardian*, 24 February 1904, reminded readers, Leslie Stephen, recognising that he had 'never really believed' in the creed took advantage in 1875 of the Clerical Disabilities Act and renounced the orders he had taken as a don at Cambridge.

17 – *I VW Letters*, no. 243, to Violet Dickinson, July 1905.

18 – *Ibid.*, no. 217, to Violet Dickinson, mid-February 1905.

19 – *Ibid.*

20 – *Ibid.*

21 – *Moments of Being*, 'A Sketch of the Past', p. 158.

22 – Quoted in *I QB*, p. 177n.

23 – *I VW Letters*, no. 206, to Violet Dickinson, early January 1905.

24 – On taking over the newly founded paper in 1902 he had invited Leslie Stephen to contribute to its pages but, according to Quentin Bell (*I QB*, p. 104), Stephen 'had been able to do little'.

25 – *V VW Diary*, 27 May 1938.

26 – *Ibid.*

27 – *I VW Letters*, no. 226, to Violet Dickinson, 30 April 1905.

28 – *Ibid.*, no. 206, to Violet Dickinson, early January 1905.

29 – *Ibid.*, no. 408, to Lytton Strachey, 22 April 1908.

30 – *Ibid.*, no. 413, to Lady Robert Cecil, May 1908.

31 – Published in *The Complete Shorter Fiction*, as are also 'The Mysterious Case of Miss V', probably written in the summer of 1906, and 'The Journal of Mistress Joan Martyn', written in August 1906.

32 – *Moments of Being*, 'A Sketch of the Past', p. 150.

33 – *I VW Letters*, no. 397, to Violet Dickinson, December 1907.

34 – *Ibid.*, no. 422, to Violet Dickinson, July 1908.

35 – *Ibid.*, no. 363, to Violet Dickinson, May 1907.

36 – *Ibid.*, no. 203, to Lady Robert Cecil, 22 December 1904.

37 – *IV VW Diary*, 28 November 1928.

38 – *I VW Letters*, no. 202, to Madge Vaughan, mid-December 1904.

Editorial Note

As has been stated in the introduction, this volume contains those essays which Virginia Stephen (otherwise referred to throughout as Virginia Woolf, or VW) is known to have published in the period from December 1904 to January 1912, that is, until her marriage to Leonard Woolf in August 1912.

Of the 109 pieces concerned, 83 have not been previously collected. All are reprinted in chronological order from the original source of publication. Source, publication date and bibliographical reference are detailed in the first note to each article; for the majority of the articles this information has been provided by B. J. Kirkpatrick's bibliography. The first note is not numbered in the text itself.

Departures from Kirkpatrick's sequence concern: newly identified articles (discussed below); a number of essays until now listed as 'doubtful' and which, on a reassessment of the evidence available have been attributed to Virginia Woolf (also discussed below); contributions to the monthly journals, the *National Review* and the *Cornhill Magazine*, which Kirkpatrick enters at the end of the year and which have now been inserted at the beginning of the month of publication; and Virginia Woolf's contribution to F. W. Maitland's *The Life and Letters of Leslie Stephen*, 'Impressions of Sir Leslie Stephen', reprinted here at November 1906, the date of publication of the book.

In addition to supplying the information already referred to, the first note states whether an article was originally 'signed'. Wherever possible it relates the article to appropriate references in Virginia Woolf's letters, a function also performed as occasion demands by the other notes. Publication details of books under review and, as available, the dates of their authors, are also provided in the first note. (Shorter reviews are referred to as notices.) Wherever Virginia Woolf wrote on the same subject more than once, or upon related subjects, the reader is cross-referred to the article or articles concerned, throughout the edition. The reader is informed where a piece has been previously collected in a volume of the author's work; and also whether there exist in relation to the essay manuscript Reading Notes. (An extensive and complete example of Virginia Woolf's note-making, preparatory to writing her review of Henry James's *The Golden Bowl*, 1904, has been transcribed from the Monks House Papers at Sussex University Library and reproduced here as Appendix III.) The notes concerned in the Monks House Papers are identified by the formula 'Reading Notes (MHP, B Ia)'; where these notes are dated, the date is given with this reference. The related notes in the Berg Collection, New York Public Library, are referred to as 'Reading Notes (Berg, XXIX)'.

The notes are otherwise intended to identify and verify Virginia Woolf's direct quotations, to annotate biographical and bibliographical references, and to elucidate other allusions, where to do so has seemed likely to be helpful to the reader. In the case of quotations, the level of annotation varies according to a number of general principles. Wholly accurate quotations are usually merely identified by chapter and page number, or other division of the work concerned, without further elucidation. But in some instances the context of the passage is quoted in the note, to suggest more fully the tone of the work under discussion or to point to material of interest which Virginia Woolf has chosen not to use. Misquotations, part-paraphrases and adaptations are identified and, where these are extensive, the original matter is quoted in the notes. Minor deviations in punctuation, the omission in a quotation of a comma, a semi-colon, or period, have been silently corrected; but where these are several they are left to stand and a statement to that effect is made. Where matter is omitted from a quotation but the omission has not been indicated in the text, ellipses have been inserted in square brackets at the appropriate point. Occasionally, where it has seemed useful to do so, the omitted matter is quoted in a note. Virginia Woolf's own interpolations are marked by angled brackets ⟨thus⟩. Wherever the source of a quotation has not been discovered, this is stated. The sole exception to this rule concerns a small number of unidentified single-word references appearing within quotation marks and which may be quoted or may have been placed between inverted commas for purposes of emphasis. House styles differ considerably between the original journals; these have been made uniform, but not to alter any significant aspect of the original.

Newly-identified articles
I am indebted to Professor S. P. Rosenbaum for bringing the following two articles to my attention.

'A Walk by Night', *Guardian*, 28 December 1905. This essay directly echoes a description of a walk at night occurring in VW's Cornwall Diary (11 August–14 September 1905), Berg Collection, New York Public Library; its conclusion: 'we were as birds lately winged that have been caught and caged' differs in only two words from the diary version which instead of 'as birds' has 'like creatures'. It is also clearly the piece of 800 words referred to as 'Night Walk' in MHP, B 1a. See p. 80.

'Portraits of Places', *Guardian*, 3 October 1906. This article takes its title from Henry James's *Portraits of Places* (1883), a work containing a number of essays on England and the English which, together with others, were reprinted in James's *English Hours* (1905). The article refers to Cornwall, where VW had stayed in August 1905, to Wales, which she had visited in 1904, and to Norfolk, whence she wrote to Violet Dickinson in August 1905: 'Read your Guardian carefully, and see if you find anything about Henry James; the first words, like [a] coin with a head on it, will tell you who wrote it.' (*I VW Letters*, no. 282.) The delay between the date of the letter and that of the article's publication cannot be factually accounted for, but no other article in the *Guardian* in the intervening period begins to answer the description, and we must conclude that it was held over or, in fact, delivered to the paper at a later date than that suggested by the letter. In its general treatment of James, and in particular in its emphasis upon the fact that he was an American, it is distinctly characteristic of VW, as, indeed, are the opening words to which she drew Violet Dickinson's attention: 'Nothing, it seems, should be so easy as to paint the portrait of a place. The sitter reclines perpetually in an attitude of complete repose outside the drawing-room windows . . . ' See p. 124.

'*The English Mail Coach*', *Guardian*, 29 August 1906, an article on Thomas De Quincey, to which allusion is made in MHP, B 1a, and which is clearly also by VW, is reprinted in Appendix 1. This article has been identified and kindly brought to my attention by Professor Rosenbaum, but, unfortunately, too late for inclusion in the main text. See p. 365.

Revised attributions
The evidence for attributing to Virginia Woolf the following five articles, which Kirkpatrick lists as 'Doubtful Contributions', has been reassessed and as a result the articles have been incorporated into the main text of this volume.

'*The Feminine Note in Fiction*', *Guardian*, 25 January 1905. This review of *The Feminine Note in Fiction* (1904) by W. L. Courtney, characteristic of VW in both tone and style, is specifically listed in her Diary (Christmas 1904–31 May 1905), Berg Collection, New York Public Library. See p. 15.

'*By Beach and Bogland*', *Guardian*, 22 March 1905. A notice of *By Beach and Bogland* (1905) by Jane Barlow, referred to in the Diary (Christmas 1904–31 May 1905) and noted in MHP, B 1a, 9 March: ' . . . Miss B. knows her Irish peasant. honest little stories. curious point of view. Life seen through a microscope . . . ', which is echoed in the article by 'every pebble and blade of grass is seen as through a microscope'. See p. 37.

'*Nancy Stair*', *Guardian*, 10 May 1905. A notice of *Nancy Stair. A Novel* (1905) by Elinor MacCartney Lane, to which reference is made in the Diary (Christmas 1904–31 May 1905) and which is noted in MHP, B 1a. The single quotation in the article, 'how little value verse-making holds to the real task of living', is recorded in the notebook. See p. 4.

'*Arrows of Fortune*', *Guardian*, 17 May 1905. A notice of *Arrows of Fortune* (1904) by Algernon Gissing, to which reference is made in the Diary (Christmas 1904–31 May 1905), and about which there is nothing uncharacteristic of VW to suggest that it was not written by her. See p. 41.

'*The American Woman*', *Guardian*, 31 May 1905. A notice of *The Women of America* (1904) by Elizabeth McCracken, to which reference is made in the Diary (Christmas 1904–31 May 1905), where the article is listed as being of 800 words, the approximate length of the piece published. See p. 46.

Appendix 11 reprints, with summary annotation, the remaining articles listed by Kirkpatrick as 'Doubtful Contributions', to enable readers to form their own judgments as to authorship. It also includes a newly located article, '*Somehow Good*', *TLS*, 2 June 1908, a review, very probably by VW, of a novel by William De Morgan. See p. 378.

Evidence received on the eve of going to press concerning the notice 'The Post-Impressionists', in the form of a letter from Vanessa Bell to VW, suggests that this piece is also almost certainly by VW. See p. 379.

Acknowledgements

For engaging me to prepare this work for publication, I am particularly grateful to the directors of The Hogarth Press and to Professor Quentin Bell and Angelica Garnett, administrators of Virginia Woolf's Literary Estate.

I am especially indebted to the Leverhulme Trustees, for awarding me a Research Grant; to my wife Diana McNeillie, who has shared in a great deal of the reading involved in annotating the essays; to Professor Quentin Bell and Anne Olivier Bell, for their kind encouragement and guidance; to Hugo Brunner for his early, and continued, support; to Professor S. P. Rosenbaum of the University of Toronto, for his advice and unstinting generosity in furnishing me with many photocopies of articles; to Professor Elizabeth Steele of the University of Toledo, Ohio, for kindly answering numerous enquiries; and to Professor Susan Dick of Queen's University, Kingston, Canada, for her advice and encouragement.

I owe a particular debt of gratitude to Nicola Edwards for her meticulous work on a number of the essays in this volume and for her continuing researches towards the completion of volume two.

I wish also to thank Christine Carswell of The Hogarth Press for her rigorous criticisms; Richard David for his expert advice on Hakluyt; and the following for generously sparing time to answer my enquiries: Elizabeth Inglis, Brownlee Kirkpatrick, Kim Richardson, Andrew Robinson and Jeremy Treglown.

I received special support in the initial stages of this project from Graham Cranfield, Head of Public Services, and the staff of the Newspaper Library, British Library, Colindale. I am similarly indebted to the Librarian, and to those who work in the periodicals and photographic departments at London University Library; and to Katherine F. Gould, Coordinator of Reference Service at the Library of Congress, and to Pat Lynagh, Reference Librarian, Smithsonian Institution, Washington D.C. I should like further to acknowledge the help of the following: Bayreuther Festspiele, Bayreuth; New York Public Library; Portrait Gallery, National Galleries of Scotland, Edinburgh; and the Richard-Wagner-Museum, Bayreuth.

For permission to publish Virginia Woolf's reading notes on *The Golden Bowl* by Henry James, I have to thank Professor Bell and Angelica Garnett, and Sussex University Library.

Abbreviations

B&P	*Books and Portraits*, ed. Mary Lyon (Hogarth Press, London, 1977; Harcourt Brace Jovanovich, New York, 1978)
CE	*Collected Essays*, 4 vols, ed. Leonard Woolf (vols 1–2, Hogarth Press, London, 1966, Harcourt Brace & World Inc., New York, 1967; vols 3–4, Hogarth Press, London, and Harcourt Brace & World Inc., New York, 1967)
CR	*The Common Reader*: 1st series (Hogarth Press, London, and Harcourt Brace & Co., New York, 1925; annotated edition, 1984) 2nd series (Hogarth Press, London, and Harcourt, Brace & Co., New York, 1932; annotated edition, 1986)
CW	*Contemporary Writers*, with a Preface by Jean Guiget (Hogarth Press, London, 1965; Harcourt Brace & World Inc., New York, 1966)
DNB	*Dictionary of National Biography*
G&R	*Granite and Rainbow*, ed. Leonard Woolf (Hogarth Press, London, and Harcourt Brace & Co., New York, 1958)
Kp	B. J. Kirkpatrick, *A Bibliography of Virginia Woolf* (third ed., Oxford University Press, Oxford, 1980)
MHP	Monks House Papers in Sussex University Library

NPD   *Newspaper Press Directory*

QB   Quentin Bell, *Virginia Woolf. A Biography. Volume One. Virginia Stephen, 1882–1912. Volume Two. Mrs Woolf, 1912–1941.* (Hogarth Press, London, and Harcourt Brace Jovanovich Inc., New York, 1972)

TLS   *Times Literary Supplement*

VW Diary   *The Diary of Virginia Woolf,* ed. Anne Olivier Bell (5 vols, Hogarth Press, London, and Harcourt Brace Jovanovich, New York, 1977–84)

VW Essays   *The Essays of Virginia Woolf,* 6 vols

VW Letters   *The Letters of Virginia Woolf,* ed. Nigel Nicolson (6 vols, Hogarth Press, London, and Harcourt Brace Jovanovich, New York, 1975–80)

W & W   *Women & Writing,* ed. Michèle Barrett (Women's Press, London, 1979; Harcourt Brace Jovanovich, New York, 1980)

The Essays

1904

'The Son of Royal Langbrith'

Mr Howells[2] is the exponent of the novel of thought as distinct from the novel of action. Men interest him primarily as thinking, not as doing, animals. *The Son of Royal Langbrith* is another experiment in this line, and one that has a singular interest. The outline of the story is this: — There was a certain Royal Langbrith, an owner of paper-mills in a New England town. He has been long dead when the book opens, so that his child knows him only through the words of the widow, which, for a good reason, are few. But the son has contrived to make a hero of his father, and a church and a village library are proofs of the munificence of the dead man. We are soon let into the secret, however, which is the property of the widow, one Dr Anther, and two others – that the public-spirited Royal Langbrith is a grotesque myth; he was in reality a scoundrel who got his wealth by appropriating the inventions of another. But, as he was not exposed in his life-time, there seems no need why the unpleasant truth should be told now, except for this reason – Dr Anther and Mrs Langbrith are old friends, and wish to marry, the fatal objection being that the son James reveres his father's memory so deeply that for his mother to remarry would be sacrilege. Mrs Langbrith is weak, and cannot face her son's displeasure, nor give him the reasons that make his father's memory anything but venerable. As he grows up he enlarges upon the paternal virtues to such an extent as to present a medallion of his father to the library. The one person from whose lips James would naturally learn his father's character is the unfortunate

3

Hawberk, whose inventions were stolen, and who was ousted from his partnership in the prosperity of the mills by a threat to disclose a slightly discreditable past to his wife. But his hardship makes him take to opium-eating, and in his dreams he cherishes the delusion that Langbrith was his best friend. Indeed, all things combine to make it necessary for the living to shield the memory of the dead man, even at their own sacrifice. The chief sufferers are Mrs Langbrith and the high-minded Dr Anther, whose conscience will not let him disabuse the son of his romantic ideal, although this ideal puts an end to his own chance of happiness. It does, in fact, happen as Anther foretold: Mrs Langbrith consents to marry him without telling her son the truth about his father. James, when he hears of the engagement, accuses both of infidelity to his father's memory. Mrs Langbrith has not the courage to withstand him, and breaks off the engagement. At this point the opium-eating Hawberk recovers, and his delusions about Royal Langbrith disappear. He decides, however, as James Langbrith is in love with his daughter, that Royal's crimes did enough harm in their day, and that there is no reason to let them affect the lives of the next generation. He dies suddenly, without breathing the secret to any one. James Langbrith, meanwhile, in disgust at his mother and Anther, had migrated to Paris; he returns on hearing of Hawberk's death, and in the train meets the fourth person who can tell him his father's true history – his uncle John. John is moved by an insulting comparison between him and Royal, who was 'at least a gentleman',[3] to show what kind of gentleman he was, which he does with great power and effect. The result is that James reaches his mother's house crushed, and prepared to accept her marriage, and learns from her that Dr Anther is just dead of typhoid. The book ends very naturally with the happy marriage of James and Hope Hawberk, and the population of Saxmills is suffered, after consideration, to revere the medallion of Royal Langbrith as that of a good man and citizen. The weak point of the book seems to us to lie in the fact of James's devotion to his father, on which the plot mainly depends. He had no materials for his worship, except a few vague words of his mother, the library, and a not very pleasant portrait. And yet it is for this reason that, over twenty years after her husband's death, he objects to his mother's remarriage. It would be more natural to object, not that his father should have a successor, but that he himself should have a stepfather. Another, however, is personally acceptable, and his sole disqualification is that he is to succeed Royal Langbirth. It is difficult to believe that a young man's devotion to a father whom he could not remember would lead him to such extravagances. However, the mere plot is not essential to a book which treats with such fineness of subtler things. The grasp of the 'dead hand'⁴ is felt in every page, and the book is full of fine observation and delicate character-drawing. It is needless to say that the whole is beautifully proportioned, and told in the reserved and expressive language of a man who has much skill in writing.

1 – A review of the *Guardian*, 14 December 1904, (Kp c01) of *The Son of Royal Langbrith* (Harper & Bros, 1904) by W. D. Howells, written on the morning of 30 November 'in ½ an hour . . . so that was pretty quick, I wont say good, work'. (*I VW Letters*, no. 197, to Madge Vaughan; see also no. 194.)
2 – William Dean Howells (1837–1920), one of the leading literary figures of his generation in the United States. He had established his reputation with the novel *The Rise of Silas Lapham* (1885) and *Criticism and Fiction* (1891). See also 'Mr Howells on Form', *II VW Essays*.
3 – Howells, ch. xxxiv, p. 326.
4 – See *ibid.*, ch. ii, p. 8: '. . . they are his children, and there must be times when he holds her in mortmain through them, when he is still her husband, still her lord and master.'

Haworth, November, 1904

I do not know whether pilgrimages to the shrines of famous men ought not to be condemned as sentimental journeys. It is better to read Carlyle in your own study chair than to visit the sound-proof room and pore over the manuscripts at Chelsea. I should be inclined to set an examination on Frederick the Great in place of entrance fee; only, in that case, the house would soon have to be shut up. The curiosity is only legitimate when the house of a great writer or the country in which it is set adds something to our understanding of his books.² This justification you have for a pilgrimage to the home and country of Charlotte Brontë and her sisters.

The *Life*, by Mrs Gaskell,³ gives you the impression that Haworth and the Brontës are somehow inextricably mixed. Haworth expresses the Brontës; the Brontës express Haworth; they fit like a snail to its shell. How far surroundings radically affect people's minds, it is not for me to ask: superficially, the influence is great, but it is worth asking if the famous parsonage had been placed in a London slum, the dens of Whitechapel would not have had the same result as the lonely Yorkshire moors. However, I am taking away my only excuse for visiting Haworth. Unreasonable or not, one of the chief points of a recent visit to Yorkshire was that an expedition to Haworth could be accomplished. The necessary arrangements were made, and we determined to take advantage of the first fine day for our expedition. A real northern snowstorm had been doing the honours of the moors. It was rash to wait fine weather, and it was also cowardly. I understand that the sun very seldom shone on the Brontë family, and if we chose a really fine day we should have to make allowance for the fact that fifty years ago there were few fine days at Haworth, and that we were, therefore, for sake of comfort, rubbing out half the shadows in the picture. However, it would be interesting to see what impression Haworth could make upon the brilliant weather of Settle. We certainly passed through a very cheerful land, which might be likened to a vast wedding cake, of which the icing was slightly undulating; the earth was bridal in its virgin snow, which helped to suggest the comparison.

Keighley – pronounced Keethly – is often mentioned in the *Life*; it was the big town four miles from Haworth in which Charlotte walked to make her more important purchases – her wedding gown, perhaps, and the thin little cloth boots which we examined under glass in the Brontë Museum. It is a big manufacturing town, hard and stony, and clattering with business, in the way of these northern towns. They make small provision for the sentimental traveller, and our only occupation was to picture the slight figure of Charlotte trotting along the streets in her thin mantle, hustled into the gutter by more burly passers-by. It was the Keighley of her day, and that was some comfort. Our excitement as we neared Haworth had in it an element of suspense that was really painful, as though we were to meet some long-separated friend, who might have changed in the interval – so clear an image of Haworth had we from print and picture. At a certain point we entered the valley, up both sides of which the village climbs, and right on the hill-top, looking down over its parish, we saw the famous oblong tower of the church. This marked the shrine at which we were to do homage.

It may have been the effect of a sympathetic imagination, but I think that there were good reasons why Haworth did certainly strike one not exactly as gloomy, but, what is worse for artistic purposes, as dingy and commonplace. The houses, built of yellow-brown stone, date from the early nineteenth century. They climb the moor step by step in little detached strips, some distance apart, so that the town instead of making one compact blot on the landscape has contrived to get a whole stretch into its clutches. There is a long line of houses up the moor-side, which clusters round the church and parsonage with a little clump of trees. At the top the interest for a Brontë lover becomes suddenly intense. The church, the parsonage, the Brontë Museum, the school where Charlotte taught, and the Bull Inn where Branwell drank are all within a stone's throw of each other. The museum is certainly rather a pallid and inanimate collection of objects. An effort ought to be made to keep things out of these mausoleums, but the choice often lies between them and destruction, so that we must be grateful for the care which has preserved much that is, under any circumstances, of deep interest. Here are many autograph letters, pencil drawings, and other documents. But the most touching case — so touching that one hardly feels reverent in one's gaze — is that which contains the little personal relics, the dresses and shoes of the dead woman. The natural fate of such things is to die before the body that wore them, and because these, trifling and transient though they are, have survived, Charlotte Brontë the woman comes to life, and one forgets the chiefly memorable fact that she was a great writer. Her shoes and her thin muslin dress have outlived her. One other object gives a thrill; the little oak stool which Emily carried with her on her solitary moorland tramps, and on which she sat, if not to write, as they say, to think what was probably better than her writing.

The church, of course, save part of the tower, is renewed since Brontë days; but that remarkable churchyard remains. The old edition of the *Life* had on its title-page a little print which struck the keynote of the book;[4] it seemed to be all graves — gravestones stood ranked all round; you walked on a pavement lettered with dead names; the graves had solemnly invaded the garden of the parsonage itself, which was as a little oasis of life in the midst of the dead. This is no exaggeration of the artist's, as we found: the stones seem to start out of the ground at you in tall, upright lines, like an army of silent soldiers. There is no hand's breadth untenanted; indeed, the economy of space is somewhat irreverent. In old days a flagged path, which suggested the slabs of graves, led from the front door of the parsonage to the churchyard without interruption of wall or hedge; the garden was practically the graveyard too; the successors of the Brontës, however, wishing a little space between life and death, planted a hedge and several tall trees, which now cut off the parsonage garden completely. The house itself is precisely the same as it was in Charlotte's day, save that one new wing has been added. It is easy to shut the eye to this, and then you have the square, boxlike parsonage, built of the ugly, yellow-brown stone which they quarry from the moors behind, precisely as it was when Charlotte lived and died there. Inside, of course, the changes are many, though not such as to obscure the original shape of the rooms. There is nothing remarkable in a mid-Victorian parsonage, though tenanted by genius, and the only room which awakens curiosity is the kitchen, now used as an ante-room, in which the girls tramped as they conceived their work. One other spot has a certain grim interest – the oblong recess beside the staircase into which Emily drove her bulldog during the famous fight, and pinned him while she pommelled him. It is otherwise a little sparse parsonage, much like others of its kind. It was due to the courtesy of the present incumbent that we were allowed to inspect it; in his place I should often feel inclined to exorcise the three famous ghosts.

One thing only remained: the church in which Charlotte worshipped, was married, and lies buried. The circumference of her life was very narrow. Here, though much is altered, a few things remain to tell of her. The slab which bears the names of the succession of children and of their parents – their births and deaths – strikes the eye first. Name follows name; at very short intervals they died – Maria the mother, Maria the daughter, Elizabeth, Branwell, Emily, Anne, Charlotte, and lastly the old father, who outlived them all. Emily was only thirty years old, and Charlotte but nine years older. 'The sting of death is sin, and the strength of sin is the law, but thanks be to God which giveth us the victory through our Lord Jesus Christ.'[5] That is the inscription which has been placed beneath their names, and with reason; for however harsh the struggle, Emily, and Charlotte above all, fought to victory.

---

1 – An essay in the *Guardian*, 21 December 1904, (Kp C02) written 'in less than 2 hours' (*I VW Letters*, no. 194, to Violet Dickinson, 26 November 1904) at Giggleswick, Yorkshire, where VW was staying with Margaret Vaughan, *née* Symonds (1869–1925), and her headmaster husband, and whence the pilgrimage to Haworth was made. Reprinted: *B&P, W&W*.

For VW's agitated reactions ('2 sleepless nights – if not 3') to reports that R. B. Haldane, the Liberal statesman and friend of Leslie Stephen, had been 'very severe' about her essay, see *I VW Letters*, no. 205, to Violet Dickinson; see also no. 206. Haldane had written to Violet Dickinson on 27 December: 'Thank you for showing me Miss S[tephen]'s article on Haworth – a place, as you know, of deep interest to me. What merits – but I think the writer can get still more inside her subject. This is a beginning however, and it shows talent . . . ' *I QB*, p. 94n). Earlier in the year, on 23 February, he had written eloquently to Virginia upon her father's death (see Frederic W. Maitland, *The Life and Letters of Leslie Stephen*, 1906, p. 490).

2 – VW returned to this theme in 'Literary Geography' below, and in 'Great Men's Houses', *V VW Essays*, in which an account is given of Thomas and Jane Carlyle's life at 5 (now 24) Cheyne Row, Chelsea: 'And it is no frivolous curiosity that sends us to Dickens's house and Johnson's house and Carlyle's house and Keats's house. We know them from their houses . . . ' The allusion to Frederick the Great refers to Carlyle's *History of Friederich II of Prussia, called Frederick the Great*, 1858–65.

3 – Elizabeth Gaskell, *The Life of Charlotte Brontë* (2 vols, Smith, Elder & Co., 1857).

4 – This is probably a reference to the New Edition, first published 1860 (VW possessed a copy of the 1865 impression), which reproduces on its title-page an etching, 'Haworth Parsonage', by W. J. Linton. But she may have had in mind the very much more dramatic, unsigned print, 'Haworth Church and Parsonage', facing the title-page of vol. 11 of the first edition.

5 – The slab referred to was erected in 1861 on the death of Rev. Patrick Brontë, whose wife Maria, *née* Branwell, had died in 1821. Their children died as follows: Maria and Elizabeth, *aetat* 12 and 11 respectively, on 6 May and 15 June 1825; (Patrick) Branwell (b.1817) on 26 September and Emily (Jane) (b.1818) on 19 December 1848; Anne (b.1820) on 28 May 1849. Charlotte Brontë (b.1816) died in 1855. The inscription is from 1 Corinthians xv, 56–7.

1905

'Next-Door Neighbours'

Mr Pett Ridge is a gentleman who finds his best entertainment in London streets. He is an open-eyed and interested observer, who overhears a few words, jots them down in his notebook, and passes on. We can imagine that he is attracted by any little street incident, and forms one of the crowd which collects round a fallen cab-horse or a drunken man. He always chooses a seat next the driver of the omnibus and likes to enter into conversation with his fellow-passengers. He has given us in this book the result of his observations in nineteen very short stories, if stories they can be called. They have no plot as a general rule, but are rather a series of brief lantern-slides which pass over the sheet and disappear. The scenes are almost all laid in London back streets, the figures are those of shopgirls, policemen, porters, and clerks at railway stations. They are, for the most part, very good-tempered, slightly commonplace people, who fall in love or don't fall in love. In either case our sympathies are not very deeply stirred. Mr Pett Ridge's plots certainly do not strike one as probable. Does a young lady behind a counter think it a point of honour to ask the fireman who rescues her to become her husband, though she is at the time engaged to another? According to Mr Pett Ridge she does, and the incident deserves to be made into a short story and bound up into a book. These nineteen stories, we are of opinion, might with advantage have been left to adorn the columns of a daily paper, for they are not of more than ephemeral interest.

1 – A notice in the *Guardian*, 4 January 1905, (Kp C03) of *Next-Door Neighbours* (Hodder & Stoughton, 1904) by W. Pett Ridge (d. 1930), a popular author likened by E. M. Forster in 1927 to 'Thomas Deloney, who wrote humorously about shops and pubs in the reign of Queen Elizabeth' (*Aspects of the Novel*, Pelican, 1976, p. 37).

On a Faithful Friend

There is some impertinence as well as some foolhardiness in the way in which we buy animals for so much gold and silver and call them ours. One cannot help wondering what the silent critic on the hearthrug thinks of our strange conventions – the mystic Persian, whose ancestors were worshipped as gods whilst we, their masters and mistresses, grovelled in caves and painted our bodies blue. She has a vast heritage of experience, which seems to brood in her eyes, too solemn and too subtle for expression; she smiles, I often think, at our late-born civilisation, and remembers the rise and fall of dynasties. There is something, too, profane in the familiarity, half contemptuous, with which we treat our animals. We deliberately transplant a little bit of simple wild life, and make it grow up beside ours, which is neither simple nor wild. You may often see in a dog's eyes a sudden look of the primitive animal, as though he were once more a wild dog hunting in the solitary places of his youth. How have we the impertinence to make these wild creatures forego their nature for ours, which at best they can but imitate? It is one of the refined sins of civilisation, for we know not what wild spirit we are taking from its purer atmosphere, or who it is – Pan, or Nymph, or Dryad – that we have trained to beg for a lump of sugar at tea.

I do not think that in domesticating our lost friend Shag we were guilty of any such crime; he was essentially a sociable dog, who had his near counterpart in the human world. I can see him smoking a cigar at the bow window of his club, his legs extended comfortably, whilst he discusses the latest news on the Stock Exchange with a companion. His best friend could not claim for him any romantic or mysterious animal nature, but that made him all the better company for mere human beings. He came to us, however, with a pedigree that had all the elements of romance in it; he, when, in horror at his price, his would-be purchaser pointed to his collie head and collie body, but terribly Skye-terrier legs – he, we were assured, was no less a dog than the original Skye – a chieftain of the same importance as the O'Brien or the O'Connor Don in human aristocracy. The whole of the Skye-terrier tribe – who, that is, inherited the paternal characteristics – had somehow been swept from the earth; Shag, the sole scion of true Skye blood, remained in an obscure Norfolk village, the property of a low-born blacksmith, who however, cherished the utmost loyalty for his person, and pressed the claims of his royal birth with such success that we had the honour of buying him for a very substantial sum. He was too great a gentleman to take part in the plebeian work of killing rats for which he was originally needed, but he certainly added, we felt, to the respectability of the family. He seldom went for a walk without punishing the impertinence of middle-class dogs who neglected the homage due to his rank, and we had to enclose the royal jaws in a muzzle long after that restriction was legally unnecessary.[2] As he advanced in middle life he became certainly rather autocratic, not only with his own kind, but with us, his masters and mistresses; such a title though was absurd where Shag was concerned, so we called ourselves his uncles and aunts. The solitary occasion when he found it necessary to inflict marks of his displeasure on human flesh was once when a visitor rashly tried to treat him as an ordinary pet-dog and tempted him with sugar, and called him 'out of his name' by the contemptible lap-dog title of 'Fido'. Then Shag, with characteristic independence, refused the sugar and took a satisfactory mouthful of calf instead. But when he felt that he was treated with due respect he was the most faithful of friends. He was not demonstrative; but failing eyesight did not blind him to his master's face, and in his deafness he could still hear his master's voice.

The evil spirit of Shag's life was introduced into the family in the person of an attractive young sheep-dog puppy – who, though of authentic breed, was unhappily without a tail – a fact which Shag could not help remarking with satisfaction. We deluded ourselves into the thought that the young dog might take the place of the son of Shag's old age, and for a time they lived happily together. But Shag had ever been contemptuous of social graces, and had relied for his place in our hearts upon his sterling qualities of honesty and independence; the puppy, however, was a young gentleman of most engaging manners, and, though we tried to be fair, Shag could not help feeling that the young dog got most of our attention. I can see him now, as in a kind of blundering and shamefaced way he lifted one stiff old paw and gave it to me to shake, which was one of the young dog's most successful tricks. It almost brought the tears to my eyes. I could not help thinking, though I smiled, of old King Lear. But Shag was too old to acquire new graces; no second place should be his, and he determined that the matter should be decided by force. So after some weeks of growing tension the battle was fought; they went for each other with white teeth gleaming – Shag was the aggressor – and rolled round and round on the grass, locked in each other's grip. When at last we got them apart, blood was running, hair was flying, and both dogs bore scars. Peace after that was impossible; they had but to see each other to growl and stiffen; the question was – Who was the conqueror? Who was to stay and who to go? The decision we came to was base, unjust, and yet, perhaps, excusable. The old dog has had his day, we said, he must give place to the new generation. So old Shag was deposed, and sent to a kind of dignified dower-house at Parson's Green, and the young dog reigned in his stead. Year after year passed, and we never saw the old friend who had known us in the days of our youth; but in the summer holidays he revisited the house in our absence with the caretaker. And so time went on till this last year, which, though we did not know it, was to be the last year of his life. Then, one winter's night, at a time of great sickness and anxiety, a dog was heard barking repeatedly, with the bark of a dog who waits to be let in, outside our kitchen door. It was many years since that bark had been heard, and only one person in the kitchen was able to recognise it now. She opened the door, and in walked Shag, now almost quite blind and stone deaf, as he had walked in many times before, and, looking neither to right nor left, went to his old corner by the fireside, where he curled up and fell asleep without a sound. If the usurper saw him he slunk guiltily away, for Shag was past fighting for his rights any more. We shall never know – it is one of the many things that we can never know – what strange wave of memory or sympathetic instinct it was that drew Shag from the house where he had lodged for years to seek again the familiar doorstep of his master's home. And it befell that Shag was the last of the family to live in the old house, for it was in crossing the road which leads to the gardens where he was taken for his first walks as a puppy, and bit all the other dogs and frightened all the babies in their perambulators, that he met his death. The blind, deaf dog neither saw nor heard a hansom; and the wheel went over him and ended instantly a life which could not have been happily prolonged. It was better for him to die thus out among the wheels and the horses than to end in a lethal-chamber or be poisoned in a stableyard.

So we say farewell to a dear and faithful friend, whose virtues we remember – and dogs have few faults.

1 – This 'obituary notice of poor old Shag', written on the morning of 8 December 1904 (*I VW Letters*, no. 200, to Violet Dickinson), appeared in the *Guardian* of 18 January 1905, (Kp c04). Reprinted: *B&P*.
'I hope,' the letter to Violet Dickinson continues, 'Mrs L.[yttelton] will print it and make poor Sophies [Sophia Farrell, cook to the Stephen family] heart glad. She never could get reconciled to Gurth [the sheepdog who usurped Shag].' See also *Moments of Being*, 'A Sketch of the Past', pp. 77–8: 'I could collect a great many floating incidents . . . how we tied Shag to a railing, and some children told the Park Keeper that we were cruel . . . '
2 – The Muzzling of Dogs Act (1871), although still enforceable at the time this article was published, was generally only imposed as a temporary local measure. (It had, however, been enforced nationally during 1897–1900 in a determined, and successful, attempt to exterminate rabies in Britain.)

'The Feminine Note in Fiction'

Mr Courtney is certain that there is such a thing as the feminine note in fiction; he desires, moreover, to define its nature in the book before us, though at the start he admits that the feminine and masculine points of view are so different that it is difficult for one to understand the other. At any rate, he has made a laborious attempt; it is, perhaps, partly for the reason just stated that he ends where he begins. He gives us eight very patient and careful studies in the works of living women writers, in which he outlines the plots of their most successful books in detail. But we would have spared him the trouble willingly in exchange for some definite verdict; we can all read Mrs Humphry Ward, for instance, and remember her story, but we want a critic to separate her virtues and her failings, to assign her right place in literature and to decide which of her characteristics are essentially feminine and why, and what is their significance. Mr Courtney implies by his title that he will, at any rate, accomplish this last, and it is with disappointment, though not with surprise, that we discover that he has done nothing of the kind. Is it not too soon after all to criticise the 'feminine note' in anything? And will not the adequate critic of women be a woman?

Mr Courtney, we think, feels something of this difficulty; his introduction, in which we expected to find some kind of summing-up, contains only some very tentative criticisms and conclusions. Women, we gather, are seldom artists, because they have a passion for detail which conflicts with the proper artistic proportion of their work. We would cite Sappho and Jane Austen as examples of two great women who combine exquisite detail with a supreme sense of artistic proportion. Women, again, excel in 'close analytic miniature work;'[2] they are more happy when they reproduce than when they create; their genius is for psychological analysis – all of which we note with interest, though we reserve our judgment for the next hundred years or bequeath the duty to our successor. Yet it is worth noting, as proof of the difficulty of the task which Mr Courtney has set himself, that he finds two at least of his eight women writers 'artists'[3] – that two others possess a strength which in this age one has to call masculine, and, in fact, that no pair of them come under any one heading, though, of course, in the same way as men, they can be divided roughly into schools. At any rate, it seems to be clear according to Mr Courtney that more and more novels are written by women for women, which is the cause, he declares, that the novel as a work of art is disappearing. The first part of his statement may well be true; it means that women having found their voices have something to say which is naturally of supreme interest and meaning to women, but the value of which we cannot yet determine. The assertion that the woman novelist is extinguishing the novel as a work of art seems to us, however, more doubtful. It is, at any rate, possible that the widening of her intelligence by means of education and study of the Greek and Latin classics may give her that sterner view of literature which will make an artist of her, so that, having blurted out her message somewhat form-lessly, she will in due time fashion it into permanent artistic shape. Mr Courtney has given us material for many questions such as these, but his book has done nothing to prevent them from still remaining questions.

1 – A review in the *Guardian*, 25 January 1905, of *The Feminine Note in Fiction* (Chapman & Hall, 1904) by W. L. (William Leonard) Courtney (1850–1928), philosopher, journalist, and sometime fellow of New College, Oxford. See Editorial Note, p. xxii.
2 – Courtney, Intro., p. xxxv.
3 – The two writers Courtney describes as artists are Mrs Humphry Ward (Mary Augusta Ward, 1851–1920): p. 32, where he talks of her work in terms of the visual arts, and p. 40, where he refers to the 'artistic excellence' of *Lady Rose's Daughter*

(1903); and John Oliver Hobbes (Mrs Pearl Craigie, 1867–1906): p. 51, and p. 53, where she is described as 'an artist assured of her powers'. The other writers he discusses are: Lucas Malet, Gertrude Atherton, Margaret Louisa Woods, Mrs E. L. Voynich, Elizabeth Robins (see '*A Dark Lantern*' below), and Mary E. Wilkins (see '*The Debtor*' below).

'A Belle of the Fifties'

I have come upon no record of any other woman of her time who has filled so powerful a place politically, whose belleship has been so long sustained, or whose magnetism and compelling fascinations have swayed others so universally as those of Mrs Clay-Clopton.[2]

So writes the lady to whom these memoirs were dictated, and to confess that one has not heard of so distinguished a person argued, at any rate, a culpable ignorance of the America of the Fifties. Indeed, Mrs Clay's memories show her – she is still alive, but the book reaches only to the year 1866 – to have been a very important person in her day, and in that day all kinds of stirring things came to pass. Her position as the wife of Senator Clement Clay, junior, and her own personal gifts gave her not only the influence of her 'belleship', as the quaint American has it, but a real political power as well. She was, in fact, an American version of our European 'great lady', with certain characteristic differences, and women of her type were commoner before than after the war. All this makes her story well worth listening to, and she tells it with the charming candour of the old who can dispense with the hesitations and self-consciousness of those who have no such reason to be sure of themselves. As we read we feel that we are one of the circle of great nephews and nieces who love to hear for the hundredth time, perhaps, what a brilliant and beautiful young woman this old lady of eighty was fifty years ago – how many distinguished men admired her, what dress she wore at Mrs Gwin's famous fancy-dress ball in '58,[3] and those sadder memories which still have power to stir her blood, of the war and the terrible days after the murder of Lincoln.

Mrs Clay, born Virginia Tunstall, came of the aristocracy of America, and was brought up in Tuscaloosa, the capital of Alabama, where the old aristocratic tradition of the South was splendidly preserved, and the planters lived the lives of great English landowners, with vast estates and retinues of slaves dependent on them. All this was pleasant and as it should be, and the little girl was brought up to honour three things religiously – her name, blood, and section; her Bible; and the *Richmond Enquirer*. She early showed herself possessed of beauty, an impulsive wit, and great power of fascination. She tells us how before she was fifteen she had her first bitter sorrow. She fell desperately in love with a hero, who proved to be already provided with wife and child, and for twelve or fourteen hours she went through an agony of disappointment. She recovered, happily, and soon afterwards married the rising young statesman, Clement Clay. Immediately after their marriage he was elected a Senator of the United States, and thus began her brilliant career in political circles at Washington. Here, although she notes as early as 1854 the growing strain between the North and the South, which made sovial civilities difficult between them, society was almost feverishly gay. The Southerners, by virtue of their inherited polish, were the leaders of society, and, as we guess, Mrs Clay was the leader of the Southerners. Washington, though the capital of a democracy, was as rigidly divided into sets, and these sets were as strictly ruled by their separate codes of etiquette as any capital that owns a court and a nobility. The foreign ministers lent an air of distinction to the diplomatic gatherings, and, says Mrs Clay, were the 'critics and mentors of the Americans, who were not so highly accomplished'.[4] In the 'mess' of the Southerners, she declares, there was 'scarcely a man who had not won a conspicuous position in the nation's affairs: hardly a woman without wit or beauty'.[5] The ladies, indeed, received tributes of admiration which are, we are told, of international fame. There was the famous trio of beauties – Mrs Pugh, the perfect brunette; Mrs Douglas, the blonde; Mrs Pryor,[6] a brunette of lighter complexion, with soft brown hair and eyes – and it was to Mrs Pugh that the Austrian Ambassador paid the compliment which is now, as it deserves to be, a 'classic in the capital':

It was at a dance at which pretty women thronged. As the Minister's gaze rested upon Miss Chalfant (afterwards Mrs Pugh) his eyes expanded with admiration. Approaching, he knelt suddenly before her, exclaiming 'Madame! I have from my Empress a piece of precious lace' – and he fumbled, alas! vainly in his pockets as he spoke – 'which her Majesty has commanded me to present to the most beautiful woman in Washington. You . . . you are, more – the most beautiful in the world! I have not with me the lace, but I will send it, if you will permit me!' And he kept his word.[7]

Then there were other ladies – Miss Walton, Madame de Bodisco, Addie

Cutts, and Mrs Pendleton[8] – whose portraits in the curls and crinolines of the Fifties are given us to make good their long-forgotten claim to belleship. Then we have the description in minute detail of the dress of fifty years ago; how 'Low necks and lace berthas were worn almost universally; panelled skirts, in which two materials, a plain and embossed or embroidered fabric, were combined, and basques with postilion backs became the order of the day.'[9] Fine dress material, we observe, had to be bought abroad and made up at home. Thanks to Mrs Clay, we are able to realise that the ladies who were covered with all this old-fashioned finery did really exist beneath the mass of artificialities which makes our own early Victorian days so strangely unreal. There is the delightful 'Lady' Crittenden,[10] for instance, who appears before us, mountainous and stately, with her dress slipping from her 'superbly moulded' shoulders and her skirt extended over a monster crinoline – a splendid monument of her time. She was wont to boast of her 'perfect happiness', which she accounts for thus:

I have been married three times, and in each alliance I have got just what I wanted. My first marriage was for love, and it was mine as fully as I could wish; my second for money, and Heaven was as good to me in this instance; my third was for position, and that too is mine. What more could I ask?[11]

There is a certain delightful freedom from restraint about the American; witness also the senator who kept a supply of soft wood in his desk in the Chamber which he whittled perpetually – on one occasion into a heart – during the sitting, and blew kisses to the Ladies' Gallery.[12] We cannot dwell further upon what are somewhat barbarously called the 'antebellum days', nor can we do justice to the famous fancy dress ball to which Mrs Clay went dressed as Aunt Ruthy Partington,[13] an American Mrs Malaprop, and where she so distinguished herself with a flow of witticisms, which did not cease all the evening, that her husband declared, 'When she married me America lost its Siddons!'[14] Mrs Clay was famous for her wit, we gather, and made so bold as to pun upon the English Ambassador's name when she asked him whether some lovely American lady was likely to be 'Lyonised'.[15] But soon came 'the saddest day of my life',[16] when, on 21 January 1861, Mr Clay took up his portfolio and left the Senate Chamber. The whole of the Southern party went with him, the capital was deserted, and the four years' war begun.

Mrs Clay was by birth and sympathy a Southerner – a lady of

vehement emotions, who took up her cause with enthusiasm. Consequently we are not allowed to weigh the questions which separated the two sides, and almost immediately we find ourselves at the Southern headquarters at Richmond. McClellan's army was gradually closing round, and the city soon took on some of the familiar aspects of a place besieged by an enemy. Nevertheless, Mrs Clay had brought some fine dresses to the front, and with undaunted energy, *The Rivals*, in which she acted Mrs Malaprop, was given by the officers and their wives to the distant boom of the Northern guns. But food and money running short, it was thought advisable for Mrs Clay and others to seek shelter in the South, and she went to stay with friends in Georgia. The old home at Huntsville was in possession of the enemy, and Mrs Clay had to picture the Northern general's daughter, Miss Mitchell,[17] mounted on her mare and dressed in her own green riding-habit. Emissaries from Europe told only of hostile feeling towards the South, and the superior resources of the North began to tell. In short, the fortunes of the South were waning, and Mrs Clay paints an attractive picture of the old plantation life as she looked on it for the last time. She stayed at the great Redcliffe estate in South Carolina, where 400 slaves were owned by one man.[18] The colony was entirely self-supporting; they had their own mills, their smithies, their farms, and their flocks and herds, and they all looked up, as did feudal retainers in mediæval England, to one lord whose word was law. Their lives were of idyllic peace and prosperity, according to Mrs Clay, and the freedom for which they were not ready was a gift that they abused.[19] After peace was made she describes how she went back to her husband's city to be jostled in the streets by the now insolent and emancipated negroes, and the conclusion she draws is, naturally, the conclusion of the deposed aristocrat.

After Lincoln's murder[20] Mr Clay, together with President Davis, was imprisoned under conditions of brutal severity at Fortress Monroe, and the rest of Mrs Clay's book is devoted to a detailed account of her efforts to secure his freedom, which hardly possess for us the interest that they naturally have for a partisan. He was finally liberated in 1866 and, here, briefly foretelling his death, worn out by services and sufferings undergone for his country, Mrs Clay brings her most entertaining book to an end. Her own brilliant part in the fortunes of her country at a critical stage of its growth was over, and we can only thank her for letting us share in the memories which she relates with such spirit and enthusiasm.

1 – A review in the *Guardian*, 8 February 1905, (Kp C05) of *A Belle of the Fifties: Memoirs of Mrs Clay, of Alabama. Put into Narrative Form by Ada Sterling* (Heinemann, 1905). Reading Notes (MHP, B 1a), dated: 24 January.

2 – Sterling, p. vii. Virginia Clay, *née* Tunstall (1825–1915) subsequently Clay-Clopton, was the wife of Senator Clement Claiborne Clay, Jnr, lawyer and Confederate diplomat. Her memoirs give an account of social and political life in Washington and the South during 1853–66, years when, at the height of the Civil War, the reviewer's father, Leslie Stephen (whose sympathies, however, lay distinctly with the North) had been in Washington and had visited the battle front.

3 – Mary, *née* Bell, second wife of Senator William McKendree Gwin; an account of the ball, early in the season 1857–58, is given in *ibid*., ch. IX, 'A Celebrated Social Event'.

4 – Sterling, p. 34, a paraphrase.

5 – *Ibid*., p. 44, which has: 'Scarcely a male member of it but had won or was destined to win a conspicuous position in the Nation's affairs; scarcely a woman in the circle who was not acknowledged to be a wit or beauty.'

6 – The trio of beauties were: Thérèse, *née* Chalfant, wife of Senator George Ellis Pugh; Adèle, *née* Cutts, wife of the Democratic leader, Senator Stephen Arnold Douglas; and Sara, *née* Rice, wife of Roger Atkinson Pryor, congressman, confederate soldier and jurist – she was the author of *Reminiscences of Peace and War* (1904).

7 – *Ibid*., pp. 44–5, which has: 'It was at a ball . . . '; and 'but, alas!', this passage being parenthesised by brackets, not dashes, in the original. (The Austrian minister to Washington concerned was Chevalier Hulseman.)

8 – Octavia Walton, afterwards famous as Mme Le Vert, Mme de Bodisco, *née* Harriet Williams, was the widow of Baron Alexandre de Bodisco, Russian minister to Washington from 1838 until his death in 1854; Addie Cutts, see n. 6 above; Mrs Pendleton, otherwise unidentified, was the wife of Senator George Hunt Pendleton.

9 – Sterling, p. 89; the matter has been edited together by VW and is quoted out of sequence.

10 – Elizabeth, *quondam* Ashley, third wife of Senator John Jordan Crittenden, lawyer and statesman, advocate of the so-called Crittenden Compromise to avert the Civil War.

11 – Sterling, p. 84.

12 – The indefatigable whittler was General Sam Houston (1793–1863), soldier and statesman of Texas; see *ibid*., p. 99.

13 – Sydney Smith's imaginary character described as vainly mopping back the ocean, transformed by the humorist, newspaperman and poet Benjamin Penhallow Shillaber (1814–90) into a national figure; see, e.g., his *Life and Sayings of Mrs Partington* (1854).

14 – Sterling, p. 136n.

15 – *Ibid*., p. 141; Richard Bickerton Pemell Lyons, 2nd Baron and 1st Earl Lyons (1817–87), British minister in Washington from December 1858 and through the critical period of the Civil War, until poor health forced his resignation in February 1865.

16 – See *ibid.*, pp. 146–8, for the origin of this apparent paraphrase.

17 – Daughter of General Ormsby Macknight Mitchel, astronomer and soldier; see Sterling, pp. 183–4.

18 – The slave owner was Senator James H. Hammond (1807–64), governor of South Carolina, 1842–4; his home was at Beech Island.

19 – Effectively on 9 April 1865, at Appomattox Courthouse.

20 – Abraham Lincoln was shot dead by the actor John Wilkes Booth on the night of 14 April 1865.

Mr Henry James's Latest Novel

Mr Henry James is one of the very few living writers who are sufficiently great to possess a point of view. We know by this time what that point of view is, and when we read a new book by him we do not expect to make discoveries, but to look once more at familiar sights through the old spectacles. And yet, though he has written so much and so well, this last book, with its all but 550 closely printed pages, gives proof that he finds the old problems as engrossing as ever, and is still toiling to say what he means, to say all he means, to leave nothing unsaid that can by any possibility complete the picture. We may dispute his theory of what a novel ought to be; but no one can deny that he brings gifts to the task which fail very little of first-rate quality, and that in using them he employs a high conscientiousness which is as admirable as it is rare. In the 550 pages of his last book there is not one, we may assert, that bears traces of haste or carelessness; there is not one that does not make one think; not one that has not its own exquisite felicity of word or thought which alone would illumine a whole chapter of an ordinary novel.

The plot, if one can call it so, is of the slightest; an episode – an incident to be disposed of by the average novelist in ten pages or less. Everything that happens in *The Golden Bowl* might have happened to a score of people one knows; but it needs skill of the very highest to make novels out of such everyday material. Mr James is one of the few who attempt to picture people as they are; his work, therefore, always commands our respect and gratitude. But, again, though he is almost over-scrupulous not to exaggerate, to see people as they are and the lives that they really lead, it is naturally through his own eyes that he sees them. Mr James's eyes, we are often led to think, must be provided with some extra fine lens, the number of things he sees is so extraordinary. It follows that his characters are similarly endowed. The 550 pages of *The Golden Bowl* are devoted to showing how four people met a certain natural difficulty which must frequently occur outside Mr James's novels, but which can hardly ever, one would imagine, produce such an amount of thinking and analysing and hair-splitting as it does within them. They are all four superlatively high-minded, and only too solicitous for each other's happiness. The book, indeed, might be called a study in the evils of unselfishness, so much pain does their care for each other inflict. The tragedy, if that is not too strong a word, is acted in dumb show. A 'scene' would have been impossible between all these well-bred and distinguished people, but Mr James has a singular power of intimating what four separate people are thinking and showing us the silent conflict of their thought without making his character speak or act. The greater part of the book is taken up with a long-drawn-out struggle for supremacy between two women; but though there are vital interests at stake and all the force of both is put into the contest, the battle and victory are eminently decorous, and when speech is necessary the words are few, and the voices are not raised.

It is, after all, a slight theme on which to spend so much ingenuity, and we suffer from a surfeit of words. For all the skill and care that have been spent on them the actors remain but so many distinguished ghosts. We have been living with thoughts and emotions, not with live people. The effect of all this marvellous accumulation of detail – all of it doubtless true, all there to see if we look close enough – obscures the main outlines. Mr James is like an artist who, with a sure knowledge of anatomy, paints every bone and muscle in the human frame; the portrait would be greater as a work of art if he were content to say less and suggest more. But Mr James tortures himself and wearies his readers in his strenuous effort to get everything said that there is to say. Many overburdened sentences could be quoted as proof of this curious sense of duty: 'This perception expanded, on the spot, as a flower, one of the strangest, might, at a breath, have suddenly opened.' 'She rubbed with her palm the polished mahogany of the balustrade, which was mounted on fine iron-work, eighteenth-century English.'[2] These are trivial instances of detail which, perpetually insisted on, fatigues without adding to the picture. Genius would have dissolved them, and whole chapters of the same kind, into a single word. Genius, however, is precisely what we do not find; and it is for this reason that we do not count Mr James's characters among the creatures of our brains, nor can we read his books easily and without conscious effort. But when we have made this reservation our praise must be unstinted. There is no living novelist whose standard is higher, or whose achievement is so consistently great.

1 – A review in the *Guardian*, 22 February 1905, (Kp c06) of *The Golden Bowl* (Methuen, 1905) by Henry James (1843–1916). The published version was substantially cut: 'It was quite good before the official eye fell upon it,' VW wrote to Violet Dickinson (*I VW Letters*, no. 217): 'now it is worthless, and doesn't in the least represent all the toil I put into it – and the book deserved a good and careful review.' See App. III where the Reading Notes for this article are reproduced. See also 'Portraits of Places' below; 'The Old Order', 'The Method of Henry James', *II VW Essays*; 'Within the Rim', 'The Letters of Henry James', 'Henry James's Ghost Stories', *III VW Essays*.

2 – James, Bk First, ch. VIII, p. 107: 'The guest had carried them to the door of the billiard-room, and their appearance, as it opened to admit them determined for Adam Verver, in the oddest way in the world, a new and sharp perception. It *was* really remarkable: this perception expanded on the spot, as a flower, one of the strangest, might, at a breath, have suddenly opened.'

Ibid., ch. V, p. 65, extracted from a more extensive example of James's 'curious overburdened sentences' (see App. III): 'She had stood a stair or two below him; where, while she looked up at him beneath the high domed light of the hall, she rubbed with her palm . . . '

The Decay of Essay-writing

The spread of education and the necessity which haunts us to impart what we have acquired have led, and will lead still further, to some startling results. We read of the over-burdened British Museum – how even its appetite for printed matter flags, and the monster pleads that it can swallow no more. This public crisis has long been familiar in private houses. One member of the household is almost officially deputed to stand at the hall door with flaming sword and do battle with the invading armies. Tracts, pamphlets, advertisements, gratuitous copies of magazines, and the literary productions of friends come by post, by van, by messenger – come at all hours of the day and fall in the night, so that the morning breakfast-table is fairly snowed up with them.

This age has painted itself more faithfully than any other in a myriad of clever and conscientious though not supremely great works of fiction; it has tried seriously to liven the faded colours of bygone ages; it has delved industriously with spade and axe in the rubbish-heaps and ruins; and, so far, we can only applaud our use of pen and ink. But if you have a monster like the British public to feed, you will try to tickle its stale palate in new ways; fresh and amusing shapes must be given to the old commodities – for we really have nothing so new to say that it will not fit into one of the familiar forms. So we confine ourselves to no one literary medium; we try to be new by being old; we revive mystery-plays and affect an archaic accent; we deck ourselves in the fine raiment of an embroidered style; we cast off all clothing and disport ourselves nakedly. In short, there is no end to our devices, and at this very moment probably some ingenious youth is concocting a fresh one which, be it ever so new, will grow stale in its turn. If there are thus an infinite variety of fashions in the external shapes of our wares, there are a certain number – naturally not so many – of wares that are new in substance and in form which we have either invented or very much developed. Perhaps the most significant of these literary inventions is the invention of the personal essay. It is true that it is at least as old as Montaigne, but we may count him the first of the moderns.[2] It has been used with considerable frequency since his day, but its poularity with us is so immense and so peculiar that we are justified in looking upon it as something of our own – typical, characteristic, a sign of the times which will strike the eye of our great-great-grandchildren. Its significance, indeed, lies not so much in the fact that we have attained any brilliant success in essay-writing – no one has approached the essays of Elia[3] – but in the undoubted facility with which we write essays as though this were beyond all others our natural way of speaking. The peculiar form of an essay implies a peculiar substance; you can say in this shape what you cannot with equal fitness say in any other. A very wide definition obviously must be that which will include all the varieties of thought which are suitably enshrined in essays; but perhaps if you say that an essay is essentially egoistical you will not exclude many essays and you will certainly include a potentous number. Almost all essays begin with a capital I – 'I think', 'I feel' – and when you have said that, it is clear that you are not writing history or philosophy or biography or anything but an essay, which may be brilliant or profound, which may deal with the immortality of the soul, or the rheumatism in your left shoulder, but is primarily an expression of personal opinion.

We are not – there is, alas! no need to prove it – more subject to ideas than our ancestors; we are not, I hope, in the main more egoistical; but there is one thing in which we are more highly skilled than they are; and that is in manual dexterity with a pen. There can be no doubt that it is to the art of penmanship that we owe our present literature of essays. The very great of old – Homer and Aeschylus – could dispense with a pen; they were not inspired by sheets of paper and gallons of ink; no fear that their harmonies, passed from lip to lip, should lose their cadence and die. But our essayists write because the gift of writing has been bestowed on them. Had they lacked writing-masters we should have lacked essayists. There are, of course, certain distinguished people who use this medium from genuine inspiration because it best embodies the soul of their thought. But, on the other hand, there is a very large number who make the fatal pause, and the mechanical act of writing is allowed to set the brain in motion which should only be accessible to a higher inspiration.

The essay, then, owes its popularity to the fact that its proper use is to express one's personal peculiarities, so that under the decent veil of print one can indulge one's egoism to the full. You need know nothing of music, art, or literature to have a certain interest in their productions, and the great burden of modern criticism is simply the expression of such individual likes and dislikes – the amiable garrulity of the tea-table – cast into the form of essays. If men and women must write, let them leave the great mysteries of art and literature unassailed; if they told us frankly not of the books that we can all read and the pictures which hang for us all to see, but of that single book to which they alone have the key and of that solitary picture whose face is shrouded to all but one gaze – if they would write of themselves – such writing would have its own permanent value. The simple words 'I was born' have somehow a charm beside which all the splendours of romance and fairy-tale turn to moonshine and tinsel. But though it seems thus easy enough to write of one's self, it is, as we know, a feat but seldom accomplished. Of the multitude of autobiographies that are written, one or two alone are what they pretend to be. Confronted with the terrible spectre of themselves, the bravest are inclined to run away or shade their eyes. And thus, instead of the honest truth which we should all respect, we are given timid side-glances in the shape of essays, which, for the most part, fail in the cardinal virtue of sincerity. And those who do not sacrifice their beliefs to the turn of a phrase or the glitter of paradox think it beneath the dignity of the printed word to say simply what it means; in print they must pretend to an oracular and infallible nature. To say simply 'I have a garden, and I will tell you what plants do best in my garden' possibly justified its egoism; but to say 'I have no sons, though I have six daughters, all unmarried, but I will tell you how I should have brought up my sons had I had any' is not interesting, cannot be useful, and is a specimen of the amazing and unclothed egoism for which first the art of penmanship and then the invention of essay-writing are responsible.

1 – An essay in *Academy & Literature*, 25 February 1905, (Kp C07). Submitted as 'A Plague of Essays', it appeared (cut by 'a good half') under the present editorially imposed title ('which means nothing') above the reviewer's name ('to which I do object'); see *I VW Letters*, no. 219, to Violet Dickinson. See also 'The Modern Essay', *IV VW Essays* and *CR1*.
2 – Montaigne's *Essais* were first published in 1580 and 1588. See also 'Montaigne', *IV VW Essays* and *CR1*.
3 – Charles Lamb, *Elia* (1823 and 1828) and the *The Last Essays of Elia* (1833).

Street Music

'Street musicians are counted a nuisance' by the candid dwellers in most London squares, and they have taken the trouble to emblazon this terse bit of musical criticism upon a board which bears other regulations for the peace and propriety of the square. No artist, however, pays the least attention to criticism, and the artist of the streets is properly scornful of the judgment of the British public. It is remarkable that in spite of such discouragement as I have noted – enforced on occasion by a British policeman – the vagrant musician is if anything on the increase. The German band gives a weekly concert as regularly as the Queen's Hall orchestra; the Italian organ grinders are as faithful to their audience and reappear punctually on the same platform, and in addition to these recognised masters every street has an occasional visit from some wandering star. The stout Teuton and the swarthy Italian certainly live on something more substantial than the artistic satisfaction of their own souls; and it is therefore probable that the coins, which it is beneath the dignity of the true lover of music to throw from the drawing-room window, are tendered at the area steps. There is an audience, in short, who is willing to pay for even such crude melody as this.

Music, to be successful in a street, must be loud before it is beautiful, and for this reason brass is the favourite instrument, and one may conclude that the street musician who uses his own voice or a violin has a genuine reason for his choice. I have seen violinists who were obviously using their instrument to express something in their own hearts as they swayed by the kerb in Fleet Street; and the copper, though rags make it acceptable, was, as it is to all who love their work, a perfectly incongruous payment. Indeed, I once followed a disreputable old man who, with eyes shut so that he might the better perceive the melodies of his soul, literally played himself from Kensington to Knightsbridge in a trance of musical ecstasy, from which a coin would have been a disagreeable awakening. It is, indeed, impossible not to respect any one who has a god like this within them; for music that takes possession of the soul so that nakedness and hunger are forgotten must be divine in its nature. It is true that the melodies that issued from his labouring violin were in themselves laughable, but he, certainly, was not. Whatever the accomplishment, we must always treat with tenderness the efforts of those who strive honestly to express the music that is in them; for the gift of conception is certainly superior to the gift of expression, and it is not unreasonable to suppose that the men and women who scrape for the harmonies that never come while the traffic goes thundering by have as great a possession, though fated never to impart it, as the masters whose facile eloquence enchants thousands to listen.

There is more than one reason perhaps why the dwellers in squares look upon the street musician as a nuisance; his music disturbs the householder at his legitimate employment, and the vagrant and unorthodox nature of such a trade irritates a well-ordered mind. Artists of all kinds have invariably been looked on with disfavour, especially by English people, not solely because of the eccentricities of the artistic temperament, but because we have trained ourselves to such perfection of civilisation that expression of any kind has something almost indecent – certainly irreticent – about it. Few parents, we observe, are willing that their sons should become painters or poets or musicians, not only for worldly reasons, but because in their own hearts they consider that it is unmanly to give expression to the thoughts and emotions which the arts express and which it should be the endeavour of the good citizen to repress. Art in this way is certainly not encouraged; and it is probably easier for an artist than for a member of any other profession to descend to the pavement. The artist is not only looked upon with contempt but with a suspicion that has not a little of fear in it. He is possessed by a spirit which the ordinary person cannot understand, but which is clearly very potent, and exercises so great a sway over him that when he hears its voice he must always rise and follow.

Nowadays we are not credulous, and though we are not comfortable in the presence of artists we do our best to domesticate them. Never was such respect paid to the successful artist as there is to-day; and perhaps we may see in this a sign of what many people have foretold, and that the gods who went into exile when the first Christian altars rose will come back to enjoy their own again. Many writers have tried to trace these old pagans, and have professed to find them in the disguise of animals and in the shelter of far-away woods and mountains; but it is not fantastic to suppose that while every one is searching for them they are working their charms in the midst of us, and that those strange heathens who do the bidding of no man and are inspired by a voice that is other than human in their ears are not really as other people, but are either the very gods themselves or their priests and prophets upon earth. Certainly I should be inclined to ascribe some such divine origin to musicians at any rate, and it is probably some suspicion of this kind that drives us to persecute them as we do. For if the stringing together of words which nevertheless may convey some useful information to the mind, or the laying on of colours which may represent some tangible object, are employments which can be but tolerated at best, how are we to regard the man who spends his time in making tunes? Is not his occupation the least respectable – the least useful and necessary – of the three? It is certain that you can carry away nothing that can be of service to you in your day's work from listening to music; but a musician is not merely a useful creature, to many, I believe, he is the most dangerous of the whole tribe of artists. He is the minister of the wildest of all the gods, who has not yet learnt to speak with human voice, or to convey to the mind the likeness of human things. It is because music incites within us something that is wild and inhuman like itself – a spirit that we would willingly stamp out and forget – that we are distrustful of musicians and loath to put ourselves under their power.

To be civilised is to have taken the measure of our own capabilities and to hold them in a perfect state of discipline; but one of our gifts has, as we conceive, so slight a power of beneficence, so unmeasured a power of harm, that far from cultivating it we have done our best to cripple and stifle it. We look upon those who have given up their lives to the service of this god as Christians regard the fanatic worshippers of some eastern idol. This arises perhaps from an uneasy foreknowledge that when the pagan gods come back the god we have never worshipped will have his revenge upon us. It will be the god of music who will breathe madness into our brains, crack the walls of our temples, and drive us in loathing of our rhythmless lives to dance and circle for ever in obedience to his voice.

The number of those that declare, as though confessing their immunity from some common weakness, that they have no ear for music is increasing, though such a confession ought to be as serious as the confession that one is colour blind. The way in which music is taught and presented by its ministers must to some extent be held answerable for this. Music is dangerous as we know, and those that teach it have not the courage to impart it in its strength, from fear of what would happen to the child who should drink so intoxicating a draught. The whole of rhythm and harmony have been pressed, like dried flowers, into the neatly divided scales, the tones and semitones of the pianoforte. The safest and easiest attribute of music – its tune – is taught, but rhythm, which is its soul, is allowed to escape like the winged creature it is. Thus educated people who have been taught what it is safe for them to know of music are those who oftenest boast of their want of ear, and the uneducated, whose sense of rhythm has never been divorced or made subsidiary to their sense of tune, are those who cherish the greatest love of music and are oftenest heard producing it.

It may be indeed that the sense of rhythm is stronger in people whose minds are not elaborately trained to other pursuits, as it is true that savages who have none of the arts of civilisation are very sensitive to rhythm, before they are awake to music proper. The beat of rhythm in the mind is akin to the beat of the pulse in the body; and thus though many are deaf to tune hardly any one is so coarsely organised as not to hear the rhythm of its own heart in words and music and movement. It is because it is thus inborn in us that we can never silence music, any more than we can stop our heart from beating; and it is for this reason too that music is so universal and has the strange and illimitable power of a natural force.

In spite of all that we have done to repress music it has a power over us still whenever we give ourselves up to its sway that no picture, however fair, or words however stately, can approach. The strange sight of a room full of civilised people moving in rhythmic motion at the command of a band of musicians is one to which we have grown accustomed, but it may be that some day it will suggest the vast possibilities that lie within the power of rhythm, and the whole of our life will be revolutionised as it was when man first realised the power of steam. The barrel-organ, for instance, by reason of its crude and emphatic rhythm, sets all the legs of the passers by walking in time; a band in the centre of the wild discord of cabs and carriages would be more effectual than any policeman; not only cabman but horse would find himself constrained to keep time in the dance, and to follow whatever measure of trot or canter the trumpets dictated. This principle has been in some degree recognised in the army, where troops are inspired to march into battle to the rhythm of music. And when the sense of rhythm was thoroughly alive in every mind we should if I mistake not, notice a great improvement not only in the ordering of all the affairs of daily life, but also in the art of writing, which is nearly allied to the art of music, and is chiefly degenerate because it has forgotten its allegiance. We should invent – or rather remember – the innumerable metres which we have so long outraged, and which would restore both prose and poetry to the harmonies that the ancients heard and observed.

Rhythm alone might easily lead to excesses; but when the ear possessed its secret, tune and harmony would be united with it, and those actions which by means of rhythm were performed punctually and in time, would now be done with whatever of melody is natural to each. Conversation, for instance, would not only obey its proper laws of metre as dictated by our sense of rhythm, but would be inspired by charity, love and wisdom, and ill-temper or sarcasm would sound to the bodily ear as terrible discords and false notes. We all know that the voices of friends are discordant after listening to beautiful music because they disturb the echo of rhythmic harmony, which for the moment makes of life a united and musical whole; and it seems probable considering this that there is a music in the air for which we are always straining our ears and which is only partially made audible to us by the transcripts which the great musicians are able to preserve. In forests and solitary places an attentive ear can detect something very like a vast pulsation, and if our ears were educated we might hear the music also which accompanies this. Though this is not a human voice it is yet a voice which some part of us can, if we let it, understand, and music perhaps because it is not human is the only thing made by men that can never be mean or ugly.

If, therefore, instead of libraries, philanthropists would bestow free music upon the poor, so that at each street corner the melodies of Beethoven and Brahms and Mozart could be heard, it is probable that all crime and quarrelling would soon be unknown, and the work of the hand and the thoughts of the mind would flow melodiously in obedience to the laws of music. It would then be a crime to account street musicians or any one who interprets the voice of the god as other than a holy man, and our lives would pass from dawn to sunset to the sound of music.

1 – An essay in the *National Review*, no. 265, March 1905, (Kp c3) published above its author's name. Although fully applauded by the editor Leo Maxse ('a paradox is always popular', *I VW Letters*, no. 228 to Violet Dickinson), it was to prove VW's only contribution to this journal (see App. IV). See also *I VW Letters*, nos 216, 218, 227.

Literary Geography

These two books belong to what is called the 'Pilgrimage' series, and before undertaking the journey it is worth considering in what spirit we do so. We are either pilgrims from sentiment, who find something stimulating to the imagination in the fact that Thackeray rang this very door bell or that Dickens shaved behind that identical window, or we are scientific in our pilgrimage and visit the country where a great novelist lived in order to see to what extent he was influenced by his surroundings. Both motives are often combined and can be legitimately satisfied; as, for instance, in the case of Scott or the Brontës, George Meredith or Thomas Hardy.[2] Each of these novelists may be said to possess a spiritual sovereignty which no one else can dispute. They have made the country theirs because they have so interpreted it as to have given it an ineffaceable shape in our minds, so that we know certain parts of Scotland, of Yorkshire, of Surrey, and of Dorset as intimately as we know the men and women who have their dwelling there. Novelists who are thus sensitive to the inspiration of the land are alone able to describe the natives who are in some sense the creatures of the land. Scott's men and women are Scotch; Miss Brontë loves her moors so well that she can draw as no one else can the curious type of human being that they produce; and so we may say not only that novelists own a country, but that all who dwell in it are their subjects. It seems a little incongruous to talk of the Thackeray 'country' or the Dickens 'country' in this sense; for the word calls up a vision of woods and fields, and you may read through a great number of these masters' works without finding any reason to believe that the whole world is not paved with cobble stones. Both Thackeray and Dickens were Londoners; the country itself comes very seldom into their books, and the country man or woman – the characteristic product of the country – hardly at all. But to say that a man is a Londoner implies only that he is not one of the far more definite class of countrymen; it does not stamp him as belonging to any recognised type.

In the case of Thackeray any such definition is more than usually absurd; he was, as Mr Melville remarks, a cosmopolitan; with London for a basis he travelled everywhere; and it follows that the characters in his books are equally citizens of the world. 'Man and not scenery,' says Mr Melville, 'was what he strove to portray';[3] and it is because he took so vast and various a subject that the only possible scene for a pilgrim in Thackeray's footsteps is the great world of London. And even in London, the scene of *Vanity Fair*, of *Pendennis*, of *The Newcomes*,[4] it is not easy to decide upon the exact shrine at which we are to offer incense. Thackeray did not consider the feelings of these devout worshippers, and left many of his localities vague. Whole districts rather than individual streets and houses seem to be his; and though we are told that he knew exactly where Becky and Colonel Newcome and Pendennis lived, the photographs of the authentic houses somehow leave one's imagination cold.[5] To imprison these immortals between brick walls strikes one as an unnecessary act of violence; they have always tenanted their own houses in our brains, and we refuse to let them go elsewhere. But there can be no such risk in following Thackeray himself from one house to another; and we may perhaps find that it adds to our knowledge of him and of his books to see where he lived when he was writing them and what surroundings met his eye. But here again we must select. Charterhouse and the Temple, Jermyn Street, and Young Street, Kensington, are the genuine Thackeray country, which seems to echo not only his presence but his spirit; these are the places that he has interpreted as well as pictured. But it needs either a boundless imagination or a mind that holds sacred the boots and umbrellas of the great to follow Thackeray with unflagging interest in his journeyings to Ireland, to America, and to all parts of the Continent; and at 36 Onslow Square, Brompton, the most devoted pilgrim might find it difficult to bend the knee.[6]

We do less violence to the truth if, in our love of classification, we describe Dickens as a cockney. We might draw a very distinct line round London – even round certain districts of London – if we wished to circumscribe his kingdom. It is true that the late Mr Kitton,[7] who brought what we must consider a superfluous zeal and a too minute knowledge to the task, begins his book with two or three pictures of Portsmouth and Chatham. We are asked to imagine the child Dickens as he looked at the stars from the upper window of 18 St Mary's Place,[8] and we are assured that he enjoyed many a ramble with his sister and nurse in the fields near Chatham. The imagination oppressed with these details has to bear an altogether insupportable load before it has followed Dickens to his last resting place. Mr Melville was wise enough to ignore the 'hundred and one places of minor importance' in writing of Thackeray and select only those that seemed to him of primary interest – from which the reader will probably make a further selection. But Mr Kitton, whose mind was a unique storehouse of facts about Dickens, lets us have the full benefit of his curiously minute scolarship. He knows not only every house where Dickens lived, but every lodging that he took for a month or two in the summer; he tells us how Dickens seemed to prefer 'houses having semi-circular frontages' and describes the inns where Dickens lodged and the mugs from which he is said to have drunk and the 'stiff wooden chair' in which he sat. A pilgrimage, if one followed this guide, would be a very serious undertaking; and we doubt whether the pilgrim at the end would know very much more about Dickens and his writings than he did at the beginning. The most vivid and valuable part of the book is that which describes the various dwelling places of Dickens as a young man before he was famous and could afford a 'frightfully first-class family mansion',[9] as he calls it. It was while he lived in these dreary and dingy back streets in Camden Town and the neighbourhood of the Debtors' Prison that Dickens absorbed the view of life which he was afterwards to reproduce so brilliantly. These early experiences, indeed, read like the first sketch for David Copperfield.[10] No one probably has ever known his London so intimately as Dickens did, or has painted the life of the streets with such first-hand knowledge. He was not really happy when he was alone. He made one or two conscientious expeditions into the country in search of local colour, but when it had yielded the words he wanted he had no further use for it. He spent his summer holidays at various seaside resorts, and in London he lived in a variety of houses which leave no single impression upon the mind. Indeed, the book is such an accumulation of detail that it is, after all, from his own writings that one must draw one's impression of the Dickens country.

And perhaps, when everything is said, this is always bound to be the case. A writer's country is a territory within his own brain; and we run the risk of disillusionment if we try to turn such phantom cities into tangible brick and mortar. We know our way there without signposts or policemen, and we can greet the passers-by without need of introduction. No city indeed is so real as this that we make for ourselves and people to our liking; and to insist that it has any counterpart in the cities of the earth is to rob it of half its charm. In the same way too the great dead come to each of us in their own guise, and their image is more palpable and enduring than any shapes of flesh and blood. Of all books therefore the books that try to impress upon the mind the fact that great men were once alive because they lived in this house or in that are those that seem to have least reason for their being, for Thackeray and Dickens, having done with earthly houses, live most certainly in our brains. If the thing must be done, however, we could not wish it better done than it is by Mr Melville. Mr Kitton, from the reasons we have given, seems to us to fail, and to injure the master whom he would honour. Both books are full of excellent pictures, to one of which only we wish to take exception. Surely Mr Melville could have found some happier portrait of Thackeray than the etching in dry point by G. Barnett Smith[11] which forms the frontispiece of his book and which gives a singularly inadequate likeness of the grand and familiar head?

1 – A review in the *TLS*, 10 March 1905, (Kp c1) – VW's first contribution to this journal – of 'two trashy books' (*I VW Letters*, no. 217, to Violet Dickinson): *The Thackeray Country* by Lewis Melville and *The Dickens Country* by F. G. Kitton (Pilgrimage Series, Adam and Charles Black, 1905). Reprinted: *B&P*, in which the concluding passage from 'If the thing must be done . . .' is omitted. Reading Notes (MHP, b 1a) dated: 15 February. See also 'Haworth, November, 1904' above, and 'Great Men's Houses', *V VW Essays* and *The London Scene* (1982).

2 – The Pilgrimage Series included works on Scott (by W. S. Crockett) and Hardy (by Chas. G. Harper) but not, at this date, on either the Brontës or Meredith.

3 – Melville, p. 5.

4 – *Vanity Fair* (1847–8); *The History of Pendennis* (1848–50); *The Newcomes* (1853–5).

5 – Melville includes among fifty full-page illustrations photographs of the originals for Colonel Newcome's house, in Fitzroy Square (facing p. 83), Becky Sharp's house,

in Curzon Street (facing p. 110), and for the chambers Arthur Pendennis shared with George Warrington, in Lamb Court, Middle Temple (facing p. 68).

6 – W. M. Thackeray (1811–63) – who was eventually to become Leslie Stephen's father-in-law – attended Charterhouse in 1822–8, and in 1831 (having come down from Trinity College, Cambridge, without a degree) entered Middle Temple, which, the law not being at all to his liking, he left the following year. He lived in apartments for a period in the 1840s in Jermyn Street; then at 13 (subsequently 16) Young Street, Kensington, 1846–53; and at 36 Onslow Square, Brompton, 1853–62. (His last home was at 2 Palace Green.)

7 – Frederick George Kitton had died in September 1904.

8 – Kitton, p. 17.

9 – Ibid., p. 58, quoting Dickens's The Uncommercial Traveller (1861, 1866).

10 – David Copperfield (1849–50).

11 – George Barnett Smith (1841–1909), biographer, journalist, poet (under the name Guy Roslyn) an intimate of Browning, and, reputedly, an accomplished etcher, examples of whose work were included in English Etchings (1884–7).

'Barham of Beltana'

Mr W. E. Norris inherits the tradition of Anthony Trollope, and like that master produces his novels punctually and copiously because it is his business in life to do so. At this time of day he is not ambitious; he is content to reproduce the surface of a certain section of contemporary English life, and he tells his simple story without any desire to discuss problems or suggest that everything is not precisely as it ought to be. He is the type of writer who regards marriage and the events that precede it as the legitimate end of a novel; and when he has satisfactorily disposed of the difficulties that are necessary to make a plot, the sound of marriage bells is the signal for a general handshaking, and we feel that we can all depart in a state of mild felicity. His last novel is not an exception to Mr Norris's ordinary rule; there is a sufficiently elaborate plot, which does not harrow our feelings unduly, because we know that it will all be happily solved upon the final page. Mr Norris would probably be the first to admit that real life is deficient in plots; but he would also quite readily agree that there is no need to take his unpretentious pictures too seriously. He has no wish, as he says somewhere, to discuss motives and analyse emotions, and therefore it is necessary for the interest of his story that certain more or less improbable things should happen. The plot of Barham of Beltana, for instance, would be very surprising if it were true, and many modern novelists would think it beneath the dignity of their art to make use of such old-fashioned stage properties. But Mr Norris does not take his art too seriously, and is a little amused by the whole business himself. His writing is always that of a gentleman quite at his ease, and whatever subject he treats he never loses his self-control or says a word more than he means. He has piloted too many heroes and heroines through their difficulties to take any very excessive interest in the performance, and his sympathies, we gather, are with the elderly fathers in the background rather than with the sons and daughters who for the moment occupy the stage. 'Some of us,' he says, 'know well enough what is ordinary in human existence and its ever-recurring developments; but we prefer not to contemplate the normal, the monotonous, the saddening.'[2] That clearly represents a middle-aged, perhaps a prosaic point of view; but if it is not profound it is certainly sane and sincere, and these are qualities which give all Mr Norris's work a charm of its own. The present novel will not sadden; it will not excite; but it will provide an hour or two of healthy entertainment; and that, we imagine, is a result with which the author would declare himself content.

1 – A notice in the *TLS*, 17 March 1905 (Kp c1.1), of *Barham of Beltana* (Methuen, 1905) by W. E. (William Edward) Norris (1847–1925); see also '*Lone Marie*' below and '*The Obstinate Lady*', 'Mr Norris's Method' and 'Mr Norris's Standard', *III VW Essays*. Reading Notes (MHP, b 1a) dated: 4 March.
2 – Norris, ch. xxix, p. 302, which begins: 'Some of us (having reached a time of life relatively equivalent to that of a mature goldfish) know well enough . . . '

'By Beach and Bogland'

Stories which illustrate the peculiarities of a certain race, whether the Scotch or the Irish, have generally an interest of their own, and the writer who wishes to preserve this charm finds it most obvious in the poorer classes of the people. The peasants who have lived on the same plot of ground for generations, and who seem, in default of other education, to have received some very intimate communication from the land itself, are the genuine natives; and whoever wishes to understand the history of Ireland must decipher these not easily intelligible characters. In Miss

Barlow we have an interpreter on whose word we feel we may depend. She does not create by force of a great imagination, but she writes from first-hand knowledge, and gives us a succession of pictures which satisfy partly because they are not ambitious. All the stories in this book describe various scenes in the lives of the peasants in far-away Irish villages; and, though the incidents in their lives are rare and unimportant, this very monotony has a charm, because we feel it to be true. The peasant very often spends a lifetime within the radius of his own little village, and every pebble and blade of grass is seen as through a microscope. The few human beings loom proportionately large. If one old lady loses a shilling it is a serious event, and the whole population turn out to look for it. The importance of shillings in such a world is something that we cannot estimate; the lack of them narrows life to its meanest boundaries. But to make up for their poverty in all the things that money can buy, the sea, the bog, the moorland, have an interest for them that is keener than any merely aesthetic pleasure. All this is faithfully painted by Miss Barlow, so that her book keeps a great deal of the charm of the wild and melancholy land, and of the people who scrape a scanty living from it.

1 – A notice in the *Guardian*, 22 March 1905, of *By Beach and Bogland* (Fisher Unwin, 1905) by Jane Barlow (author also of the book of verse *Bog-Land Studies*, 1892). Reading Notes (MHP, B 1a): dated 9 March. See Editorial Note, p. xxii.

'The Fortunes of Farthings'

The Fortunes of Fathings by A. J. Dawson has little in common with the average modern novel. The point of view throughout strikes one as old-fashioned. The characters are of the conventional type of hero and villain, and they play their parts with simple-minded consistency. The date of the story has perhaps something to do with this; it took place in the beginning of the eighteenth century, and the scene is laid in Dorset. In those days, apparently, the bottle was the inseparable companion of the old English gentleman, and the squire who had any pretensions to humanity ended the day beneath the dinner-table. The villain kept sober, but this is but another proof of the coldness of his heart. This sober gentleman was 'wizened as a forgotten russet apple in spring time, his nose was sharp as a ferret's, and his sound eye was a grey green gimlet in a pink frame; the other was a forbidding blank.'[2] He is in short everything that an English gentleman of that date ought not to be, and his machinations supply the plot of the book. Mr Dawson draws a more pleasant and truthful picture when he describes the life of the country people of the time, which he has studied 'in cosy chimney-corner talk, over cider mugs dipped into by venerable cronies, among yellow old letters'.[3] His style, which is pleasant and diffuse without being distinguished, is more suited to the farm and the simple country life than to the complexities of the human character. The picture of Dorset of 200 years ago is the most successful part of the book, but unfortunately the one-eyed squire contrives, for good reasons of his own, that our hero shall be kidnapped and carried off on board ship. The ship is taken by Sallee Rovers, and the hero finds himself a Christian slave in the possession of the Sultan of Morocco. The hardships which he underwent in this capacity, and the amazing brutalities of his master fill the last half of the novel. Mr Dawson is a conscientious novelist; not only does he give his authority for every instance of the Sultan's cruelty from contemporary writers, but he tells us that before inflicting a certain penance on his hero he tried it on himself! But such learning and endurance are quite secondary qualities in a novelist, and divert our sympathies from the characters themselves. It is, perhaps, for this reason that we are not deeply interested in the pair of faithful lovers who, after going through many painful experiences, are happily united at last and enjoy all the good fortune they deserve. Mr Dawson has no very strong grasp of character, and he easily lapses into sentimentality and a patriotism which tends to be ridiculous. But if the reader wants a long, amiable, and pleasantly garrulous novel to take to bed with him *The Fortunes of Farthings* will serve his purpose.

1 – A notice in the *TLS*, 31 March 1905, (Kp C1.2) of *The Fortunes of Farthings* (Harper Bros, 1905) by A. J. (Alec John) Dawson. Reading Notes (MHP, B 1a) dated: 18 March.
2 – Dawson, p. 3.
3 – *Ibid.*, p. 49.

'Nancy Stair'

At the outset of this book the reader is met by a problem which should by this time be familiar – whether the story is true, as it purports to be. Biographical dictionaries throw no light on the matter, for, though there are many earls of Stair, not one had a daughter who would correspond with the gifted Nancy of this volume, the poetess and friend of Burns. However, it matters little, for the title-page proclaims the book a novel, and the further one reads the more one is convinced that Miss Mac-Cartney Lane has not been studying the dictionaries. The story is acted in the last half of the eighteenth century; Scotland is the scene; and thus we are at liberty to be as romantic as we like. Nancy Stair is everything that a heroine ought to be, beautiful, witty, a genius at making verses moreover. But it is as a child that we think her most charming, when she reminds us not a little of that other brilliant Scottish child, Marjorie Fleming.[2] She is motherless, and her unusual gifts determine her father to give her a man's education, in spite of a friend's warning that women are not meant to be civilised, and that it is useless to attempt it. The experiment certainly succeeds, in that by the time she grows up the world is at her feet and her poems are famous. But, unfortunately, Miss MacCartney Lane will not let her escape the orthodox doubts as to woman's mission which were to become fashionable a hundred years later. Verse-making had seemed to her the most important thing in the world till she met Burns, who opened her eyes to the fact that divine genius is consistent with very human failings. She realises 'how little value verse-making holds to the real task of living',[3] and understands the real task of living to mean, for a woman at any rate, marriage and motherhood. The genius for poetry seems to be incompatible with the duties of wife and mother, and, as the least important, Nancy has no hesitation in quenching it in order to marry and live happily ever afterwards. This is the eighteenth-century solution of the doubts of the nineteenth century. Such a solution is, of course, the popular one, and it is right, perhaps, that a novelist should take a sentimental point of view and rejoice at the conventional ending. The prosaic mind may be tempted to suggest that the world might, perhaps, be considerably poorer if the great writers had exchanged their books for children of flesh and blood. But Miss Lane does not go very deeply into these problems, and she prefers the romantic to the probable. The scheme of the book, indeed, is too ambitious, and, in spite of footnotes with ostentatious facts and figures, the characters strike us as weak and unreal. But if you represent brilliant young women, great poets, and noble dukes, you have need of an imagination to match your daring. Miss Lane fails in this; but, nevertheless, contrives to write a lively and amusing story.

1 – A notice in the *Guardian*, 10 May 1905, of *Nancy Stair. A Novel* (Heinemann, 1905) by Elinor MacCartney Lane (d. 1909). Reading Notes (MHP, B 1a), undated. See Editorial Note, p. xxii.
2 – Margaret Fleming (1803–11), Sir Walter Scott's 'Pet Marjorie', author of a poem on Mary, Queen of Scots and other verses.
3 – Lane, ch. XIX, p. 244.

'Arrows of Fortune'

The reviewer of Mr Algernon Gissing's last book need not spend much time in criticism of his characters. Their names speak for them. Sir Philip Scorton and Marian Kellbrook are, on the face of it, hero and heroine; Crispin Cragg is obviously the villain. In the first chapter an old book is found in which Marian's dead father has registered his curse and demand for vengeance upon Crispin Cragg, who has apparently done him great wrong in his lifetime. The law-courts, however, had decided that Crispin was within his rights. But Marian is a heroic young woman, and determines, at whatever personal risk, to punish the infamous Cragg. We do not know what precise form her vengeance is to take, because at the first hint of her determination Crispin has her conveyed to a convenient desert island somewhere near the Isle of Man, where she stays for three weeks concealed in a secret room in a smuggler's cottage. She is rescued by the knightly youth, Sir Philip Scorton, who proposes to marry her. She cannot consent to spoil his life because she well knows that she must give herself up to the destruction of Cragg. An alternative is, however, suggested which shall close the feud – that she shall marry Hartley, the son of Cragg. This, with noble self-sacrifice, she consents to do; Sir Philip is fetched from Oxford in the nick of time to overhear a conversation behind a rock at Solway between Marian and Hartley, and the result is that the three take an evening stroll together. Sir Philip and Marian are suddenly seized by rough hands who are in the employment of Hartley, and would, we understand, have conveyed Marian to Bristol – 'for what ultimate destination nobody knew'[2] – but for the intervention of Rhoda Grike, the widow of the smuggler on the desert island. In the scuffle one of the 'Arrows of Fortune' strikes Hartley dead. Marian is naturally accused of his murder, but is acquitted in a Scotch court of law. Crispin has still to be disposed of before the feud can be closed, and Marian comes to the pacific conclusion to let bygones be bygones. Crispin is alarmed less the race of Cragg should become extinct, and proposes to prolong the line by marriage with Rhoda Grike. To this, with a meritorious desire for peace, she consents, on an occasion when the whole party, Marian and her brother Julius, Crispin, and herself seek shelter from a storm in a shed. Marian in each flash of lightning states that she will not consent to this sacrifice, but will end the feud by burning the book herself. Crispin then most opportunely walks out into the storm, where he is struck by the second arrow in the form of a thunderbolt. It only remains for Julius to marry Rhoda and for Marian to become engaged to Sir Philip, who by this time was no longer a boy, 'as a year ago he had begun to shave'.[3] Marian and Philip make a bonfire in a wood into which they drop the evil book (it was, as we suspected, always concealed about her person), where we can only hope that it was burnt to ashes.

1 – A notice in the *Guardian*, 17 May 1905, of *Arrows of Fortune: a tale* (Arrowsmith, 1904) by Algernon Gissing (1860–1937). See Editorial Note, p. xxii.
2 – Gissing, ch. XXI, p. 299.
3 – *Ibid.*, ch. XXXIV, p. 334.

'A Dark Lantern'

Of this novel it can be said without exaggeration that every page interests. If such a thing were possible, it might almost be added that it is too interesting, or, perhaps, that the interest it excites is not quite of the right quality. Miss Robins has the gift of charging her air with electricity, and her readers wait for the expected explosion in a state of high tension. This is partly due to the fact that she is always in earnest – that she is one of the few novelists who can live in their characters. But it is also true that her work would be finer if its intensity were, not less, but, so to speak, diffused over a greater surface. As it is, she is too closely interested in her characters to be able to take a dispassionate view of them. A character like that of Garth Vincent, for instance, comes near failure because of this tendency to a kind of passionate concentration on the part of the novelist. He is one of the many versions of Rochester. The argument applied once more by Miss Robins seems to be that, if you want a man to be excessively masculine, you have only to take certain of the conventional masculine qualities and develop them to the desired strength. The result has overpowering effects within the covers of the novel; but, outside, the hero is more melodramatic than impressive. In the woman's character Miss Robins shows far more sense of proportion, and we protest that if Miss Katherine Dereham had met Mr Garth Vincent under normal conditions she would not have allowed herself to take him seriously. A great part of the book is devoted to the medical details of a nervous breakdown and a rest cure, in which Mr Garth Vincent is the doctor in attendance. Here, too, Miss Robins seems to have had some purpose in her mind which leads her to insist, rather more emphatically than is artistic, upon the faults of hospital nurses and the incidents of physical illness. The defects of the book seem to us to be the persistent atmosphere of the sick-room; of morbidity, whether of body or mind; and the lack of a sense of humour. But there can be no doubt that few living novelists are so genuinely gifted as Miss Robins, or can produce work to match hers for strength and sincerity.

1 – A notice in the *Guardian*, 24 May 1905, (Kp C1.3) of *A Dark Lantern* (Heinemann, 1905) by Elizabeth Robins (1862–1952), the American actress and feminist, pioneer of Ibsen on the London stage; she was a friend of Leslie and Julia Stephen (and of Oscar Wilde) and, in later years, of Leonard and Virginia Woolf. She had already published several novels under the pseudonym C. E. Raimond; her play *Votes for Women* also appeared in 1905. 'She is a clever woman', VW wrote to Violet Dickinson (*I VW Letters*, no. 277), 'if she weren't so brutal.' Reading Notes (MHP, B 1a), undated. See also 'The Mills of the Gods', *III VW Essays*.

Journeys in Spain

Before going on a journey the question of a guide-book naturally suggests itself. Your need is not altogether simple, and, though many profess to supply it, few, when put to the test, are found to succeed. Baedeker settles your hotel and the amount you are expected to tip the waiter; but one suspects Baedeker as an art critic. The asterisk with which he directs you to the best picture and tells you to a superlative how much praise you must be prepared to expend seems too simple a solution of the difficulties of criticism. But though you consult him surreptitiously it is often solely upon him that you come to depend. His work, as generations of grateful travellers can testify, is a necessity, though hardly a luxury. No one thinks of reading him for pleasure, for the reason, perhaps, that his is the most impersonal of books, and even tourists like to be treated as human beings. He provides materials in abundance, but expects you to draw your own conclusions. Thus the traveller when he comes to choose finds that guide-books separate themselves into two classes, and neither gives him completely and compactly what he wants. Books of the type of those that lie before us disclaim, if they do not despise, the name of guide-book. Sterne, when he invented the title of Sentimental Journey,[2] not only christened but called into existence a class of book which seems to grow more popular the more we travel and the more sentimental we become. It is their aim to provide all that Baedeker ignores; but as their aim is more ambitious so is their success very rarely so complete. The Sentimental Journeys that succeed are among the most delightful books in the language; Sterne succeeded and so did Borrow, and Kinglake, and Lord Dufferin, and Mr Henry James.[3] But the list, if we count the competitors, is not a long one. Theirs are books that we may read with almost equal pleasure in the country that they describe or seated a thousand miles away with no prospect of ever seeing the place except with the mind's eye. They owe their success not to any strangeness in the things they saw or to any adventures they met with on the way, but to the faculty of seeing they had in them and of interpreting the sight to others. A book such as this is as much a guide-book to the mind of the man that wrote it as it is to any definite region of the earth's surface. At the same time, the balance is kept even; the sentiment is not allowed to displace the fact, however

44

deeply it colours it. *The Bible in Spain*, for instance, gives a clear portrait both of Borrow and of Spain, but it would be hard to say where Spain ends and Borrow begins. Such an amalgamation demands rare literary genius, and it is no harsh criticism of the writers before us if we say that the secret is not theirs.

Mr Thirlmere gives us two substantial volumes of *Letters of Catalonia*, in which there is considerably more information about Mr Thirlmere than about Catalonia. Catalonia, we gather, is a place which, like many others, possesses sunsets and stars and mosquitoes and cathedrals. Mr Thirlmere has a great deal that is pleasant to say upon all these subjects, and they give rise to reflections which lead us in many directions not marked upon the map of Spain. The sentiment is out of all proportion to the journey. It is but fair to say that we are warned beforehand that many changes will be rung on certain subjects, 'such as sunsets, rustic wit, Germany, politics, and so forth';[4] and when he reaches his 800th page Mr Thirlmere is genuinely surprised to find how seldom he has found it necessary to allude to Catalonia. The book then consists of a miscellaneous collection of meditations and facts and personal opinions which conceal any definite outline of Catalonia as behind a shifting veil. The traveller will still need his Murray;[5] but the two large volumes, though they make no special appeal to travellers, can be read with pleasure by anyone who has a taste for light reading of a miscellaneous nature. The value of the book is much increased by the many excellent reproductions of pictures and photographs of Spain, especially of the drawings of Mr Frank Brangwyn.[6]

Mr Somerset Maugham's single volume, *The Land of the Blessed Virgin*, is slim and reticent. He writes of Andalusia, and, so to speak, edits the country carefully. He selects certain scenes which have remained in his mind as typical and illustrative of the country which he knows so well, and they are not necessarily those prescribed by the guide-book. In his work, too, the personal element preponderates; he is content in more than one instance to let an impression stand as a permanent record which was admittedly coloured by facts of purely personal significance. But he has his pen well under control, and strikes out pictures now and again which are true in themselves and yet could have been so seen by one person only. 'Ah, the beautiful things which I have seen which other men have not!'[7] he exclaims, and he has a sincere desire to find the right word for the beauty which he genuinely loves and which, consequently, interests him more than any peculiarities in the individual who observes it. His book thus, even when the desire is beyond his power of satisfying it, has a value of its own, both for the traveller and for the reader who remains in his study chair.

1 – A review in the *TLS*, 26 May 1905 (Kp C2) of *Letters from Catalonia and Other Parts of Spain* (2 vols, Hutchinson, 1905) by Rowland Thirlmere (John Walker, 1861–1932) and *The Land of the Blessed Virgin: Sketches and Impressions in Andalusia*, etc. (Heinemann, 1905) by W. S. Maugham (1874–1965) – ' . . . 3 fat books . . . a peace offering . . . You will be surprised to hear that I am an authority upon Spain – but so it is' (*I VW Letters*, no. 226, to Violet Dickinson, 30 April). Reprinted: *CW*. Reading Notes (MHP, B 1a) dated: 28 April. See also 'An Andalusian Inn' below and 'To Spain', *III VW Essays*.
2 – Laurence Sterne, *A Sentimental Journey through France and Italy* (1768). See also '*The Sentimental Traveller*' below.
3 – The works alluded to here are: George Borrow, *The Bible in Spain* (1843); Alexander Kinglake, *Eōthen* (1844); Frederick Temple Hamilton-Temple Blackwood, Marquis of Dufferin and Ava, *Letters from High Latitudes* (1857). Henry James wrote several volumes of travel sketches, including *Portraits of Places* (1882) – see 'Portraits of Places' below.
4 – Thirlmere, Foreword, p. 3.
5 – Richard Ford, *Murray's Hand-Book for Travellers in Spain* (John Murray, 1845; subsequently 'revised on the spot with additions' in several editions down to 1898).
6 – Frank (François Guillaume) Brangwyn (1867–1956), travelled widely during the 1880s and 1890s on commissions in Europe, the Near East and South Africa; he had been elected A.R.A. in 1904 and was later made R.A. and knighted.
7 – Maugham, ch. XXXVII, p. 209 which has: 'But I liked Jerez towards evening, when the sun had set and the twilight glided through the tortuous alleys like a woman dressed in white . . . We walked through the deserted streets, I and the woman dressed in white . . . And Jerez was wrapped in a ghostly shroud. Ah, the beautiful things I have seen which other men have not!'

================

The American Woman

Miss McCracken, in her investigations into the natural history of the American woman, travelled over nearly the whole of the United States, in a journey which occupied six months, which she found to be all too short. She came home with her boxes full of pamphlets and calendars and her notebooks full of statistics. But when she began to write she found it best to put aside all these and to draw her picture from life. Instead of a scientific treatise on the nature of woman or a blue-book upon her place in the national life, she gives us fourteen snapshots of the woman herself as she works or plays, in whatever position she happened to be found. This method is admittedly superficial, but in the space of one short volume we are taken over a great distance of country and shown many queer people living out-of-the-way lives.

There are many types of the American woman – more, perhaps, than of the English woman – but they have a curious unity. We begin with the pioneer who is set down in the Western prairie where 'one need not yet keep to the path, for there is none. You make your own trail.'[2] She and her husband have to make their own house, their home, and their town, and the woman's work here is even more important than the man's. 'I want to help try new ways,'[3] says one of these pioneer women who lived in a small cattle-ranch thirty-five miles from the nearest town. 'We have our whole lives before us [...] And [...] we intend to make them good.'[4] The woman in the small town does, perhaps, the most important work done by women in America. America, says Miss McCracken, is a nation of small communities, and the influence of home, which is the influence of woman, is paramount here. It is significant that almost all the public libraries in these towns were founded by women, their librarians were usually women, and the women read almost exclusively 'real books'.[5] In the South she found that the women who had suffered most in the war were teaching the negroes and fitting them for public life.

Miss McCracken is a cordial admirer of her own sex, and in only one case does her sympathy fail. For the last ten years the women of Colorado have had the ballot, and, while she admits that they have done good work publicly by means of it, she thinks that it has been at the expense of their own womanliness. Charitable acts are done with a view to votes, and the woman's perception of right and wrong has been dulled. But it is open to remark that the same might be said as emphatically of the male politician, and that the real question is whether the use made by women of political freedom is sufficiently valuable to justify the alleged injury. It is characteristic that the American woman's club is almost invariably a kind of Charity Organisation Society for the improvement of themselves and others, and the democratic motto of one of them, 'Of all, by all, for all,'[6] is appropriate to many. Indeed, the American view of charity is typical and peculiar. A charitable English lady, for example, may read to the blind in her village; but the work is personal, and probably ceases in the case of her illness or death. An American woman in the same circumstances at once organised a society from the members of her club to help the blind. Then, not content with this, she got a commission appointed by the State of Massachusetts to inquire into the condition of the blind, with the result that the State will probably institute schools for the training of the blind at public expense. There are many other illustrations of the same genius for organisation, and of the peculiar nature of American charity, which is not satisfied with relieving suffering, but must find out and, if possible, eliminate the cause of it.

We have not space to comment upon the many interesting lines of thought that Miss McCracken opens up. One remark of hers seems to us to suggest the essential difference between American and other women, which gives them their special interest, and which has made it possible to paint such a sketch as this of a whole race with marked and recognisable features. The province of the American writer, she says, is the short story, because American life lends itself to 'instantaneous portraiture'. 'It is so young, without any deep furrows on its face.' 'The oldest of us in America are still rather new',[7] said one lady, who went on to say that they were not old enough yet to be even really democratic. A mother can point to her own mother, herself, and her daughter as representing three stages of development, and can lay her finger on the causes which have made them different. So many causes have combined to make an Englishwoman, that it is impossible to trace their effects, and the succession of influences may well have neutralised each other. But everything that alters her own or her country's life at present tells upon the American woman, and to watch the process is a study of exceeding interest.

1 – A review in the *Guardian*, 31 May 1905, of *The Women of America* (Macmillan Co., 1904) by Elizabeth McCracken. See Editorial Note, p. xxii.
2 – McCracken, ch. 1, p. 3, which has: 'Here you do not need to keep to the path, for there is none. You may make your own trail.'
3 – *Ibid.*, p. 12.
4 – *Ibid.*, p. 13.
5 – *Ibid.*, ch II, p. 51.
6 – *Ibid.*, ch V, p. 115.
7 – The three quotations here are from, respectively: *ibid.*, ch. VIII, p. 220; p. 221; ch. XIV, p. 389.

'Rose of Lone Farm'

Miss Hayden, it is clear, knows the country and loves it. Something of its charm, at any rate, is reproduced in these pages, and also something of the oddity of the life of the country people. She is not so sure of herself when she treats of the hero and heroine who are drawn tamely after the conventional pattern. Miss Hayden's gift seems to lie in close and humorous observation of the details of life on a country farm. The character of the 'fogger' Esau, for instance, is the most faithful bit of work in the book. But she is trammelled by the limitations of the novel form, and is at her best when she describes what she has seen and forgets the necessity of telling a story. The story in this case serves merely as an excuse for introducing us to a circle of south country farms, where we are mildly entertained by the gossip of the farmer's wife and the blunders of the good lady who tries to use 'dixshonry' words. The tendency here is, perhaps, to exaggerate these peculiarities at the expense of the truth; and, if we look to the proportions of the book as a whole, we must complain that many of the scenes are too obviously given as specimens of country manners without connection with the main theme. But these little pictures have a certain value of their own which the more ambitious scenes are without.

1 – A notice in the *Guardian*, 19 July 1905, (Kp C2.01) of *Rose of Lone Farm* (Smith, Elder & Co., 1905) by Eleanor G. Hayden (author of a number of books on rural subjects). Reading Notes (MHP, B 1a) dated: 24 June.

An Andalusian Inn

Hotel-keepers are apparently subject to that slight and amiable obliquity of the moral sense which goes by the name of loyalty. Thus, when we asked whether we should find good quarters for a night's rest at a certain little country town in Andalusia where we had to sleep we were assured that the hotel there was good. Not, of course, a first-class establishment such as the palatial building in which we stood, but, nevertheless, a good second-class inn, where we should be made comfortable and provided with beds of the cleanest. At half past nine, then, when after a long day's loitering through the country the train finally came to a stop and announced its intention of going no further, the hotel-keeper's word sounded comfortable in our ears. We should be content with little, we reflected, and during the last stages of the journey, as the orthodox dinner hour passed uncelebrated and the wick which swam in the oil-lamp committed suicide – and its life had not been happy – we dwelt much upon the terms of this recommendation and the good second-class inn became an epitome of all that is desirable in life. Here we should meet with a simple-hearted welcome; we pictured the innkeeper and his wife coming out to greet us, eager to take our bundles and our wraps – bustling about to prepare our rooms and catch the fowl who was to make our dinner. For the night's rest between clean and scented sheets the plain but delicious dinner and the excellent breakfast before our early start they would ask some ridiculously small sum. We should be made to feel that silver is a most vulgar coin in which to pay such hospitality, and that that noble virtue – long dead among the innkeepers of our own country – still flourishes in Spain.

In thoughts like these we passed the time till the train had reached the station where we were to be rewarded for all our joltings and fatigues. It was a little disconcerting to find that the porters, at any rate, were evidently surprised that two travellers with heavy luggage should be deposited on the platform at this time of night. The inevitable crowd came running to stare at us, and gaped when we produced the careful arrangement of Spanish words in which we signified our desire for an inn. A sentence in a conversation-book is something of the nature of an extinct monster in a museum: only the specially initiated can tell you that it is related to the live animal. It was at once obvious that our specimen was hopelessly extinct, and, further, a terrible doubt insinuated itself that it was the nature of what we asked as much as the language in which we asked it that was unintelligible. At length, after much Spanish, French, and English had clashed unprofitably, it dawned upon the natives that we did not speak their language, and the powers of gesticulation were tried upon us. Presently an official appeared who informed us that he could speak French. Our request for an hotel was joyfully translated into that language. 'The train goes no further to-night,' answered the interpreter. 'We know that, and therefore we wish to sleep here,' we said. 'To-morrow morning, at 5.30.' 'But to-night, an hotel,' we insisted. The gentleman who spoke French produced a pencil with an air of resignation, and wrote large and very black the figures 5 and 30. We shrugged our shoulders, and vociferated 'hotel' first in French and then in three different kinds of Spanish. The crowd had by this time made a complete circle round us, and every one was translating for the benefit of his neighbour. We then bethought us of a Spanish dictionary, which had consistently refused to be left behind, and the Spanish equivalent for the English word 'hotel' was found and emphasised with a forefinger. As many heads as could be pressed together gazed blankly at the spot thus indicated, and the interpreter was struck by a brilliant idea. He lost the place and searched feverishly for a word of his own among the Ss and the Zs. We helped him to the Spanish department of the dictionary, and left him to prolonged, but, as it turned out, fruitless researches.

Meanwhile we repeated our solitary word in the chance that it might somewhere fall upon fertile soil. At every utterance a buzz of good Spanish rose from the crowd; finally, when we were trying to define hotel with an umbrella, a small old man forced himself upon our notice. To the inevitable question he answered by laying his hand upon his breast and bowing profoundly. We asked him three times in succession, and he always answered in the same way, as though in his solitary person he combined all the qualities we needed. Public opinion seemed to be unanimous that we should accept him as the representative of dinner and bed, and a few last attempts at the Spanish for 'inn' were answered by hands stretched in his direction. To settle the matter he gripped us by the arm and drew us outside the station to the edge of a sandy desert grown wth tufts of reeds and lighted by a large moon. On one side was a steep hill, crowned by a Moorish castle, and at a little distance we saw a solitary cottage. The choice apparently lay between the two, and neither seemed precisely what we had expected. We looked at the old man, and observed not without relief that he was both old and small. One of our doubts, at any rate, was soon at an end, for it was clear that the white cottage was to be our lodging, and that the hotel-keeper at Granada had had the imagination of an artist. We were shown into a room where a lamp burnt, and where several men and women sat round a fire drinking and talking.[2] There was a pause, in which several eyes inspected us at their leisure, and we were led into an ante-room, in whose honour that word 'hotel' had been applied to the cottage. There was a bed and a canvas partition to serve as door, water to wash in, if we chose to keep up that respectable farce, and a candle in case we wished for light. Food, it was clear, must be sought at the station; and we were by no means unwilling to go out into the fresh air again. When at the hour of eleven we were tired of the Spanish desert, and the Moorish castle, and the conversation of the gentleman who could speak French, but did not think it essential to understand that language, we returned to the inn and began what promised to be a somewhat weary vigil. The company sat late and talked loud. Scraps of vehement Spanish penetrated the canvas partition, and somehow seemed to be concerned with us. Spanish is a fierce and bloodthirsty language when heard under these conditions. The figure of our small friend with his perpetual bows and finger laid on his breast became towards midnight of a very sinister aspect; we remembered his ominous silence, his persistent determination that we should be parted from our luggage. Country people of honest conscience, we reflected, should have been in bed long before this. The only precaution possible to us was to stand the solitary chair on its hind legs against the door. That must have had a strangely composing effect upon our minds, for, thus fortified against the murderous assault which we expected, we fell asleep in our clothes, and dreamed that we had found the Spanish word for 'inn'.

The sound that finally awoke us at half past four in the morning was certainly an assault upon the door; but when we cautiously looked out there was no one more hostile than the peasant woman with a basin of goat's milk in her hands.

1 – An essay in the *Guardian*, 19 July 1905, (Kp C2.02) based on VW's experiences during a visit with her brother Adrian Stephen to the Iberian Peninsula in April 1905. She had thought of sending her article, 'my Spanish rubbish', to Leopold Maxse at the *National Review* and thanked her stars 'that it hasn't already gone to the High Church parsonesses [the *Guardian*]' (*I VW Letters*, no. 228, to Violet Dickinson). 'I am touching it up a little,' she continued, 'and adding a final chapter; do you really think it good enough to send – because I needn't? As a matter of fact, I didn't mean to write any articles this summer under my name, which is becoming rather thread bare.' But in the event it did go to the 'parsonesses' and whether the article was read by Maxse for the *National Review* is not known. See also 'Journeys in Spain' above and 'To Spain', *III VW Essays*.

2 – Cf. *I VW Letters*, no. 224, to Violet Dickinson, 24 April 1905: 'Then we had to travel 24, or 48 hours to Lisbon, and slept one night at a little country wayside inn – where the fire burnt in the middle of the room, and the company of Spanish peasants sat around and stared at us . . . '

A Priory Church

You see Christchurch from afar like a ship riding out to sea. The land all round is flat as water; if the sun shines it may light up a little gleam of river or of the sea itself, because, as soon appears, the church is almost an island in the midst of waters. The sun when we made our expedition was not visible, but in spite of that the whole air was full of light. It was as though a white curtain had been drawn across the sky, by which the sunbeams as they fell were filtered to a pure white light. There was on the horizon a rim of sky like tarnished silver, but, otherwise, there was no slit in the curtain. The town of Christchurch resolves itself into one long street, which rises very slightly, and bursts at the top into its flower, which is the Priory Church. The church is built on the pattern of a small cathedral, and, perhaps, because of its comparative insignificance, has suffered very little from reformers and restorers. The stonework within has worn very white, and has crumbled in places, but for the most part the chiselling is as sharp as though it had just left the mason's hand. Much of the carving is of exquisite delicacy, and so perfect that one needs the assurance of the date inscribed on it to realise that the work is more than three hundred years old. But the most beautiful possession of the old church – and it has many both beautiful and curious – is the view from the square tower. Here out on the leads, with the sharp spine of the church running out beneath you, you look to the sea on two sides; and directly at your feet the rivers Stour and Avon loop and cross and entangle themselves like a silver chain. The church is one of the few great churches that has not chosen to plant itself on a hill; the stream laps at its feet, and it looks as though an extra large wave would roll across the land and break against the church walls. Only a breadth of flats, dun-coloured with feathery bulrushes, separates the land from the water; looking east there is no hill, and on the horizon an undulating shadow marks the beginning of the New Forest.

1 – A note published in the *Guardian*, 26 July 1905, (Kp C2.03) on Priory Church, Christchurch, at the edge of the New Forest. The Forest was a popular resort of the Stephen family. VW had last visited it for Christmas and the New Year, 1904–5, staying with her sister and two brothers at Lane End, Bank, Lyndhurst, the home of Sarah (Aunt Minna) Duckworth (Julia Stephen's sister-in-law). In a letter from there

to Violet Dickinson in early January, VW refers to '2 little articles ... one on Christchurch – the other on the forest – which I've tried to make good and careful' (*I VW Letters*, no. 206). The article on the Forest does not appear to have been published.

The Letters of Jane Welsh Carlyle

There is happily no longer any temptation for the reader of these letters to use them merely as so much material for a brief on one side or another of a very unpleasant dispute. Mrs Carlyle's letters must rapidly lose, if they have not already lost, the interest which they had for a generation that had seen Carlyle in the flesh and had the morbid appetite of contemporaries for personal gossip. 'These seem to me about the cleverest letters I ever read,' wrote Carlyle,[2] and although other issues for the moment obscured that verdict, a later generation finds it sound.

Few people, indeed, have been able to cast so brilliant an image of themselves upon paper. And yet it is noteworthy that she has not taken advantage of the usual method of self-portraiture that recommends itself to letter-writers; she seldom talks of herself as other than an active and practical human being. Letters of the 'inner woman' sort, 'all about feelings',[3] anything that savoured of self-analysis or introspection she checked ruthlessly. But in spite of this reserve, which drove her to make her letters out of facts, they were facts which did more to illuminate herself than most people's feelings. She could not go for a drive or meet a neighbour without bringing back two or three precious words of description. Her letters, for example, are full of 'coterie speech',[4] little phrases which she has picked up for something odd in the expression, or for something characteristic of the speaker in them, as a connoisseur with a fine eye might collect curiosities. This, though it was done so swiftly and faultlessly, demands an insight into character and a power of seizing on the essential, which is creative as well as critical, and, in her, amounted to genius. It meant that out of all the talk she heard, and all the sights she saw, she could infallibly select the one word or scene which, written down, brings the spirit of the past before us. She made no claim to style in the modern sense of the word; but if a manner of speech which is perfectly expressive of the thought and of the thinker deserves such a title, she never wrote six lines without it. Quotation is difficult because she seldom concentrated her wit into flashes, though it plays everywhere abundantly, and is often brilliant. But such coruscations as we find in the letters of Charles Lamb, for instance, are seldom spontaneous;[5] and Mrs Carlyle wrote as easily and copiously as she talked. She was in all things a practical woman, and would have despised a letter which was not content with its simple mission.

Carlyle was writing for his biographer, she supposed, when he sent her descriptions of scenery instead of some humbler but more necessary details. Her own letters are emphatically genuine letters in the sense that she had always some definite object in writing them at a particular moment to a particular person. Thus, though she read widely, and was educated beyond the standard of her time, she seldom writes a word of literary criticism. She was content to make her letters out of simple things; the fact that she had a higher ambition made her always ironically alive to the smallness of mere letter-writing. But if there were such a branch of learning as the study of human nature Mrs Carlyle would have been one of its most distinguished professors. While her husband sat upstairs in the sound-proof room deciphering the motives and characters of the actors in some long-forgotten drama, Mrs Carlyle was practising the same art over her teacups. Occasionally the live bodies were treated a little too much as though they were dried inscriptions on parchment who might be made to yield an amusing sentence in the next letter. Her dark eyes had a dangerous light in them, as Mr Froude says,[6] and her wit, we gather, generally had its victim. But this power of sarcasm and of administering a shrewing of which we hear so much was in some degree a measure of protection; she was very sensitive and had an inner woman to defend. She had constant reason, too, to recover her balance in the emotions of life with a man of genius by some strong, possibly caustic, effort of common sense. 'This world looks always the more absurd to me the longer I live in it'[7] was a reflection that was often at the back of her mind, and that was called forth particularly by anything exaggerated or insincere. 'The style which suits me best is the natural and simple style, and . . . my soul cannot be thrown into deliquium by any hundred horse-power of upholstery or of moral sublime.'[8] Thus she was a harsh critic of the class who have most time to deal in superlatives and was merciless to bores. But her bores were bores by reason of some pretentiousness or pomposity; simple stupidity did not sharpen her tongue, though she might note its symptoms with amusement.

On the other hand, there is ample proof that she could be the most faithful and sympathetic of friends where her sympathy was genuinely needed. Take, for instance, a scene from her notebook, in the first volume of the *Letters and Memorials*, which is typical of many. She has visits from Count d'Orsay and Lord Jeffrey, 'the prince of dandies and the prince of critics',[9] and sketches brilliant little pictures of both. Then she goes on to ask, 'Why does every miserable man and woman of my acquaintance come to me with his and her woes, as if I had no woes of my own, nothing in the world to do but to console others?' 'Here has been that ill-fated C.J.' Then she goes out of doors and finds in the King's Road a child 'of "the lower orders" in the act, it seemed, of dissolving all away in tears'. She takes the child back with her to Cheyne Row, to wait investigations, and finds a note from a lady who feels it 'due to herself to make some disclosures to me'. 'It was a desperate interview.' The disclosures end in tears and embraces, also in some advice – 'she will not, of course, follow a syllable of it'. The child meanwhile 'munched away unconscious in the tragic scene', 'drowning its recent sorrows in bread and butter'.[10] Mrs Carlyle, like the true humorist she was, has eyes for all sides of the little dramas that enact themselves in her drawing-room and never loses her sense of proportion.

To the poor, the sick, the unhappy, to any one who depended on her, Mrs Carlyle could show the deeper and more tender side of her character. She did not want for dependents – humble people, for the most part, who would not appreciate her wit. But the basis of her wit, as they knew well, was a substantial common sense, a power of seeing things as they are, which gave the sting to her words, and, at the same time, made her effective in all practical ways. She had the same attraction for 'mad people or miserable people', she writes, 'that amber has for straws'.[11] She could sympathise, but her sympathy never blinded her to the facts of the case or made her lower her own high standard. Some one declared her to be a 'cross betwixt John Knox and a gipsy',[12] and the austere preacher in her was not slow to denounce any 'sumptuosity' or indolence that came in her way. 'Oh, dear me! I wonder why so many people wish for high position and great wealth' when it merely emancipates them 'from all the practical difficulties, which might teach them the facts of things, and sympathy with their fellow-creatures'.[13] 'I ... could not be other than perfectly miserable in idleness, world without end.'[14] Thus, when she had to give up her ambition to work with her pen she worked none the less hard, though in humbler ways. Her practical difficulties were some of them sordid enough, but she made them yield the very best that was in them. Her battles with crowing cocks and barking dogs, barrel-organs and household repairs are grotesque enough in themselves, but as she writes of them they become a real significance. 'The facts of things' might be found in unexpected places. She might sometimes resent the fate which had driven her to squander all her gifts on such apparently trivial ends – 'the eternal writing of little unavoidable notes'[15] and the rest – but that is not a reflection that will occur to her readers. Under other conditions she might have written more; she could hardly have written better.

1 – An article in the *Guardian*, 2 August 1905, (Kp C2.1) largely based on *Letters and Memorials of Jane Welsh Carlyle* (3 vols, Longmans, 1883) – a work prepared for publication by Thomas Carlyle (1795–1881) and edited by James Anthony Froude (1818–94), his intimate friend, and as it proved, controversial biographer, whose sympathy for Mrs Carlyle (1801–66) and her grievances was thought by some to have caused him to malign her husband. VW also consulted *New Letters and Memorials of Jane Welsh Carlyle*. Annotated by Thomas Carlyle, Ed. Alexander Carlyle. Introduced by Sir James Crichton-Browne (2 vols, John Lane, 1903); and probably Froude's *Thomas Carlyle: A History of His Life in London 1834–81* (2 vols, Longmans, 1884). She may well also have read Leslie Stephen's article on Carlyle in the *DNB*.
  'I have been sent the proof of Mrs Carlyle,' VW wrote to Violet Dickinson. 'O Lord, – it is bad – such an ugly angular piece of writing, all jagged edges. ¶ Do you feel convinced I *can* write?' (*I VW Letters*, no. 244; see also nos 233, 237, 240, 242). See 'More Carlyle Letters' below, and 'Geraldine and Jane', *V VW Essays* and *CR*2.
2 – Sir James Crichton-Browne, *New Letters and Memorials*, Intro., quoting Carlyle's Journal, April 1868: 'These seem to me about the cleverest letters I ever read; but none except me can interpret their allusions, their coterie speech (which are often the most ingenious part of the rapid, bright-flowing style), or give them a chance even of far-off intelligibility to readers.'
3 – The source of the reference to the 'inner woman', if it is not a phrase of VW's, has not been traced; the expression 'all about feelings' occurs at least three times in the correspondence, e.g., *Letters and Memorials*, vol. II, pp. 51, 70, 257.
4 – See n. 2 above; see also *Letters and Memorials*, vol. I, p. 23, Carlyle's note to Letter 7.
5 – Cf. *I VW Letters*, no. 237, to Violet Dickinson, July 1905: 'I say in my Carlyle article "coruscations are more in letters"!!'
6 – The source of this allusion has not been discovered.
7 – *Letters and Memorials*, vol. I, p. 128, Letter 27, to Mrs Stirling, 8 January 1841, slightly adapted.
8 – *Ibid.*, vol. II, pp. 393–4, Letter 204, to Mrs Russell, 30 December 1858, slightly adapted.
9 – *Ibid.*, vol. I, Mrs Carlyle's Notebook, 13 April 1845, p. 300, adapted.

10 – For Mrs Carlyle's complaints at being put upon and the resulting experience of the child of the lower orders, *ibid.*, April, pp. 302–6.

11 – *Ibid.*, vol. II, Letter 204, to Mrs Russell, 30 December 1858, p. 393, which has 'and for', not 'or'.

12 – *Ibid.*, vol. II, from Mrs Carlyle's narrative 'Much Ado About Nothing', p. 54; the comparison was made by the Liberal statesman William Edward Forster (1818–86).

13 – *Ibid.*, vol. I, Letter 84, to Mrs Russell, 30 December 1845, p. 361.

14 – *Ibid.*, Letter 85, to Mrs Aitken, April 1846, p. 364.

15 – *Ibid.*, vol. II, Letter 109, to Mrs Aitken, May 1849, p. 39: 'But the great business of life for a woman like me in this place is an eternal writing of little unavoidable notes.'

The Value of Laughter

The old idea was that comedy represented the failings of human nature, and that tragedy pictured men as greater than they are. To paint them truly one must, it seems, strike a mean between the two, and the result is something too serious to be comic, too imperfect to be tragic, and this we may call humour. Humour, we have been told, is denied to women. They may be tragic or comic, but the particular blend which makes a humorist is to be found only in men. But experiments are dangerous things, and in trying to attain the humorist's point of view – in balancing himself on that pinnacle which is denied his sisters – the male gymnast not infrequently topples over ignominiously on to the other side, and either plunges headlong into buffoonery or else descends to the hard ground of serious commonplace, where, to do him justice, he is entirely at his ease. It may be that tragedy – a necessary ingredient – is not so common as it was in the time of Shakespeare, and therefore the present age has had to provide a decorous substitute which dispenses with blood and daggers, and looks its best in a chimney-pot hat and long frock-coat. This we may call the spirit of solemnity, and if spirits have a gender, there is no doubt that it is masculine. Now, comedy is of the sex of the graces and the muses, and when this solemn gentleman advances to offer his compliments she looks and laughs, and looks again till irresistible laughter comes over her, and she flies to hide her merriment in the bosoms of her sisters. Thus humour very rarely comes into the world, and comedy has a hard fight for it. Pure laughter, such as we hear on the lips of children and silly women, is in disrepute. It is held to be the voice of folly and frivolity inspired neither by knowledge nor emotion. It gives no message, conveys no information; it is an inarticulate utterance like the bark of a dog or the bleat of sheep, and it is beneath the dignity of a race that has made itself a language to express itself thus.

But there are some things that are beyond words and not beneath them, and laughter is one of these. For laughter is the one sound, inarticulate though it be, that no animal can produce. If the dog on the hearthrug groans in pain or barks for joy we recognise his meaning and it has nothing strange in it, but suppose he were to laugh? Suppose that when you came into the room he did not express his legitimate joy at the sight of you by tail or tongue, but burst into peals of laughter – grinned – shook his sides and showed all the usual signs of extreme amusement. Your feeling then would be one of shrinking and horror, as though a human voice had spoken from a beast's mouth. Nor can we imagine that beings in a higher state than ourselves laugh; laughter seems to belong essentially and exclusively to men and women. Laughter is the expression of the comic spirit within us, and the comic spirit concerns itself with oddities and eccentricities and deviations from the recognised pattern. It makes its comment in the sudden and spontaneous laugh which comes, we hardly know why, and we cannot tell when. If we took time to think – to analyse this impression that the comic spirit registers – we should find, doubtless, that what is superficially comic is fundamentally tragic, and while the smile was on our lips the water would stand in our eyes. This – the words are Bunyan's[2] – has been accepted as a definition of humour; but the laughter of comedy has no burden of tears. At the same time, though its office is comparatively slight compared with that of true humour, the value of laughter in life and in art cannot be over-rated. Humour is of the heights; the rarest minds alone can climb the pinnacle whence the whole of life can be viewed as in a panorama; but comedy walks the highways and reflects the trivial and accidental – the venial faults and peculiarities of all who pass in its bright little mirror. Laughter more than anything else preserves our sense of proportion; it is for ever reminding us that we are but human, that no man is quite a hero or entirely a villain. Directly we forget to laugh we see things out of proportion and lose our sense of reality. Dogs, mercifully, cannot laugh, because, if they could, they would realise the terrible limitations of being a dog. Men and women are just high enough in the scale of civilisation to be intrusted with the power of knowing their own failings and have been granted the gift of laughing at them. But we are in danger of losing this precious privilege, or of crushing it out of our breasts, by a mass of crude and ponderous knowledge.

To be able to laugh at a person you must, to begin with, be able to see him as he is. All his cloak of wealth and rank and learning, so far as it is a superficial accumulation, must not blunt the keen blade of the comic spirit which probes to the quick. It is a commonplace that children have a surer power of knowing men for what they are than grown people, and I believe that the verdict that women pass upon character will not be revoked at the Day of Judgment. Women and children, then, are the chief ministers of the comic spirit, because their eyes are not clouded with learning nor are their brains choked with the theories of books, so that men and things still preserve their original sharp outlines. All the hideous excrescences that have overgrown our modern life, the pomps and conventions and dreary solemnities, dread nothing so much as the flash of laughter which, like lightning, shrivels them up and leaves the bones bare. It is because their laughter possesses this quality that children are feared by people who are conscious of affectations and unrealities; and it is probably for this reason that women are looked upon with such disfavour in the learned professions. The danger is that they may laugh, like the child in Hans Andersen who said that the king went naked when his elders worshipped the splendid raiment that did not exist. In art, as in life, all the worst blunders arise from a lack of proportion, and the tendency of both is to be over-emphatically serious. Our great writers blossom in purple and roll in magnificent periods; our lesser writers multiply their adjectives and luxuriate in the sentimentalism which in a lower class produces the sensational placard and the melodrama. We go to funerals and to sick-beds far more willingly than to marriages and festivals, and we cannot rid our minds of the belief that there is something virtuous in tears and that black is the most becoming habit. There is nothing, indeed, so difficult as laughter, but no quality is more valuable. It is a knife that both prunes and trains and gives symmetry and sincerity to our acts and to the spoken and the written word.

1 – An essay in the *Guardian*, 16 August 1905, (Kp C2.2).
2 – *The Pilgrim's Progress* (1678), pt. I, Christian's meeting with 'a grave and beautiful Damsel named Discretion': 'So she smiled, but the water stood in her eyes; and after a little pause she said, I will call forth two or three more of the Family.' (Everyman, 1973, p. 49.)

Their Passing Hour

'A witty woman', says George Meredith, 'is a treasure; a witty beauty is a power.'[2] The volume before us gives us ample reason to ponder this saying and goes to prove that there were at least eight separate instances in which it once held good. It is melancholy to be forced to change the present tense to the past and to confess that we can no longer proclaim ourselves the subject of that sway. No beauty, it seems, is too great to perish; no wit long outlives the echo of the voice that speaks it. Mr Fyvie's eight chapters, indeed, are responsible for some sombre reflections. We cannot doubt that the power of which they speak was real enough in its day and that these ladies wielded it for the most part in circumstances of truly regal splendour. The fact, then, is all the more strange that when we come, some fifty years or so later, to ask in what the secret of their rule consisted we must confess ourselves not a little puzzled to account for it. 'She was splendidly handsome,' we read. 'She had rich colouring and blue-black braids of hair.'[3] The memoirs and the diaries seldom achieve any portrait that is more striking than that; or: 'She was extremely epigrammatic in her talk,'[4] we are told, when we ask for a specimen of the famous wit. There is also considerable difference of opinion; the same lady[5] is at once 'an enthusiastic angel from heaven'[6] and – if we look at her from another point of view – 'bold, forward, coarse, assuming and vain'.[7] You must reconcile both these extremes before you can make any likeness of the woman who captivated Nelson.

The paradox has challenged considerable and distinguished attention; four at least of the eight famous women who are sketched here have had their champions and their enemies; more than one has snatched her fame at the cost of her reputation; all have thrown down their gauntlets to the world in one way or another. But the problem still fascinates, partly perhaps because the solution must always escape us. The secret of the spell seems to have died in each case with its possessor; it could not be transmitted to another. That fatal condition was attached to it, but the effect was all the more concentrated because it could not be prolonged. If it survives the grave at all, it is as some phantom and elusive will-o'-the-wisp, which flits through the vague regions of Victorian memoir-writers and leaves us with empty hands when we try to grasp it. Such a book as this spurs us on to the pursuit once more by its sober recapitulation of the miracles that were accomplished by some such intangible force. The means seem so slight in proportion to the results which they achieve that we are forced to imagine the presence of some subtle quality which is now lost to us. At the same time, when we are inclined in sheer despair to belittle the miracle, we must remember that we have substantial proofs before us. We find, for instance, that enigmatic lady, Mrs Fitzherbert,[8] the daughter of a small country squire, winning for herself a power second only to that of the queen; and there is the blacksmith's daughter who without manners or wit could rule our greatest admiral and command the fleet. The book supplies us with not a few instances of the kind. This apparent discrepancy between her powers and her fame may become merely pathetic when we are in a position to test the lady's gifts by some authentic product that remains to us.

We have the 'Essay on the Genius and Writings of Shakespeare',[9] for example, if we wish to inquiry into Mrs Montagu's title to fame, but it is charitable to remember, before we form our verdict, that Johnson said of the author: 'She diffuses more knowledge in her conversation than any woman I know or, indeed, almost any man.'[10] The book, we must suppose, in this case, as in many others, is no adequate substitute for the talk. Mrs Lennox, on the other hand, survives, if she survives at all, by virtue of *The Female Quixote, or the Adventures of Arabella*,[11] which, we take Mr Fyvie's word for it, is 'unquestionably a work of genius'.[12] The poor lady might have succeeded better with a witty tongue; she lived in poverty, and a friend had to pay the expenses of her burial. We must not, it is plain, turn to the ladies' literary works to help us to account for their celebrity. The pen, in two cases at least, was merely a useful drudge driven late into the night by beautiful women who must, unfortunately, earn their bread. Lady Blessington and Mrs Norton[13] both contributed copiously to these Keepsakes and Books of Beauty in which rank and fashion might use their brains without demeaning themselves. Mrs Norton was styled on a famous occasion 'The Empress of Fiction':[14] her novels had enormous vogue. And now – save for one or two of her poems which have been rescued by the anthologists – the rubbish-heaps of tarnished finery remain undisturbed. It was, as we have noted, the nature of these women's genius that it seemed inseparable from the living voice and the smile of the lips; it evaded the grosser interpretation of pen or pencil.

We must look for our portrait, then, not so much in any substantial token that has been left us, as in the reflection of the splendour which we can still discover on the face of contemporary society. We catch our best glimpse of Lady Blessington in those remarkable parties at Gore House[15] in the youth of the last century, when all the lions of the season were collected round her. She made an art of such entertainments, and believed that they could yield really important results. Mrs Grote,[16] too, held a salon of the same kind. London society, it seems, was then of such proportions that the different sets could be made to revolve round some appropriate drawing-room centre, and women of high natural gifts thought it no mean ambition to occupy the position of authority. It asked no small artistic genius, they might have claimed, though their work must be anonymous. Lady Eastlake, again, was not only a hostess of 'great conversational powers' but an art critic of high reputation. Her criticism of John Ruskin, for instance, makes very good reading still, and would be accepted with little alteration, we believe, by the artist of the present day.[17]

There is, happily, no need for us to construct for ourselves any laborious portrait of the most brilliant of these eight women, the Hon. Mrs Norton. We need not attempt to put flesh on such bare bones as are thrown to us by contemporary observers, when we have *Diana of the Crossways* upon our shelves. Mr Meredith, as we know, desires his work 'to be read as fiction';[18] but the word fiction applies only to the unessential facts, and it is safe to predict that generations to come will read the truth of this famous woman and of many like her in the pages of a novel. Genius alone can preserve for us the wit that has been spoken and the beauty that has long faded, by creating them afresh. We must be grateful, however, for Mr Fyvie's addition to our materials, although we still await the wizard who shall transform them into flesh and blood. Thanks must be given, too, for eight very interesting illustrations.

1 – A review in *Academy & Literature*, 26 August 1905, (Kp C2.3) of *Some Famous Women of Wit and Beauty. A Georgian Galaxy. With eight illustrations* (Constable & Co., 1905) by John Fyvie.
2 – *Diana of the Crossways* (1885), ch. 1; (Virago, 1980, p. 2). Fyvie's penultimate portrait is of 'The Real "Diana of the Crossways" (The Hon. Mrs Norton)'.
3 – Fyvie, p. 225, quoting Fanny Kemble on Caroline Norton, *née* Sheridan (see n. 14 below): 'She was splendidly handsome, of an un-English character of beauty, her rather large and heavy head and features recalling the grandest Grecian and Italian models, to the latter of whom her rich colouring and blue-black braids of hair gave her an additional resemblance.'

4 – *Ibid.*, p. 225: 'Mrs Norton was extremely epigrammatic in her talk, and comically dramatic in her manner of narrating things.'

5 – Emma, Lady Hamilton (1761?–1815), daughter of Mary and Henry Lyon, of Nesse in Cheshire, and the subject of Fyvie's second portrait, 'Nelson's Lady Hamilton'.

6 – Fyvie, p. 66, quoting from the *Journal of Rear-Admiral Bartholomew James:* '. . . for in the ecstasy of singing "God save the King" in full chorus with the whole ship's company she tore her fan to pieces, and threw herself into such bewitching attitudes that no mortal soul could refrain from believing her to be an enthusiastic angel from heaven, purposely sent down to celebrate this pleasant, happy festival.'

7 – Fyvie, p. 75, quoting Mrs St George (later Mrs Trench) on meeting Lady Hamilton at the British Embassy in Dresden, an event recorded in her *Journal kept during a Visit to Germany in 1799–1800.*

8 – Maria Anne Fitzherbert (1756–1837), wife of George IV, youngest daughter of Walter Smythe, Esq., of Brambridge, Hampshire, portrayed in Fyvie's first chapter, 'The Unacknowledged Wife of George IV'.

9 – *Essays on the Writings and Genius of Shakespeare with the Greek and French Dramatic Poets, with some Remarks upon the Misrepresentations of Mons. de Voltaire* (1769) by Mrs Elizabeth Montagu (1720–1800), who is portrayed in Fyvie's third chapter, 'The Queen of the "Blue-Stockings"'.

10 – Fyvie, p. 114.

11 – Mrs Charlotte Lennox (1720–1804), the subject of Fyvie's fifth portrait, 'The Female Quixote'; her novel was published in two vols in 1752.

12 – Fyvie, p. 167.

13 – Marguerite, Countess of Blessington (1789–1849), whose works include *Grace Cassidy, or the Repealers* (1833), *The Two Friends* (1835) and *Conversations with Lord Byron* (1834). She was the editor for a period from 1834 of *The Book of Beauty.* The Hon. Mrs (Caroline Elizabeth Sarah) Norton (1808–77), poet and novelist, a granddaughter of Sheridan, upon whom Meredith based the character of Diana Warwick (*née* Merion) in *Diana of the Crossways* (1885). Her works include *Stuart of Dunleath* (1851), *Lost and Saved* (1863), *Old Sir Douglas* (1867), and the poem *The Lady of La Garaye* (1862).

14 – The famous occasion is not referred to by Fyvie and has not been identified.

15 – Gore House, Kensington, which stood where now stands the Royal Albert Hall, was Lady Blessington's home from 1836.

16 – Mrs (Harriet) Grote, *née* Lewin (1792–1878), biographer, wife of the historian and politician George Grote, both of whom were associated with the Philosophical Radicals. See Fyvie's sixth portrait, 'A Radical of the Last Generation'.

17 – Elizabeth, Lady Eastlake, *née* Rigby (1809–93), wife of Sir Charles Lock Eastlake (1793–1865), president of the Royal Academy. For Fyvie's comment on her powers of conversation see his final portrait, 'A Tory Lady of the Last Generation', p. 261. Lady Eastlake's celebrated hostile criticism of Ruskin's *Modern Painters* appeared in the *Quarterly Review*, no. CXCVI, March 1856.

18 – Fyvie, p. 223: 'In a brief prefatory note to one of his finest books, Mr George Meredith says: "A lady of high distinction for wit and beauty, the daughter of an illustrious Irish house, came under the shadow of a calumny. It has latterly been

examined and expressed as baseless. The story of *Diana of the Crossways* is to be read as fiction."'

'The Letter Killeth'

It is almost inevitable that the story of a religious phase in its moment of crisis should sound unreal and somewhat distasteful to a generation far outside its influence; and it needs rare skill to interpret the religious fanatic so that he is sympathetic to those who do not share his enthusiasm. The subtler marks of character seem to be obliterated by the one mastering passion; and the novel which has such persons for its chief figures tends, unless it can infect the reader with its own fervour, to become a little flat and monotonous. Such a criticism seems to apply to *The Letter Killeth*, by A. C. Inchbold, which gives a picture of the early days of the Wesleyan revival on the coast of Sussex. For, in spite of the fact that the author writes well and can give us an interesting study of the effect of the sudden stimulus upon the illiterate peasants, the main characters are coldly conceived and have little likeness to palpable human beings. A sense of humour, unfortunately, is no necessary part of excellence, and the tension of strict virtue is but seldom relaxed. The famous preacher George Gilbert and his son are not much more than lay figures upon which the conventional virtues hang stiffly enough; and though the character of Naomi, the visionary enthusiast, is drawn with greater delicacy, the actors seem for the most part to live in a rarefied atmosphere among shadows. The minor characters are drawn with greater freedom and force and provide some welcome relief. The plot hinges upon the inevitable conflict between the fleshly and the spiritual loves, which must be combined harmoniously before the nature even of a Wesleyan minister can be considered perfect. The means by which this result is reached are of the ordinary kind, and the author does not attempt to penetrate beneath a somewhat elementary conception of character. Within these modest limits the book is simply written and pleasantly free from exaggeration.

1 – A notice in the *TLS*, 27 October 1905, (Kp c2.4) of *The Letter Killeth: a romance of the Sussex Downs* (S. W. Partridge & Co., 1905) by A. Cunnick

Inchbold (Mrs Stanley Inchbold, who also published a romance of Napoleon, 1906, as well as books of European and Middle-eastern archaeology and travel). Reading Notes (MHP, B 1a) dated: 7 October.

'Lone Marie'

The novel-reader who sees the familiar name of Mr W. E. Norris upon the title-page can dismiss all doubts as to the quality of his entertainment. No problems will perplex him; no tragedies will disturb his peace; and if the serenity of the atmosphere tends at times to become a trifle soporific few will be so unreasonable as to complain of boredom. Indeed, it sometimes puzzles the reader to decide why it is that with so many rare and indisputable gifts for his calling Mr Norris has never achieved any work of first-rate importance. His last novel, *Lone Marie*, once more proves him a master of technique; once more we find ourselves perpetually surprised by some felicity of expression or subtlety of insight which would seem to hint at the presence of a talent more than ephemeral in value. But the depths thus indicated remain unrevealed. In the present book the characters, so far as they go, are suggested with admirable ease and delicacy of touch, but the wise reader will ask no more than a suggestion if he does not wish to be disappointed. Gordon Heneage, the loveable rascal, Marie Ludlow, even Mrs Strover, are all of them excellent studies of their kind; Mr Henry James might have noted them down for future use in some brief sketch-book. There is the same economy of incident, and restraint of treatment, and even a trace of Mr James's marvellous penetration. And if the likeness ends there it is not obscured on Mr Norris's part by any supervening defect; the fact is merely that he is ready to stop when Mr James is just prepared to begin. Even so we have every reason to thank Mr Norris for a delightful and delicate piece of work which if it does not reach the highest standard of contemporary fiction is still further removed from the average level.

1 – A notice in the *Guardian*, 1 November 1905, (Kp C2.5) of *Lone Marie* (Macmillan, 1905) by W. E. Norris (1847–1925), the second of his books VW wrote about this year: see '*Barham of Beltana*' above; and see also '*The Obstinate Lady*', 'Mr Norris's Method' and 'Mr Norris's Standard', III *VW Essays*. Reading Notes (MHP, B 1a) dated: 17 October.

'The Devil's Due'

Mr Burgin tells us at starting that it is his intention to draw an 'unrepentant villain'[2] and if the reader is fond of villains he will have no reason to complain. Unfortunately nature is less consistent than novelists would wish her to be, and seldom achieves a saint or a villain who is not spoilt for artistic purposes by some taint of vice or virtue. It is necessary also if you have drawn one character above life-size to heighten the others in due proportion, so that although Mr Burgin makes praiseworthy attempts to descend to the level of ordinary life, we must confess that they seem strangely unnatural. When you have tuned your mind to believe in a deserted wife who follows her husband disguised as a man, works in his employment for months, haunts the neighbourhood as a disembodied voice, and is partly drowned in a cellar beneath the villain's dinner-table, Canadian humour seems more than usually out of place. Mr Burgin has facility of expression, and can describe Canadian scenery vividly, but the picture he draws of life and manners in the village of Four Corners is, we hope and believe, imaginary. The story might be played on the stage with success, but it hardly endures the cold light of print.

1 – A notice in the *Guardian*, 1 November 1905, (Kp C2.6) of *The Devil's Due. A romance* (Hutchinson & Co., 1905) by George Brown Burgin. Reading Notes (MHP, B 1a) dated: 14 October.
2 – In dedicating his book to his 'Dear Mother', Burgin wrote: 'There is an unrepentant villain in this book – just the sort of villain we used to revere when we had visions that I should one day write books.'

'The House of Mirth'

The first pages of this novel make it obvious, even if the writer's name had not conveyed the information, that we have to consider a serious work of fiction. It is serious, not in the sense that it has any definite purpose to expound, but in that the writer has chosen her subject with deliberate foresight, and has spared no pains to make her delineation exact. The moral may be left to the reader. She gives us, as we do not remember to have seen it given before, a picture of that 'set' in New York society which contains not only all that is wealthiest, but also all that, for whatever reason, is most exclusive. The members of the community in which the heroine, Lily Bart, is placed are bound together not only by the possession of wealth, but also by a certain gift, which has its equivalent with us, too, perhaps – 'a force of negation which eliminated everything beyond their own range of perception'.[2] However we define them, there is no doubt that these 'affinities', as Mrs Wharton calls them, which bring the elect together, produce a curiously cold and vicious society. We are invited to watch this force at work upon a girl who, though by birth a member of the set, is partially disqualified by her poverty. The story traces her gradual descent, how, in the first instance, she loses money at bridge, and has to recoup herself by allowing a friend's husband to speculate for her; how her name is involved in a scandal, her friends desert her, and finally, the necessary sleeping-draught brings a death which, if not sought, is at least not unwelcome. In outline this is unpleasant; in detail it is tragic, because, though the girl has many of the faults of her surroundings she has a capacity for better things which is never to be exercised. There is no doubt that Mrs Wharton has so illuminated the House of Mirth for us that we shall not soon forget it.

1 – A notice in the *Guardian*, 15 November 1905, (Kp C2.7) of *The House of Mirth* (Macmillan & Co., 1905) by Edith Wharton (1862–1937). Reading Notes (MHP, B 1a) dated: 25 October.
2 – Wharton, pp. 73–4: 'But the deeper affinity was unmistakable: the two had the same prejudices and ideals, and the same quality of making other standards non-existent by ignoring them. This attribute was common to most of Lily's set: they had a force of negation which eliminated everything beyond their own range of perception.'

'The Debtor'

Miss Wilkins, to use the name with which we are familiar, was known originally as the writer of very brief and delightful New England stories. They were unpretentious in theme and slight in construction, but, thanks to the skill and charm of the workmanship, they managed to outlive much that was apparently more robust. Since that time she has surprised us more than once by producing a compact work of fiction which so far as the size is concerned has nothing in common with those eminently short stories of an earlier date. Her new book, *The Debtor*, is a substantial volume of some 560 closely printed pages, which are all, moreover, spent upon a single subject. But on closer inspection it seems that Miss Wilkins has not changed her method so greatly as this might lead one to expect. The story is placed in one of those American villages which correspond with our English Cranford, but in this case Banbridge, the town in question, is within range of the lights of New York. In reproducing the minute humours of the little place, the rivalries and intimacies of its inhabitants, Miss Wilkins is at her best. In the midst of this rural innocence and simplicity a Southern family of the name of Carroll has taken up its lodging. Arthur Carroll, the father, is a man of good birth and great personal charm, who, having been cheated of his rights in early youth, has since considered himself the creditor of society at large and has no scruples in exacting the debt. To Banbridge he figures first as a rich man; later he fails to meet his bills; and in the end he is forced to get a living by dancing as a negro on the stage. The descent is slow and illustrated from every possible point of view. The characters of the debtor himself, of his wife and children, of his creditors, of any one remotely connected with him are drawn in with a curious elaboration. And yet the effect is not wholly successful. Occasionally we are given a chapter which, complete and detached as it is, might stand for a short story by itself, but these scenes are linked together by pages of close description and unessential detail which should have been transacted silently in the writer's brain. As it is the novel seems to lack unity, and in spite of much subtlety and fine workmanship the effect is that of a succession of disconnected studies of character rather than of a single and well-proportioned whole.

1 – A notice in the *TLS*, 17 November 1905, (Kp c2.8) of *The Debtor: a novel . . .* Illustrations by W. D. Stevens (Harper & Bros, 1905) by Mary E. (Eleanor) Wilkins (1852–1930), American short-story writer and novelist whose reputation was established with the publication of her two collections: *A Humble Romance, and Other Stories* (1887) and *A New England Nun, and Other Stories* (1891).

'A Flood Tide'

It has been maintained that an interval of sixty years places a novelist at the most satisfactory distance from his characters. At closer quarters he is liable to be confused by a multiplicity of detail, and if he withdraws too far from his creations they are likely to lack vitality. Miss Mary Debenham in placing her story, *A Flood Tide*, some hundred and thirty years back lays herself under certain limitations; but she has made use of the corresponding advantages in such a way as to justify her choice. Indeed, for a novelist who desires dramatic situations and richness of colouring rather than psychological subtlety the eighteenth century is incomparably superior to the nineteenth. In *A Flood Tide*, for example, we are busied from the first page to the last with the intricacies of two main plots, one political and the other private, which are further complicated with echoes of the Stuart cause and a lavish supply of the usual romantic element. A novelist with such extravagant tastes must clearly look to the past to satisfy them. It says much for Miss Debenham's dexterity that she can combine all these different threads not only without confusion but so that they seem to spin themselves naturally from the circumstances of the time. Of the plot it is not necessary to say more than that it is concerned with the peace of 1763[2] and with a hitherto unpublished conspiracy on the part of the French which was to bring it prematurely to an end. The gentlemen charged with this affair contrive to get involved in the family difficulties of an English country squire, and the mixture of political and private intrigue results in some sufficiently dramatic situations. The incidents indeed are occasionally too closely crowded for comfort; but, on the whole, Miss Debenham has given us a very spirited picture of the time. Like most novelists who deal with a period other than their own, she lays a little too much emphasis upon the superficial distinctions of custom and manner, and is inclined to forget that even in that picturesque age men and women were made of something more substantial than powder. As a novel of adventure rather than of character, the book is successful and a very good specimen of its class.

1 – A notice in the *TLS*, 17 November 1905, (Kp c2.9) of *A Flood Tide* (Edward

Arnold, 1905) by Mary H. Debenham. Reading Notes (MHP, B 1a) dated: 23 October.

2 – Under the Treaty of Paris, concluding the Seven Years' War, 1756–63.

'The Making of Michael'

The Making of Michael, by Mrs Fred Reynolds, is the history of the career of a child who from his infancy showed unmistakable signs of genius. In the first chapter he asks an elderly spinster whether she knows what love is. He goes on with the same amazing precocity to distinguish between photographs and real pictures, and further declares that sound and colour are the two best things in the world. Later chapters chronicle other remarkable statements and actions, until it becomes obvious that he must either die prematurely or develop into one of those surprising geniuses who are not uncommon in novels. Happily, his genius is of such an order that it is essential that he should impart its message, and he becomes finally the greatest violinist of his time. Such a nature as this is not to be judged by ordinary standards, and the book therefore which portrays it is scarcely a novel in the sense that it attempts a sober study of life or character. The vagueness with which the different persons are described is indicated by the fact that they are seldom endowed with proper names, but are dubbed 'Stranger' or 'Dreamer' or 'Musician', as though they were possessed of only one quality apiece. The 'Child' himself passes through the various stages of existence – 'Dawn', 'Growth', 'Experience', and so on, each symbolised by some significant event, till finally he becomes 'The Man'. This method, if somewhat elementary, has the merit of simplicity, and the writer who is not concerned with the exact truth may be picturesque where another must be prosaic. On the other hand, it needs great imaginative force as well as rare powers of language to embody the truth in beautifully coloured symbols. Mrs Reynolds has tried to create a character at once real and ideal; he is to be as other boys and yet to typify a pure and inspired genius. The result is that he is neither one thing nor the other, and in spite of a certain grace of style the picture is too vague to leave other than a shadowy and fantastic impression upon the mind.

1 – A notice in the *TLS*, 17 November 1905, (Kp C2.10) of *The Making of Michael*

(George Allen, 1905) by Mrs Fred (Amy Dora) Reynolds. Reading Notes (MHP, B 1a) dated: 29 October.

A Description of the Desert

Mr Watson might echo the delightful claim which another writer of whom we are occasionally reminded put forward on behalf of his book. 'I believe I may truly acknowledge,' wrote Kingslake, 'that from all details of geographical discovery . . . from all historical and scientific illustrations, from all useful statistics, from all political disquisitions . . . the volume is thoroughly free.'[2] That is the spirit, we believe, in which journeys ought to be undertaken, as it is certainly the spirit in which many people choose to have them chronicled. And yet if we judge by results it must be obvious that few travellers who write share this simple faith. A new country to most is simply a sheet of statistics upon which they can decipher the annual returns of rice or tea or tobacco, and upon which are inscribed in terms as brief the 'habits' of those whom we call indiscriminately 'the natives'. It is much to Mr Watson's credit that he has not once glanced upon this page, but has trusted to his own powers of observation.

From Biskra in Southern Algeria he travelled to Tougourt, on the edge of the desert of Sahara; it is not a great distance on the map, nor was his path interrupted by adventures. But when the reader has submitted himself to the charm of the narrative he is quite content that it should be uneventful, and is only disappointed that it should not be prolonged. Mr Watson is master of a leisurely and graceful style well suited to the spirit of the story, and when he chooses he can make it yield little pictures of real beauty. The vast desert appears to soothe the mind into a state of philosophic calm, and from the serene height of a camel's back you behold all things dispassionately and yet with a humorous sense of their incongruities. All day the little caravan moves on through 'the high sea of the desert';[3] a troop of horsemen drift past with courteous salutation on their lips, or a bride passes in her golden palanquin journeying with her kinsfolk to her husband's village. At midday the praying-rugs are stretched on the sand, and, standing upright or bending till their foreheads touch the ground, the Arabs pray to Allah. By nightfall the green line on the horizon is reached, and they seek shelter in the oasis as in 'an open boat upon the rolling desert sea'.[4] This metaphor of the sea is one that recurs so often that by degrees the two ideas of the desert and the ocean rise and blend spontaneously in the mind. The immense solemnity, indeed, might become monotonous were it not for an artifice by which the sameness of the journey is relieved, and by which also the spirit of the South becomes articulate. Mr Watson was attended by two Arabs, Athman, the guide, and Abdullah, the owner of the camels. Athman had negro blood in his veins, of which he was deeply ashamed, but the mixture of dignity and simplicity which the two different strains produced, made him a curiously interesting companion. He was a poet, and beguiled the way by reciting from the manuscripts which were packed in large quantities about his person; he was always gay, kind, and demonstrative, but there were some subjects which he felt too deeply to discuss. One of these was his religion. Once Mr Watson caught him busied with several superfluous parcels of candles. Careful questioning revealed the fact that a light was to be offered at each tomb of a Marabout that was passed on the journey, and the vow was kept faithfully even when the shrine had long been tenanted by jackals. With this piety he combined a delightful strain of childlike credulity. Mr Watson tells us that he possessed a beautiful meerschaum pipe carved into the head of a laughing negro. For this pipe Athman conceived a curious affection, and his sympathy was genuine when it was explained to him that the negro had once been white, but would become entirely black in the course of continuous smoking. One day, before this process was complete, Mr Watson found the negro's head severed from his body; the culprit was Athman, who had taken this decisive step to rescue the negro from the ignominious fate in store for him.

Tougourt, on the edge of the great desert, was the goal of the journey, and here Mr Watson hired a house and took up his lodging for some time. The expedition so far as we are concerned ends here with the fantastic disappearance of Athman. For by chance he saw a dancer who as she danced expressed in some mysterious way that voice of the South, to which the Arab, as he had once explained, can never be deaf. To follow her he left his master and his friends, and rode away from Tougourt into the desert. Whether we accept this and much that is like it as fact or fiction, there is no doubt that Mr Watson has managed to convey to us something of the mystery and charm of the strange land where such things happen.

1 – A review in the *Guardian*, 6 December 1905, (Kp C2.11) of *The Voice of the South* (Hurst & Blackett Ltd, 1905) by Gilbert Watson. Reading Notes (MHP, B 1a) dated: 30 October.
2 – Alexander Kinglake, *Eōthen* (1844), preface to the first edition.
3 – Watson, ch. xv, p. 89.
4 – *Ibid.*, ch. xv, p. 98.

'The Brown House and Cordelia'

This volume contains two stories which one may infer to be the work of an immature writer who has not yet mastered the technical difficulties of her profession. The first pages of 'The Brown House' offer but cold welcome to the tentative reader. We are presented with genealogical problems before we can have the least interest in their solution, and we are hurried from one fresh character to another with uncomfortable rapidity. But when these introductions have been conscientiously performed, the author is free to exercise a talent that is both delightful and original. The scene is laid, in both cases, in an English country house, and the story concerns itself with the normal lives of its inhabitants and the incidents of the village world around them. Miss Booth has set herself a difficult task, for the whole interest of the book depends upon the skill with which the different shades of character can be revealed. To achieve this she relies almost entirely upon dialogue, and shows herself possessed of a real talent for conceiving talk that is at once natural and characteristic. She is at her best in conveying the atmosphere of family life, and the delicate distinctions of temperament which a keen and humorous observer is able to detect in it. She is scarcely so happy when she has to face some more emphatic situation, and is clearly hampered by the intricacies of the necessary plot, but it is not rash to expect that she will give us something still better in the future.

1 – A notice in the *Guardian*, 6 December 1905, (Kp C2.12) of *The Brown House, and Cordelia* (Edward Arnold, 1905) by Margaret Booth – a daughter of Charles Booth, the social reformer, and friend of the Stephen family: in 1906 she was to marry William ('Billy') Ritchie, son of Sir Richmond and Anne Thackeray (VW's 'Aunt Anny') Ritchie. Reading Notes (MHP, B 1a) dated: 18 October.

'Delta'

That a very dusty little volume dated 1828 should blossom in all the fairness of a new edition at this prolific season of the twentieth century seems a somewhat impudent defiance of the laws of nature, for it must be owned that *Mansie Wauch* was among the least substantial of that ghostly company of the books which are no longer read. And yet, as piety alone would not be responsible for this resurrection, the curious will look further and ask not only who is this 'Mansie Wauch', of surprising vitality, but also whose is the name that stands upon the title-page.

David Macbeth Moir was born of 'respectable' parents at Musselburgh in 1798. His education was good, and his boyhood in no way extraordinary, except that, besides playing games energetically, he also saved his pocket-money to buy books. The result of buying books is often the writing of books, and at the age of fifteen poems began to accumulate in his desk, while *The Cheap Magazine*, a local sheet, printed some very early works in prose. But instead of developing along these orthodox lines Moir was early apprenticed to a Musselburgh doctor, and henceforth medicine was his profession, and literature was only a hobby, to be indulged when his patients allowed. Indeed, his profession was a very serious matter. The death of his father left his mother dependent on him, and when, in 1817, he became the partner of Dr Brown, of Musselburgh, he was kept so closely at work that he was not free till nine or ten at night. His brother, who shared a bedroom with him, tells us how literature was served when the day's task was over. 'After supper a candle was lighted and the work of the desk begun ... With that loving kindness of heart and tender care for others',[2] which many remarked in him, Moir would first persuade his brother to go to bed; often, however, when the night was far spent, the boy woke and saw the candle burning and the figure still bent over the open books and the half-written sheets. By the light of that midnight candle he wrote the rhyming epistles, mock heroic translations from Horace, parodies, and cockney love songs which supplied many magazines till the long and fruitful connection with *Blackwood's Magazine* was firmly established. But it is probable that among all these miscellaneous occupations Moir took most pride as well as pleasure in the serious poetry to which alone he affixed his hieroglyphic 'Delta'.

By one of those ironies with which most writers are familiar, the work which cost the writer least trouble and gave him least satisfaction is that by which he was best known in his lifetime and is solely remembered now. The *Life of Mansie Wauch* was, as he writes, 'dashed off' as 'a mere sportive freak', and for years he hesitated to acknowledge it.[3] It began as a series of chapters in *Blackwood* in 1824, and ran on for the three following years. It was instantly popular, so that Mr Aird tells us of 'districts where country clubs waiting for the magazine met monthly and had *Mansie Wauch* read aloud amidst explosions of congregated laughter'.[4] It came out as a volume in 1828, and was accepted – again we quote the biographer – as a standard classic of humour, not only in Scotland but in England and America also, 'giving Moir for all time to come a uniqueness of fame as a novelist'.[5]

To-day we have more sympathy with the author's own judgment, except that we are inclined to put the prose work above the poetry. It is a very simple-minded performance – the narrative of a tailor in Dalkeith, who tells the story of his life in the pleasant Scottish dialect. If it still has power to please, it is more because we feel the good humour and kindly simplicity of the writer than because we can join very heartily in the 'congregated laughter' which the story of the deacon who sat down on the cat or of the bailies who ate their cigars,[6] called forth from a less sophisticated age. But it is noticeable that when Moir speaks in the person of the tailor he writes with a force and humour which are lacking in the smoothly conventional periods of his educated prose, and for this reason the story has a certain humble value by virtue of which it has endured to our day.

But any one who writes of Moir as a literary man alone must remember that he is speaking only of evenings and odd moments, and that the working daylight was spent in labour of a different sort. To Musselburgh – where he was born, lived, and died – Moir was known as the devoted doctor who had nursed the town through the cholera epidemic of 1832, the member of the town council, the elder of the church; it was to this good citizen that a statue was raised on the banks of the river Esk by his fellow-townsmen. He was too good a doctor to be a poet; he prescribed employment of the mind as the best method of dispelling the vapours, and might have treated genius itself as some symptom of physical disease. But this sanity, if it was opposed to inspiration, was almost medicinal in its simplicity; the savage Jeffrey wrote that one of Moir's poems had excited 'soothing and, I hope, bettering emotions' in him; 'it was so tender and true, so sweet and natural as to make all lower recommendations indifferent';[7] and Carlyle, on hearing of his death, exclaimed, 'A fine, melodious nature.'[8]

1 – A review in the *Guardian*, 13 December 1905, (Kp C2.13) of *The Life of Mansie Wauch, Tailor in Dalkeith. Written by Himself* (Blackwood, 1905) by 'Delta' (David Macbeth Moir, 1798–1851). Refs are here identified in the original edition of 1828. Reading Notes (MHP, B 1a) dated: 9 November.
2 – Thomas Aird, *The Poetical Works of David MacBeth Moir*. Ed. With a memoir of the author (2nd ed., Blackwood, 1860), p. 8, which has ' . . . after supper the candle was lighted in his bed-room, and the work of the desk began'; and p. 9, which has: 'With that tender care for others, which was the distinguishing feature of his character, he used to persuade me to retire to rest . . .' Thomas Aird (1802–76), was a poet, and a friend of Moir.
3 – *Ibid.*, p. 44; Moir writing to Aird, 12 April 1845, slightly paraphrased.
4 – *Ibid.*, p. 16, slightly adapted.
5 – *Ibid.*
6 – 'Delta': for the account of Deacon Paunch, who squashed the cat 'as flat as a flounder, and as dead as a mawk!!!', see ch. IX, p. 81; and for the bailies who ate cigars, ch. II, p. 26.
7 – Aird, p. 92: Lord Jeffrey (1773–1850), founder and, until 1829, editor of the *Edinburgh Review*, on Moir's 'Domestic Verses'.
8 – *Ibid.*, p. 82.

Two Irish Novels

Dan the Dollar, by Shan F. Bullock and *The Red-Haired Woman: Her Autobiography*, by Louise Kenny both treat of the Irish people, and even – an important addition – of the same Irish people. Mr Bullock's peasants come from the county of Fermanagh, and the O'Currys in Miss Kenny's book have their ancestral mansion on the coast to the west of the Shannon. As far as the map is concerned, then, there is little difference between them, and although both writers are unlike in all else, they have yet one substantial point in common. They both agree that this geographical fact is all important and that the type which it produces is so original as to be worth study as a type alone. Mr Bullock's novel, indeed, makes scarcely any effort at an interest independent of its interest as a picture of Irish peasant character. There is an Irish farmer and his wife, their niece, and a farm-hand. They live in great poverty, but with a certain frugal grace and charm of their own. The farmer, Felix, is a lovable and imaginative man, who is incapable of work, but who meets bad luck and poverty always with the same pious, half humorous, acquiescence in the ways of fate. 'Och, och, that's bad. But sure it was to be'[2] is the bitterest complaint he knows, for after all life has so many compensations. We hear the familiar voice of the Celtic poet issuing not incongruously from his lips:

We go about working, or fretting . . . and we kind of forget all the big things that are happening everywhere about us. No matter what we be at the autumn comes at the right minute, and the sun keeps on rising later every day, and we have frosts and dews, and whether we like it or not the hedges wither and burst out again . . . Ah, it's wonderful strange.[3]

With such a philosophy it is not surprising that the farmer and all connected with him gradually sink deeper and deeper into poverty. They are rescued by a son, Dan the Dollar, who has emigrated at an early age to America and now returns, a rich man. Is it possible that America will turn the son of a dreaming Irishman into a strenuous business man in whom all the characteristic qualities of the Anglo-Saxon are pre-eminent? 'The boy wants us all to be like himself, grand and prosperous. But how could that happen in a country like this and with people like ourselves?'[4] asks Felix. That is one of the many questions which Mr Bullock suggests to us; he is too fine an artist to press an answer upon us, but it is not unlikely that his candour conceals one.

Miss Kenny in *The Red-Haired Woman* deals also with life in the west of Ireland, and, like Mr Bullock, she is always, both consciously and unconsciously, pointing her finger at the peculiarities of the Irish temperament. But it is curious to see how differently that temperament appears to two observers presumably of the same nationality. We may adjust the two points of view to some extent by considering that, while Mr Bullock scarcely leaves the peasant's cottage, Miss Kenny is at home in the landlord's great house; the two views are opposed, but each to some degree supplements the other. The 'I' in Miss Kenny's book is Miss Peggy O'Curry, daughter and heiress of O'Curry of the Dunes, 'the offset of a thousand princes and gentlemen of Ireland'[5] on her father's side and a Dane on her mother's. This, to begin with, is an important distinction; she is not of the people who are 'rooted to the soil';[6] on the other hand, perhaps as a result of her foreign blood, she is conscious in every fibre of her noble Irish descent. Miss Kenny's peasants, so far as we have anything to do with them, are of the conventional 'Moonlighter' type, and in every way her conception of character is more emphatic and less subtle than Mr Bullock's. In place of the delicately natural life of the peasants, the O'Currys masquerade with all the properties of an ancient family; they talk of their 'Luck', apostrophise their ancestors, and keep an ancestral corpse embalmed on the top of their tower. All this might be Scottish as it might be Irish. The writer seems to have absorbed a strange miscellany of facts, legends, and theories, which she has poured out without any regard to form or coherency. Why, we ask, did Miss Kenny burden herself with the pretence of a plot or the pretence of characters? For we are constantly tantalised by signs of an original mind stored with interesting knowledge struggling to express itself in an uncongenial medium. A patient reader, however, will find much that illuminates the Irish character in the labyrinths of Miss Kenny's novel.

1 – A review in the *TLS*, 15 December 1905, (Kp c2.14) of *Dan the Dollar* (Maunsel & Co., 1905) by Shan F. Bullock and *The Red-Haired Woman: Her Autobiography* (John Murray, 1905) by Louise Kenny. Reading Notes (MHP, B 1a) dated: 21 and 24 November.
2 – Bullock, p. 27, slightly adapted.
3 – *Ibid.*, p. 58.
4 – *Ibid.*, p. 123.
5 – Kenny, Bk Second, ch. x, p. 380.
6 – *Ibid.*, ch. 1, p. 259.

'The Tower of Siloam'

This novel, like many others, purposes to give a picture of that aristocratic section of English society which seems to exercise so strong a fascination over the modern novelist. There are some, like Mr E. F. Benson and Mr Anthony Hope,[2] who find it frankly amusing, but not otherwise eccentric, and there are others, like Mrs Graham, who conceive that nobility of birth implies not only a certain superficial difference of manner, but also a radical distinction of character and morality. Those who incline to the more emphatic belief are generally of opinion that the distinction is wholly discreditable to the aristocrat, and if we are to believe in the truth of Mrs Graham's portrait we must come to the same conclusion. But it must be confessed that in whatever light you consider her characters it is difficult to believe in the fidelity to life. It is true that they race, gamble, and play bridge, and reflect with considerable sentimentality at intervals that 'it is the heart that matters most, whether its owner lives in Whitechapel or in Mayfair',[3] but the atmosphere of the book is both morbid and artificial, and an occasional promise of cleverness is not fulfilled.

1 – A notice in the *Guardian*, 20 December 1905, (Kp C2.15) of *The Tower of Siloam* (Alston Rivers, 1905) by Mrs Henry Graham (Ellen Graham, *née* Peel, who in 1908 married George Ranken, later Baron, Askwith). Reading Notes (MHP, B 1a) dated: 24 October.
2 – E. F. Benson (1867–1940), author of *Dodo* (1893), etc.; Anthony Hope (Sir Anthony Hope Hawkins, 1863–1933), author of *The Prisoner of Zenda* (1894), etc.
3 – Graham, p. 128, on the character of Mrs Judeney, which has: 'She might be fat and red and stupid, unsuited to her present position. But she had a heart, and that is what matters most . . . '

A Walk By Night

On an expedition reaching to a certain fold in the coast to the west of St Ives, known as Trevail, the autumnal dusk fell before the party had fairly started homewards. And indeed the view, still solid in the twilight, was such as to draw one's silent and steadfast attention. There stood out into the sea a solemn procession of great cliffs fronting the night and the Atlantic waves with what seemed an almost conscious nobility of purpose, as though yet once more they must obey some immemorial command. Now and again a far lighthouse flashed its golden pathway through the mist and suddenly recalled the harsh shapes of the rocks. The sight was sufficient to indicate the lateness of the evening in view of those six or seven miles which must yet be traversed on foot; and so vague, moreover, was the surrounding country that it seemed prudent not to forsake the road. In half-an-hour's time even the white surface beneath us swam like mist, and our feet struck somewhat tentatively as though they questioned the ground. A figure withdrawing itself some yards wavered for a moment and was then engulfed as though the dark waters of the night had closed over it, and the voice sounded like one reaching across great depths. It was noticeable that though we walked in close companionship and tried to defy the dark with cheerful argument our voices sounded strange to each other, and the most cogent reasoning lacked authority; insensibly we glided into such topics as are suitable to sombre and melancholy places.

In those silences which came too frequently the identity of the figure walking beside one seemed to merge in the night; one strode on alone, conscious of the pressure of the dark all around, conscious, too, that by degrees resistance to it grew less and less; that the body carried forward over the ground was some thing separate from the mind which floated away as though in a swoon. The road, even, had been left behind, and we had struck - if a word implying definite action can be used of anything as indefinite as our course now became, across the fields of the daytime – the trackless ocean of the night. From time to time it was advisable to test the ground beneath the feet in order that its substance might be proved indisputably. Both eyes and ears were fast sealed, or, for the pressure on them was of something intangible, had grown numb insensibly, so that the apparition of several lights beneath us had to be realised almost with conscious effort. Could one really see, as in the daytime, or was this some vision within the brain like those stars which a blow scatters before the eye? There they hung, floating without anchorage, in soft depths of darkness in a valley beneath us; for directly that the eye had proved them true the brain woke and constructed a scheme of the world in which to place them. There, too, must be a hill, a town beneath it, the road winding round as we remembered it; a dozen lights can do much to solidify the world. The strangest part of our pilgrimage was over, for something visible had emerged; we had a proof before us. Moreover, we found ourselves upon a road, and walked forward more freely. There were human beings down here too, though they were not as the people of the daytime are. Suddenly a light burnt close at our side, and even as we saw it bearing down upon us a wheel crunched, and a man in a cart was lit up before us; in a second his lights were out and his wheels were dumb; no voice of ours could have reached him. Again, as though scenes were passed swiftly before us and withdrawn, we found ourselves in a farmyard, where a lantern swung an unsteady disc of light over the huddled shapes of cattle, and even discovered parts of our submerged persons. The voice of the farmer bidding us goodnight recalled us as though a firm hand had grasped ours, to the shores of the world, but in two strides the immense flood of darkness and silence was over us again. Yet once more lights stood beside us, as though they had approached with silent steps like the lights of ships passing at sea – the lamps that we had seen from the hill-top. The village was quiet, but not asleep, as though it lay wide-eyed in tacit conflict with the dark; we could distinguish forms leaning against the house-walls, men apparently, who could not sleep with that weight of night pressing against their windows, but must come forth and stretch their arms in it. How puny were the rays of the lamp against the immeasurable waves of darkness surging round them! A ship at sea is a lonely thing, but far lonelier it seemed was this little village anchored to the desolate earth and exposed every night, alone, to the unfathomed waters of darkness.

And yet, once accustomed to the strange element, there was great peace and beauty in it. It seemed as though only the phantoms and spirits of substantial things were now abroad; clouds floated where the hills had been, and the houses were sparks of fire. The eye might bathe and refresh itself in the depths of the night, without grating upon any harsh outline of reality; the earth with its infinity of detail was dissolved into ambiguous space. The walls of the house were too narrow, the glare of the lamps too fierce for those thus refreshed and made sensitive; we were as birds lately winged that have been caught and caged.

1 – An essay in the *Guardian*, 28 December 1905, an earlier version of which, including almost the exact last words, occurs in VW's Cornwall Diary (11 August–14 September 1905), Berg Collection, New York Public Library. See Editorial Note, p. xxi.

1906

A Nineteenth-Century Critic

Canon Ainger's *Lectures and Essays* give rise to some reflections which are only indirectly inspired by the text. It is no disparagement to the author to say that we find his volumes of greater interest as a revelation of his point of view than as a criticism of the subjects which he professes to treat. His point of view, by which we may understand the personal attitude towards literature as distinct from the intellectual, was far more clearly marked than his critical gift. And this attitude is interesting not only in itself, but because, as Ainger would have been the first to agree, it is much less common to-day than it was yesterday, and the nineteenth century is already yesterday. Canon Beeching says with obvious truth that 'Ainger's interest in literature was in the main ethical.'[2] He goes on to attribute this characteristic to the fact that he lived in 'one of the great ages of creative impulse',[3] and the writers of such an age, he says, are chiefly concerned with ideas. But the distinction of the writers of the nineteenth century, so far as we are now able to judge them, seems to be that the ideas which interested them were, roughly speaking, ethical rather than aesthetic. If for this reason alone then, Canon Ainger seems to us a typical product of the nineteenth century, the more so because his individual gift was not of sufficient strength to colour or confuse his faithful reflection of the bent of contemporary thought.

The reader is driven to some such general criticism of the present collection of essays and lectures; by the form of work as well as by its nature. The lectures are considerably in the majority, and anyone who has had the misfortune to be lectured knows that certain defects are almost inherent in the form. The sense has to be adapted to the understanding of the least intelligent among the audience, and points must be made far more obvious to the ear than they need be to the eye. Again, as Canon Beeching points out, Ainger was ready to make some sacrifice of his style 'for the sake of the lessons to be taught',[4] and the publication of the present volumes has been undertaken partly because, in the editor's opinion, these lessons still need to be enforced. Here we are reminded that Canon Ainger possessed a 'professional bias',[5] and we feel inclined to echo the criticism which he anticipated for himself, 'Sermoni propriora' – these things are 'properer for a sermon'.[6] But a man is a clergyman because he upholds certain principles; he does not, certainly if he is Canon Ainger, don them with his black coat and his shovel hat. In his case the bias was innate and unconscious; it affects every view upon life or literature that is expressed in these volumes; but it is only occasionally that we feel that the lecturer is speaking by virtue of his office. However we may account for it, the reader of these lectures and essays will have to consider this point of view seriously; it is part of the lesson. Many quotations might be found to illustrate it. In his lecture upon the ethical element in Shakespeare, for instance, Ainger quotes with approval a saying of Coventry Patmore to the effect that a good poet must first be a good man.[7] Byron, he says, might have written the lines:

> To me the meanest flower that blows can give
> Thoughts that do often lie too deep for tears[8]

but if Byron had written them they would not have 'affected our imagination and evoked the kind of response in our hearts'[9] as they do when we know that they were written by Wordsworth. The reason is that 'we are, in fact, whatever our theories upon this head, affected in our estimate of some beautiful and touching thought by our acquaintance with the personality of the author of it'.[10]

Canon Ainger goes on, of course, to point out that we draw our conception of an author's 'personality' from the whole body of his work and not from isolated phrases. This estimate would not be altered by any knowledge of the actual facts of his life, because the man and his work are indivisible. But as it is true that we can judge a man's character from his writings, so we can lay emphasis upon that element in his work which reveals his character; the ethical element that is in preference to the purely intellectual. In the case of Shakespeare we have no evidence that affects our estimate of him save that which is supplied by his works; but with other writers it is not so. It is tempting, in many instances, to use our knowledge of a man's life to interpret his work, and the result may be not only that we lay too great a stress upon the ethical element with which it is allied. This, we must confess, seems to us the weakness inherent in all Canon Ainger's writing; his chief aim in criticism seems to be to institute an anxious inquiry into the state of the writer's morals. Shakespeare thus was chiefly superior to Marlowe because he had 'a dominating sense of the supremacy and beauty of goodness'.[11] Mr Stephen Phillips is not a great poet because the ethical element is absent from his plays;[12] Tennyson is superior to Shelley and Keats because his sympathies are 'in close touch with man, his sorrows, his hopes, his eternal destiny'.[13] No one will deny that a man may reasonably hold these judgments, but no one will feel that they are comprehensive. We may even assert that they imply some intellectual confusion. The upshot of it is that Canon Ainger, we feel, gives undue prominence to moral excellence in literature; his literary judgment is swayed by what he knows of a man's life, and his affection for a writer blunts his critical insight. One might almost sum up his position by the advice which he gives to those who aim at 'being pleasant in conversation'. 'Take care of the heart and the intellect will take care of itself.'[14] Such advice, as he knew well, would be held merely amazing by a generation which is more concerned with the state of its art than with the state of its soul. Thus he found himself in the position of one who has to teach a lesson; he detected grave faults in the new age; and he did not hesitate to condemn them. But though we cannot agree in the value of the lesson which he consciously sets forth, we believe that unconsciously he has taught a lesson well worth learning. The picture of the man himself is the best thing in these volumes, for though no one will call him a great critic, all will agree that he reverenced letters; that he possessed a mind of singular culture and sincerity; and that his sympathy was with everything both in life and in letters that he held to be sweet and true. For these reasons it seems that he had something of that 'secret of charm' which he defined to be 'the presence of the moral element; that is, "the human element – the ear that hears ... the still sad music of humanity" and responds to it.'[15]

1 – A review in the *Speaker*, 6 January 1906, (Kp C3.1) of *Lectures and Essays* (ed. H. C. Beeching; 2 vols, Macmillan & Co., 1905) by Canon Alfred Ainger (1837–

1904), writer, humorist, and divine. While at Trinity Hall, Cambridge, 1856–9, Ainger had been considerably influenced by Henry Fawcett and by the newly appointed junior tutor, Leslie Stephen. Indeed, it was Stephen who did much to encourage him to take holy orders. Reading Notes (MHP, B 1a) dated: 3 December.
2 – Ainger, vol. I, p. ix; Henry Charles Beeching (1859–1919), Ainger's friend as well as editor, was Canon of Westminster, 1902–11, and in due course Dean of Norwich.
3 – *Ibid.*, p. x.   4 – *Ibid.*, p. ix.
5 – *Ibid.*, p. xi.
6 – See *ibid.*, vol. II, 'True and False Humour', p. 250, which has: 'When I insist (perhaps *ad nauseam*) that the salt of all humour worthy the name is sympathy and reverence, I have to risk the objection of approaching the subject from too professional a view, and of being taunted with Lamb's translation of Coleridge's Horatian motto – *Sermoni propiora* ("Properer for a sermon").'
7 – *Ibid.*, vol. I, 'The Ethical Element in Shakespeare', p. 98; Ainger paraphrases rather than quotes Coventry Patmore.
8 – *Ibid.*, p. 99; the lines conclude Wordsworth's 'Ode On Intimations of Immortality'.
9 – *Ibid.*, p. 98.
10 – *Ibid.*, which has 'on', not 'upon'.
11 – *Ibid.*, p. 117.
12 – *Ibid.*, vol. II, 'Some Aspects of Mr Stephen Phillips's New Tragedy', p. 178; the work discussed is *Paolo and Francesca* (1900).
13 – *Ibid.*, 'The Death of Tennyson' (whom Ainger had known at Cambridge), p. 117.
14 – *Ibid.*, 'The Art of Conversation', p. 292.
15 – *Ibid.*, 'The Secret of Charm in Literature', pp. 129–30.

'After His Kind'

The stories which make this volume all treat of the different aspects of love. But Mrs Henderson has chosen in every instance an unusual point of view. She has not tried to elaborate plots or to analyse character; rather she has taken up her story at some point of emotional crisis and has dropped it when the crisis is past. And the crisis comes where you do not expect it. Her stories then are very short and in most cases very intense. They are even occasionally abrupt; we are left standing on the edge of a precipice as it were. But however brief and elliptical, every story manages somehow to hold the attention, often to puzzle it. The people are strange, their actions are odd, their speech is unwonted – everything about them is a little harsh and angular. But this austerity, when it is due to discrimination, has a force of its own; the story of the Italian priest and the Madonna, of the preacher in the docks, of the don and Jane Austen, for example – and we could quote others – express much more than they say. And even when the writer is not so successful she yet interests us by the directness and originality of her touch. The book, in short, stimulates our appetite, and we hope that Mrs Henderson will give us more.

1 – A notice in the *Guardian*, 10 January 1906, (Kp C3.2) of *After His Kind* (Duckworth & Co., 1905) by M. Sturge Henderson. Mrs Henderson – one of the authors of VW's stepbrother Gerald Duckworth – did not, it appears, write more in this vein, but she did later publish books on rural subjects. Reading Notes (MHP, B 1a) dated: 17 December.

The Sister of Frederic the Great

The sister of Frederic [*sic*] the Great left behind her not only a considerable mass of correspondence, but also, according to the habit of her age, a memoir, which she had never been able to finish to her liking. After her death the manuscripts fell into the hands of publishers, and various editions with different claims to authenticity excited for the time considerable interest and controversy. Wilhelmina, it appeared, had used her pen freely, some thought unscrupulously, and the critics were quick to convict her of disloyalty as a friend and of inaccuracy as a writer. Nevertheless, Carlyle, with his keen eye for worth, finds it 'a human book . . . a veracious book, done with heart, and from eyesight and insight'.[2] To Sainte-Beuve it revealed talents no less remarkable than those of her famous brother.[3] Miss Cuthell, although her method is at times too crude and colloquial to be altogether pleasing, has given us a picturesque and readable account of a woman who is invariably interesting.

On her mother's side Wilhelmina was a granddaughter of George I of England and of Sophia Dorothea, the prisoner of Ahlden.[4] Her father's mother was more pleasantly distinguished as the friend of Leibnitz and Bayle,[5] who did her best to kindle something of the brilliancy of Parisian salons in Charlottenburg. The parents of Frederic and Wilhelmina had done little to deserve two such children, and the relationship was from the first strangely incongruous. Frederic William, the father, with many solid claims to respect, treated his children with a grotesque brutality which suggested insanity; Sophia Dorothea, the mother, was a stern and ambitious woman, who, like her husband, was too much dominated by her own wishes to have much independent affection for her children. Wilhelmina was a precocious child, but, save for one circumstance, an unhappy one. The happiness of her childhood, as to a great extent of her whole life, depended upon her brother Frederic, who was born three years after her: they had two bodies and one soul, he wrote in later years. They were 'inseparable in the nursery':[6] at six years old Wilhelmina had impressed the eye of a painter with one attitude that was to be characteristic of her future life; she lays her hand on Frederic's arm to restrain him from some infantine campaign on which he is bent with his big drum.[7] But in the nursery Wilhelmina had to suffer from the tyranny of nurses and the erudition of scholars. The Queen was already ambitious for her daughter, and, not content with the simple teaching of governesses, procured a tutor who could instruct in 'six modern languages without counting Slav and Basque dialects and Oriental tongues including Chinese'. With this gentleman Wilhelmina absorbed 'universal history' with such thoroughness that it took her four years of steady toil to reach the eighth century starting from 'before the Deluge'.[8] She was so good a linguist that, as Sainte-Beuve says, she might have written her memoirs in English or German had she not chosen to write them in French;[9] but, unfortunately, she was taught neither Greek nor Latin, and with her deep interest in the classics only knew them through translations. All this learning, however, so far as the Queen was concerned, was but an instrument to fit Wilhelmina for marriage. Her marriage engrossed her thoughts while she was still strumming her scales and learning her declensions, for thus early the Queen had chosen Frederic, Prince of Wales as the most desirable suitor for her daughter. To further the match she condescended to intrigues and secret negotiations in which Wilhelmina soon became an accomplice, for, although both mother and daughter ignored the wider issues that were at stake, the King considered the English marriage from its political aspect only. The part that this intrigue played in Wilhelmina's early life seems curiously out of proportion to its intrinsic importance, or perhaps we may complain that Miss Cuthell has followed the complications too laboriously. After six years of scheming and diplomacy the negotiations were broken off by the King in a sudden fit of rage: and, before

Wilhelmina knew what was to become of her, the Crown Prince's plot to escape to France was discovered. It was natural that Wilhelmina should be suspected of complicity, and after a violent scene with her father she was sent to prison and bidden to reflect on the merits of her two suitors, the Duke of Weissenfels and the Hereditary Prince of Baireuth [sic]. Her mother was still of opinion that 'a prison is better than a bad marriage',[10] but Wilhelmina, when her brother's pardon was promised on condition of her consent, was weak enough to give in. She agreed to marry the Prince of Baireuth, and received two letters from her parents, in one of which her 'faithful father' promised that he would never forsake her, and in the other her mother exclaimed: 'I swear you an eternal hatred, and will never forgive you.'[11] In spite of the fervour of this statement the Queen proved herself fairly consistent.

So far the brutal and cumbersome machinery of the court had effectually obscured the finer shades of Wilhelmina's character. Her love of her brother was the most individual trait in her nature, except for a habit she had, when ill in bed or locked up in prison, of reading and writing and composing music. But now that she was married she could expand more freely, although the atmosphere was still sufficiently harsh. The little court of Baireuth was humble compared with that of Berlin, and Her Royal Highness seemed both to herself and others too grand a lady for such simplicity. The Margrave, her father-in-law, moreover, was as economical as her own father, and less respectable. He might have been induced to die, thought Frederic, 'if only he was sure that they distilled brandy in Heaven'.[12] But Wilhelmina was happy in her husband, who to some extent shared her cultivated tastes. A daughter, their only child, was born to them and named Frederica after her uncle. The Margrave died in 1735, and with her accession began the few happy years of Wilhelmina's life. As Margravine she had some scope for her energies, although in many ways they were still pitiably circumscribed. Her husband consulted her in the affairs of the government and she began to meditate plans for transforming Baireuth into a centre, or at least a reflection, of intellectual brilliancy. She corresponded with her brother about Italian actors and musicians, and the rustic taste of Baireuth was trained by the performance of French plays and operas. Her intellectual tastes were revived and stimulated; she read philosophy and expounded her views upon the theory of atoms and the existence of God. She began to build extravagantly, in the classical style. This, it is clear, was the real Wilhelmina: the woman of brilliant and volatile intellect, eager for knowledge and experience and craving above all the stimulus of companionship. She stayed once at Rheinsberg when Frederic was King, and the days passed in music, acting, and the conversation that she loved. There she met Voltaire, and began an intimacy which lasted her lifetime. But the King left this brilliant company for the opening campaign of the war of the Austrian succession and henceforward the Margravine's life was never free from anxiety. 'My great joy,' she had written, 'has always been study, music and above all the delight of society.' All her life, with one or two brief exceptions, she was only to know this joy through translations. The music and the society of Baireuth she found 'detestable'.[13] Nor was she to enjoy her studies and the companionship of her husband for long. Wilhelmina's beauty faded as her health became increasingly frail, and her husband was drawn into an intimacy with her greatest friend, Dorothea von Marwitz. Wilhelmina, in spite of her sarcastic tongue, was distinguished by a certain proud loyalty where her friends were concerned, and for a long time would see no ill. The effect of her disappointment when she could no longer ignore it was to concentrate her affections still more exclusively upon her brother. He inspired the most profound feeling in a nature too fastidious to be passionate. She threw herself into the intellectual reform of Baireuth, founded a university and anticipated the present opera house. Baireuth was sufficiently gay to attract Frenchmen from their metropolis; Voltaire, with whom the Margravine corresponded, paid her the high compliment of coming himself. But all this activity was carried on in defiance of the failing health which obliged her to winter in the South. To Wilhelmina the journey was an intellectual pilgrimage to be performed in a spirit of due reverence, but the account so faithfully recorded by Miss Cuthell is not more interesting than such itineraries generally are. Wilhelmina at the age of forty-five preserved an insatiable appetite for the sights of the world.

The last years of her life were years of physical and mental suffering. She tried to negotiate a peace for her brother, and failed. She had to hear of his defeats and to read of his desire to kill himself. 'Medieval barbarism'[14] she thought was to engulf the little spot of light and reason which she had tended with so much care. Her daughter's marriage proved a failure. But her mind, as she wrote in her last letter to her brother, 'is always with me',[15] and she might have added, always occupied with others. She died in October 1758, aged forty-nine, and 'Vanity of Vanities' was by her own choice the text of her funeral sermon. Miss Cuthell's book is full of interesting materials for any one who cares to preach it.

1 – A review in *Academy & Literature*, 13 January 1906, (Kp C3.3) of *Wilhelmina Margravine of Baireuth* (2 vols, Chapman & Hall Ltd, 1905) by Edith E. Cuthell. Reading Notes (MHP, B 1a) dated: 11 November.

2 – Carlyle, *History of Friederich II of Prussia, called Frederick the Great* (6 vols, Chapman & Hall, 1858 etc.), vol. 1, bk. IV, ch. I, p. 384.

3 – Sainte-Beuve, *Causeries du Lundi*, 'Le Margrave de Bareith. Sa correspondance avec Frédéric' (lundi 1er septembre 1856): 'L'élévation de coeur en effet, la noblesse de sentiments qui était inherente à sa nature et qui, dans ses Mémoires, est masquée par l'esprit de plaisanterie et de satire, se prononce davantage dans les lettres . . . et c'est aussi par ces côtés sérieux et moins connus que nous prendrons plaisir à la dégager et à la dessiner en face de son frère.' This is not quoted by Cuthell.

4 – In 1694 the Electress of Hanover, Sophia Dorothea, had been divorced by the Elector George Louis (King of Gt Britain and Ireland 1714–27) and until her death in 1726 was kept a prisoner at Ahlden – a circumstance which did little to endear George to his British subjects.

5 – Wilhelmina's paternal grandmother was the wife of Frederick I of Prussia, a patron of the philosophers Leibnitz and Bayle.

6 – Cuthell, vol. 1, p. 19.

7 – *Ibid.*, pp. 27–8; from a painting by the French artist Pésne, bearing the caption 'Wilhelmina and Frederic, aged six and three. "Jamais tendresse n'a égalé la nôtre"', reproduced facing p. 27.

8 – For Wilhemina's learning, *ibid.*, pp. 28–9; the tutor was one La Croze, an ex-monk from St Germain-des-Près, librarian of the Royal Library at Berlin.

9 – Sainte-Beuve, *op. cit.*: 'La Margrave de Bareith qui avait eu une education très-soignée, qui savait les langues modernes, l'histoire, la littérature, et qui aurait pu écrire ses Mémoires en anglais aussi bien qu'en allemand, les a écrits en français, de même que c'est en français qu'elle correspondait toujours avec son frère. C'est donc un écrivain Français de plus que nous avons en elle, et un écrivain peintre tout à fait digne d'attention.' (The last sentence is quoted by Cuthell, vol, 1, p. XVIII.)

10 – Cuthell, vol. 1, p. 200.

11 – For these parental responses, *ibid.*, p. 202; p. 203.

12 – *Ibid.*, p. 259.

13 – For the Margravine's delights and detestations, *ibid.*, vol. II, p. 7.

14 – *Ibid.*, p. 356.

15 – *Ibid.*, p. 379, a letter dictated 25 September 1758.

'The Scholar's Daughter'

The picture of a girl, young, beautiful, and gifted, brought up solely among learned scholars who are preparing a colossal dictionary of the English language attracts attention at the outset in *The Scholar's Daughter* by Beatrice Harraden. But afterwards we complain that the author has been satisfied with the obvious reading of the situation, so that its attraction and promise remain on the surface. Perhaps it is impossible to feel much sympathy for the self-possessed young woman with her high spirits and her slang; or perhaps the scholarly atmosphere with which she contrasts is but a very diluted version of the real thing. The three bookworms with their tender hearts and their tempered love of philology are not convincing as men or scholars, if, as Miss Harraden would have us, we must make that distinction. The book, indeed, seems to fall between two stools; either Miss Harraden might have concentrated her powers upon the sufficiently amusing intricacies of the plot and turned out a well-filled short story, or, had she chosen to expound the characters more elaborately, she might have given us an interesting study of the conflict of one temperament with another. But, as it is, if we consider the book as a serious novel its superficiality irritates us, or if we take it as a short story we are wearied by the protracted explanations. If it is said that in spite of this it is easy to read *The Scholar's Daughter* with interest and amusement it is obvious how much more might have been expected of the writer than she has given us here.

1 – A notice in the *TLS*, 16 February 1906, (Kp c3.4) of *The Scholar's Daughter* (Methuen, 1906) by Beatrice Harraden (1864–1936), prolific popular author, graduate of London University and a devoted feminist. Reading Notes (MHP, B 1a) dated: 10 February.

'A Supreme Moment'

It is not easy to account for the impression that *A Supreme Moment* by Mrs Hamilton Synge leaves upon the mind; even during the process of reading one is conscious of a little amazement at the result which is being achieved by apparently simple means. A commonplace stretch of English country, dotted with substantial country houses and snug vicarages, will either be described, one expects, quite frankly as it stands or made the scene of some violent and romantic contrast. But Mrs Synge, starting, as it seems, to go patiently over the familiar ground of mothers' meetings and village scandals, somehow contrives always to skip what we expect and to show us something different. Nothing more happens than that a girl, brought up with some freedom abroad, comes to stay with a quiet English family; but her coming slightly changes the perspective all round. The girl herself is not much more than a shadow; but she has the property of proving that the characters among whom she passes are living flesh and blood. The gradual unfolding of Agatha, the staid Englishwoman of middle age, when brought into contact with something unlike what she has ever known is the real achievement of the book; for without any crudeness or improbability we are shown the way in which, with all the odd reserves and simplicities of her type, she alters the point of view which education and tradition have given her. Thus by the end of the book she has become a new person with hardly any alteration in the facts of her life to accentuate the change which has taken place within. Mrs Hamilton Synge's method is carefully simple; she always understates and often omits what we expect to be put in; but, in spite of the fact that some of her characters are hints rather than people, each stroke makes its impression, and the result is that the book as a whole is undeniably memorable among its fellows.

1 – A notice in the *TLS*, 16 Febuary 1906, (Kp C 3.5) of *A Supreme Moment* (Fisher Unwin, 1905) by Mrs Hamilton Synge. Reading Notes (MHP, B 1a) dated: 3 February.

'The House of Shadows'

In many novels the situation seems to have been suggested by the author's desire to introduce certain characters; in others the writer seems to have conceived his scheme first and to have made his characters its creatures. Mr R. J. Farrer, in *The House of Shadows*, has written a novel under the stress of an idea; and although his method has certain drawbacks it has undoubtedly produced a book remarkable for its force and continuity. The story is concerned with an old Yorkshire house and its squire, Ladon by name, who has nursed his eccentricities and his pride in solitude with an only son since the death of his wife twenty-five years ago. The son has never mixed with the world; and the first visit that he pays to London sends him back to Yorkshire with a wife. Between this vulgar, but beautiful and passionate, woman and her morose old father-in-law things go wrong from the first; indeed, in his fierce headaches his dislike of her becomes almost insane. Then he is suddenly told by a specialist that he is suffering from a disease that must kill him after a year of increasing agony. A niece, guessing that her symptoms are the same as her uncle's, poisons herself; and he resolves to do the same thing, but that his religion forbids suicide. His son refuses to administer the draught, and he determines to exact this deed in revenge from his daughter-in-law. The situation verges upon the melodramatic; but the reserve and humour with which it is treated keep it in proper proportions. The same purpose, that is, links all the chapters together, and each adds something of its own to the single impression. And that impression is so consistently gloomy that it is possible to resent the power with which it is expounded. For the writer seems possessed with the idea of physical pain, and its conflict with the forces of the human soul – with love and religion; and it is pain that conquers. The drawback of the concentration which is the result of the scheme of the book is naturally that the characters are always seen under some kind of distortion, and that at intervals the idea behind comes too prominently and crudely to the foreground. The author harangues us on occasion as though he were speaking from the pulpit. And the defect that is allied to the subject of the book qualifies our admiration at its strongest; the pain and conflict are inevitably degraded by the taint of the merely bodily anguish from which they proceed. But these are the limitations of a remarkable book, and in some degree spring from its strength. Moreover, pleasure of a less sardonic kind can be taken in Cousin Coralie the Countess, the Reverend Mr Lancaster, with his devout respect for titles, and Mrs Bolpett, of the ancestral Bolpetts. Mr Farrer clearly is a writer to be remembered.

1 – A notice in the *TLS*, 9 March 1906, (Kp C3.6) of *The House of Shadows* (Edward Arnold, 1906) by R. J. (Reginald John) Farrer. Reading Notes (MHP, B 1a) dated: 17 February.

'Blanche Esmead'

Mrs Fuller Maitland calls her novel *Blanche Esmead*, a study of diverse temperaments; the frail and exquisite Blanche Esmead has married an honest country parson who can talk only of the Clothing Club and of the drunkenness of Hoggins. The diversity, however, between the parson and his wife manifests itself in such very trivial ways – he likes cold beef, for instance, and his wife cannot bear it – that a catastrophe of any kind between them seems quite unnecessary. For some reason we do not realise that there is an essential gulf between the two, of which these trifles are the superficial indication. But then Mrs Fuller Maitland writes so gracefully and evolves her story with such smooth skill that we are content to remain on the surface and laugh at trifles. There is no need to take anybody or anything very much to heart. Good John Esmead was no doubt a very worthy man; but as he will quote proverbs on every occason, call his wife 'the wifie', knock over the ink, and tread upon the dog, what can we do but laugh at him? Every village in England must be supplied with such a vicar and such a Mrs Crowle who cuts out the clothes and manages the societies and is full of intolerance and virtuous wrath, if we are to believe the novelists. Somehow it seems conceivable that the novelists have been satisfied with a traditional conception of these parts, and that the pattern may have changed since it was first originated. But Mrs Fuller Maitland is quite content with things as they are, or may conveniently be supposed to be. Then there is, of course, the great lady of the neighbourhood, who on this occasion is a lady of doubtful reputation; and Zéphine, the fashionable widow from London in whom Blanche confides. There is a little flavour of the disagreeable, some discomfort; 'neuralgia of the soul' as Blanche calls it.[2] But Blanche is too refined to be wicked, and when the crisis comes prefers to die gracefully of influenza – until her good husband somehow suggests to her that a coffin and a grave are necessary parts of death, upon which she eats her dinner and recovers. It is then obvious that John must collide with a motor-car, and so set his wife free in the eye of the law to marry her irreproachable lover Basil Forde. All this naturally is treated in a facile and frivolous style, in which pet dogs and paper knives seem of equal value with men and women. But within its limits – the limits of a fashionable drawing-room – this is a graceful and entertaining novel, and the action is swift and sparkling from first to last, if it is also shallow.

1 – A notice in the *TLS*, 23 March 1906, (Kp C3.7) of *Blanche Esmead: a story of diverse temperaments* (Methuen, 1906) by Mrs Fuller Maitland – Charlotte Elizabeth ('Ella'), *née* Squire (d. 1931), wife of J. A. Fuller Maitland (1856–1936), musical critic and connoisseur. Reading Notes (MHP, B 1a) dated: 17 March.
2 – Maitland, ch. LIII, p. 255: '"If I have neuralgia, it is neuralgia of the soul," Blanche answered, with a half-wishful, half-amused, and wholly mournful expression, which was not calculated to put her friend's apprehensions to rest.'

'The Face of Clay'

Mr H. A. Vachell could hardly have chosen a happier setting for his novel *The Face of Clay* than the fishing village of Pont-Aven in Brittany. The rustic barbarity of the peasant life becomes something primitive and beautiful when it is set against the mysterious background of the sea. It is as though the presence of this great force at their doors simplified and lent dignity to the lives which are so constantly risked upon it. Certainly Mr Vachell has caught the spirit of the place and conveyed it to us in a quantity of delicate and vivid pictures of the sea and of the characters bred beneath its influence. His heroine, Téphany Lane, belongs in a double sense to the twofold life of the town and its colony of artists; on her mother's side she comes of an old Breton family, and her father was an English painter who is drowned, as the book opens, in the sea almost beneath his daughter's eyes. But it is the Breton element in her that predominates, and her strong inheritance of Breton instincts and superstitions that gives its meaning to the story. Indeed, the first half of the book, in which the life of both peasant and artist is illustrated with great charm and an indication of perfect fidelity, attracts us more than the development of the story itself. Michael Ossory, the painter of genius, who leads a life of failure and misanthropy in remorse for a mysterious crime committed early in life, is not a figure who convinces one of his truth, or impresses one with his supreme capabilities. The touch of mystery and superstition, which seems natural in a Breton peasant, becomes slightly melodramatic in the character of an English gentleman. For this reason the second half of the book, in which the story of the crime, symbolised by the face of clay, is confessed and cleared up, is less successful than the perfectly natural and sincere opening. Mr Vachell is conscious perhaps that he has a moral to expound, and he becomes, therefore, a little solemn and emphatic. 'Clinton Carne,' he remarks, 'walks out of these pages a better man than he entered them, and a finer artist.'[2] That may be true, but the conclusion ought to have been so closely woven into the texture of the story that there was no need to sum it up in so many words. But though there are some weak passages, especially, it seems, in any crisis of emotion, the book is interesting not only as a study of curious beliefs and superstitions, but in a wider sense as a study of the life that is not limited to peasants. The subsidiary characters of Mary Machin, and Johnnie Keats, the delightful Satellite, are observed with such humour and sympathy that they make a very severe touchstone by which to test the other characters in the book. And the story of Yannik, the peasant girl, whose caste forbids her to sit as a model, and the grandmother who craves for the 'fat five-franc pieces'[3] in order to save her sons' souls, is observed with such delicacy that it touches the reader perhaps more than anything else in the book.

1 – A notice in the *TLS*, 13 April 1906, (Kp c3.8) of *The Face of Clay: an interpretation* (John Murray, 1906) by H. A. (Horace Annesley) Vachell (1861–1955), a prolific author, who had in 1905 achieved 'great popular success' (*DNB*) with *The Hill*. Reading Notes (MHP, B 1a) dated: 8 April.
2 – Vachell, ch. XVI, p. 323.
3 – *Ibid.*, ch. III, pp. 40–1.

The Poetic Drama

It is at least encouraging to see with what energy people can still devote themselves to poetry even in its most arduous and ambitious branches. No less than three of the seven volumes before us are seriously concerned with the drama, and merit our respect, therefore, however we may rate their achievement. Mr Dillon, indeed, has given us not only a play but a trilogy – a threefold illustration of the life of William the Conqueror. It is a tremendous theme, and the author has attacked it vigorously, but his vigour is spasmodic rather than sustained, and he never reaches those equable heights to which the masters of blank verse seem to rise without effort. Thus he can keep up to a fair level of dignity for a passage at a time, and then the strain becomes too tense and he drops to a metaphor like this:

> 'These words are gridirons whereon we lie stretched
> In lingering agony . . .'[2]

Or this:

> 'Let me gather up the shreds,
> The potsherds of the broken crock, my son'[3]

and the spell is rudely broken. But it would be unfair to criticise a work of such magnitude by single phrases. The general impression left upon the mind of the reader is somewhat fragmentary and confused, as though a great many scenes and characters had passed across the stage without much order or continuity.

Mr Spencer Moore is more successful in the narrower limits of his *Aurelian*. He has used his materials more completely and has the advantage of a skilled and mellifluous pen. His gift, it is true, is more for a picturesque rhetoric than for the imaginative depths of poetry. Passages like the following abound:

> 'The sun in golden plashes beats upon
> My battlemented glory! Do you not hear
> The waves of adulation lapping me?'[4]

And that is not poetry. But in the mouth of Zenobia, Queen of Palmyra, the lines are not inappropriate; or at any rate we can accept them in default of better. Mr Moore, moreover, can make his drama move with some swiftness and dramatic skill so that it is not hard to read him, even with some degree of pleasure. It is curious, indeed, to hear a Roman Emperor address his son as 'sonny' and speak of a 'protégé'; while Zenobia, adjusting her diadem after her submission, asks, 'Is it on straight?'[5] The insight into feminine nature that is shown in the last touch is hardly permissible in a poet who is not Euripides. But with the exception of a few slips like these the play is vivid and occasionally eloquent.

With Mr Douglas Fox we draw nearer our own time and the change is welcome. For both the dramatists we have passed in review respect the splendid surface of their kings and queens too deeply to credit them with human subtleties. Mr Fox shows traces of a warmer sympathy. He takes five scenes from the life of Sir Thomas More and leaves him on the scaffold with the axe about to fall. The drama moves gently and melodiously, with no very great vigour but without consistent dignity of thought and expression. There are lines, too, which suggest that he has it in him to produce something more than lengths of irreproachable English, as, for instance, the concluding lines of the fine speech on page 22:

> '... rather march
> With souls attuned to heavenly purposes
> And fortified by stout fidelity
> To ancient, high, and venerable things,
> Beneath old banners into lands unknown.'[6]

The figure of Dame More is excellent. Sir Thomas himself is a little too flatly and evenly drawn to excite much sympathy.

Miss von Herder leaves the solid world and takes us beneath the sea. But it must be confessed that her mermaidens, and her Sea Queen in particular, would do credit to Belgravia, and that is a disappointment. Matthew Arnold, in his 'Forsaken Merman',[7] made the sea and its people both true and mysterious, but Miss von Herder makes the fatal mistake of adding a tail to the ordinary mortal and thinking that she has created a mermaid. However, the tails are an excuse for much pretty and fantastic verse, and if the sound and the sense are somewhat thin, it is all thoroughly sweet and amiable.

Of Mr Upson's 'poem-drama', again, it is difficult to speak enthusiastically, though it would be unjust not to speak respectfully. Unfortunately it is possible to write a great number of lines in perfect taste and rhythm without saying anything that has not been said before. Any one with sufficient culture and leisure might be expected to write as Mr Upson has written with no other or rarer gift from the gods. *The City*, in which he has for his theme the story of Abgar, King of Edessa, and of his appeal to Christ, is not so successful as the shorter pieces which succeed it. Culture is less able to deal with such far-off things than with the gentle meditations inspired by an Oxford garden. Here Mr Upson is pleasantly at his ease, and muses not unmelodiously.

The claim which Mr Hookham makes for his book is doubtless justifiable; it is 'the individual expression of an individual mind'[8] and no plagiarism either in thought or expression. Whether the individual mind is so interesting that we wish to have an exact copy of it may be a matter of opinion. So long as the poem flows easily among familiar thoughts it is

graceful enough, but directly the writer has to face a crisis his imaginative force gives out, and he takes refuge in the conventional and obvious.
This is sufficiently clear from the *Sappho*, where there are some
genuinely graceful passages; while in *The Cup and the Lip* (written in
conjunction with Mr Edward Ferris) the exigencies of the plot are
painfully beyond the strength of the verse. Indeed, we get the impression
that the drama was written primarily for the stage, and that the authors
have not considered how crudely their work reads in the paler light of
the study. For the rest Mr Hookham has paraphrased a great number of
La Fontaine's fables, and has also written some shorter original pieces.
These show him to be possessed of a sincere and appreciative mind,
which reflects thoughtfully upon such themes as *Spring and Age, The
Snowdrop, Equality*, and so forth.

We have left to the last the volume which has given us the clearest
impression of original talent. Miss Travers is a young writer who
publishes for the first time. She is at the stage, evidently, of revolt and
intolerance; of question rather than of answer. She reads as though she
wrote under some sort of compulsion, and not merely because words
can be made to rhyme. In the 'Arcady in Peril' and the 'Suburbiad' she
lashes the ugly surface of modern life with satire, often pointed but
sometimes shrill. But in spite of this tendency to see the merely ridiculous
side of things – perhaps because of it – she is equally sensitive to the
underlying beauty:

> 'These shift and pass; the Unknown Powers remain
> The Everlasting Voices linger yet
> By field and flood.'[9]

In other poems, notably 'The Enemy Within', 'The Cliff Head', 'The
Tramp', Miss Travers lets her imagination dwell on subjects that are
more congenial to it, and proves that she can see clearly, passionately,
and with her own eyes. Such gifts make this little book noticeable among
its fellows, for they promise work to come no less original and more
deeply imaginative than that which we have in the volume before us.

1 – A review in the *Guardian*, 18 April 1906, (Kp C3.9) of: *King William I* (Elkin
Mathews, 1905) by Arthur Dillon; *Aurelian: a drama of the later Empire* (Longmans, 1905) by Spencer Moore; *Sir Thomas More: an historical play in five acts*
(Constable & Co., 1905) by Archibald Douglas Fox; *The Little Mermaid: a play in
three acts . . . suggested by Hans Andersen's fairy tale . . .* (Elkin Mathews, 1906
[1905]) by Alexandra von Herder; *The City: a poem-drama, and other poems*

(Macmillan & Co., 1905) by Arthur Upson; *Plays & Poems* (Kegan Paul & Co., 1905) by Paul Hookham; and *The Two Arcadias: plays and poems ... with an introduction by Richard Garnett* (Brimley Johnson & Ince, 1905) by Rosalind Travers. Reading Notes (MHP, B 1a) dated: 16 January.

2 – *King William I*, pt II, sc. III, p. 78, spoken by Edith Swan-neck, which has a 'death', not 'agony'.

3 – *Ibid.*, pt III, sc. I, p. 183, spoken by Gutha.

4 – *Aurelian*, act II, sc. I, p. 59, spoken by Zenobia, Queen of Palmyra. '(*with sudden exaltation*)'.

5 – *Ibid.*, act I, sc. I, p. 25, Aurelian to Flavius; act IV, sc. I, p. 119; and act II, sc. I, p. 77, Zenobia to Zara.

6 – *Sir Thomas More*, actually on p. 23, spoken by Sir Thomas.

7 – In *The Strayed Reveller and other Poems* (1849)

8 – *Plays & Poems*, p. v.

9 – *The Two Arcadias*, 'The Suburbiad', pp. 60–1.

Poets' Letters

If it were possible to condense into set phrases that mist of felt rather than spoken criticism which hangs round all the great names in literature, it is tolerably certain what result we should reach in the case of Mrs Browning.[2] We should have to interpret some brief decision to the effect that she was a bad poet, and that our fathers were strangely mistaken when they exalted her to the place which she holds, in theory at least, at the present day. It is true that a candid inquirer would have to enlarge and qualify such a verdict considerably before it could be allowed to stand; but in its rude way it points to a fact that need not be made the subject of inquiry here, that Mrs Browning, as a poet, has ceased to play much part in our lives.[3]

The appearance of Mr Lubbock's book, however, makes one wonder whether the method which he has applied to her letters might not be applied with equally happy results to the voluminous body of her poetry. For her letters, especially we must own the famous volumes of love letters, are responsible for a great deal of our partly instinctive distrust of her poetry. It was dreadful, the sensitive said, to overhear; but if one did sin, the more callous suggested, it was as well to be guilty of a pleasant crime. And the eavesdropper became so weary of those emphatic voices, protesting and asseverating, uttering commonplaces with dreadful distortion of the lips and drowning even the simple emotions in a twisted torrent of language, that he might surely consider that his fault was expiated as soon as committed. Mr Lubbock, then, has done Mrs Browning and her readers a substantial service. With singular discretion and tact he has gone through the many volumes of her correspondence, prompting her as it were to speak just those words which explain herself and connecting them with admirably intelligent comments of his own. In the compass of one modest volume we have all the passages we could wish to see preserved, and, when thus skilfully pieced together, it is seen that they compose a finished and brilliant portrait of the writer. And then it appears how summary would have been that decision which disposed of her merely as an extravagent freak of early Victorian taste and denied her any more permanent claim on our attention.

For, paradoxically enough, it is more easy to understand what was meant by her genius when we study her life than when we read those works that were the legitimate expression of it. It is as though the pure and intense flame which we detect when we read or hear of her had been blown into all kinds of vague and diffuse gusts, more of smoke than of fire when she yielded herself in her enthusiastic way to the inspiration of poetry. But when we approach her work through a knowledge of her life, something of the disappointment is explained, although the pity of it is deepened. It is one of the merits of Mr Lubbock's book that the familiar facts of Mrs Browning's life, of her unmarried life in particular, are so arranged that they seem to gather a new and significant force. In hands less just and discriminating the story becomes so monstrous that its real effect upon Mrs Browning is obscured. But as it is told here, with the perpetual illustration of the letters, it becomes clearly a thing that did really happen and that had an immense but calculable influence on the victim's life. We see how, gradually, after those first years of astonishing precocity, Elizabeth was silently secluded from the world, forced to acquiesce in her position as a life-long prisoner in a London house, guarded by a mad gaoler in the person of her father, and nourished almost solely upon books and her own writings. Without definite disease she was relegated by family consent to a sofa in a single room, which she scarcely left for five years. It is true that she saw a few visitors who could be smuggled upstairs without meeting her father, and she carried on a voluminous correspondence with mild literary gentlemen who were anxious to direct her talent. But it was hardly possible, as she knew herself, that sane poetry should issue from such conditions.

You ⟨she writes to Browning⟩ seem to have drunken of the cup of life full, with the sun shining on it. I have lived only inwardly, or with *sorrow* for a strong emotion. Before this seclusion of my illness, I was secluded still, and there are few of the youngest women in the world who have not seen more, heard more, known more, of society than I, who am scarcely to be called young now. ⟨When she was supposed to be dying she thought⟩ that I had stood blind in this temple I was about to leave – that I had seen no human nature, that my brothers and sisters of the earth were names to me, that I had beheld no great mountain or river, nothing in fact . . . And do you also know what a disadvantage this ignorance is to my art? . . . that I am in a manner, as a *blind poet*? Certainly, there is a compensation to a degree. I have had much of the inner life, and from the habit of self-consciousness and self-analysis I make great guesses at human nature in the main. But how willingly I would, as a poet, exchange some of this lumbering, ponderous, helpless knowledge of books, for some experience of life and man, for some . . . '[4]

The vigour with which she threw herself into the only life that was free to her and lived so steadily and strongly in her books that her days were full of purpose and character would be pathetic did it not impress us with the strength that underlay her ardent and sometimes febrile temperament. Indeed, there is no questioning her deliberate and reasonable love of literature and all that the word contains. Not only was she a very shrewd critic of others, but, pliant as she was in most matters, she could be almost obstinate when her literary independence was attacked. The many critics who objected to faults of obscurity and technique in her writing she answered indeed, but answered authoritatively, as a person stating a fact, and not pleading a case. 'My poetry,' she writes to Ruskin, 'which you once called "sickly" . . . has been called by much harder names, "affected", for instance, a charge I have never deserved, for I do think, if I may say it of myself, that the desire of speaking or spluttering the real truth out broadly, may be a cause of a good deal of what is called in me careless and awkward expression.'[5]

The desire was so honest and valiant that the 'splutterer' may be condoned, although there seems to be no reason to agree with Mrs Browning in her tacit assertion that the cause of truth would be demeaned by a more scrupulous regard for literary form. But it is not possible to consider what she might have done had her life been propitious – had not one half of it dwindled in a London sick-room – had not the other been exposed suddenly to the fierce Italian sun and Robert Browning. Or, if we are to speculate, we must remember her own consolation. 'I love poetry better than I love my own success in it.'[6]

We may all know now, if we choose to finish the poem in prose, what became of Waring; that he was Alfred Domett, CMG; that he went to New Zealand, rose to be Prime Minister there, and 'came back the other day after thirty years' absence, the same as ever – nearly … with a poem'.[7] Browning, moreover, wrote to him frequently for some years, and the letters, with some from another friend, Joseph Arnould,[8] are now printed together in a small volume. Browning, it is clear, was not what is called a good correspondent. We can almost hear the groan with which he sat down to his task when 'Chris Dowson' called to bid him 'Get a letter ready, seeing that the ship is ready for it.'[9] One may guess that as a poet he grudged the use of his fine tools upon such rude and trivial work as letter-writing. 'Consider these scratches but as so many energetic "kickings of the feet", and that what they mean is God bless you',[10] is the kind of phrase that constantly testifies his dissatisfaction with the scrawled sheets in front of him. But although he strives like a giant in chains with the conventional 'hopes and anxieties and good wishes',[11] he gets his meaning expressed in the end with his usual energy. Almost all the letters are written early, before his marriage, and the atmosphere is full of hope and defiance. 'The true best of me is to come, and you shall have it.'[12] 'Expect more and better things'[13] are phrases called out by his friend's enthusiastic trust in him. 'I believe as devoutly as ever in *Paracelsus*, and find more wealth of thought and poetry in it than in any book, except Shakespeare,' writes Arnould.[14] In return for this confidence, Browning expounds some of his aims and theories in his own cryptic and abundant method, which may not be quoted here. Few and fragmentary though the letters are, all lovers of Browning will feel that they add some vigorous strokes to the poet's familiar portrait.

1 – A signed review in the *Speaker*, 21 April 1906, (Kp C4) of *Elizabeth Barrett Browning in her Letters* (Smith, Elder, 1906) by Percy Lubbock and *Robert Browning and Alfred Domett* (Smith, Elder, 1906) ed. F. G. Kenyon – see *I VW Letters*, no. 264. Reading Notes (MHP, B 1a) dated: 2 and 5 April. See also '*Aurora Leigh*', *V VW Essays* and CR2.
2 – Elizabeth Barrett Browning (1806–61); Robert Browning (1812–89).
3 – See '*Aurora Leigh*': 'Nobody reads her, nobody discusses her, nobody troubles to put her in her place.'
4 – Lubbock, pp. 81–2, 20 March 1845; also quoted in '*Aurora Leigh*'.
5 – *Ibid.*, p. 327, 2 June 1855, which has 'spluttering' in italics.
6 – *Ibid.*, pp. 69–70.
7 – Kenyon, p. 145. Alfred Domett (1811–87), colonial statesman, whose departure

for New Zealand Browning mourned in his poem 'Waring', first published in *Bells and Pomegranates* (1842). The poem with which Domett returned to England was his epic of New Zealand *Ranolf and Amohia* (1872).

8 – (Sir) Joseph Arnould (1813–86), who won the Newdigate Prize while at Oxford with a poem on 'The Hospice of St Bernard', and later became Judge of the Supreme Court at Bombay.

9 – Kenyon, p. 91.

10 – *Ibid.*, p. 108.

11 – *Ibid.*, pp. 91–2.

12 – *Ibid.*, p. 37.

13 – *Ibid.*, p. 51.

14 – *Ibid.*, p. 86; Browning's poem *Paracelsus* was published in 1835.

Wordsworth and the Lakes

Wordsworth[2] wrote his *Guide to the Lakes* in 1810, to preface a work by the Rev. Joseph Wilkinson,[3] who had drawn a folio volume of select views. But the drawings were, as Wordsworth was the first to pronounce, so 'intolerable'[4] that he had his preface severed from the main volume and published separately. In spite of its popularity in this shape, however – some one asked him whether he had written anything else – the book has not been reprinted as a separate volume since 1864; and many readers will have reason to thank Mr de Sélincourt for his letter of introduction to a new and happily permanent friend. In his excellent preface, which, besides furnishing all facts, suggests the right way of approaching them, Mr de Sélincourt tells us something of the sentimental history of the Lakes. In 1810 they were already the subject of curiosity, although they had not been domesticated in the sense that they are to-day. The people who went went in the conscious spirit of explorers, to bring back tales of what they had seen and to figure hereafter as travellers, rather than as private people who might keep their emotions to themselves. It was the custom to preserve these experiences in prose or verse; but these volumes do not as Mr de Sélincourt says, 'afford invigorating reading'.[5] There was, perhaps, some affectation in their appreciation, and a tendency to approach lakes and mountains with a mind on the defensive against any attacks upon its sensibility. Mountains are 'horrid',[6] and when praise is given, the curiously obsolete and artificial sound of it suggests that it is inspired by a wish to save the writer's reputation as a man of taste rather than by a simple desire to write the truth.

Wordsworth, coming after these somewhat perplexed and perfunctory tourists, wrote with the calm authority of one who had lived for all but three years of his life among the scenes he describes. He has all the courtesy and consideration of an old inhabitant who does the honours of the place to a stranger, and who not only undertakes to show him the beauties, but will explain from his abundant and well-ordered knowledge any fact of history or geography that seems to him worth observation. He is jealous for his country's credit, but his familiarity with the place is so perfect that no view will drive him into hasty exaggeration; he admires what he has seen and tested during a lifetime and knows to deserve and require every word he bestows. At first, it is true, the readers may detect some old-fashioned formality in his guide; he uses still the somewhat rigid vocabulary that was then thought proper for natural things; he will talk of a view that is 'rich in a diversity of pleasing or grand scenery',[7] of 'prospects' and 'situations', and he condescends more than a poet should to direct you how best to secure beds at the inn, 'as there is but one, and it is much resorted to in summer'.[8] But this very sedateness has its value, and seems to prove that the beauty is real enough to suffer examination by a perfectly candid and conscientious temper. These sober details, moreover, give a tone of solidity to the whole, and suggest the rough surface of the earth, which is as true a part of the country as its heights and its splendours.

Let us station ourselves in a cloud, he begins, hanging midway between Great Gavel or Scawfell; 'we shall then see stretched at our feet a number of valleys, not fewer than eight . . . diverging from the point . . . like spokes from the nave of a wheel.'[9] After this general survey he goes on to follow out certain paths in detail, making general observations on the form of the country and gradually narrowing his gaze till he gives us those closely observed trifles which only a very penetrating eye after long search could have selected and described. He knows not only the scientific reasons why the rocky part of a mountain is blue or 'hoary grey', with a tinge of red in it 'like the compound hues of a dove's neck',[10] but also which shade of green is due to the lichen and which to the fern that grows when the first grass is faded. But all through this minute and scrupulous catalogue there runs a purpose which solves it into one coherent and increasingly impressive picture. For all these details and more 'which a volume would not be sufficient to describe'[11] are of such interest to him because he sees them all as living parts of a vast and exquisitely ordered system. It is this combination in him of obstinate truth and fervent imagination that stamps his descriptions more deeply upon the mind than those of almost any other writer. 'Days of unsettled weather', he says, 'with partial showers, are very frequent, but the showers, darkening or brightening as they fly from hill to hill, are not less grateful to the eye than finely interwoven passages of gay and sad music are touching to the ear.'[12] Or again, 'There is also an imaginative influence in the voice of the cuckoo, when that voice has taken posses- sion of a deep mountain valley'.[13] Or 'We observed the lemon-coloured leaves of the birches, as the breeze turned them to the sun, sparkle, or rather flash like diamonds, and the leafless purple twigs were tipped with globes of shining crystal.'[14] He suggests, moreover, in a curious way, the loneliness of nature; how one may think 'of the primaeval woods shedding and renewing their leaves with no human eye to notice, or human heart to regret or welcome the change.'[15] 'Flowers, the most brilliant feathers, and even gems, scarcely surpass in colouring some of those masses of stone which no human eye beholds except the shepherd or traveller be led there by curiosity; and how seldom must this happen!'[16]

But a more characteristic passage, perhaps, is that in which he reflects why it is that a lake carries you 'into recesses of feeling otherwise impenetrable. The reason of this is that the heavens are not only brought down into the bosom of the earth, but that the earth is mainly looked at and thought of through the medium of a purer element.'[17] A thought like that, he seems to suggest, must be common to every tourist; it is as easy for him to see heaven in the earth as to see grass and stones there. Indeed, his quiet assumption that not only mountains, trees and lakes, but the most minute changes of leaf and herb, are the seriously important things in all lives, amusing as it is at first, persuades us in the end that it is, or should be, really so. For in Wordsworth's eyes this spectacle of the countryside which we find variously pleasant or delightful as a relief from other things is the most solemn truth that exists. It is no mere curiosity or a taste for the picturesque that drives him to walk out among the hills, and to know all that can be known about the things that grow there. Rather he is trying to read the signs which, whatever their meaning, are to him never made in vain. And, conscious as he is of a beautifully adjusted symmetry in all natural things, his condemnation is most severe of those whose arrogance leads them in any way, by their buildings or plantations, to violate that order. His usual austerity almost breaks into tenderness when he speaks of the little republics of shepherds and farmers which lie among the hills. Theirs was the perfect life whose constitution had been 'imposed and regulated by the mountains which protected it'; and theirs, also, were the perfect dwelling places which seem 'to have risen, by an instinct of their own, out of the native rock' and 'appear to be received into the bosom of the living principle of things'.[18] This belief, so gravely and reverently worshipped, one may almost say, in the live force which lies beneath woods and hills and is perpetually working in them for good, gives to this little book its tone of solemn enthusiasm. You draw from it the impression that a walk among the lakes is to be undertaken in a spirit of reverence, for the sights which rejoice the eye also minister to the soul.

It is scarcely fair perhaps to take Canon Rawnsley as a sequel to Wordsworth. There are few who would not seem to write diluted English after the terse veracity of the poet's prose. The Canon's style, moreover, starred as it is with a great variety of pretty words and fashioned into innumerable conceits, seems, if not impertinent, at least irrelevant when you remember the respect with which Wordsworth subordinated his pen to the truth. The snowdrop, for instance, becomes in Canon Rawnsley's hands 'a fair maiden of February', who conceals a secret 'that . . . deep below in the ground is marvellous activity. By every rootlet's tiniest mouth, in the great laboratory of growth in which the Spring is chief chemist,'[19] and so on, and so on. Elsewhere we read of meres and tarns, 'like sapphires . . . to-morrow they will be as white as a dead man's face'.[20] When the sun strikes a rhododendron bush it seems as though 'coloured fire was springing in a fountain from the ground'; the sun is a 'rosy jewel'; the bracken in August is like 'torrents of green verdure'; clouds are 'white galleons that come sailing into seas of sapphire'.[21] Indeed, although the Canon devotes a chapter to every month, the dazzling colours in which he sees them prevent us from realizing what stage of the year we have reached, and the individual features of plant and tree are wholly lost in a shower of light. If there are any dark days they are cheered by 'Bands of Hope meetings, parish room concerts, magic lantern entertainments, and tea drinkings'.[22] In December, finally, we feel that we have passed a very innocent and brightly coloured year, although we are not quite sure that we have been at the Lakes.

1 – A review in the *TLS*, 15 June 1906, (Kp C5) of *Wordsworth's Guide to the Lakes*. Fifth ed., 1835. With an introduction and appendices and notes ... by E. de Sélincourt (Henry Frowde, 1906) and of *Months at the Lakes*. With nine illustrations (James Maclehose & Sons, 1906) by Rev. H. D. Rawnsley [1851–1920], Honorary Canon of Carlisle.

'The good Times,' wrote VW (*I VW Letters*, no. 271, to Violet Dickinson, June 1906), 'wants me to write 2 columns on the Lakes for them! I have never been there – but the Imagination, as the poet says, has wings.' Reading Notes (MHP, B 1a) dated: 21 and 25 May. See also 'Wordsworth Letters' below; 'Past and Present at the English Lakes', *II VW Essays*; and 'Dorothy Wordsworth', *V VW Essays* and CR2.

2 – William Wordsworth (1770–1850).

3 – *Select Views in Cumberland, Westmorland, and Lancashire* (1810); the preface was published anonymously.

4 – *Wordsworth's Guide*, Intro., p. iv, quoting Wordsworth writing to Lady Beaumont, 10 May 1810.

5 – *Ibid.*, p. xi.

6 – *Ibid.*, p. xiii: 'Thus William Gilpin ... upon Dunmail Raise ... "The whole view ... is entirely of the horrid kind. With a view to adorning such a scene with figures, nothing could suit it better than a group of banditti."'

7 – *Ibid.*, p. 6, which has: 'But the whole road from Bowness is rich in diversity ...'

8 – *Ibid.*, p. 2.

9 – *Ibid.*, p. 22.

10 – *Ibid.*, p. 28.

11 – *Ibid.*, p. 30, which has 'volumes', not 'a volume'.

12 – *Ibid.*, p. 45.

13 – *Ibid.*, p. 95, which continues: ' ... very different from anything which can be excited by the same sound in a flat country.'

14 – *Ibid.*, p. 127.

15 – *Ibid.*, p. 52.

16 – *Ibid.*, p. 116.

17 – *Ibid.*, p. 47.

18 – *Ibid.*, p. 68; p. 62; p. 63.

19 – *Months at the Lakes*, p. 18, which has 'fair maidens of February'.

20 – *Ibid.*, p. 30.

21 – *Ibid.*, p. 56; p. 93; p. 99 (which has 'torrents of dark verdure'); p. 118.

22 – *Ibid.*, p. 213, adapted.

'The Compromise'

The skilful description, with which *The Compromise* by Dorothea Gerard opens, of a slate quarry in the highlands, gives fair promise of what is to come. The author writes with such ease that to read her is a safe and pleasant undertaking. As an experienced novelist she models her material with a certain largeness and simplicity of touch that defies conventional boundaries. Thus she skips from generation to generation, tells ghost stories, and shows a comfortable forgetfulness at times of the necessity of going on with the story. It needs a large stage upon which to show the workings of a compromise made between the flesh and the spirit; it is necessary to see John M'Donnell first as a slate worker, then as a student at Glasgow, then as a minister married to a shallow and worldly wife. She plays the part of the flesh in the compact with considerable vitality. When he proposes to dedicate his life to the people, she is thinking of reforming the dinner-table; he has brothers and sisters in the slate quarries, while she recognises the bishop and the 'county people' only. Soon – too soon for the reader's pleasure – she dies, and leaves her husband with three children, who embody the discord between their parents. The elements of a very interesting study are here, but somehow they are suggested rather than discussed. Dorothea Gerard keeps upon the outskirts of the problem and therefore upon the outskirts of her characters; but at the same time she must be allowed the credit of keeping the balance humorously poised between all extremes. She tempers her characters in a way that is pleasantly like nature. The weakness of John M'Donnell, for instance, makes it credible that marriage should represent to him that Pride of Life[2] which necessitates a compromise. He is only completely happy and effective when at the end of the book he is left without wife or child, 'glorying in his isolation'.[3] It is because you are moving all the time in an atmosphere that is cool and natural if in no way stimulating that the considerable length at which the story is told does not become tedious; and the writing, if somewhat diffuse, keeps to a consistently high level. It is in short a spacious and temperate book, which is satisfactory rather than exciting, but which even within these limits must be treated with respect.

1 – A notice in the *TLS*, 15 June 1906, (Kp C5.1) of *The Compromise* (Hutchinson

& Co., 1906) by Dorothea Gerard. Reading Notes (MHP, B 1a) dated : 10 June.
2 – Gerard, ch. XVI is entitled 'The Pride of Life'.
3 – *Ibid.*, ch. XXVII, p. 367: '"At last I understand," said Father Grey. ¶ Immediately after, and with a rather knowing little smile upon his lips, he glanced up into the face of the man so barefacedly glorying in his isolation.'

'Mrs Grundy's Crucifix'

The motive, if we may call it so, of Mr Vincent Brown's novel, *Mrs Grundy's Crucifix*, is suggested upon the fifth page of the volume, when the mention of a certain Mrs Gilpin leads Walter Ingram to denounce her, or rather the institution of which she is a type, in words which seem to proceed from the author himself. 'She is the only immaculate thing the British people have ever done ... She expresses the immortality of money and respectability ... She is the high priestess of the Philistines," and the torrent continues vigorously, if in somewhat well-worn channels, for another page or so. The reader may guess what this prologue implies. A good woman who has been unfortunate will be sacrificed to Mrs Gilpin; and the characters in the book will be divided into those who minister to the Idol and those who deny her divinity. And it is very soon clear that this portentous old lady dominates her immediate world in such fashion that a happy English village is transformed into a community – with one or two exceptions – of abject devotees. We are introduced to a scene which is already familiar; it is that circus of a small country town in which parson and patron and spinster go through their staid and irreproachable antics, if not to our applause, at least to our comfortable acquiescence. But in this case, though all the figures are in their places, they suffer some malicious twist before the performance starts. We watch all the wits in the town feverishly and ignobly at work upon the reputation of a woman whom they have vague reasons for believing to be disreputable; and finally she is confronted with the truth in a scene where the horror is grotesque and the pathos is sentimental. The vulgarity and the spite might be there, but surely they would be more subtly mixed. And at the risk of joining the worshippers of Mrs Gilpin we confess that it seems to us possible that there was some excuse for them. A woman who says, 'It is true. I have a little boy at school, I have never been married,'[3] may be the victim of harsh social laws; but at the same time the fact here stated does not seem sufficient by itself to prove that she is the noblest of her sex. Indeed Mr Brown has given one more proof of the danger of the novel that undertakes a crusade. So much of natural human nature, so many lights and shades, so much truth, in short, must be sacrificed altogether if you insist upon your crucifix and your crucified. And in the end, it must be said regretfully, we feel small love for the injured woman, in spite of her sins, and her rescuer is little more than a tract which has been put somewhat crudely into a human case. This is all the more to be regretted because Mr Brown is a clever writer, and has made one character, Harry Albemarle, with whom the reader's sympathies are genuine.

1 – A review in the *TLS*, 22 June 1906, (Kp C5.2) of *Mrs Grundy's Crucifix* (Hutchinson, 1906) by Vincent Brown. Reading Notes (MHP, B 1a): dated 27 May.
2 – Brown, ch. I, p. 5; p. 6; p. 7.
3 – *Ibid.*, ch. XVI, p. 211, which continues: 'They were both looking into the fire now. It was going out, and Ingram put on another log. To do this he went down on one knee. He remained in a kneeling posture at her feet; his head bowed in reverence before her; it was as though he could not rise . . . He got up and moved slowly away. Her terrible sob followed him out into the shrouded world.'

The Bluest of the Blue

Every one who lived in the age of Johnson seems to have possessed a little of his genius for sitting for his portrait. Ladies and gentlemen not otherwise distinguished had the gift of arranging themselves, with a certain deliberation and simplicity of pose, as though they were draping themselves becomingly for the eye of posterity. The group thus formed by those famous ladies, the Blues, has been often reproduced in the mass, but it seems questionable whether the single figures will stand isolation in the way that Miss Gaussen has attempted in the present book. There is clearly very little to be said about Mrs Carter unless you possess a real gift for the interpretation of character, and Miss Gaussen is content with the more superficial part of a biographer's duties. There is no doubt that the pose which Elizabeth Carter adopted was from the first that of the learned woman. No affectation or pretension need be implied by such a statement, for if a woman knew Greek in that age she was immediately set apart from her sex and supplied with a character in life from which she could hardly deviate. And perhaps it was the consciousness of this separation that made the learned lady so very learned; as she must give up all distinctions of another sort, she might as well specialise in learning, and in the eccentricities which go with it. When she was a mere girl Elizabeth seems to have made up her mind to be a thorough prodigy; not only did she learn the essential Greek and Latin, but also Hebrew, Italian, Spanish, German, Portuguese, and finally Arabic, although she did not profess to understand the last sufficiently well to read it without a dictionary. So much learning needed and inspired heroic qualities. She had to struggle with a vigorous frame which slept soundly and loved exercise. To conquer sleep she had a bell tied to the head of her bedstead to which a string was attached, leading through a 'crevasse'[2] in her window to the garden below. At four or five in the morning a friendly sexton tolled the bell, Elizabeth sprang from her bed and worked at her books till six, when she took a stick and tramped the countryside till it was time for breakfast. Her walking was as vigorous as her reading, and she claimed to be one of the best walkers in England. Snuff, and green tea, and wet towels were called in to goad her brain to its task, and no one can assert that her fame was easily earned.

The fruit of this immense energy was the publication in 1758 of her translation of Epictetus,[3] and the reception with which it met proved that it was worthwhile to be learned in those days. Not only did she make £1000 by it, but it introduced her to the Blues and established her in an oracular position for life. She did not escape the faults which are common to oracles; she could utter common sense as though it were the inspired wisdom of the gods. But good judges have put it beyond doubt that she was a very able woman – a sound scholar, and a shrewd and sensible friend. The place she took in the society of the time was rather that of a monitor and instructress, apparently, than of a wit. When it was proposed to form a government of women, Johnson appointed 'Carter', to be Archbishop of Canterbury – 'Who is there', he wrote, 'that you cannot influence?'[4] Although she had to prove herself a true woman by producing a shirt and a pudding, it was evident that Nature meant her to be learned. She was shy and shortsighted, and came into a room with an 'idiot look', and felt, as she said, like 'a dog in a dancing school'.[5] But her sense and kindliness made her oddities delightful, and her learning, which was so thorough that she was never conscious of it, gave her a place of real authority among her friends. Fine ladies like Mrs Montagu and Mrs Vesey[6] depended on her, and the world held no puzzle for her that common sense could not solve or childlike faith accept. She deliberately made up her mind that marriage was 'a very good scheme for everybody but herself', and broke off the one connection which might have ended in matrimony because the gentleman wrote some verses 'of which she could not approve'.[7] She 'dreaded nothing so much as irregularity', and, being strictly High Church, had the courage to 'forbear reading any book, however sound and sober, which proceeded from any other quarter'.[8] With such qualities it is not surprising that her fortunes were equable rather than exciting, and that her life was as long as even she could desire. She died in 1806 in her eighty-ninth year, and left instructions characteristic of her brave common sense – that she was to be buried wherever she died 'with as little expense as possible'.[9]

1 – A review in the *Guardian*, 11 July 1906, (Kp C5.3) of *A Woman of Wit and Wisdom: a memoir of Elizabeth Carter, one of the 'Bas Bleu' Society, 1717–1806* (Smith, Elder, 1906) by Alice C. C. Gaussen. Reading Notes (MHP, B 1a) dated: 18 March.

2 – Gaussen, ch. I, p. 12.

3 – *All the Works of Epictetus which are now extant &c*, published by guinea subscription in April 1758.

4 – For Johnson on Carter, Gaussen, ch. VII, pp. 5–7.

5 – *Ibid.*, ch. VI, p. 129; p. 135.

6 – Elizabeth Montagu, *née* Robinson (1720–1800), authoress, wife of Edward Montagu, a son of the 1st Earl of Sandwich; and Elizabeth Vesey, *née* Vesey (1715?–91), wife of the Irish M.P. Agmondesham Vesey – both leading figures in the 'blue-stocking' coterie of literary women, as were Hester Chapone (1727–1801) and Hannah More (1745–1843).

7 – *Ibid.*, ch. III, p. 60; pp. 62–3.

8 – *Ibid.*, ch. XII, p. 249: 'To Mrs [Hannah] More, though she loved her honest, correct heart, cultivated intellect, and calm orderly mind, Mrs Carter appeared to be "most strictly High Church", for she dreaded nothing so much as irregularity, and scrupulously forebore reading any book, however sound and sober, which proceeded from any other quarter.'

9 – *Ibid.*, ch. XII, p. 253.

'Coniston'

The reader of Mr Winston Churchill's new novel, *Coniston*, will be struck once more, as he has probably been struck many times already, by a certain shabbiness in American fiction when it deals with the natives in their own land. And in saying this we refer to a quality in the men and women themselves and in the atmosphere of the place, and not to the peculiar manner of the novelist. They seem to be dressed by nature in clothes of the last generation which do not exactly fit them. In this novel, for instance, we are introduced to the primitive society of Coniston, a New England village in the time of President Grant, where politics are as complicated and apparently as corrupt as in the capital. But the glitter and resonance with which such manoeuvres are made attractive in European states are entirely absent here. Their corruptness is so uncouth indeed that you must suspect some hidden virtue. A tanner, Jethro Bass by name, becomes, with the help of bribery, the 'senior selectman' of Coniston, and thereby forfeits the affections of the minister's daughter. The reader, it is clear, must know something of village politics in New England in order to give these phrases their meaning. But Mr Jethro Bass, with his ungainly name, and his stammer and his twang, is a man of great force and ability, who studies the life of Napoleon and proposes to imitate him in America. His career is successful, although his victories are not won upon the battlefield, and he becomes finally the most important man in his state. He has, that is, carried to such perfection his system of collecting mortgages that he controls the votes of the countryside and can get his bills through the State House, and can appoint his own men to the official posts. But to follow the transactions of these shrewd men of business, who, in Mr Churchill's words, 'found so many chinks in the Constitution to crawl through and steal the people's chestnuts, that the era may be called the Boss Era',[2] is a very long and somewhat obscure business; and Mr Churchill's novel swells considerably beyond the normal limit. Mr Bass has a habit of repeating the last words of his sentences, which his biographer seems to have caught from him. The book is as long and loose-limbed and deliberate as one of the characters themselves, and it seems also to have copied the shapelessness of a people whose latent energies are not yet properly fashioned for use. There is a considerable amount of latent energy in Mr

Churchill's book, but it must be dug out of the unchiselled mass. He chronicles with infinite patience not only the intricacies of railway politics, but the gossip of humorous villagers and the love affairs of young men and women. It is love finally that triumphs over Jethro's corrupt practices and drives him to sacrifice some very substantial advantages for a sentimental consideration. Mr Churchill finally admits that he has 'grown to love'[3] his characters, and is reluctant to leave them. It seems an affection born more of habit than of passion, and he is not able or does not care to observe his old friends too closely. But the simplicity of the process and the candour with which he confesses 'I do not know why I have dwelt so long on such a minor character as Bijah, except that the man fascinates me,'[4] induces the reader to agree that such reasons for writing are quite sufficient. A confession of this kind, however, points to Mr Churchill's limitations as an artist; he transcribes rather than creates, and his effects are got by plodding equally ahead with his narrative rather than by any flash of inspiration. But the system is pleasant as it is pleasant on a lazy summer's day to listen to a story told by a native in the rustic dialect. You rise with the impression that you have absorbed a great deal of the raw material of history, and in this case it is a history that will make strange reading.

1 – A review in the *TLS*, 13 July 1906, (Kp c5.4) of *Coniston*, with illustrations by Florence Scovel Shinn (Macmillan & Co., 1906) by Winston Churchill (1871–1947), the American novelist. Reading Notes (MHP, B 1a) dated: 9 July.
2 – Churchill, p. 1. In 1903 and 1905 Churchill was a member of the New Hampshire legislature and an outspoken critic of the machinations of the political bosses of his time.
3 – *Ibid.*, p. 540.
4 – *Ibid.*, p. 104.

'The Author's Progress'

We have an uncomfortable impression that the author of this book wrote it under some kind of wager not to leave off till the due number of pages was accomplished. There is so little you can tell a writer about writing, so little even that you can tell him about publishing. Or it may be that the subject is so essentially depressing that the briefest statement is sufficient, and an elaboration of the theme is almost more than the reader can bear. For here we have the ugliest form of 'shop' expounded, garnished with innumerable jokes and topical allusions, solidified with calculations and figures, and presented with all the sober conviction of print. There is no escaping the fact that a great many people write, and most of them write for money, and that there are ways of increasing that wage of which the 'dear young author',[2] as Mr Lorimer calls him, would do well to take account. Let him write to the publisher on good paper stamped with the family crest; let him employ no agents; let him refuse his photograph to the world, but in all other ways let him advertise himself as loudly as he can. The result may be – Mr Lorimer has worked out the sales and the expenses and the royalties – so many pounds and shillings and pence of hard cash. It is affected to pretend that this form of 'shop' is without its interest, as it is unreasonable to complain that it is for the most part concerned with very base things. The root of the matter is that the confusion between art and trade must always be ugly, and that the confusion – since writing is sold as boots are sold – is inevitable. Mr Lorimer's book states the case very plainly, and all that goes to make a book successful independently of the book itself may be learnt in his pages.

1 – A notice in the *Guardian*, 25 July 1906, (Kp C5.5) of *The Author's Progress; or the Literary Book of the Road* (Blackwood & Sons, 1906) by Adam Lorimer (William Lorimer Watson) – VW's first professional encounter with what she was later to call the 'underworld' (*I VW Diary*, p. 159), her version of Grub Street.
2 – Lorimer, ch. IX begins: 'Dear young Author, for the Publisher's Reader we bespeak your kindliest charity.'

Sweetness – Long Drawn Out

There has been lately a rage for the memoirs of respectable or disreputable ladies of the eighteenth century, not unlike the fashion which rose at the same time for mezzotints from Sir Joshua's portraits of women. It was not necessary that they should have possessed remarkable minds or should have lived irreproachable lives. But it was essential that they should move in brilliant circles, should sweep through the world in satin and powder, and should charm their way from one splendid height to another by virtue of smiles and courtesies and little exquisite phrases which brought peers and princes to their knees. Their prosaic descendants were expected to do homage also at the mere recollection of those vanished charms. How far such a creature was possible it is scarcely fitting to ask; but if she lived at all, and lived by means of such graces as these, it must surely have been in the age when Sir Joshua painted her. But then the biographer must approach her with peculiar tact, for words pierce beneath paint, and the souls of Pompadours may look fairer upon the surface.

The difficulties of the task are great, we may admit; and Miss Marie Hay seems to have complicated them still further by the method which she has adopted in her *Extraordinary History of Wilhelmine von Grävenitz*. It is a true story, dug, we are told, from official archives, but the facts briefly stated with 'colourless reticence'[2] by the lawyers have been expanded and embellished in Miss Hay's imagination till they are certainly not reticent, and there is plenty of colour, although it is not always in quite the right place. But her compromise between history and fiction is maintained throughout; she is always guiding herself by authentic facts, and her emotions are regulated by the documents at her side. And here lies the defect of the system. She cannot give her imagination free rein, and yet she may indulge it to such an extent that the reader does not know when he is reading history and when he is reading fiction. This is an awkward frame of mind, and the artistic merits of the book suffer from the compromise. It is easy to suggest that the figure of Wilhelmine invited treatment in one of two ways: she might have made an interesting study if her biographer had kept strictly to the truth and allowed her to speak in her own words, or she might have posed for a very picturesque portrait in the manner of Sir Joshua. But here we have a composite production, where the truth has the vagueness of fiction and the fiction is diluted with fact.

Wilhelmine was the sister of a courtier at the palace of Duke Eberhard Ludwig of Wirtemberg. The book opens in the year 1705 when this gentleman, finding that he cannot afford to live there any longer, sends for his sister to captivate the Duke, dethrone the old favourite, and raise her own family to the heights with her. She is a poor girl, of great beauty, with the eyes of a witch and the voice of a nightingale, and her triumph is instant and complete. '"Ah Mademoiselle ⟨says the Duke at their first meeting⟩ will you leave the Duke here on the balcony, and come and look at the stars with the ridiculous poet-fellow?" ... Who could resist him, this man with the pleading eyes and deep, strong voice?'[3]

Wilhelmine, at least, had no intention of resisting him, and the intimacy, begun poetically under the stars, was continued in all its extravagant and familiar phases for some twenty years. It is not difficult in the early stages to be thrilled in the right places by all the cumbersome ceremonial of the little German court: the eye is pleased with the pageantry of dance and festival, and the ear is flattered with the 'Monseigneurs' and 'Highnesses' that drop from the lips of profoundly obeisant great ladies and gentlemen. Wilhelmine has the gift of appearing suddenly in the doorway, robed in the 'Grävenitz yellow';[4] all eyes are fixed upon her and she achieves some triumph or passes unmoved with her snake glance through some terrible insult. But there comes a time when the sensational moment fails to thrill, and the sarcasm of the outraged ladies, which generally takes the form of suggesting that the favourite has had the smallpox very badly, is not sufficiently pointed to draw our blood. To make the interest endure when the brilliant surface has worn thin, we want to feel that Wilhelmine was a high-spirited, romantic woman in spite of her morals, that the Duke had some lovable quality that touched her heart and not merely her ambition; in short, that the whole set of decorous eighteenth-century figures were driven by human passions, and were not the puppets of some elaborate court machine. But in spite of many picturesque passages it is difficult to move with any swiftness through the long-drawn vicissitudes of the favourite's career. They tend to repeat themselves and to twist and turn with languid motion in the familiar channels. A novelist here would have been at liberty to select and epitomise; but Miss Hay, with the burden of documents on her shoulders, follows the story patiently, and engrafts upon the bare outline a lavish but indiscriminate wealth of description and conversation which seems not to be spun from the legitimate source of inspiration in her brain, but to be the spurious outcome of research in official archives. It does not reveal character, that is, but encumbers it.

It is enough to say that the favourite rose to be Prime Minister as well as mistress, accumulated lands till the peasants called her the 'Land-despoiler',[5] and surrounded herself with splendours of marble and satin that were to rival Versailles. But it remained a German copy till the end. We catch glimpses of her beneath all this shifting mass of finery, and of other figures more visionary still, but they move in a drifting atmosphere where the laws that bind live men and women can scarcely be applied. It is not possible to try their conduct by any ordinary standard, nor does their biographer attempt to pronounce the moral verdict. Wilhelmine falls, and we read how in the end 'A soft evening breeze came stealing round her. The long Spring twilight faded, night drew near – and the Grävenitz turned away. "Farewell," she said aloud, "the night comes. Farewell Spring."'[6]

And is that the voice of the dismissed courtesan or of her biographer?

'Like a faint fragrance of faded rose-leaves,' we read, 'a breath of this woman's charm seems to cling and elusively to peep out of the curt record of her crimes.'[7] But the ordinary reader will question whether the record of Wilhelmine might not give off a more pungent odour to other nostrils; and still more will he doubt whether this vagrant air is potent enough to steep three-hundred-and-fifty-odd pages in its fragrance. A magazine article or a sonnet were the proper vessel for such sweetness.

1 – A review in *Academy & Literature*, 28 July 1906, (Kp c5.6) of *A German Pompadour. Being the Extraordinary History of Wilhelmine von Grävenitz, Land-hofmeisterin of Wirtemberg. A narrative of the Eighteenth Century* (Constable & Co., 1906) by Marie Hay. Reading Notes (MHP, B 1a) dated: 27 June.
2 – Hay, Pref., p. vii.
3 – *Ibid.*, p. 80.
4 – Grävenitz yellow appears to have been a bright yet delicate shade; it was the colour of both clothing (*ibid.*, p. 218) and curtains (p. 228).
5 – *Ibid.*, Pref., p. vii.
6 – *Ibid.*, p. 358.
7 – *Ibid.*, Pref., p. vii.

Trafficks and Discoveries

Whoever has read Hakluyt from those five cumbrous volumes in which the printers of 1811[2] thought good to entomb him will have felt the need of the preface or chart which Professor Raleigh's book provides. It was possible, like one of those early seamen, to have one's head so gloriously confused with the medley of rich names and places, of spices and precious stones, of strange lands and monsters, of regal charters and proclamations that the hard outlines of the earth swam and melted in a gorgeous mist. The reader could never detach himself sufficiently from the yellow page with its decorative spelling, to supply the spectators comment, and see the whole pageant in its proper proportions. Like one groping in the dark he stumbled about the world, knocking suddenly against America or beating fruitlessly up and down that long barrier which separated him from Cathay and all the splendours of the East. The five volumes swung only a warm disc of light over that romantic ambiguity, without map or index or editorial footnote to point the way. Professor Raleigh is one of the few writers from whom we can bear illumination, and one of whom we can say that although he orders and establishes this miscellaneous world he rather increases than impoverishes its beauty. To know that it was all founded on hard truth, that the voyagers were substantial Elizabethan seamen, and that the whole makes a consecutive chapter of English history checks the tendency which we feel towards a vague enthusiasm, but founds it on a real and permanent basis. And the more detailed our knowledge of the men and their adventures the more potently they touch our imaginations.

The story, as Professor Raleigh points out, is by no means simple; there were missionaries and empire builders, merchants, and men of science among the seamen, and you find traces of all these different interests woven into the great theme of adventure and discovery. But there is in common to all an immense belief that the unknown world holds what they seek, that the future and the veiled continent are alike rich with portentous shadows hardly to be traced by the hand of that age. Wherever you open the volumes you are struck by the wide-eyed credulity of the Elizabethan sailors and the largeness of their imaginations, stretched to hold any miracle undoubtingly. The poets, too, accompanied these journeys in the spirit and wrought their discoveries into the texture of plays and poems:

If the voyagers explored new countries and trafficked with strange peoples, the poets and dramatists went abroad too, and rifled foreign nations, returning with far-fetched and dear-bought wares; or explored lonely and untried recesses of the microcosm of man. One spirit of discovery and exultant power animated both seamen and poets. Shakespeare and Marlowe were, no less than Drake and Cavendish, circumnavigators of the world.[3]

But it is not, as Professor Raleigh goes on to remark, in literature that we must look for the influence of the Elizabethan voyagers. Their actions were not handed down to us in poetry, nor are they dependent upon poetry for their survival. The charm of Hakluyt's great book, indeed, does not lie in any meditated felicity so much as in its air of rough and unsophisticated simplicity, so often made a matter for apology by the writers themselves. They have neither learning nor leisure to 'vary or multiply words'.[4] But their laborious pens, dipping into the stately vocabulary which was common to seaman and poet, build up such a noble structure of words in the end that the effect is as rich and more authentic than that got by more artistic processes. The frequent lists of 'commodities' even have a strange charm. 'And in all these countries there are oak, and bortz, ashes, elms, arables, trees of life, pines, prussetrees, cedars, great walnut trees, and wild nuts, hasel trees, wild pear trees, wild grapes, and there have been found red plums. And there are goodly forests wherein men may hunt. And there are great store of stags, deer, porkpicks, and the savages say there be unicorns.'[5] All the pleasant roots and spices of the earth are massed together with sweet-scented trees and gold and silver and precious stones till a fragrance seems to rise from the page itself. In these long lists, moreover, little landscapes are let in, all the more romantic because they have been observed with the same sober and veracious eye and inscribed with the same stiff pen. You read of perilous woods, of the strange thunder of waters, of a mighty cataract, 'with diamonds and other precious stones on it', which 'shine very far off',[6] of a 'most beautiful country' with 'fair green grass ... the deer crossing on every path, the birds towards evening singing on every tree, cranes, and herons of white crimson and carnation perching in the rivers side, the air fresh with a gentle easterly wind, and every stone that we stooped to pick up promised either gold or silver by his complexion'.[7] The lustre of that promise is upon all these southern voyages, till in Drake's voyage round the world it breaks into a blaze of splendour. The progress of the *Pelican* and the fleet along the coast of the Pacific was, as Professor Raleigh says, 'a carnival of plunder'.[8] Silver and gold in wedges and bars 'of the fashion and bigness of a brickbat', silk and fine linen, china ware and precious stones, crucifixes set with 'goodly greaf emeralds'[9] poured into the ships in a continuous stream. Great Spanish vessels waited them, laden from the kingdom of Peru, lying innocently at anchor without guard or suspicion. The tale reads like some coloured opium dream. But the intoxication does not spring solely from the material glitter of the words. The profusion of the earth itself seems typical of the whole age, and the grosser counterpart of that opulence of the imagination which was now yielding treasures of another sort. The bleak voyages to the north and the north-east bear such sentences as that quoted by Professor Raleigh: 'There is no land unhabitable, nor sea innavigable'.[10] Gilbert, in the teeth of the storm, is seen by those in the *Hinde*, 'sitting abaft with a book in his hand' and crying, 'We are as near to Heaven by sea as by land.'[11] Suddenly the ship's lights went out, and they were seen no more. Wherever you open the book you may find some rough phrase to be tuned to such melody, and as you go along you may be your own poet.

Professor Raleigh meanwhile keeps the larger scheme of the work before you, and makes these phrases its natural ornament. Anyone, then, who owns the original text will wish to complete it with this luminous and authoritative comment.

1 – A review in the *Speaker*, 11 August 1906, (Kp C5.7) of *The English Voyages of the Sixteenth Century* (James MacLehose & Sons, 1906) by Professor Walter Raleigh. This work was first published as an introduction to the last volume of *The Principal Navigations, Voyages, and Discoveries of the English Nation* (12 vols, MacLehose, 1903–5) by Richard Hakluyt (1552?–1616). Reading Notes (MHP, B 1a) dated: 23 March. See also the article of the same title and 'Sir Walter Raleigh', *II VW Essays*, and 'The Elizabethan Lumber Room', *IV VW Essays* and CR1.

2 – *Hakluyt's Collection of the Early Voyages, Travels and Discoveries of the English Nation. A new edition with additions* (5 vols, R. H. Evans, 1809–12), vol. III of which is dated 1811. It is not clear from which edition of Hakluyt direct quotation is made; references have been identified in both the Evans and MacLehose editions, in neither of which is the spelling modernised as here.

3 – Professor Raleigh, p. 155.

4 – The source of this quotation has not been discovered.

5 – See the account of the coast of Canada and the eastern States by Alphonse of Xanctoigne, chief pilot to Jean François de la Roche, or 'Roberval', who made his voyage in 1542 (Evans, vol. III, p. 282, ll. 25–8 and 29–31; MacLehose, vol. VIII, p. 282, ll. 19–23 and 25–8). There should be an ellipsis after 'red plums' to mark the omission of the sentence: 'And very faire corne groweth there, and peason grow of their owne accord, gooseberries and strawberries.'

6 – Berreo's account of the 'mountain of crystal' in Sir Walter Raleigh's 'Discovery of Guiana' (Evans, vol. IV, p. 150, ll. 26–7; MacLehose, vol. X, p. 418, ll. 21–2).

7 – Sir Walter Raleigh's description of the shores of the Caroli river, also in 'Discovery of Guiana' (Evans, vol. IV, p. 144, ll. 15–19. MacLehose, vol. X, p. 404, ll. 14–22).

8 – Professor Raleigh, p. 94.

9 – From 'Drake's Circumnavigation'; the wedges (of silver not gold) were taken from three barks at the plundered town of Arica (Evans, vol. IV, p. 238, ll. 35–6; MacLehose, vol. XI, p. 114, ll. 14–15). The crucifix came from a bark taken between Lima and Panama just before the capture of the treasure ship *Cacafuego* (Evans, vol. IV, p. 239, l. 2; MacLehose, vol. XI, p. 116, l. 9).

10 – Professor Raleigh, p. 33; Master Robert Thorne's dismissal of the perils of the north.
11 – *Ibid.*, p. 59; the dying moments of Sir Humphrey Gilbert (1539–83) off the coast of Newfoundland.

Portraits of Places

Nothing, it seems, should be so easy as to paint the portrait of a place. The sitter reclines perpetually in an attitude of complete repose outside the drawing-room windows; he is there whenever you want him; he submits to any amount of scrutiny and analysis; and, moreover, there is no need to trouble about his soul. We press the point too far, indeed, when we suggest that he has a sex. Such a representation of the duties of a landscape artist, must, of course, be entirely insufficient, because, acting upon it, writers have produced by no means encouraging results. Indeed, it is safe to say that if you want to know the look of some town in Cornwall or Wales or Norfolk the best plan will be to get a map and study its portrait there. For some reason there is more of the character of a place in this sheet of coloured paper, with its hills of shaded chocolate, its seas of spotless blue, and its villages of dots and punctures than in all the words of an ordinary vocabulary, arrange them how you will. The swarm of names, the jagged edge of the coast-line, the curves that ships make ploughing round the world, are all romantic grains of fact brewed from the heart of the land itself, and sluggish must be the mind that would refuse to work with such tools as these. And the reason is, perhaps, that, after all, the country is a very solid and ancient place, and a page stamped with printed words skims off but a thin and superficial slice on the top of it. The swiftest portrait carried off by the eye has a great many different elements in its composition, although the brain may never separate them or call them by their right names. There are associations – things you have read or imagined, or had driven into you – blending with all the blues and greens of the turf and the sky; there is scarcely a field in England that is not, as Mr Henry James has it, 'richly suggestive'[2] and not easily to be expounded. Indeed, the psychology of the land becomes so increasingly complex the more you think of it that the wonder is that any written picture should do more than cast a flimsy and ineffectual veil over the surface. The first touch of the real thing, a name with crossed swords over it, a cottage with a date upon the door, will be sufficient to tear the fabric asunder.

Who, then, of living writers, can present upon his page a spectacle so tremendous, with such memories and emotions and experiences seething and blending beneath the placid face that we know so well? If any one is fit for the task, it must be the same writer who has made such astonishing discoveries beneath other tranquil surfaces. Indeed, it is possible to read Mr Henry James upon various aspects of the English countryside not only with pleasure, and possibly with profit, but also certainly with amusement. Forgetting for the moment the purpose with which we set out of finding a picture that does justice to our own land, it is really entertaining to find that we ourselves are part of the show. Indeed, we may be said to be the flower of it. And as clearly such a flower is only to be plucked by hands from without, Mr James starts with one initial advantage over the native chronicler. He sees us as the natural and most significant result of all that has gone before, and our actions and attitudes point morals and draw pictures that are imperceptible to the shortsighted eye of a person immediately concerned in them. Perhaps it is this deficiency that makes our own statements of the same kind look so bare. And, as an American stranger, he enjoys yet another advantage, for he comes to most of our sights and institutions with an eye that is unblunted by custom. Add to this his individual gifts of perception and description and you have every right to expect from him a picture that is both pleasant and perspicacious.

Indeed, the pleasantness of Mr James's writing is never more serene and persuasive than when he is dealing with countries that are not his own. His attitude is that of an irresponsible guest who may look upon the whole of Europe as an entertainment preserved, long after its original use has disappeared, for his own diversion. All his duty to his host consists in keeping an open eye for picturesque attitudes and impressions, and it would be really harmful to the tact and discrimination of his taste if it were biased by any racial or political prejudices. Besides, it is none of his business to advise. The spectacle of a profesional amateur wandering over the world with his brain exposed like a very sensitive photographic film to the outward aspects of things has a singular charm, and no little value, in this serious age. The process seems so simple and so little fatiguing. You need merely lounge in front of a picture, or ramble at your will about a church, or stroll through a town, and meanwhile all kinds of pictures are depositing themselves in your brain to be smoothed out upon a sheet of paper when the occasion presents itself. It is only what we could all of us do, we may say, if we chose to keep our eyes at the proper focus; but, unfortunately, if you are a native there is always something to startle you out of the proper detachment. Only an American can be really impartial where sights of ancient interest are concerned. Only an American could have written so widely and tenderly and humorously of Warwickshire as Mr James has done, because no English person could forget so happily that Shakespeare was born there. Mr James, it is true, does not entirely ignore the fact; but he contrives to suggest that that was, after all, what might have been expected from the landscape. Certainly and that is the important thing – you are convinced that he was 'on the point of going into one of the ale-houses to ask Mrs Quickly for a cup of sack'.[3] And then he passes quite naturally and decorously, as though he were offering a suggestion about the sonnets, to discuss the temperaments and appearances of certain young English women who are playing tennis in the parsonage garden. They possess, according to him – no Briton could have said it! – 'something that he can best describe as an intimate salubrity'.[4] 'The face of this fair creature had a pure oval, and her clear, brown eye a quiet warmth . . . The young man stood facing her, slowly scratching his thigh, and shifting from one foot to the other. He had honest, stupid, blue eyes, and a simple smile that showed his handsome teeth. He was very well dressed. "I suppose it's pretty big," said the beautiful young girl. "Yes; it's pretty big," said the handsome young man. "It's nicer when they are big," said his interlocutress, and for some time no further remark was made.'[5]

No English writer would have thought that scene worth recording, nor would any Shakespearian scholar have believed that it threw any light upon his text. But as Mr James tells it, it illuminates all kinds of things. For it is not the descendant of centuries of such conversations in English gardens, and English castles; and were not the same things said in the time of Shakespeare, and was not Shakespeare himself a link in the same interminable chain? It is a little surprising, it must be owned, to find from Mr James's pages how spectacular we are; and were it not for the grace and urbanity with which the show is exhibited, we might fairly resent the position in which we are placed. We are, according to him, enormously old; we are full of ancient mannerisms and antiquated phrases; we have accumulated such a deposit of tradition and inheritance on top of us that the original substance is scarcely to be discovered. At any rate, it is so thoroughly steeped in associations of all kinds that the commonest handful of English earth, like the most ordinary young man or woman at a country tea-party, is something venerable and subtle, and probably more than a little quaint. We were not conscious, perhaps, of the extreme richness and complexity – to use two favourite adjectives – of our temperaments, and it is not altogether pleasant to be treated with such respect by the young. But we may comfort outselves, if need be, by making an addition to the title of the book, and reading 'or the portrait of an American' after *Portraits of Places*, for both are there. Still, we have no reason to complain if, demanding a picture of ourselves, we see a good deal of America reflected in our own face, when that portrait is, after all, so charming and so true.

1 – An article in the *Guardian*, 3 October 1906, which takes its title from Henry James's *Portraits of Places* (Macmillan & Co., 1883), a work containing a number of essays on England and the English which, together with others, were reprinted in *English Hours* (Heinemann, 1905). See Editorial Note, p. xxi and 'Mr Henry James's Latest Novel' above.
2 – *Portraits*, p. 220, *Hours*, p. 162: 'Viewed in this intellectual light the polluted river [Thames], the sprawling barges, the dead-faced warehouses, the frowsy people, the atmospheric impurities, become richly suggestive.'
3 – *Portraits*, p. 250, *Hours*, p. 190.
4 – *Portraits*, p. 254, *Hours*, p. 195.
5 – *Portraits*, pp. 255–6, *Hours*, pp. 196–7; the subject under discussion is a boat.

Impressions of Sir Leslie Stephen

My impression as a child always was that my father[2] was not very much older than we were. He used to take us to sail our boats in the Round Pond, and with his own hands fitted one out with masts and sails after the patterns of a Cornish lugger; and we knew that his interest was no 'grown-up' pretence; it was as genuine as our own; so there was a perfectly equal companionship between us.[3] Every evening we spent an hour and a half in the drawing-room, and, as far back as I can remember, he found some way of amusing us himself. At first he drew pictures of animals as fat as we could demand them, or cut them out of paper with a pair of scissors. Then when we were old enough he spent the time in reading aloud to us. I cannot remember any book before *Tom Brown's*

School Days and *Treasure Island*;[4] but it must have been very soon that we attacked the first of that long line of red backs – the thirty-two volumes of the Waverley Novels, which provided reading for many years of evenings, because when we had finished the last he was ready to begin the first over again. At the end of a volume my father always gravely asked our opinion as to its merits, and we were required to say which of the characters we liked best and why. I can remember his indignation when one of us preferred the hero to the far more lifelike villain. My father always loved reading aloud, and of all books, I think, he loved Scott's the best. In the last years of his life, when he was tired of reading anything else, he would send one of us to the bookshelf to take down the first of the Waverley Novels that happened to present itself, and this he would open at random and read with quiet satisfaction till bedtime. He put *Guy Mannering* before most of the others because of Dandie Dinmont, whom he loved, and the first part of *The Heart of Midlothian*[5] he admired so much that his reading of it cannot be forgotten. When my brothers had gone to school, he still went on reading to my sister and me, but chose more serious books. He read Carlyle's *French Revolution*, and stopped in the middle of *Vanity Fair*, because he said it was 'too terrible'.[6] He read Miss Austen through, and Hawthorne and some of Shakespeare and many other classics. He began too to read poetry instead of prose on Sunday nights, and the Sunday poetry went on till the very end after the nightly reading had been given up.

His memory for poetry was wonderful; he could absorb a poem that he liked almost unconsciously from a single reading, and it amused him to discover what odd fragments and often quite second-rate pieces had 'stuck' to him, as he said, in this way. He had long ago acquired all the most famous poems of Wordsworth, Tennyson, Keats, and Matthew Arnold, among moderns. Milton of old writers was the one he knew best; he specially loved the 'Ode on the Nativity',[7] which he said to us regularly on Christmas night. This was indeed the last poem he tried to say on the Christmas night before he died; he remembered the words, but was then too weak to speak them. He loved, too, and knew by heart since he had first read it, George Meredith's 'Love in the Valley',[8] and he made us remark – and this was a rare instance of its kind – the beauty of Mr Meredith's metres and his mastery over them. As a rule he disliked criticism of technical qualities, and, indeed, disliked being drawn into criticism of any kind. He often repeated, too, with enthusiasm, some of

Sir Alfred Lyall's *Verses written in India.*[9] His taste in poetry was very
catholic, and if he liked a thing, it did not matter who had written it or
whether the writer was unknown; it 'stuck' to him, and was added to his
large store. He knew many of Mr Rudyard Kipling's ballads by heart,
and shouted Mr Henry Newbolt's 'Admirals All'[10] at the top of his voice
as he went about the house or walked in Kensington Gardens, to the
surprise of nursery-maids and park-keepers.[11] The poets whose work he
most cared to recite were, I think, Wordsworth, Tennyson and Matthew
Arnold, whose 'Scholar Gipsey'[12] was one of his greatest favourites. He
very much disliked reading poems from a book, and if he could not
speak from memory he generally refused to recite at all. His recitation,
or whatever it may be called, gained immensely from this fact, for as he
lay back in his chair and spoke the beautiful words with closed eyes, we
felt that he was speaking not merely the words of Tennyson or Wordsworth but what he himself felt and knew. Thus many of the great English
poems now seem to me inseparable from my father; I hear in them not
only his voice, but in some sort his teaching and belief.

After my mother's death,[13] my father was very anxious to take her
place and to teach us as she had taught us, and for some years he gave up
two of his precious morning hours to the drudgery of the schoolroom.
Later on I read with him some Greek and some German. His method of
teaching a language was always the same. He put all grammar on one
side, and then, taking some classic, made straight for the sense. He once
said that he owed Eton a grudge for not having made a scholar of him. In
his last years he did not, I think, read any of the Greek or Latin classics by
himself, except his little *Plato*, which, being of a convenient size for his
pocket, went with him on his journeys, and travelled to America and
back.[14] He read German, but seldom read it for pleasure, except Heine
and Goethe. During his last illness he read French books by the score.

1 – From ch. XXI, 'The Sunset (1902–4)' of F. W. Maitland's *The Life and Letters of
Leslie Stephen* (Duckworth & Co.) published on c. 8 November 1906 (Kp B1). VW
wrote to Violet Dickinson on 22 October 1904 that she thought she could 'write
something worth adding' to Maitland's life of her father (*I VW Letters*, no. 184). By
the following February she had evidently done so, as her jubilant letter of the 28th
reveals: 'As I can make my boasts in public, I must send a line to say that I have heard
from Fred Maitland, and he says my thing is "beautiful. Really it is beautiful, and if
this were a proper occasion I would write a page of praise. But of course I know that
this is not what you would like and I can only say that what you write is just what
your Father would have wished you to write. Whether all of it will be printed I

cannot yet say; but you well know that my inclination will be to print as much as possible".' (*I VW Letters*, no. 219, to Violet Dickinson). The passage is introduced thus: 'Before I tell the little that remains to be told of Stephen's life a few such words as could be written only by a member of his household will be welcome. One of his daughters kindly allows me to repeat what follows.'

Frederic William Maitland (b. 1850), Downing Professor of the laws of England at Cambridge, was, like Leslie Stephen, an oarsman, an alpinist, and one of that fraternity of walkers known as the Sunday Tramps; he died on 19 December 1906. See also 'Leslie Stephen, the Philosopher at Home: A Daughter's Memories', *VW Essays*.

2 – Sir Leslie Stephen (1832–1904).

3 – See also *Moments of Being*, p. 77: 'There was a great day when my Cornish lugger sailed perfectly to the middle of the pond and then . . . sank suddenly; "Did you see that?" my father cried, coming striding towards me . . . Then my mother made new sails; and my father rigged it . . . ; and how interested he became and said, with his little snort, half-laughing, something like "Absurd – what fun it is doing this!"'

4 – Thomas Hughes, *Tom Brown's School Days* (1857); R. L. Stevenson, *Treasure Island* (1883).

5 – Sir Walter Scott, *Guy Mannering* (1815), *The Heart of Midlothian* (1818).

6 – Thomas Carlyle, *The French Revolution* (1837); W. M. Thackeray, *Vanity Fair* (1847–8).

7 – 'Ode on the Morning of Christ's Nativity' (1629).

8 – 'Love in the Valley', 1851 and 1878. George Meredith (1828–1909) and Stephen were intimate friends and Stephen a model for Vernon Whitford in Meredith's novel *The Egoist* (1879).

9 – Sir Alfred Comyn Lyall (1835–1911) whose *Verses Written in India* was published in 1889.

10 – Rudyard Kipling (1865–1936); Sir Henry Newbolt (1862–1938), whose *Admirals All and Other Verses* appeared in 1897.

11 – Maitland here interpolates: 'The same classes in the same district had been surprised some sixty years ago by a little boy who was shouting "Marmion".' *Marmion: A Tale of Flodden Field*, 1808, by Sir Walter Scott.

12 – Matthew Arnold, *The Scholar-Gipsy*, 1853.

13 – Julia, *née* Jackson, *quondam* Duckworth (b. 1846), Leslie Stephen's second wife, died on 5 May 1895.

14 – Leslie Stephen visited America on three ocassions, in 1863 to observe the Civil War at first hand rather than as reported in *The Times* (whose coverage of the war he was to attack in a famous pamphlet in 1865); in 1868 to visit James Russell Lowell, and in 1890, the last time he saw Lowell, to receive an honorary doctorate from Harvard University.

1907

'The Private Papers of Henry Ryecroft'

When *The Private Papers of Henry Ryecroft* first came out in 1903 attentive ears recognised the accent of a true book that would endure when the clamour of a season of books was passed away. Here was a voice that spoke straight and shapely words at its natural pitch, and carried their meaning by the impulse of some rare sincerity to the recesses of the mind. Since that date much has been said of the author, who was held in this little volume to have spoken for the first time in his proper person. The novelist, it was said, had dropped his mask, and the sight of the real man beneath had a peculiar interest for readers who had long known the conjuror. But that the book has an interest for many who are without this incentive to read it seems proved by the fact that later editions are called for, and many to whom the novels of George Gissing are unknown read the reflections of Henry Ryecroft. It is not necessary that you should identify the two men and prove them to have one personality apiece, when Henry Ryecroft, without other background or circumstance than those he chooses to reveal, stands solidly on his own feet, and needs no exterior support. For, with whatever name you christen him, there is no doubt that the man who wrote these *Papers* wrote down what he thought, and that, in this sense, it is the most genuine of all autobiographies. The interest of the book, indeed, proceeds to many readers not from the beauty of its writing, the sweetness of its humour, or the maturity of its knowledge, but from the impression that it leaves of a live, human creature, who has not scrupled to let us know his foibles, and his failings, and his imperfect human shape. It is in no sense a confession, but into the sensitive outline much may be read that reticence forebore to state.

He was a man, we learn, who had to make his living by writing, and to support others; for many years his pen and a scrap of paper were the tools with which he had to fashion food and house and clothing. Finally, in middle life, when he was beginning to fear that he could hold out no longer, a friend died and left him an annuity of £300. It was then for almost the first time, and certainly for the last, that he wrote because he wished it, and left as final bequest these notes of the thoughts and books which came in the end to mean most to him. The charm of the writing then is of the sober and tranquil kind, like the grey light which comes after the sunset and has no future illumination to hope for or to dread. And yet the final impression is by no means melancholy; it seems on the whole a creditable thing that a life so bare of outer luxuries should find within itself gifts that could be sufficient by themselves. He was born with qualities that are neither rare nor splendid: good brains, for instance, and a passion for books; but it is inspiring to see how these two gifts in their naked austerity – for neither ever attracted anything foreign to it – are able to supply all that a man wants; at any rate, all that he needs to be a respectable, independent, and harmless human being. If one must feel that such epithets applied to a strenuous life are somewhat meagre, they have yet the charm of flawless integrity. It seems as though Henry Ryecroft had pared down every emotion, every thought, and every book until the pith of it only remained – as if poor men may not afford to feel or to think insincerely. And the residue is the pure metal, of such strong and equable heat that it will irradiate the whole of a man's life, so that it becomes worth living. It is hard that even such a talent for economy of both kinds was not sufficient to keep him possessed of the few things he wanted. He had to sell books in order to buy warmth and light, and he had to go without the pleasures of the country. And these are sacrifices that imply many others. Then, again, he had to sell his brains, and in a double sense, for if he had had the means to use them respectfully they might have kept their value undiminished. All this paring down did, it cannot be doubted, cut him to the quick, for his capacity for happiness was radically weakened when the chance for using it came. The harsh fights in his youth, when he struggled for the little ray of joy there might be in reading and walking, had strained his muscles, so that he could not grasp firmly the beautiful and abundant treasures that surrounded him at the end. His delight in the spring at last, when he has time to know it, is made tremulous by the knowledge that haunts him of the few that can enjoy it with him; and he must ask himself 'whether I shall not have to pay, by some disaster, for this period of sacred calm'.[2]

Still, one must ask, what would have been his lot had he been a rich man – had he been able even to feed his brains on all the things they craved? He might have been an 'owl-eyed pedant',[3] a don who had never left his college walls – and that may have been what Nature meant in shaping the sensitive, meditative man; but, had she been consistent, we should never have had the sight, grotesque and painful, but deeply inspiring also, of this owl turned out among the harsh lights and rough corners of the world. He would have had no need to measure books with life, to know men as well as letters, and to come finally to a philosophy of his own that was lean and muscular and serviceable in every strand of it. The result of such training was that the smallest sum that left him in peace to read by himself in the country was such a competence to him as it could not have been had he learnt even unconsciously to buy things with money. Given food and clothing, and his own brain would do the rest. And thus it is that the picture of a middle-aged literary man sitting in a Devonshire garden and reading all day long is not the mild, benevolent portrait that we know, but something even heroic. His daily life, his food, his servant, his room are all worn down till every superfluous quality is gone, and only what poverty has taught him to be essential remains. Nothing that he owns is without its beauty of use and scrupulous refinement. 'My house is perfect. Just large enough to allow the grace of order in domestic circumstance . . . The fabric is sound . . .[4] In the garden I can hear singing of birds, I can hear the rustle of their wings. And thus, if it please me, I may sit all day long and into the profounder quiet of the night . . . Oh! blessed silence!'[5] How much, one may ask, must one not have suffered to appreciate these things? How much must one not have read! For when all else has been attenuated and economised, the love of books alone has grown strong and lusty. Only with the weary cynicism of a man who has failed, he is inclined to put more trust in books than in people. It might be said that books are to him no relief from life or comment upon life, but are life itself, save for some stretches of the English countryside, where he has the strength to walk and botanise. And even these he sees instinctively through some veil of written words. Like all exquisitely literate minds, his brain plays a kind of battledore and shuttlecock with life and literature; a passage of print suggests a sunny meadow, or a lighted window in the evening lane sends him thirsting to *Tristram Shandy*.[6] He wakes in a strange place at night and hears church bells. 'Then a glow came over me. "We have heard the chimes at midnight, Master Shallow!"'[7]

This enriching process is never complete; there are always strange, new islands floating somewhere in remote seas to be explored and plundered of their treasures. There is the 'ancient geography of Asia Minor';[8] there is Egypt; there are all the histories that call up pictures out of the abyss and let them slip again. But it does not matter. 'Perhaps the last fault of which I shall cure myself is that habit of mind which urges me to seek knowledge.'[9] And at the end he could wish for 'many another year';[10] not because the years would bring him new things, but because they might let him live on thus, with a passive body and a mind ranging over the world and coming back to settle in that corner of it which he had chosen. This is the kind of freedom, so delightful and so sufficient, that all might desire, and the charm of the book is that it suggests, not only that such a power exists, but that it lies within the grasp of most of us. A book, a pen, a cottage in the country, and the world is at your feet.

1 – An article in the *Guardian*, 13 February 1907, (Kp C5.8) on *The Private Papers of Henry Ryecroft* (Constable & Co., 1903) by George Gissing (1857–1903). Reading Notes (MHP, B 1a), undated. See also 'The Novels of George Gissing' below; 'An Impression of Gissing', *III VW Essays*; and 'George Gissing', *V VW Essays* and CR2.
2 – Gissing, 'Spring', ch. XXIV, p. 74.
3 – *Ibid.*, 'Winter', ch. XVI, p. 264.
4 – *Ibid.*, 'Spring', ch. II, p. 7.
5 – *Ibid.*, p. 6.
6 – For Gissing's sudden thirst for Sterne's *Tristram Shandy* (1760–7), *ibid.*, 'Autumn', ch. II, p. 158.
7 – *Ibid.*, 'Summer', ch. XIX, p. 129, for this allusion to 2 *Henry IV*, iii, 2, 228.
8 – *Ibid.*, 'Winter', ch. XVI, p. 263.
9 – *Ibid.*, 'Winter', ch. XVII, p. 266.
10 – *Ibid.*, 'Winter', ch. XXVI, p. 292; 'I could wish for many another year; yet, if I knew that not one more awaited me, I should not grumble.'

'Temptation'

Mr Richard Bagot has one advantage over the ordinary novelist; he has a knowledge of Italy which allows him to take that land for his stage and its people for his actors. In his new book *Temptation*, for instance, there is a great charm, superficially at any rate, in the mere change of scene; the life is so different, the manners are so picturesque, and over all lies such a magic of place that you are willing to concede much to the novelist who can produce the illusion. But on a closer inspection the result is not quite so satisfactory; for, with all the appreciation and understanding of an admirer, Mr Bagot is still the sympathetic stranger, interested in habits, and observant of differences. There is a hint that the purpose of the book is to illustrate Italian life for our instruction, and we are to compare and draw conclusions. But apart from this formality – and it is less noticeable as the story proceeds – the book is interesting as an able study of character, and whether it is Italian character or English character matters but little. There is a certain Count Ugo Vitali, the head of an ancient family of the provincial nobility, who lives in his ancestral palace at Viterbo. He has married beneath him a woman whose beauty and whose passions hint at the peasant blood in her veins. She is ambitious of all the things that her husband distrusts, for he is a simple country gentleman of aristocratic instincts, with the interests of his people much at heart. Then there is the cousin from Rome, who comes to stay and talks philosophy. Cristina listens and finds the philosophy pleasant; she is terribly bored by her husband; finally she brings herself to believe in his disloyalty. The end – and the plot is slight – is very much what you might expect from the woman's character, and if we add that the end is violent it will be seen that Mr Bagot has written skilfully. With less restraint of treatment the last chapters might be not only unpleasant, but also incredible. And we certainly believe all that we are told. The truth is that we could believe something more. Mr Bagot spends so much care on the few characters whom he introduces, and offers so close an explanation of their motives, that we are prepared both for greater vigour of action and greater subtlety of speech. But he seldom drops his attitude of the grave observer pondering wide issues. In any case, however, it is an interesting book: you lay it down not infrequently, but you open it with respect.

1 – A notice in the *TLS*, 22 February 1907, (Kp C5.9) of *Temptation* (Methuen, 1907) by Richard Bagot – 'such is my prudery, that when temptation is written out in plain English, I throw my book under the sofa,' wrote VW to Violet Dickinson, 15 February 1907 (*I VW Letters*, no. 347).

'Fräulein Schmidt and Mr Anstruther'

Fräulein Schmidt and Mr Anstruther by the author of *Elizabeth and her German Garden*, contains the letters of 'an independent woman' one Rose-Marie Schmidt, of Jena, to Mr Anstruther, of the Foreign Office in London, to whom for a brief period she was engaged. They broke off their engagement, but she still went on writing to him; she may well be writing to him now; she is probably writing to some one else, and the final 'I shall not write again'² is a mere pause for breath, as who should say 'You must wait a moment, while I change my dress.' Mr Anstruther does not appear once, even as a reflection in the mirror, and there is cause to believe that this is for the good reason that he does not exist. It is Rose-Marie then who is important; but why should she be called Fräulein Schmidt and supplied with the troublesome properties of her part when she is really Elizabeth in a German lodging house, or Princess Priscilla, or any other cultivated woman with a taste for poetry and a fluent pen? That this is so points, of course, to serious limitations, for it means that the book is merely a record of personal impressions veiled but scarcely coloured by a few conventions of name and circumstance, and that these are so thinly laid upon the surface that you may shift them altogether if you choose. Rosie-Marie was not in love, nor was she poor, nor did she know how to cook; but to say precisely what she was is more difficult, and it is probable that different readers will answer differently. She was charming, all would agree; or why should we read – with various degrees of pleasure it is true – a whole volume of her meditations which are without form, often shallow, sometimes slipshod, and never inspired? But she writes so freshly and sensibly and happily that to ask for a closer attention to these matters would be like asking a thrush, for example, to whistle a Bach fugue. She follows her moods, and delights in them: 'The weather, time of day, the light in the room . . . the scent of certain flowers, the sound of certain voices – the instant my senses become aware of either of these things I find myself flung into the middle of a fresh mood.'[3] The violets in Schiller's garden, the beans in the Englishman's field, Stevenson, Whitman, the notes of a violin – she is at the mercy of all these sounds, and smells, and her ecstasies carry her buoyantly, as on the back of curving waves, which never rise too high for comfort, over all the experiences of life. The experiences that admit of this treatment best are homely ones; vegetarianism, for example, and servants, and the pettiness of life in a small German town. There the humour is exhilarating and sufficient; but it does not lift more weighty matters successfuly. 'The muse never seized and shook him ⟨Goethe⟩ till divinenesses dropped off his pen without his knowing how or whence.'[4]

Perhaps what you really want most is a prolonged dose of Walt Whitman[5] . . . the faint breath of corruption hanging about Christina Rossetti's poetry makes me turn my head the other way . . . And at least in one place she gives directions as to the proper use of green grass and wet dewdrops upon her grave – implying that dewdrops are sometimes dry.[6]

Is this the place?

> Be the green grass above me
>   With showers and dewdrops wet;
> And if thou wilt, remember,
>   And if thou wilt, forget.[7]

We turn our heads away too. But if you accept the point of view there is, as we began by saying, charm in the frankness and simplicity, in the verbosity even, with which it is written down; as though you listened to vivacious talk and conceived an affection for the talker for the sake of tones and gestures, not to be called reasons, and not always to be defined. That is why this book will be popular with many, and why to many criticism will seem beside the point.

1 – A review in the *TLS*, 10 May 1907, (Kp C5.10) of *Fräulein Schmidt and Mr Anstruther. Being the Letters of an Independent Woman* (Smith, Elder, 1907) by Elizabeth von Arnim, *née* Mary Annette Beauchamp (1886–1941), whose more celebrated work *Elizabeth and her German Garden* had been published anonymously in 1898. 'Here is a review, which was originally long and vigorous,' VW wrote to Violet Dickinson (*I VW Letters*, no. 363); 'the Times have cut it down and tamed it. I wanted to scourge that Fine Lady the Baroness . . . it is chatter and trash.'
2 – Arnim, letter LXXXI, Fraulein Schmidt's last 'letter', in its entirety.
3 – *Ibid.*, letter VIII, p. 33.
4 – *Ibid.*, letter IV, p. 18.

5 – *Ibid.*, letter XXXI, p. 111.
6 – *Ibid.*, p. 108.
7 – From the first stanza of 'Song' ('When I am dead, my dearest'); the first line of which is quoted in 'I am Christina Rossetti', *V VW Essays* and *CR2*.

'The Glen o' Weeping'

Miss Marjorie Bowen writes a preface to her new book, *The Glen o' Weeping*, in which some rather emphatic opinions upon the proper writing of history are flung together – in haste, as it seems. 'The unconscious historian is the only one that may be trusted ... the letters, in fact, of the world's statesmen and women.'[2] Hume and Smollett are 'pernicious' because 'they merely chronicle "opinions" that the dogma of the prejudiced and the acceptance of the unthinking have converted into what are known as "historical facts"'.[3] Drink your history neat, in short; but beware, we might add, lest the fumes are too strong for your head and colour historical facts no less queerly than the spectacles of the scientific historian. But this is an old quarrel, and only pertinent here because Miss Bowen has cast aside her Hume and her Smollett and uses the same sarcastic commas for the massacre of Glencoe and for these 'opinions' and 'facts'. Probably no true novelist makes it his business to administer strict historical justice; and we think him successful in the best sense if he can set people talking and fighting once more, and thinking even, as they did and do to this very day. But, although there are only two 'absolute liberties with facts',[4] honestly confessed, and the truth of the matter is a question, we cannot go on to say that Miss Bowen has written a book which we must believe though all the doctors in Oxford cried shame on us. And yet she possesses some of the gifts that should make a novelist. People group themselves before her; she sees lonely figures watching on the shore, and solitary horsemen on deserted roads; the picture forms itself instinctively; it is there in every chapter. And we must add with speed that there is a great deal more than this, and we should even find it hard to give an intelligible sketch of the plot. There is the feud of the Campbells and the Macdonalds; the Jacobite plots, the Orange plots, and, above all, the Master of Stair. Miss Bowen is as daring in her way as one of her own conspirators; she shirks no crisis, she is lavish of adventures and escapes, and a murder is undertaken with the utmost indifference. Still, while we admire her spirit, it is difficult to feel that all this 'slightly grandiloquent magnificence'[5] is satisfactory; it is a rich cloak, but it does not take the place of bones and flesh.

1 – A review in the *TLS*, 24 May 1907, (Kp C5.11) of *The Glen o' Weeping* (Alston Rivers, 1907) by Marjorie Bowen (Gabrielle Margaret Vere Campbell), a book reprinted several times, in 1936 by Penguin Books – see *I VW Letters*, no. 363, to Violet Dickinson: 'I have reviewed a novel The Glen o' Weeping; damned it, and now all the other reviewers are exclaiming, and there is a second edition.'
2 – Bowen, Pref., p. vii; David Hume (1711–76), *History of England* (1762, etc.), a work continued by Tobias Smollett (1721–71).
3 – *Ibid.*, p. ix.
4 – *Ibid.*, p. x.
5 – *Ibid.*, ch. x, p. 103.

Philip Sidney

So simple and complete is the image that we have of Sir Philip Sidney that we use his name almost as an adjective, as we speak of Don Quixote, when we wish to give a figure to a cluster of closely related qualities. The cup of water and the phrase 'Thy necessity is yet greater than mine',[2] though very nearly the last of his actions and his speeches, have inspired all that went before them in the imaginations of most; for not many, it is likely, draw their information from the *Arcadia*,[3] and the Life by Greville (unless this reprint attracts as much attention as it deserves) is not known to the ordinary reader at all. And yet the life of which we have here a reprint, edited and annotated by Mr Nowell Smith, is the first authority for that phrase, and, as seems likely, the original though hidden source of much that is scarcely so articulate. Sir Fulke Greville was the author of several plays and poems, 'political treatises rather than plays,' says Lamb, and poems 'frozen and made rigid with intellect'.[4] So you might go on to qualify the term 'life' as applied to this pamphlet which professes to be a dedication and is a volume; which has much of Spain and Elizabeth and Greville in it, and very little of the life of any one, unless we choose to divorce the word from the hard framework of date and fact to which in our day it has grown so close. But if this is not the method of biography of which we approve, if we like letters and dates and events all ranged in order, surely we must admit that in good hands it has advantages, and that in the case of Sidney particularly it is the only way in which the rare stuff of his life could be preserved and made of value. Sir Fulke began, as we said, to dedicate his poems; but the name of Philip Sidney so wrought upon his imagination that he could not stay till he had fashioned a monument to him, carved and decorated it, twisted and plaited it, in the best style of the early sevententh-century prose.[5] And, like other sepulchral monuments, it celebrates the virtues of the dead and traces the outlines of their form with a smooth and generous hand. But it is neither mere panegyric such as you speak to patrons, nor is it the mournful eulogy that is chanted appropriately over the bodies of heroes; and yet it has much of the exaltation and largeness of period that are common to both these styles. Even so, perhaps, it still seems natural to write of Philip Sidney.

The figure of Sidney, alive, making love, making war, writing poems, or walking in the gardens at Wilton, cast upon the minds of his contemporaries the same image, only infinitely brighter, that is still visible before us. They did not see a poet or a soldier or a statesman, but a man who somehow held all these qualities latent in his mind, but so fused that no one of them issued separately. The difficulty of writing his life at all was that there was no point to indicate to the eye of posterity as the sufficient reason of Sidney's fame; but all qualities rather must be kept melting and mixing in their confinement, beautiful in their sum and in their harmony rather than in the supremacy of any single one of them. And yet that was also the reason of writing; for there was need to fear that a future age with no proof before it might disbelieve that any such man had ever lived; and that death might have more power over a frame so exquisitely composed than over one made in a coarser pattern. For to know the perfection of Sidney's nature it is clear you must have known him in the flesh; only the minutes and the seconds of daily life were fine enough in texture to receive the impression of so rare a spirit. Such was the task that Greville set himself 'to the end that in the tribute I owe him, our nation may see a sea-mark, rais'd upon their native coast, above the level of any private Pharos abroad'.[6] So, happily careless of detail where the mass was so admirable, Greville stands back from his model, and composes the full-length figure as a work of art, detached from time and matter, like a Greek statue, where the foot is necessary to the head.

The familiar course of Sidney's life followed the pattern usual to young men of his rank; he travelled the Continent in the suite of a nobleman, conversed with emperors and men of letters, learnt to ride, and finally attached himself to the Court of Elizabeth. But as it seemed to Greville and to all who knew him – and we must acquiesce – he was never 'possessed of any fit stage for eminence to act upon';[7] all his virtues were but hinted or spilt by the way in pamphlets and *Arcadias* to the anger, and pride too, of his friends; if he had chosen to economise, what might he not have done, and yet such is the carelessness of wealth. As a boy, even, he was always for enlarging the task given him to do and for expanding the ceremonies of diplomacy, so as to make them include matters of vital interest to his country. His stage became steadily wider; it spread over England, Ireland, and Spain and, had fate allowed, it was to embrace the 'main of America' as 'an Emporium for the confluence of all nations that love, or profess any kinde of vertue, or Commerce'.[8] And this was undertaken from no mere opulence of spirit, but gravely, like all his plans, with the sagacity of a far-sighted statesman. Had he lived, so we may guess with Greville, his nature would have found its proper scope in rule and statecraft, for it was in the temper of a magistrate after all that he approached the peaceful arts. He was not so much a poet or a romance writer as an explorer of fresh tracts for other men to cultivate, and, in the best sense of the word, a patron of poets. One may figure him still leading at Wilton or at Leicester House, with Spenser and Greville for followers, and indicating as from some summit above his men the noble land which they are to press on and occupy. So he reclaimed classic metres strange to English verse, and pronounced his eloquent *Defence of Poësie*.[9] 'But the truth is, his end was not writing, even while he wrote.'[10] Such was the characteristic opinion of his friend, at any rate, who perhaps had two ends in his mind. It was one 'end' to conceal sound political philosophy within the bodies of fantastic princes living in Arcadia; 'in all these creatures of his making his intent and scope was to turn the barren philosophy precepts into pregnant images of life'.[11] Modern readers will be less alive to the moral and will endow Sidney with a greater measure of purely literary inspiration than Greville thought due to him or entirely to his credit. But there was another end, not to be reached by pen and ink; for we may agree that his knowledge was 'not moulded for table or schools; but both his wit and understanding bent upon his heart, to make himself and others, not in word or in opinion, but in life and action, good and great, in which Architectional art he was such a master, with so commending, and yet equall waies amongst men, that wheresoever he went, he was beloved, and obeyed'.[12]

The temptation is to copy out still more of one of the many noble passages in the book; and it is hard too to resist a temptation not altogether so innocent. For, upborne upon such stately pinions it would be easy to glide in serene air, to exalt and magnify till the figure of Sidney became of colossal proportions, and we might find ourselves in the end mouthing fine periods about a man who had ceased to exist. But Greville was not only a statesman and a philosopher, but also a writer of fine English prose. He had, of course, the vices of his time in that he used a medium not yet refined for utilitarian purposes, and he is often closely throttled in the embraces of a sinuous metaphor. Mr Nowell Smith has had to perform – and most adequately has he done it – the task of an editor of a corrupt classic, and on more than one occasion the meaning must still be left an open question. But the obscurities arise from a congestion of precious metal; ideas and images and learning collide and block the way; but when the stream runs clear it is both swift and deep. 'In these passages', says Mr Nowell Smith, 'he haunts the ear with that solemn and rich and varied rhythm which is the peculiar glory of Elizabethan and Jacobean prose.'[13] And he goes on to point out the beauty of one particular chapter and paragraph. But, pleasant as it is for the cultivated modern to find in Greville's book a collection of rare old curiosities to be handled separately, it has a higher value perhaps as a complete work in which the whole figure is embalmed, and there is no rent perceptible in the encircling envelope. For, although Sidney is raised a little beyond the ordinary human stature so that his outline runs free unchecked by petty interruptions, and has become a 'sea-mark' and a standard for men to sail by, it is due to his friend's art that it is still a solid figure which we may feel warm to our touch. If it is true that he is a type and has something of the general and public nature of a type, the type after all was closely allied with the particular. For it is the virtue of the Elizabethan age, unless imagination is too partial, that such heroes should have space to expand there to their natural circumference, and men can stand back and gaze at them. So that when Sidney died, at the age of thirty-two, his death was but the final harmony of a life that was too short, but that was complete; indeed, the shortness of such lives seems in some way a necessary part of their perfection. Poets sang of him as an ideal fit for worship; and other countries besides his own lamented as though some image common to them all had been withdrawn from sight. Best of all is the tribute of his friend, for there you hear a sterner note than eulogy and see the exact countenance that was then deemed heroic:

Indeed he was a true modell of Worth; A man fit for Conquest, Plantation, Reformation, or what Action soever is greatest, and hardest amongst men; Withall, such a lover of Mankind, and Goodnesse, that whosoever had any real parts, in him found comfort, participation, and protection to the uttermost of his power; like Zephyrus he giving life where he blew.[14]

1 – A review in the *TLS*, 31 May 1907, (Kp c5.12) of *Sir Fulke Greville's Life of Sir Philip Sidney* (1652). With an introduction by Nowell Smith (Tudor & Stuart Library, Clarendon Press, 1906).
2 – *Ibid.*, ch. XII, pp. 129–30.
3 – *The Countess of Pembroke's Arcadia* (1590); see VW's essay of this title, V VW *Essays* and *CR2*.
4 – For his views on 'Fulke Greville, Lord Brooke' see Charles Lamb, *Specimens of English Dramatic Poets who lived about the Time of Shakespeare* (Longman, 1808), p. 295; also in *Works* (1818).
5 – Cf. I VW *Letters*, no. 355, 22 March 1907, in which VW recommends *Greville's Life of Sidney* to Clive Bell: ' . . . it has some passages of the ripest melody, like plaited columns of marble, if I may mix my metaphors and confuse my sense. And if there are such books in the world I shall continue to read.'
6 – *Greville's Life*, ch. I, p. 3; which continues: 'and so by a right Meridian line of their own, learn to sail through the straits of true vertue, into a calm, and spacious ocean of humane honour'.
7 – *Ibid.*, ch. IV, p. 38.
8 – *Ibid.*, ch. X, p. 117; p. 118.
9 – *Defence of Poesie* also published as *The Apologie for Poetrie*, both in 1595.
10 – *Greville's Life*, ch. I, p. 18; for the continuation of this passage, see n. 12 below.
11 – *Ibid.*, ch. I, p. 15.
12 – *Ibid.*, ch. I, p. 18, which has: 'But the truth is: his end was not writing, even while he wrote; nor his knowledge moulded for tables, or schooles; but both his wit, and understanding bent upon his heart, to make himself and others, not in words or opinions, but in life, and action, good and great . . . '
13 – *Ibid.*, Intro., p. xxi.
14 – *Ibid.*, ch. III, p. 33.

Lady Fanshawe's Memoirs

The memoirs of Lady Fanshawe are probably the memoirs of many other ladies of her time who did not go to the trouble of writing them down. Such were the stories that were current in halls and manor houses all over England in the luxurious Restoration days; how 'your father was the tenderest father imaginable', how he loved hospitality, which he thought 'wholly essential for the constitution of England';[2] was loyal, honest, and walked often with a poetry book in his hand; listen, then, while I tell you how he lived, so that you may live like him, and grow up true and charitable and discreet. The writer, in this instance, might go on to speak of grandfathers and uncles and aunts, all of them 'honest, worthy, virtuous men and women who served God in their generation[s]'[3] and lay now obscure beneath their tombs. Indeed, she could hint at far generations, doubtless once practising the same virtues, who had accumulated in the chancel of the church at Dronfield, and bore the same name, spelt variously ffaunchel, ffauncall, or Fanshawe, above them. Nor would it be hard for a stranger who finds himself in that churchyard, or comes upon the low little stone house from which they issued, to perceive a family history running alongside of all seasons of English life, inconspicuously, as a murmured accompaniment. So set humming, the whole land seems to swim in a pleasant kind of harmony, in which no age is more present than another, and all are of the one piece.

Lady Fanshawe's memoirs serve but to freshen colours now grown dim; one might read them beneath the yew tree on a hot summer day with no sense of incongruity, no discordancy. She was the daughter of Sir John Harrison, and, through her mother, cousin already of the Fanshawe family;[4] her father was a member of five parliaments, and a devoted servant of the Royal cause, which, as a rich man, he supported with his purse. Ann was educated in 'working all sorts of fine works with my needle, and learning French, singing, the lute, the virginals, and dancing'; but a vigorous love of 'active pastime[s]' breaking through these restraints made her 'that which we graver people call a hoyting girl'.[5] At Oxford, where they had come with the Court, she married her husband, Sir Richard Fanshawe,[6] the talk of battles in her ears, sickness and the spectacle of war before her eyes; and immediately the turbulent business that was to last their life together began. She makes, as perhaps she once made on her knees, some solemn little preface to this undertaking – 'as faith is the evidence of things not seen, so we upon so righteous a cause cheerfully resolved to suffer what that would drive us to'.[7] And, without further meditation, she began her voyages and shipwrecks and adventures, till, having lavished herself with characteristic profusion – bearing eighteen children in twenty-one years, for example, and losing most of them – she was laid in the church of Ware beside her husband. It is the lack of meditation in proportion to so much action that strikes the reader, and colours, if we do not mean rather washes with a single shade, the whole book. The atmosphere is singularly clear; you see what happens now and what comes next, the clothes Sir Richard wore, the wondrous fruits that drooped from trees, the commodities of the land, the detail and solidity of things as in a child's story of adventure. It is a method full of charm; a method, it seems, that marks another age. Indeed, we should miss a great deal if we tried to convict Lady Fanshawe of much fine feeling; it is precisely her candour and simplicity that are valuable, adding nothing to the fact, but, at the same time, in no way obscuring it.

In October, as I told you, my husband and I went into France by way of Portsmouth, where, walking by the seaside . . . two ships of the Dutch shot bullets at us, [. . .] so near that we heard them whiz by us; at which I called my husband to make haste back, and began to run. But he altered not his pace, saying, if we must be killed, it were as good to be killed walking as running.[8]

An attitude of mind which Lady Fanshawe gives us to understand is proper to a nobleman on all occasions. Such is the rather serene and florid spirit, easily to be made visible to the eye, in which the whole drama is presented – the two embassies to Madrid, the shipwrecks, the escape from Cork, the imprisonment of Sir Richard.[9] Their adventures stir in them no petty feelings of resentment against men or against nature; it is the lot of gallant knights to tilt nobly against obstacles, as the knights in *The Faery Queene*[10] proved their chivalry against the monsters of allegory. So, when they part with Charles I:

I prayed God to preserve his Majesty . . . He stroked me on the cheek and said, 'Child, if God pleaseth it shall be so; but both you and I must submit to God's will . . . ' Thus did we part from that glorious sun that within a few months after set, to the grief of all Christians that were not forsaken by God.[11]

The phrase is round; it gives the surface and the ceremony, much as a curtsey duly regulated expresses what it is proper to feel in the presence of the Sovereign; but the pen is scarcely more subtle than the knee. After all we must allow that in an age when there was so much ceremony, so much action needed merely to cross to Spain – 'we saw coming towards us with full sail a Turkish galley, well manned, and we believed we should all be carried away slaves'[12] – it would have needed a deeper mind than Lady Fanshawe's to accept all these events and stain them in any peculiar dye, or crack them open and show what was inside. As it is, there is so much of a likeness between one thing and another as they appear in this medium that we give almost the same value to the story of the little Portuguese boy who was rolled in honey[13] as to the Restoration of Charles II. On both occasions it is the show that the writer lays before us, without comment, almost without arrangement. But the charm of such unconsciousness is that it permits her to make statements plainly which most writers would in some way distort; and the reader has the pleasure of filling in the picture with fresh colours. 'I found a twenty shilling piece of gold which nobody owning that was by, I kept.'[14] Of Irish ghosts: 'She spake aloud, and in a tone I never heard, thrice "Ahone"; and then with a sigh more like wind than breath she vanished ... Your father entertained me with telling how much more those apparitions were usual in Ireland than in England.'[15]

It is something of a surprise to find that this candid tale with its air of something naturally completed, a statement as round and as detached as a bird's song, is in need of five appendices and nearly 350 closely printed pages of notes. The supplement includes not only the minute comment of history but the still more minute additions of family pride; and both together make Lady Fanshawe's memoirs a matter of far greater or other importance than she or her readers were aware. The perspective is changed of a sudden, and instead of vague 'business' into which she did not inquire too narrowly, you have accurate texts faithfully recovered from the originals in the British Museum, the Bodleian, the Public Record Office, and from nearly a thousand printed volumes. You have what Pepys wrote and Evelyn;[16] distances measured on the map; a precise examination of dates and Christian names, for Lady Fanshawe was casual even as to her own children; a little biography of every name she mentions and often a genealogy as well; till the family of Fanshawe seems to cast itself like an intricate net over the entire population of England. The curiosity of such speculations is great; some one with a fiery imagination might fuse the text and its notes into such a whole as should constitute a complete little globe of human life; meanwhile the book remains curious, delightful so far as Lady Fanshawe is concerned, elaborate and admirable so far as we can absorb her editor. The touch, 'a real personage, whose memory is specially dear to the family of her husband', colours much very pleasantly that we are apt to call mere antiquarianism. Lady Fanshawe, it seems, is still a grandmother.[17]

1 – A review in the *TLS*, 26 July 1907, (Kp c6) of *The Memoirs of Ann Lady Fanshawe. Wife of the Honble. Sir Richard Fanshawe, Bart., 1600–72*. Reprinted from the original manuscript in the possession of Mr Evelyn John Fanshawe of

Parsloes . . . (John Lane, 1907). ' . . . Lady Fanshawe is rather disappointing,' VW wrote to Violet Dickinson on 20 July (*I VW Letters*, no. 371); 'only a thread of a story, and some nameless descendant has tied a volume of dry little notes to her tail; and the Times say they must have my article at once, and that flurries me . . . ' See also *I VW Letters*, nos 369, 373 and 374.

2 – See Lady Fanshawe, p. 5: 'He was the tenderest father imaginable, the carefulest and most generous master I ever knew. He loved hospitality, and would often say it was wholly essential for the constitution of England.'

3 – *Ibid.*, p. 17.

4 – Lady Fanshawe (1625–80) was the fourth child and elder daughter of Sir John Harrison (c.1589–1669) of Balls Park, Hertfordshire, and his wife Margaret (1591–1640), daughter of Robert Fanshawe of Fanshawe Gate and thus her son-in-law's first cousin.

5 – For all three quotations, *ibid.*, p. 22.

6 – In 1644, at Wolvercote Church. Sir Richard Fanshawe's dates, according to the *DNB*, are 1608–66 and not as given in the subtitle to the *Memoirs*.

7 – Lady Fanshawe, p. 30.

8 – *Ibid.*, p. 47.

9 – Sir Richard was taken prisoner at the battle of Worcester in September 1651 and detained at Whitehall until 28 November; he was placed thereafter under what amounted to house arrest at Tankersley Park in Yorkshire.

10 – Edmund Spenser, *The Faery Queene*, 1589 and 1596.

11 – Lady Fanshawe, p. 46.

12 – *Ibid.*, p. 63.

13 – *Ibid.*, p. 109: 'The porter . . . took this boy and pulled off his rags and anointed him all over with honey, leaving no part undone, and very thick, and threw him into a tub of fine feathers; which as soon as he had done set him on to his legs and frighted him home to his mother who seeing this thing . . . ran out into the city, the boy screaking after her, and all the people in the street after them, thinking it was a devil or some strange creature.'

14 – *Ibid.*, p. 123.

15 – *Ibid.*, p. 58, which has: 'I pulled and pinched your father . . . Neither of us slept more that night; but he entertained me with telling how much more those apparitions . . . '

16 – Samuel Pepys (1633–1703); John Evelyn (1620–1706) was a cousin of Sir Richard Fanshawe.

17 – VW appears to have had a wild stab at translating '*Par nobile conjugum/ grato animo recordantes/ eiusdem gentis posteri/ hoc marmor ponendum curaverunt*' (Lady Fanshawe, Notes, p. 588) which brought upon her head '12 sheets from Mr Fanshawe this morning, who says I did no justice to the gravestone . . . and how can I say "Lady F. it seems is still a grandmother" when no grandson of hers is alive.' (*I VW Letters*, no. 374, to Lady Robert Cecil, August 1907).

'The New Religion'

No one has any right, perhaps, with a title like *The New Religion*, and the additional clause 'A Modern Novel' and the dedication 'For those who are sick – for those who believe they are sick', and so on,[2] to be very much surprised by what follows; and yet there are moments of illusion. A beautiful young woman waiting her husband's return in a country garden, soft, affectionate, pure-minded; a faithful business man, submitting tenderly to the punctual button-hole, whose years confirm his sincerity – here is the stuff for close domestic analysis, combined, perhaps, with some debate of current heresies. But before this picture has established itself it is clear that the interest does not lie in those regions at all, but, to begin with, in the state of Mrs Lomas's health. She is ill, and there is a country doctor who hints at a possible complication; then there is a specialist, and then another specialist, and then we see that it is not Mrs Lomas's health that we are to be interested in, but health in general, and doctors of all kinds. Each character is introduced in turn with some familiar phrase on his lips; they come so swift and so pat that the reader has to abandon any original desire to follow the fortunes of individuals, and must devote all his agility to taking the points as they rise; a restless, exacting duty, not, however, to be forgone. He will have to listen to private conversations between Dr Russett, 'the greatest living nerve specialist',[3] and his wife. 'The whole thing's just a big financial and social spec,'[4] he remarks when his wife murmurs something about the cause of humanity. Next a boy proves the victory of prayer over surgery; and an old gardener pleads the cause of charms and simples. When all these points have been made with considerable vivacity, Mrs Lomas is pronounced to be suffering from general debility, and Dr Russett prescribes a year in a sanatorium in the Vaudois Alps, which will cure her if, as he remarks in the hall, she has not a spine complaint which is incurable. At Gringinges-sur-Aulches there is a vast establishment dedicated to the 'Return to Nature'.[5] The founder, Dr Vourray, has discovered that man is nearly allied to the apes; and 'Live as the monkey, and you will regain your lost strength'[6] is the creed. Here Mrs Lomas was shut in a dark room, with a nurse who exhibits, submissively but as pointedly as the rest, the vices of her class; while Henry Lomas undergoes the treatment prescribed for apoplexy, since, as the doctor discovers, his symptoms point to that disease. To bring down the whole of this colossal imposture Henry Lomas is suddenly stricken with consumption; and a mad patient breaks into Mrs Lomas's isolation at night-time while her nurse sleeps. The next task, then, is to exhibit the fallacies that are current with respect to consumption; 'dosimetry'[7] in this case, and the Riviera. But the proof this time requires that the invalid shall die; and another symptom directly takes his place, in the person of Mrs Lomas's divorced father, who suffers from something that we are now perhaps permitted to call 'Angelina Pectoris'.[8] For in truth the point of view has once more shifted. The satire of the earlier chapters was after all directed against the solid bodies of doctors and faiths, and it was possible for Mr Maartens to inspire them with rigorous rhetoric – 'Tis the new religion', cried Dr Russett. 'Nobody listens to the poor dead parsons. *We* are the new infallible priests,' and so on;[9] and though we have heard this before, we feel that we ought perhaps to believe in it. But now the connexion with things that are shaped somewhat after the fashion of life is blown aside, and Mr Maartens indulges a delightful irresponsible mood which neglects all the missions, and charges nobody with the disagreeable duty of abolishing shams. Can we believe, for example, in the doctor who, to refute the germ theory of disease, swallows a tinful of tubercles and calls his daughter 'Microbe d'Amour; my cabbage, she infecteth nobody'?[10] But it is amusing. Again, shall we conceive a millionaire endowed with sufficient imagination to cruise among the Aegean islands in search for a prophet with miraculous powders that either cure you or kill you? But the story is one of the most charming in the book. At last we are entertained with a wild jumble of the different creeds in conflict, issuing from the lips of valets, and ladies' maids, and sea captains; and the babble of petroleum pills, biblical texts, and auto-suggestion is the exhilarating effervescence into which all the sense and satire of the book boil over. It is a mistake to impose a solid ending upon such chaos; nor do we believe that Dr Russett cedes the Lomas property upon which he had built his gigantic sanatorium, his culminating fraud; or that young Russett, after proving his devotion by swallowing a powder, marries Mrs Lomas, with the chronic spinal complaint; or that his final vow is 'to succour the sick.'[11] We have not believed in the loves or the diseases; nor have we profited by the satire; but we have been very much entertained, and wit and fantasy are good, call them what you will.

1 – A review in the *TLS*, 6 September 1907, (Kp c6.1) of *The New Religion. A Modern Novel* (Methuen, 1907) by Marten Maartens (Joost Marius Willem van der Poorten-Schwarz, 1858–1915, sometime lecturer in law at Utrecht University). 'Once more I have a letter from B. Richmond asking me to review a novel by Marten Maartens at once, at some length, for Friday's Times . . . ' (*I VW Letters*, no. 381, to Violet Dickinson, 1 September 1907.)

2 – The dedication continues: 'For those who want to live longer than other people. For nobody else.'

3 – Maartens, p. 47, which has: 'Dr Nathanael Russett, the great nerve specialist. The greatest living.'

4 – *Ibid.*, p. 55, which has: 'You know as well as I do, Isabella, the whole thing's just a big financial spec.'

5 – *Ibid.*, p. 106.

6 – *Ibid.*, p. 110.

7 – *Ibid.*, p. 190; p. 196.

8 – *Ibid.*, p. 279.

9 – *Ibid.*, p. 127, which continues: ' . . . that ban and threaten a trembling world!'

10 – *Ibid.*, p. 184, which has: 'He would call his sweet Euphrosyne "Microbe d'Amour": "my cabbage, she infecteth nobody," he said.'

11 – *Ibid.*, p. 384.

'A Swan and Her Friends'

Macaulay, so we read in those marginal notes of his that have just been published, once amused himself by going through the six volumes of Miss Seward's letters with a pen in his hand.[2] Surely no more effective and economic way could be found – nor does it need great subtlety – of disposing of such a rubbish heap, and of preserving any trifle of value that may chance to lie hid there. One quotation, for quotation has already been made in these columns,[3] will be enough. The Latins, Miss Seward remarks (rebuking 'pleasant Mrs Piozzi'[4]) place their lyric Horace next to their epic Virgil, much more on account of his odes than of his satires. 'What Latins?' asks Macaulay; 'There is not a word of the sort in any Latin writer.'[5] Then it was her grammar, then her taste. Finally we have the verdict, 'Was ever such pedantry found in company with such ignorance?'[6] which we should do well perhaps to couple with some softer phrase to the effect that she could write simply when (for example) she was describing the last illness of her tiresome old father. But this is not the way that seems good to Mr Lucas; and we agree with some of his reasons for thinking that Miss Seward and her friends deserve an ampler investigation. Not only were their views on most matters of literature and life repulsive to us, but they were, as Mr Lucas points out, 'acclaimed with enthusiasm' by the mass of the intelligent people of their time.[7] What kind of society that was, and the nature of the revolution that destroyed it, is surely an interesting topic enough; and in this case the extravagance of the contrast and the delightful emphasis with which the old monstrous doctrine was expressed make it as lively a subject as the wittiest could desire.

But Mr Lucas is neither historian nor satirist; he is content with the simpler duties of the caricaturist, with the useful but modest art of the maker of amusing books. Let us grant at once that the portentous Swan tempts the parodist if any one ever did; her writing is of the kind that you feel to be almost too good to be true; another touch and it is incredible. That touch would have come from some convincing correspondence between her life and her work, and we cannot bring ourselves to believe that she ever gave it. And a true humorist would also refrain; he would lead us, as Miss Bates[8] leads us, to the very limits of comedy, suffer us perhaps to glance at the ridiculous, and then, by means of some skilful light upon another side of the character, he would draw us smoothly away, give our comic sense a respite, and urge it forth again with a fresh start. Thus the character would float buoyantly all the time within its proper limits. But Mr Lucas is not careful of limits, he wishes us to laugh, to laugh almost incessantly; and so the chance he had of drawing in these three hundred pages an exquisitely comic figure typical not only of Lichfield and the time, but of something vast and enduring in human nature is lost; we have instead the conventional buffoon. For she could be made, of course, to comport herself precisely as the caricaturist would have her; so that it is possible, as Mr Lucas has proved, to let her mouth forth a whole volume of autobiography in what he calls 'Sewardese'. But how much of it is characteristic of her? How much is merely the exaggerated manner in which all second-rate writers parody the temper of their age? What, in short, is really the flesh and blood behind this drapery, the idea that this particular pose represents? Mr Lucas deals lightly with a few of these questions. Why should Miss Seward need a biography? Because 'it is interesting to mark changes ... and nothing could be less ⟨sic⟩ out of place in the present day than Anna Seward's pontifical confidence, her floridity, and her sentimentalism'.[9] Why was she admired? Because she was a pioneer, because a fashion for poetry was in the air. 'There are certain phases of human incompetence that really are worth examination,' and Miss Seward, it is added, was 'the last and greatest of the unhumorous women'.[10] And then we hear what Lamb said about Miss Benjay;[11] we read, not perhaps for the first time, Miss Pinkerton's letter in *Vanity Fair*;[12] and we are told what, it is true, we did not know before – that 'I entered Lichfield in a station omnibus filled otherwise with a commercial traveller and three rural deans'.[13] The first ten or twenty pages of the performance are so comic for one reason or another that we are ready to sink all our objections to the method. The Swan, as Mr Lucas says, 'sprang from the egg almost fully fledged'.[14] She began by writing verses at the challenge of Erasmus Darwin, who doubted whether she could really do all that fame protested.[15] At once the verses spout, profuse and pompous, with the same capital letters, the same platitudes, rounded and rhymed, that were to serve her all her life for poetry. Unfortunately, however, it was not until 1784 that she kept copies of her letters, and there is little record of a time that was not, perhaps, completely obscured by the full development of her style. But even at the age of twenty-one this was the way in which life was arranged; she describes the engagement of a younger sister:

I stood by her toilet while she dressed ... she sighed often, and once or twice exclaimed, 'Ah! Heaven!' in a pensive, languid tone, and with an emphatic shake of the head, as she put on her light hat and ribands. 'Bless me,' said I, 'one would think thou wert adorning a victim and not a mistress. If that idea has passed across thy mind, prithee, put a stop to this business at once! ... Study a pretty harangue of dismissal ... '[16]

and so on and so on. There is one shrewder phrase: – 'I grew so saucy to my mother ... that she took her pinch of snuff first at one nostril and then at the other.'[17] But after that we have superabundant reasons for knowing how she thought that she ought to think, and how she trained herself to express it. It would be easy and delightful to quote – to make her illustrate every vice that is known to literature, to indicate most of the vices that can infect the character. We are gorged with falseness of every description; the whole society echoes her accents; the Hayleys, the Ansteys, the Whalleys, and the Potters deluge us with bad criticism, bad poetry, and bad emotion.[18] We laugh till we are bored, and we are bored because we are still conscious that this is all too far removed from life to give us much reason to dislike or love or know them more than any other tedious and prolix people much at the mercy of their pens. We are only curious to know why it is that clever people, as these were, ever thought it right to submit to such a convention. For there are touches that remind us that they had brains and that they lived; we hear Miss Seward dub herself a 'fat cook maid', and laugh in private with 'the Bard of Sussex' over her lameness and her figure. Scott, who received her letters 'with despair', 'really liked' her when he met her and heard her talk 'with the keenness and vivacity of youth . . . with a ready perception of the serious and the ludicrous',[19] and listened to her admirable mimicry of Johnson. It is this that tantalises the reader; for, here we feel and dimly see that it is a toweringly humorous figure who did contrive to embody with over-whelming success an ideal of the moment, because, among other reasons, she embodied it with more vigour than other people. Ten pages are enough to prove to us that she was ludicrous; but the essential point of her — that her letters half cover and half express a genuine attitude towards life — is what Mr Lucas with all his vivacity fails to show.

1 – A review in the TLS, 14 November 1907, (Kp C7) of A Swan and Her Friends (Methuen, 1907) by E. V. Lucas. Ann Seward (1747–1809), the 'Swan of Lichfield', was the daughter of Thomas Seward (1708–90), Canon of Lichfield and of Salisbury, and Elizabeth, née Hunter (d. 1780), whose father had been headmaster of Lichfield Grammar School and Dr Johnson's teacher. She lived at Lichfield from 1754 until her death, pursuing her literary interests and caring for her valetudinarian father.
2 – See Marginal Notes by Lord Macaulay selected and arranged by the Rt. Hon. Sir George Otto Trevelyan, Bart (Longmans, Green, 1907).
3 – Marginal Notes was extensively reviewed in the TLS, 31 October 1907: 'Little did Macaulay dream that these insults were to bring Miss Seward the greatest compliment her name will ever receive.'
4 – Marginal Notes, p. 6.
5 – Ibid., p. 7.
6 – Ibid., p. 7, which has: 'Now I understand. She calls her sonnets "centennial" because there were a hundred of them. Was there ever such pedantry . . . '
7 – Lucas, ch. 1, p. 2: 'Indifferent writers are still often the darlings of the great-hearted public; but there is no such praise reserved for them now as was poured out upon Miss Seward. The answer to the question, Why was she acclaimed with such enthusiasm? also answers the question, Why should this book be written? Because she was a pioneer, and pioneers are not negligible.' See also n.9 below.
8 – In Jane Austen's Emma (1816).
9 – Lucas, ch. 1, p. 2, which has: 'I think the answer is that it is always amusing, not only in life but in literature, to mark changes; and nothing could be less out of place in the present day . . . '
10 – Ibid., p. 4, which concludes: ' . . . just as Miss Austen was the first of the humorous ones.'
11 – Elizabeth Ogilvy Benger (1778–1827), author of The Female Geniad (1791)

and *On the Slave Trade* (1809), concerning whom Charles Lamb wrote to Coleridge: 'Tea and coffee, and macaroons – a kind of cake – much love. We sat down. Presently Miss Benjay broke the silence, by declaring herself quite of a different opinion from *D'Israeli*, who supposes the differences of human intellect to be the mere effect of organisation . . . ' (Lucas, pp. 5–6).

12 – Lucas, ch. I, p. 7; the letter, quoted in full from Thackeray's *Vanity Fair* (1847–8) is that to Miss Amelia Sedley's mother from Barbara Pinkerton (whom Lucas sees as a fictional descendant of 'the Swan').

13 – *Ibid.*, ch. I, p. 10.

14 – *Ibid.*, ch. III, p. 27.

15 – *Ibid.*, ch. II, pp. 24–5; the talents of the Cygnet Seward were put to the test when Erasmus Darwin (1731–1802), the botanical poet, invited her to complete a poem for which he provided impromptu an opening stanza.

16 – Lucas, ch. II, pp. 28–9; the sister, Sarah, died 'a day or so' (*ibid.*, p. 36) before her wedding day – she was to have married a stepson of Dr Johnson. The punctuation here differs slightly from that in the original.

17 – *Ibid.*, p. 33.

18 – These were the principal 'Bath-Easton poets' – among whom Anna Seward was the leading poetess – cultivated and published (in *Poetical Amusements at a Villa Near Bath*, 1775, etc.), by Anna, Lady Miller (1741–81), herself the author of verses: William Hayley (1745–1820), poet, dubbed 'the Bard of Sussex', and more notably autobiographer, friend of Cowper, Blake, Southey, and of the painter Romney, whose *Life* he wrote; Christopher Anstey (1724–1805), author of *The New Bath Guide* (1766); Rev. Thomas Sedgwick Whalley (1746–1828), anonymous author of *Edwy and Edilda*, a poetic tale in five parts (1779); Rev. Robert Potter (1721–1804), translator of Aeschylus. For the Swan's commemoration of these see Lucas, ch. VIII, pp. 143–5.

19 – Lucas, ch. X, p. 192; for 'the Bard of Sussex' see n. 16 above; *ibid.*, ch. XV, p. 316 (Scott to Lockhart: 'The despair which I used to feel on receiving poor Miss Seward's letters, whom I really liked, gave me a most unsentimental horror for sentimental letters'); *ibid.*, p. 314, paraphrased.

William Allingham

Are we on the whole to regret the fortune that left William Allingham's autobiography unfinished, and gave us the chance of reading his diaries and notebooks unprepared as he wrote them? The finished narrative covers his childhood and the first years of his youth; a time that seems always most happily treated by people of imaginative temper, because the view is broad, and there are at the same time events of inexplicable interest which seem to sum up long trains of thought and experience suddenly in some quaint symbol, persistent all through life. Allingham remembered certain trees that grew in the garden at Ballyshannon, one 'leafy spray that touched my face was an enchantment beyond all telling', vague, 'warm scented white roses' and fig trees with crooked boughs, stables with forks and curry-combs, 'where perpetual twilight reigned';[2] and all these things shaped and coloured his life with their odd meanings far more than the real people about him. But when these first impressions have ceased to come together into pictures and the world intrudes 'obstinate questionings'[3] and much dull action which must be recorded, then, in default of the supreme artist, Mr Allingham's plan of short spontaneous notes seems happiest.

In spite of his appointment in the Customs in Ireland, he found time for frequent visits to London, where, in 1847, he knew first Leigh Hunt, a friendly, communicative man, who was ready to bestow all the wealth of the age upon the boy who had an enthusiasm for letters. '"Dickens," he exclaimed, "a pleasant felow! Carlyle – I know him well. Browning lives at Peckham because no one else does! I will take an opportunity of asking Dickens, Carlyle, and Browning to meet you." (Gracious powers!)'[4] Indeed, whether it was due to Leigh Hunt, or to his own merits, or to the convenient nature of literary society in those days, Allingham was soon admitted to all the great men and able to talk with them familiarly of their friends and their writings. He met Tennyson at Twickenham in 1851, 'a tall, broad-shouldered man', 'strange and almost spectral' in appearance, who began reading Allingham's own poems aloud in 'rich slow solemn chant' and spoke of George Meredith's poems lately sent him – 'author only twenty-three' – 'I thanked him for it and praised it – "Love in the Valley" the best.' When Allingham lived at Lymington some years later he saw much of Tennyson, and has to record not so much definite stories of him as an impression of the whole vast nature of the man, his odd, simple ways and direct speech. They came to a 'large tangled fig tree ... "It's like a breaking wave," says I. "Not in the least," says he.' Then, as his thought swept round, '"Man is so small! but a fly on the wheel [. . .] Allingham, would it disgust you if I read 'Maud'? Would you expire?"' As he read he cried, '"This is what was called namby pamby! That's wonderfully fine",' and so on. But it is Carlyle as usual, if we are to choose, whose sentences cut from the context and dulled by time still burn brightest. It is sometimes the obverse side of him that shows; when, for example, Allingham stands at the door and Carlyle is heard from within, 'Go away, Sir! I can do nothing with you!' But for the most part he was generous and accessible and lavish of his uncompromising judgments. 'Shelley had not the least poetic faculty. I never could read anything he wrote. It was all a shriek merely.' Of Swinburne, 'There is not the least intellectual value in anything he writes.' Whistler was 'the most absurd creature on the face of the earth'. Of Whitman, 'It is as though the town bull had learnt to hold a pen.' But of Shakespeare, 'The longer I live the higher I rate that much belauded man.' And he described 'like an imaginative child,' as George Eliot said, the murmur that went up in the theatre when *Othello* was played. 'The voices of the men rising – in your imagination – like a red mountain, with the women's voices floating round it like blue vapour.'[5] It is curious to read that he judged *Sartor* a book of very little value, and cared most for his *Cromwell*.[6] But the volume might yield many more stories than those we have taken; and most of them are true in the best sense of the word. How often, in the future, biographers will come here who want to know exactly what Carlyle said of Browning, or how it was that he disposed of his old pipes! An index makes all these facts available; and the book has several interesting portraits from the brush of Mrs Allingham.[7]

1 – A review in the *TLS*, 19 December 1907, (Kp c8) of *William Allingham. A Diary*. ed. H. Allingham and D. Radford (Macmillan & Co., 1907). Apart from the volume of poems referred to by VW, William Allingham (1824–89) also wrote *Day and Night Songs* (1854), *Laurence Bloomfield in Ireland* (1864) and *Songs, Ballads and Stories* (1877). His circle of eminent acquaintances also included Leslie Stephen (1832–1904) and his brother James Fitzjames Stephen (1829–94), brief accounts of both of whom appear in the *Diary*.
2 – Allingham, ch. I, p. 4; p. 5; p. 6.
3 – William Wordsworth, *Ode. On Intimations of Immortality* . . . stanza IX, I, 145 (not quoted in Allingham).
4 – Allingham, ch. II, p. 36, paraphrased; an account of his first meeting with Leigh Hunt (1784–1859), to whom Allingham dedicated his first book, *Poems* (1850).
5 – For Allingham on Tennyson, *ibid*., ch. IV, p. 60 (which has 'a tall, broad-shouldered swarthy man.'); *ibid*., p. 61; ch. V, p. 89; ch. VII, p. 117, p. 118; on Carlyle, ch. IX, p. 165; ch. XIV, p. 242; on Swinburne, ch. XVI, p. 258; on Whistler, ch. XIII, p. 227; on Whitman, ch. XII, p. 212; on Shakespeare, *ibid*., p. 206; and for George Eliot, and *Othello*, ch. XVIII, p. 286.
6 – Thomas Carlyle, *Sartor Resartus: The Life and Opinions of Herr Tenfers-dröckh* (1833–4); *Oliver Cromwell's Letters and Speeches* (1845).
7 – Helen, *née* Paterson, who married Allingham in 1874.

1908

'The Sentimental Traveller'

It is, perhaps, the confession of a narrow spirit, but have we not heard a little too much lately about this pervasive *Genius Loci*? Nature has innumerable beauties and defects; the smallest congregation of cottages is of profound significance; and the more we feel this or see how it can be felt the more we resent the incessant evocation by one writer after another of a spirit that we believe to be in its purity both remote and austere. Vernon Lee, who gives us *The Sentimental Traveller*, in particular boasts the utmost familiarity with this demon; she looks out of a train window, or parts her bedroom curtains of a morning, and the picture, compounded partly from the shape of the land, partly from such expression as human habitation has given it, composes itself at once. But this is the bodily form only in which the genius manifests itself; the spirit of the sight travels everywhere, and wakens echoes in her mind of people, of her childhood, of music, of books, or perhaps she is led by it to consider some deep question of life or morality. Her method then, so far as the portrait of the place is concerned, is purely impressionist, for if she were to concentrate her mind upon the task of seeing any object as exactly as it can be seen there would be no time for these egotistical diversions. And who but pedants and antiquaries want to know when a palace was built, or the exact style of its architecture? To separate herself emphatically from such worthies she will indulge in quite gratuitous ambiguities. 'To the earlier Greeks, navigating the dangerous Adriatic, the sun sets visibly among the seagirt cones; hence Phaeton, Icarus, and

Geryon, who, if you remember, was in some manner connected with the Hesperides . . . ''[2] The dots are a characteristic device, and part of an artistic system that prevails throughout. If only, in travelling, you will open your mind to receive all impressions and force your imagination to track down the most fugitive of suggestions, something charming and valuable, because original, will be recorded. This is perhaps the course that any sensitive mind adopts naturally, though it does not always go on to trace it out upon paper. But what art is needed to give such perishable matter an enduring form! – the art of Charles Lamb or of Henry James. Vernon Lee, with much of the curiosity, the candour, and the sensitiveness to trifles of the true essayist, lacks the exquisite taste and penetrating clearness of sight which make some essays concentrated epitomes of precious things.[3] Such phrases as 'that bathing-place of dim Napoleonic Grecian-Pilaster and lyre-backed-chair fashionableness' or 'the poor, pomatum-locked, faintly moustachioed, wasp-waisted grandson'[4] attempt to snatch the essential; but they surely light on something quite different. Or when the process is reversed, and a waistcoat button is made the centre of branching avenues of thought, do we feel that they strike inevitably from the spot of heat in the middle? 'That he ⟨Goethe⟩ should have brought back just this basket seems so human and touching, opening vistas of the kind of memories he, like some others among us, would clutch at; mornings in Verona market-place, and such like. Or perhaps . . . '[5] That is slipshod thinking, and if it does stumble on the truth we feel inclined to congratulate ourselves on the accident. The question as to what exactly distinguishes the truth from the falsehood in such work is a delicate one, and the value of the book depends entirely upon our immediate certainty – this is precisely right. We can hardly appeal to any standard but that of our own taste in such matters; why, for instance, does an image like the following satisfy us – 'That melancholy sunset, the smell of torn-up seaweed and wet sands, has always remained in my mind as symbolical of a soul's shipwreck' – when the comparison that follows between the shell-fish and the human beings seems altogether forced and unimaginative? 'Of such quivering slime we also are made up; and our microscopic realities steep in our living liquids as these creatures in the sea.'[6] Perhaps the most satisfactory essays in the book are those that treat of real people, for their characters are more profoundly realised, and are not too fragile to stand a delicate and sure examination.

1 – A review in the *TLS*, 9 January 1908, (Kp C9) of *The Sentimental Traveller. Notes on Places* (John Lane, Bodley Head, 1908) by Vernon Lee (Violet Paget, 1856–1935, who lived in Florence and chiefly wrote about Italian culture). Reprinted: *CW*. See also 'Art and Life' below.
2 – Lee, ch. XVI, pp. 141–2.
3 – See also *I VW Letters*, no. 397, to Violet Dickinson, December 1907: 'I am sobbing with misery over Vernon Lee, who really turns all good writing to vapour, with her fluency and insipidity – the plausible woman! I put her on my black list, with Mrs Humphry Ward. But though this is true as truth, as the Sage said in the fairy tale, still it can't be said in print; anymore than I can sit to Dodd naked.'
4 – Lee, ch. I, pp. 6–7; ch. VI, p. 52.
5 – *Ibid.*, p. 60, which continues: 'Or perhaps the basket had held the last oranges picked in that South he would never revisit.'
6 – For these marine comparisons, *ibid.*, ch. XVIII, pp. 156–7.

Thomas Hood

At the same time that Keats and Lamb were writing there flourished – so thick that even men like these showed little higher than the rest – a whole forest of strenuous and lusty human beings, journalists, artists, or people simply who happened to live then and rear their children. What profuse clamour, what multitudinous swarms of life a wise biographer can call up for us from fields long since shorn and flat if he will take for his subject one of these mortals it is really bewildering for a moment to consider. A student of letters is so much in the habit of striding through the centuries from one pinnacle of accomplishment to the next that he forgets all the hubbub that once surged round the base; how Keats lived in a street and had a neighbour and his neighbour had a family – the rings widen infinitely; how Oxford Street ran turbulent with men and women while De Quincey walked with Ann.[2] And such considerations are not trivial if only because they had their effect upon things that we are wont to look upon as isolated births, and to judge, therefore, in a spirit that is more than necessarily dry. Mr Jerrold's life of Thomas Hood[3] gives rise to a number of such reflections, both because he has written with delightful good taste and discrimination and because his subject, after all, belonged almost the whole of him to the race of the mortals. If it had not been for his two or three poems perhaps he would have sunk with the rest of them, with the load of albums and annuals and their makers, or would have survived as some half-mythical comic figure, the father of a few good stories and the author of innumerable puns. There is even something nugatory about the facts of his life; they suggest, in the easy ordinary way in which they fit and succeed each other, that there were hundreds of Thomas Hoods, sons of middle-class parents, apprenticed to engravers, with a turn for writing verse or prose; kindly domestic young men, who if they did take to letters – their parents were well advised in dissuading them – would make no mark there, but fill endless columns satisfactorily. Such, to a great extent, was the life of Hood; but there was just that exaggeration of temper or fortune in it that made him, while he was one of a class, typical of it also. He was impelled by his gifts and his failings to travel the whole course that slighter men trod partly, until he achieved something significant and completed his symbol.

As a boy he showed an abnormal facility; if he went away on a holiday he sent home profuse letters full of descriptions. Already the surface show of life tickled him with its incongruities; and at a time when most boys are aping some older writer he was simply observing with a lively eye what went on round him and scribbling it down in sheets of fresh easy prose. He laughed at his fellow lodgers, or stood at the window and took off the people whom he saw passing on their way to church. 'The study of character (I mean of amusing ones) I enjoy exceedingly,' he wrote when he was sixteen, and in the same spirit he dashed off a long poem on the town of Dundee, in imitation of the *New Bath Guide*.[4] No one could doubt where his gift would lead him, in spite of the engraving;[5] and when he was twenty-two some papers, accepted by the *London Magazine*, definitely determined him, as Mr Jerrold thinks, to trust entirely to his pen. From that time onward his life was the complex life of a busy journalist. There was no respite, scarcely any partition; for where are we to seek the events of his life but in his writings? And when we read him we must remember his wife and children, his ill-health, the ceaseless pressure of money cares. If a particular style pleased the public he must continue it, though the mood was spent; and as his first success was made in the *Whims and Oddities* he had still, as he says, to 'breathe his comic vein'. 'Could Hood at his moment have taken some editorial appointment ⟨writes Mr Jerrold⟩ we might have had more of his best and less of that journeyman work.'[6] That is a very moderate statement of the regret that bursts from our lips at many stages of this panting, hard-driven career; but in our desire to round the picture, to possess our tragedy, are we not inclined to fall into the fallacy to which Thackeray gave shape in his paper 'On a joke I once heard from the late Thomas Hood'? He speaks of the grinning and tumbling, 'through sorrow, through exile, poverty, fever, depression', 'the sad marvellous picture of courage, of honesty, of patient endurance, of duty struggling against pain'[7] – until in our compassion we forget very likely the true spirit of the man, his exuberance and brilliancy, the odd vulgar humour of a cockney life, the practical jokes and the supper parties. 'O Hood, Hood, you do run on so!' exclaimed poor Mrs Hood, half inarticulate, at one of these feasts.[8] The very fact that he gave himself with such pliancy to the drudgery of a journalist's life proves that there was something in the nature of his gift and temperament akin to it.

And when we turn to his writing we can surely discover there signs, not only of work 'pumped out', but of ideas springing gladly to the surface at the cheerful command of throbbing presses and fast falling sheets. No other invitation could have sounded quite so aptly to a man with a brain full of puns. But it is largely on account of these puns, we are told, that Hood is now so little read. Indeed, the portent is one that strikes the attention directly, and it must be held to typify something fundamental in the constitution of his mind. For his puns divide themselves into two classes or degrees; the greater part of them are simply happy matchings of sound in which there is so thin a burden of meaning that the contrast is almost purely verbal.

> Alas; they've taken my beau Ben
> To sail with old Benbow[9]

But there are others in which the pun is the result of some strange association in Hood's mind of two remote ideas, which it is his singular gift to illustrate by a corresponding coincidence of language.

> Even the bright extremes of joy
> Bring on conclusions of disgust;
> Like the sweet blossoms of the May,
> Whose fragrance ends in must.[10]

These lines are taken from one of his most serious poems, that on Melancholy, and serve to illustrate, compactly, a remarkable tendency – perhaps it is the remarkable tendency – of his thought. They show how the original leaning of his mind was really to wild and incongruous associations, grotesque and monstrous conceits, not in words only, but in human life, such as those we see so strikingly displayed in poems like

'Eugene Aram', 'The Haunted House', and 'The Last Man'.[11] And also we may discover a certain superficiality of conception, which suffers him to find such contrasts as the verbal one of 'may' and 'must' adequate, and makes him so supersensitive to the surface inflections of language as he was sensitive to the influence of contemporary writers. The influence of Lamb is clear in his prose, of Keats in his verse, and Coleridge one may guess affected his thought more deeply then either.

From these poems Sir Francis Burnand has lately published in the Red Letter Library a selection which gives a fair representation of the different moods in which Hood sang. They are broadly farcical, or romantic, or satirical or wildly fantastical; and there are the two famous poems which admirers of Hood will scarcely classify at all except by calling them inspired. The 'Song of the Shirt' in particular makes Sir Francis 'positively disinclined to dwell upon any other serious poems of Hood's be it even the "Bridge of Sighs"'; and he has some quarrel with Thackeray for the way in which he dwelt upon Hood's perverse love of 'comicalities'.[12] He points out that it was the jesting that paid, and that Hood was forced to make an income. But what perhaps is overlooked is the necessary relationship between Hood's fun and Hood's tragedy; you could not have the one without the other – if he laughed in this way he must cry in that – and the faults which we find in this light verse surely reproduce themselves in his serious poems. Thus, the reason why we cannot, with deference to Sir Francis Burnand, accept the 'Song of the Shirt' as an enduring masterpiece is because of the slight cheapness of effect, tending to the melodramatic, which has something in common, with the verbal dexterity, the supersensitive surface of mind already noticed. Such lines as

> Sewing at once, with a double thread,
> A shroud as well as a shirt.

or,

> A little weeping would ease my heart,
>   But in their briny bed
> My tears must stop, for every drop
>   Hinders needle and thread![13]

go straight, as he says, to our hearts; but not to the noblest part of them. 'Ruth' or 'The Death Bed' touches a higher note.[14] You must honour and pity so fine a nature, so honest and brilliant a mind, stung now to impulsive and passionate utterance by the sorrows of the world, now to irrepressible showers of merriment by its oddities. But in the most solid of his work the sharp blade of his own circumstance is always wearing through. You do not find all of him in his work; you rise from it unsatisfied, to ask what were the accidents of his life that made him write so. Mr Jerrold's book, then, is a valuable addition to our knowledge of Hood, and any one who has had occasion to consult the Memorials[15] by his son and daughter will perceive at once how much all readers in the future must be indebted to Mr Jerrold's laborious research and good judgment. A life was needed, and he has provided it.

1 – A review in the TLS, 30 January 1908, (Kp C10) of *Thomas Hood. His Life and Times* (Alston Rivers, 1907) by Walter Jerrold; and of *Poems* by Thomas Hood. With an introduction by Sir Francis Cowley Burnand (Red Letter Library, Blackie & Son, 1907). Reprinted: *B & P*.

2 – John Keats (1795–1821), Charles Lamb (1775–1834). For De Quincey's Ann – one of 'those female peripatetics who are technically called street-walkers' – see *Confessions of an English Opium-Eater* (1822), 'Preliminary Confessions'.

3 – Thomas Hood (1799–1845).

4 – Jerrold, ch. III, p. 35, from a letter written at Dundee, September 1815 to Miss Sands; for the imitation of Christopher Anstey's *The New Bath Guide* (1766), ibid., pp. 36–8. Hood stayed in Scotland for the benefit of his health, during the period 1815–8.

5 – Hood was articled as an engraver on his return to London from Scotland but this did not suit his health and by 1821 he had embarked on his literary career in earnest.

6 – *Whims and Oddities. In Prose and Verse*, 1st and 2nd series (1826 and 1827 respectively). Both quotations are from Jerrold, ch. VII, p. 183.

7 – W. M. Thackeray, *Roundabout Papers* (Smith, Elder, 1877), p. 70; p. 71, which has 'Oh, sad, marvellous picture of courage . . . '

8 – Jerrold, ch. IX, p. 244, which has: ' . . . true to his humorous nature, he loved to tease her with jokes and whimsical accusations which were only responded to by "Hood, Hood, how can you run on so?"' Charles and Mary Lamb were the Hoods' principal guests on this occasion.

9 – 'Faithless Sally Brown. An Old Ballad', *Whims and Oddities*, 1st Series, ll. 29–30. The stanza concludes: 'And her woe began to run afresh/ As if she'd said Gee woe!'

10 – 'Ode to Melancholy', *The Plea of the Midsummer Fairies . . . and Other Poems* (1827), ll. 113–6.

11 – 'The Dream of Eugene Aram, The Murderer', first published in 1829 in *The Gem*, which Hood edited; 'The Haunted House: A Romance', *Hood's Magazine*, January 1844; 'The Last Man', *Whims and Oddities*, 1st Series.

12 – Burnand, Intro. p. ix; p. vii; 'The Song of the shirt' was originally published in 1843 in the Christmas number of *Punch*; 'The Bridge of Sighs', first published in *Hood's Magazine*, May 1844.

13 – 'The Song of the Shirt', stanza 4, ll. 31–2; and the last stanza.

14 – 'Ruth' ('She stood breast high amid the corn'), first published in 1827 in *Forget-*

me-not; 'The Death-Bed' ('We watch'd her breathing thro' the night'), *Englishman's Magazine*, August 1831.

15 – *Memorials of Thomas Hood, Collected, arranged and edited by his Daughter* (1860).

The Memoirs of Sarah Bernhardt

There are good reasons why, when an actress promises to give us her memoirs, we should feel an unusual interest and excitement even. She lives before us in many shapes and in many circumstances, the instrument of this passion and of that. Meanwhile, if we choose to remember it, she also sits in passive contemplation some little way withdrawn, in an attitude which we must believe to be one of final significance. It might be urged that it is the presence of this contrast that gives meaning to the most trivial of her actions, and some additional poignancy to the most majestic. We know, too, that each part she plays deposits its own small contribution upon her unseen shape, until it is complete and distinct from its creations at the same time that it inspires them with life. And when she undertakes to show us what manner of woman this has become, should we not feel an exceptional gratitude and an interest that is more than usually complex?

Perhaps no woman now alive could tell us more strange things, of herself and of life, than Sarah Bernhardt. It is true that when she comes to this final act of revelation she makes use of certain conventions, poses herself with greater care than we could wish, before she allows the curtain to rise; but that, too, is characteristic, and, to drop all metaphor, her book surely should do what none of her parts has done, and show us what cannot be shown upon the stage.

She was brought up in the Convent of Grands Champs at Versailles, and her life at once forms itself into separate and brightly coloured beads; they succeed each other, but they scarcely connect. She was so intensely organised even then that there were explosions when she came into contact for the first time with hard things in the world outside her. When she was confronted by the sad walls of the convent, she exclaimed: 'Papa, papa! I won't go to prison. This is a prison, I am sure.' But at that moment a 'little round short woman' came out veiled to the mouth. After she had talked for a time she saw that Sarah was trembling, and with some strange instinct she raised her veil wholly for a second. 'I then saw the sweetest and merriest face imaginable . . . I flung myself at once into her arms.'[2] Her actions within the walls were as sudden and as passionate. Her hair, for example, grew thick and curled, and the sister who had to comb it in the early morning tugged callously. 'I flung myself upon her, and with feet, teeth, hands, elbows, head, and indeed all my poor little body, I hit and thumped, yelling at the same time.'[3] The pupils and the sisters came running, they muttered their prayers and waved their holy signs, at a distance, until the Mother Prefect had recourse to a further charm and dashed a spray of holy water over the active devil of Sarah Bernhardt. But after all this spiritual display it was the good Mother Superior, with her sure instinct for effect, who conquered by no more potent charm than 'an expression of pity'.[4] But such tempers were partly the result of the extreme fragility of her health. It is more significant to read how she built up for herself the reputation of a 'personality' among her fellows. She carried about with her little boxes full of adders and crickets and lizards. The lizards generally had their tails broken, for, in order to see whether they were eating, she would lift the lid and let it fall sharply 'red with surprise' at their assurance in rushing forwards. 'And *crac* – there was nearly always a tail caught.'[5] So, while the sister taught she was fingering the severed tails and wondering how she could fasten them on again. Then she kept spiders, and when a child cut her finger, '"Come at once," I would say, "I have some fresh spider web, and I will wrap your finger in it."'[6] With such strange crafts and passions, for she was never good at her books, she touched the imagination. And of course all this intensity of feeling went, in the convent, to paint some beautiful dramatic picture in which she acted the chief part as the nun who had renounced the world, or the nun who lay dead beneath a heavy black cloth, while the candles flared, and the sisters and pupils cried out in delightful agony. 'You saw, O Lord God,' she prayed, 'that mamma cried, and that it did not affect me!' for 'I adored my mother, but with a touching and fervent desire to leave her . . . to sacrifice her to God.'[7] But a violent escapade which ended in a bad illness finished the religious career that promised so well. She left the convent, and though she still cherished only one ambition, to take the veil, it was decided in the most casual fashion in a remarkable family council to send her to the Conservatoire. Her mother, an indolent charming woman, with mysterious eyes and heart disease and a passion for music, who was at any rate no ascetic, was in the habit of assembling relations and advisers when any family business had to be transacted. On this occasion there were present a notary, a godfather, an uncle, an aunt, a governess, a friend from the flat above, and a distinguished gentleman, the duc de Morny. Most of these people Sarah had some reason to hate or to love – 'he had red hair planted in his head like couch grass',[8] 'he called me *ma fil*'[9] – 'he was gentle and kind . . . and occupied a high place at Court.'[10] They discussed whether, with the 100,000 francs which her father had left her, it would not be best to find her a husband. But upon this she flew into a passion and cried, 'I'll marry the Bon Dieu . . . I will be a nun, I will,'[11] and grew red and confronted her enemies. They murmured and expostulated, and her mother began to talk in a 'clear drawling voice like the sound of a little waterfall . . .'[12] Finally the duc de Morny was bored, and rose to go. 'Do you know what you ought to do with this child?' he said. 'You ought to send her to the Conservatoire.'[13]

The words, as we know, were to have tremendous consequences, but it is worth while to consider the whole scene apart from them as an example of that curious gift which gives to so many passages in this autobiography the precision and vitality of coloured and animated photographs. No emotion that could express itself in gesture or action was lost upon her eye, and even though such incidents had nothing to do with the matter in hand, her brain treasured them and could, if necessary, use them to explain something. It is often something quite trivial, but for that reason, perhaps, almost startling in its effect. Thus the little sister was sitting on the floor 'plaiting the fringe of the sofa'; Mme Guérard came in 'without a hat; she was wearing an indoor gown of *indienne* with a design of little brown leaves'.[14] Later, a little drama is given thus. 'My godfather shrugged his shoulders, and getting up, left the box, banging the door after him. Mamma, losing all patience with me, proceeded to review the house through her opera-glasses. Mlle de Brabender passed me her handkerchief, for I had dropped mine and dared not pick it up.'[15] That perhaps may be taken as a simple example of the way in which it is natural for an actress, be she only twelve years old, to see things. It is her business to be able to concentrate all that she feels into some gesture perceptible to the eye, and to receive her impressions of what is going on in the minds of others from the same tokens also. The nature of her gift becomes increasingly obvious as the memoirs proceed, and the actress matures and takes her station at this point of view. And when, as is here the case, the alien art of letters is used to express a highly developed dramatic genius, some of the effects that it produces are strange and brilliant, and others pass beyond this limit and become grotesque and even painful. On the way back from her examination at the Conservatoire, in which she had been successful, she prepared a scene for her mother. She was to enter with a sad face, and then, when her mother exclaimed 'I told you so,' she was to cry 'I have passed!'[16] But the faithful Madame Guérard spoilt the effect by shouting the true story in the courtyard. 'I must say that the kind woman continued so long as she lived . . . to spoil my effects . . . so that before beginning a story or a game I used to ask her to go out of the room.' Not seldom we find ourselves in the same position as Madame Guérard, although perhaps we might be able to offer an excuse. There are two stories, out of a bewildering variety, which will serve to show how it is that Sarah Bernhardt sometimes crosses the boundary, and becomes either ludicrous or painful – or is it that we, like Madame Guérard, should leave the room?

After her astonishing exertions in the Franco-Prussian war she felt the need of a change, and went accordingly to Brittany.[17] 'I adore the sea and the plain . . . but I neither care for mountains nor for forests . . . they crush me . . . and stifle me.'[18] In Brittany she found horrid precipices, set in the 'infernal noise of the sea', and rocks to crawl beneath, which had fallen there 'in unknown ages, and were only held in equilibrium by some inexplicable cause'.[19] There was a crevasse also, the Enfer du Plogoff, which she was determined to descend in spite of the mysterious warnings of her guide. Accordingly she was lowered by a rope attached to a belt, in which additional holes had to be pierced, for her waist 'was then but forty-three centimetres'.[20] It was dark, and the sea roared, and there was a din as of cannons and whips and the howling of the damned. At last her feet touched ground, the point of a little rock in a swirl of waters, and she looked fearfully about her. Suddenly she saw that she was observed by two enormous eyes; a little further, and she saw another pair of eyes. 'I saw no body to these beings . . . I thought for a minute that I was losing my senses.' She tugged violently, and was slowly raised; 'the eyes were lifted up also . . . and while I mounted through the air I saw nothing but eyes everywhere – eyes throwing out long feelers to reach me . . . "Those are the eyes of the shipwrecked ones,"' said her guide, crossing himself. 'I knew very well that they were not the eyes of shipwrecked ones . . . but it was only at the hotel that I heard about the octopus.'[21] It might puzzle a scrupulous chronicler to assign their original parts in this drama to the octopus, the fisherman, and to Sarah Bernhardt; for the others it does not matter.

Then, again, 'my dear governess, Mlle de Brabender', was dying, and she went to visit her.

'She had suffered so much that she looked like a different person. She was lying in her little white bed, a little white cap covering her hair; her big nose was drawn with pain, her washed-out eyes seemed to have no colour in them. Her formidable moustache alone bristled up with constant spasms of pain. Besides all this she was so strangely altered that I wondered what had caused the change. I went nearer, and bending down, kissed her gently. I then gazed at her so inquisitively that she understood instinctively. With her eyes she signed to me to look on the table near her, and there in a glass I saw all my dear old friend's teeth.'[22]

There is one quality that most of the stories she tells have in common: they are clearly the productions of a very literal mind. She will accumulate fact upon fact, multiply her octopuses indefinitely, in order to achieve her effect, but she will never invoke any mystical agency. How could one manage 'the souls of the drowned'?[23] All the vast unconscious forces of the world, the width of the sky and the immensity of the sea, she crinkles together into some effective scenery for her solitary figure. It is for this reason that her gaze is so narrow and so penetrating. And although her convictions as an artist hardly enter these pages, it may be guessed that something of her unmatched intensity on the stage comes from the capacity which she shows for keen and sceptical vision where character is concerned; she is under no illusions. 'I had played badly, looked ugly, and been in a bad temper.'[24] One figures her the most practical of women when she chooses, a cheapener of fowls with the best of them, who will only suffer herself to be cheated from the same cynicism with which, no doubt, she would cheat herself if she wished it. For so clear an insight does not seem in her case at least consistent with a very exalted view of her kind; if she had it by nature she may have found that it would not lend itself easily to the resources of her art, that the effects to be got by it were uncertain, and it is her glory to make any sacrifice that her art demands. Certainly, when you have read some way in the book you become aware of a hardness and limitation in her view, which perhaps may be accounted for by the fact that all these violent scenes are the result of certain well-contrived explosions which serve but to illumine the curious face, so unlike any other face, of the actress. And in a world thus lit for us in lurid bursts of violet and crimson light the one figure in all its poses is always vivid enough, but the others which fall just outside the circle are strangely discoloured. Thus, she saved a lady from falling downstairs on board ship, who murmured 'in a voice that was scarcely audible "I am the widow of President Lincoln" . . . A thrill of anguish ran through me . . . her husband had been assassinated by an actor, and it was an actress who prevented her from joining her beloved husband. I went to my cabin and stayed there two days.'[25] And what was Mrs Lincoln feeling meanwhile?

Such a multiplication of crude visible objects upon our senses wearies them considerably by the time the book is finished, but what we suffer – it is the final triumph of 'the personality' – is exhaustion and not boredom. Even the stars, when she draws her curtain at night, shine not upon the earth and the sea, but upon 'the new era' which her second volume will reveal to us also.[26]

With our eyes dazzled by this unflinching stare we are urged to say something of the revelation – and vainly, no doubt. For the more you are under the obsession of a book the less of articulate language you have to use concerning it. You creep along after such shocks, like some bewildered animal, whose head, struck by a flying stone, flashes with all manner of sharp lightnings. It is possible, as you read the volume, to feel your chair sink beneath you into undulating crimson vapours, of a strange perfume, which presently rise and enclose you entirely. And then they draw asunder and leave clear spaces, still shot with crimson, in which some vivid conflict goes forward between bright pigmies; the clouds ring with high French voices perfect of accent, though so strangely mannered and so monotonous of tone that you hardly recognise them for the voices of human beings. There is a constant reverberation of applause, chafing all the nerves to action. But where after all does dream end, and where does life begin? For when the buoyant armchair grounds itself at the end of the chapter with a gentle shock that wakes you and the clouds spin round you and disappear, does not the solid room which is suddenly presented with all its furniture expectant appear too large and gaunt to be submerged again by the thin stream of interest which is all that is left you after your prodigal expense? Yes – one must dine and sleep and register one's life by the dial of the clock, in a pale light, attended only by the irrelevant uproar of cart and carriage, and observed by the universal eye of sun and moon which looks upon us all, we are told, impartially. But is not this a gigantic falsehood? Are we not each in truth the centre of innumerable rays which so strike upon one figure only, and is it not our business to flash them straight and completely back again, and never suffer a single shaft to blunt itself on the far side of us? Sarah Bernhardt at least, by reason of some such concentration, will sparkle for many generations a sinister and enigmatic message; but still she will sparkle, while the rest of us – is the prophecy too arrogant? – lie dissipated among the floods.

1 – A signed article in 'The Book on the Table' series, *Cornhill Magazine*, February 1908, vol. XXIV, (Kp C22) of *My Double Life. Memoirs of Sarah Bernardt [1845–1923]. With many portraits and illustrations.* (Heinemann, 1907). Reprinted: *B&P*.
2 – For her reactions to the convent, see Bernhardt, ch. III, p. 17.
3 – *Ibid.*, p. 22, which has: 'I flung myself upon the unfortunate sister . . . '
4 – *Ibid.*, p. 23.
5 – *Ibid.*, p. 24, which has: 'I shut the box very quickly, red with surprise at such assurance, and *crac*! in a twinkling, either at right or left, there was nearly always a tail caught.'
6 – *Ibid.*, pp. 24–5.
7 – *Ibid.*, ch. IV, p. 36; the order of the quotations has been reversed.
8 – *Ibid.*, ch. VI, p. 49; this refers to 'the Maitre C—. the notary from Hâvre, whom I detested . . . ', a bitter enemy of her father.
9 – *Ibid.*, p. 50, which has: ' . . . M. Meydieu . . . an old friend of the family, and he always called me *ma fil*, which annoyed me greatly, as did his familiarity.'
10 – *Ibid.*, p. 49; Charles Auguste Louis Joseph, duc de Morny (1811–65), the French statesman.
11 – *Ibid.*, p. 51.
12 – *Ibid.*, p. 52, which has: 'It was like the sound of a waterfall as it flows down babbling and clear, from the mountain, dragging with it the gravel, and gradually increasing in volume with the thawed snow until it sweeps along rocks and trees in its course. This was the effect my mother's clear drawling voice had upon me at that moment.'
13 – *Ibid.*
14 – For this scene, *ibid.*, p. 50.
15 – *Ibid.*, p. 57; the occasion was a visit to the Théâtre Français, made after the decision that Sarah should attend the Conservatoire: ' "Well, what do you think of it?" asked my godfather when the curtain fell. I did not answer . . . big tears were rolling slowly down my cheeks . . . ¶ My godfather shrugged his shoulders . . . '
16 – *Ibid.*, ch. VIII, p. 71, which has: 'I felt she would say, "Oh, I am not surprised, my poor child, you are so foolish!" and then I should have thrown my arms round her neck and said, "It isn't true, it isn't true; I have passed!" '
17 – Sarah Bernhardt had helped care for the wounded during the siege of Paris in the Franco-Prussian War, 1870–1. The sequence of events in this passage is somewhat dislocated; the immediate reason for her visit to Brittany had been her illness following the death of her sister Regina, *ibid.*, ch. XXII, p. 259: 'I was ordered to the south for two months. I promised to go to Mentone, and I turned immediately towards Brittany, the country of my dreams.'

18 – *Ibid.*, ch. v, p. 38 – on an earlier visit, to Caterets, in the Pyrenees – which has: 'I adore the sea and the plain, but I neither care for mountains nor for forests. Mountains seem to crush me and forests to stifle me. I must, at any cost, have the horizon stretching out as far as the eye can see and skies to dream about.'

19 – *Ibid.*, ch. XXIII, p. 260.   20 – *Ibid.*, p. 261.

21 – For this incident, *ibid.*, p. 264; the last extract is slightly paraphrased.

22 – *Ibid.*, ch. XIII, pp. 124–5.

23 – The source of this quotation has resisted discovery.

24 – *Ibid.*, ch. XXX, p. 332: 'The Press did not praise me, and the Press was quite right. I had played badly, looked ugly, and been in a bad temper, but I considered that there was nevertheless a want of courtesy and indulgence with regard to me.'

25 – *Ibid.*, ch. XXXII, p. 354, paraphrased.

26 – *Ibid.*, ch. XXVIII, p. 440: 'That night left me without sleep, for I wished to catch a glimpse in the darkness of the small star in which I had faith. ¶ I saw it as dawn was breaking, and fell asleep thinking over the new era that it was going to light up.' No second volume of these *Memoirs* was published.

'The Inward Light'

An Englishman travelling for business in Burma fell from his pony and broke his leg. The monks from the monastery above found him and laid him in a dim room, and bound his head with leaves. He slept and woke in peace, and looked from his windows over a great valley and heard only the murmur of cattle, and the cries of peasants, down below, and at dawn and sunset the melodious chant of Gregorian prayers. When his own people came to carry him away with them he begged to be left where he was, telling them of all the things round him – the fields, the air, the monks, the children who sang – that refreshed him, and added 'I am quite happy'.[2] Indeed, when he was recovered and could walk out in the country the simplest and most usual sights delighted and surprised him; not only had they a fresh beauty of their own, but he became aware that each plant or animal had in it a soul akin to his soul which made of the earth one coherent and harmonious whole. To share in this gave a new meaning to life; 'To live was good'. And then, as readers of Mr Fielding Hall's works will expect, the Englishman of the present volume 'began to think'.[3] Why should this accidental stay at a wayside monastery so change the view of a mature man, who had spent his life in various travel and effort and had achieved success? Again he resisted the invitation of his friends to return to them, and met their half scornful questioning with gentle but resolute replies. He determined that he would set himself to learn the clearly visible faith which makes the Eastern life so different from the Western, and decided that the fundamental difference was to be found in the consciousness, which the Burmese at least still cherish, of the live presence, the message, of nature. Inspired with this belief he lived on in the midst of the people and put to them the questions that no European asks of another: 'What is it you think of life? What is man's soul?'[4] The state of civilisation in which these questions are naked and urgent provides also an atmosphere of such clarity that very broad answers are possible. In the same spirit, Mr Fielding Hall makes use again and again, with gentle persistency, of the old images; life is a stream, a wind; it is a shaft of sunlight – composed of separate beams, indeed, but you may not part them and bid one burn in the lamp and another in the grate. It is a tide flowing in different measure, but not in different kind, through every living thing, through plants and beasts and man; and they are not units in themselves, but 'fractions of ⟨infinity⟩ and must be joined to make One'.[5] That is something of what people told him, and of what was borne in upon him by the sight of their simple ways, and the voice, for such it became, of the beautiful and happy world of nature. He was further told, in answer to his questioning, that the soul of man had been evolved, but the soul has a separate consciousness of its own which is not transmitted to the children of its body, with their physical form. What then happens to it? Is it merged in the wind? No; the monk shook his head. 'It goes on for ever, until – until – . . . Why should we wish to know?'[6] A steamer coming up the river soon afterwards, 'a myriad-jewelled water creature breasting the stream', provided the parable of the lamp with the light in it, which it put out, and the energy that made it goes – who knows where? 'Tout lasse, tout casse, tout passe. Et tout renaît.'[7]

Such fragments of wisdom, though expressed with all Mr Fielding Hall's usual charm of diction, will never perhaps satisfy a mind which asks for counsel earnestly; they are too vague, too slight, too humble. But then, as the author himself would urge, he has never desired to impose the faith of 'this little people in their Eastern valley'[8] upon the virile and indomitable West. He is the first to recognise its limitations; but also he is convinced of the value of certain qualities which he finds in the one belief and not in the other. And, as we are all concerned with the business of living, though few consider it philosophically, the impressions of so sensitive an observer have charm and value also. There are, it seems, two distinguishing qualities in the Burmese faith – it makes them happy and it keeps them unafraid. It teaches them that the life of the world from the beginning has been a continuous procession of all its parts towards the infinite light, and that none of the attributes of life are important compared with the capacity for life which is in each; for it is that, the simple living in the midst of other live things, that confers the supreme happiness. Thus they make no distinction between one class and another; their sexes, with different duties, are of equal value; no sharp division of creed or race can separate men who all breathe alike. In order that you may realise the purity of this existence the better, a European who has become a Burman in religion without adopting their conception of the whole passes through one of their merry festivals, and painfully disturbs it; his face is sharp and white and sad. He has come from a land where the faith is dry and formal, as a thing enclosed in sealed vessels; his soul cannot melt into the universal harmony; it is a 'little nut within a changing kernel'.[9] So, when the famine came it found a meek and acquiescent victim in the race which had no fear of death; 'Famines come and go – only the soul lasts on';[10] and, when the Englishman listened to the prayers of men and women tortured and left desolate, he did not hear bitter words of revolt or hopeless words of submission, but a peaceful sound 'like the murmur of the pigeons on the flags'.[11] Indeed, the impression which the book leaves, in part perhaps unconsciously, is one of singular peace, but also of singular monotony. The continued metaphors in which their philosophy is expressed, taken from the wind and light, waters, chains of bubbles and other sustained forces, solve all personal energy, all irregularity, into one suave stream. It is wise and harmonious, beautifully simple and innocent, but, if religion is, as Mr Hall defines it, 'a way of looking at the world',[12] is this the richest way? Does it require any faith so high as that which believes that it is right to develop your powers to the utmost?

1 – A review in the *TLS*, 27 February 1908, (Kp cii) of *The Inward Light* (Macmillan & Co., 1908) by Harold Fielding Hall (1859–1917) who had served in Upper Burma, as a political officer, 1887–91, famine officer, 1896–7 (he wrote a *Famine Manual*), and district magistrate, 1901. Reprinted: *CW*. See also '*One Immortality*' below.

2 – Fielding Hall, ch. ii, p. 18.

3 – *Ibid.*, p. 21; p. 22.

4 – *Ibid.*, ch. vi, pp. 58–9.

5 – *Ibid.*, ch. xi, p. 116: 'All the innumerable "I's" of every form of life are but fractions of that Unit and must be joined to make One.'

6 – *Ibid.*, ch. VI, p. 63.

7 – *Ibid.*, p. 65; p. 67 (repeated on pp. 157, 165).

8 – *Ibid.*, ch. I, p. 12.

9 – *Ibid.*, ch. V, p. 55: ' . . . can it be that the soul preserves for ever one unbroken entity? Is it a little nut within a changing kernel?'

10 – *Ibid.*, ch. XIII, p. 143, which has: '"Famines come and go, and so does pestilence and war and conquerors. Only the soul lasts on".'

11 – *Ibid.*, ch. XV, p. 165.

12 – *Ibid.*, ch. XIV, p. 155: 'Religion is a way of looking at the world. This is the Eastern way. And it must be remembered that all this comes from Buddhism.'

Shelley and Elizabeth Hitchener

Lovers of literature have once more to thank Mr Dobell[2] for discharging one of those patient and humble services which only true devotion will take the pains to perform. Shelley's letters to Miss Hitchener have already been printed, indeed, but privately; and now we have them issued in a delightful shape, enriched with an introduction and with notes by Mr Dobell himself, so that one more chapter in the life of Shelley becomes plainer and more substantial. Nor can it be objected that the piety in this instance is excessive, for although the letters are chiefly remarkable because they illustrate the nature of a boy who was, five or six years later, to write consummate poetry, still Shelley's character is always amazing. And in spite of the verbosity and the pale platitudes of his style in 1811, it is impossible to read the letters without an exquisite sense of faded scenes come to life again, and dull people set talking, and all the country houses and respectable Sussex vicarages once more alive with ladies and gentlemen who exclaim, 'What! a Shelley an Atheist!'[3] and add their weight to the intense comedy and tragedy of his life.

Elizabeth Hitchener was a schoolmistress at Hurstpierpoint, and Shelley first knew her in 1811 when he was nineteen and she was twenty-eight. She was the daughter of a man who kept a public house and was, or had been, a smuggler; and all her education was due to a Mrs Adams, who is called, in the language of the letters, 'the mother of my soul'.[4] Miss Hitchener was thin, tall, and dark, an austere intellectual woman with a desire for better things than the society of a country village could afford her, although she was not, as Shelley was eager to assure her, a

Deist and a Republican. But she was probably the first clever woman he had met; she was oppressed, lonely, misunderstood, and in need of some one with whom she could discuss the pleasant agitations of her soul. Shelley rushed into the correspondence with enthusiasm; and she, no doubt, though a little mystified and awkward in her flight, was touched and anxious to prove herself as passionate, as philanthropic, and almost as revolutionary as he was. Shelley's first letter indicates the nature of the friendship; he speaks of certain books which, in the manner of ardent young men, he had thrust upon her – Locke, *The Curse of Kehama*, and Ensor's *National Education*.⁵ He goes on to attack her Christianity, exclaims that 'Truth is *my* God,' and ends up, 'But see Ensor on the subject of poetry.'⁶ It would be delightful if we could have Miss Hitchener's letters also, for some allusions in Shelley's answers show the way in which, on occasion, she would try to cap his speculations. 'All nature,' she wrote, 'but that of *horses* is harmonical; and *he* is born to misery because he is a horse.'⁷ An 'Ode on the Rights of Women' began,

> All, all are men – women and all!⁸

But it is clear enough, without her replies, that Shelley was not anxiously concerned with the state of her mind. He assumed easily that she was of a more exalted temper than he was; so that it was not necessary to investigate details, but he might pour forth to her, as to some impersonal deity, the surprising discoveries and ardent convictions which come, with such bewildering rapidity, when for the first time the world asks a definite question and literature supplies a variety of answers. The poor schoolmistress, we can gather, took vague alarm when she found to what a mate she had attached herself, to what speculations she was driven, what opinions she must embrace; and yet there was a strange and not laughable exhilaration in it, which urged her on. The relationship, moreover, was soon justified by Shelley's marriage with Harriet Westbrook, and her approval of the correspondence. It was to be a spiritual companionship, in no way inspired by carnal love of that 'lump of organised matter which enshrines thy soul';⁹ and, further, there was the insidious bait which Shelley offered, with his curious lack of humanity, in the letter which explains why he married Harriet. He begged the 'sister of his soul' to help him in educating his wife. 'Blame me ⟨for the marriage⟩ if thou wilt, dearest friend, for *still* thou art dearest to me; yet pity even this error, if thou blamest me.'¹⁰ Miss Hitchener, it is clear, was keenly susceptible to praise of her mind which so subtly implied a closer tie; her letters became voluminous, and showed, so Shelley declared, 'the embryon of a mighty intellect'.[11] But the prophetess kept one shrewd and sensible and, it must be added, honourable eye upon the earth; she was well aware that Harriet might become jealous, nor could she disregard the mischievous chatter of Cuckfield gossips and attend only, as Shelley bade her, to the majestic approval of her conscience. Tragedy, of a sordid and substantial kind, was bound sooner or later to dissolve this incongruous alliance between the rushing poet, whose wings grew stronger every day, and the painstaking but closely tethered woman. The illusion was only sustained because for so long Shelley was in Wales or Cumberland or Ireland, and the lady remained at Hurstpierpoint, earning her living, which was noble in itself, and teaching small children, which was yet nobler; for to teach is 'to propagate intellect ... every error conquered, every mind enlightened, is so much added to the progression of human perfectibility'.[12] Then the first of the poet's illusions was terribly destroyed; Hogg's treachery was discovered; and poor Shelley, more in need than ever of understanding, turned wholly to his 'almost only friend', as he calls her in the letter which tells her of the blow.[13]

His desire, reiterated with the utmost emphasis, was that Elizabeth should join his wandering household directly; and Harriet, in some of the most interesting letters in the volume, was made to add her entreaty to his, in a tone that tried, with some pathos, to imitate his enthusiasm and generosity, but would lapse easily, it is clear, into plaintive commonsense when he was out of hearing. Miss Hitchener for a long while declined, for a variety of reasons; she would have to give up her school, her only support, depend entirely on Shelley, defy her father, and, besides, people would talk. But these arguments, coming on the top of so much impassioned rhetoric, were inadmissible; 'the hatred of the world,' Shelley declared, 'is despicable to you. Come, come, [–] and share with us the noblest success, or the most glorious martyrdom [. . .] Assert your freedom[14] . . . Your pen . . . ought to trace characters for a nation's perusal.'[15] Whatever the reason, she yielded at length, and set off in July 1812, on her disastrous expedition to Devonshire. For a time all acted up to their high missions; Portia (for 'Elizabeth' was already sacred to Harriet's sister), discussed 'innate passions, God, Christianity, etc.' with Shelley, walked with him, and condescended so far as to exchange the name Portia, which Harriet did not like – 'I had thought it would have been one more common and pleasing to the ear'[16] – for

Bessy. Professor Dowden gives us a singular picture of the time; Shelley and the tall dark woman, who is taken by some for a maidservant, wander on the shore together, and set bottles and chests stuffed with revolutionary pamphlets floating out to sea, uttering words of ecstatic prophecy over them. Within doors she wrote from his dictation and read as he directed. But the decline of this artificial virtue was inevitable; the women were the first to discover that the others were impostors; and soon Shelley himself veered round with childlike passion. The spiritual sister and prophetess became simply 'The Brown Demon', 'a woman of desperate views and dreadful passions',[17] who must be got rid of even at the cost of a yearly allowance of a hundred pounds. It is not known whether she ever received it; but there is a very credible tradition that she recovered her senses, after her startling downfall, and lived a respectable and laborious life at Edmonton, sweetened by the reading of the poets, and the memory of her romantic indiscretions with the truest of them all.

1 – A review in the TLS, 5 March 1908, (Kp C12) of Letters from Percy Bysshe Shelley [1792–1822] to Elizabeth Hitchener. With an Introduction and Notes by Bertram Dobell (Bertram Dobell, 1908). Reprinted: B&P.

2 – Bertram Dobell (1842–1914), bookseller, pioneering editor and publisher, notably of works by James Thomson, Shelley, Goldsmith and Traherne.

3 – Letters, Notes, Elizabeth Hitchener to Shelley, p. 331. See n. 4 below.

4 – Ibid., Intro., p. xxiv: '. . . but she owed much to her schoolmistress, Miss (or Mrs) Adams, whom she termed "the mother of her soul".' It was she who had exclaimed, 'What! a Shelley an Atheist!'

5 – Ibid., letter I, 5 June 1811, p. 3; The Curse of Kehama (1810) by Robert Southey (1774–1843); National Education (1811) by George Ensor (1769–1843), a writer noted for his advanced political and religious views.

6 – Ibid., p. 4; p. 5.

7 – Ibid., letter IV, 25 June 1811, p. 23.

8 – For Miss Hitchener, her ode and its effect on Shelley, see The Life of Percy Bysshe Shelley (2 vols, Kegan Paul, 1886) by Edward Dowden, vol. I, ch. VII, p. 314.

9 – Letters, letter X, 16 October 1811, p. 50; Shelley and Harriet Westbrook were married at Edinburgh on 28 August 1811.

10 – Ibid., letter XII, 26 October ?1811, p. 69; the expression 'sister of my soul' occurs here and on pp. 52, 54 and 65.

11 – Ibid., letter XXVIII, 29 January 1812, p. 208: 'I perceive in you the embryon of a mighty intellect which may one day enlighten thousands.'

12 – Ibid., letter XII, 26 October ?1811, p. 66, which has: 'When may I see the woman who indeed deserves my love, if she was thy instructress? . . . I already reverence her as a mother. How useful are such characters! how they propagate intellect, and add to the list of the virtuous and free! Every error conquered . . .'

13 – Ibid., letter XIII, 8 November ?1811, passim; the treacherous affair of Harriet

and Thomas Jefferson Hogg (1792–1862), friend and biographer of Shelley, caused a breach in the two men's relations. The phrase quoted is from p. 77.

14 – *Ibid.*, letter XXVII, 29 January 1812, p. 211.

15 – *Ibid.*, letter XXIV, 2 January 1812, pp. 159–60: 'Your pen – so overflowing, so demonstrative, so impassioned – ought to trace characters for a nation's perusal, and not make grammar-books for children.'

16 – *Ibid.*, letter XLII, 6 June 1812, p. 300; and letter XXXVI (written by Harriet), 14 March 1812, p. 270.

17 – Dowden, vol. I, ch. VII, p. 313, Shelley writing to his friend Edward Williams, 30 March 1813; the sentence concludes: '. . . but of cool and undeviating revenge'.

The Memoirs of Lady Dorothy Nevill

Sometimes, coming home at night through dark streets, you may see vanishing round the corner the curved shape of a ghostly chariot; it must be on its way surely to some brilliant festival where the lights have been out these hundred years. But no – the omnibus driver points too; it is Lord So-and-So's coach. That great nobleman, then, has still the imagination to conceive himself properly conveyed down Regent Street, on a muddy night, in a swinging crystal box, with angels adoring a coat of arms on the panels, and two symbolical footmen erect behind him to ward off all the perils of the dark – and it is a great achievement, which deserves our gratitude. For assuring ourselves that it is April, shall we say, in the year nineteen hundred and eight, and that the white blaze among the trees over there is symbol of a royal court, we may go on to indulge ourselves in a number of exquisite scenes, shut hitherto between the covers of books. When the chariot stays the serving men leap down, and stand with uncovered heads as the Lord and his Lady step through them, and into the great white hall. Hand in hand they mount the staircase, and bow, and curtsey, and pass on leisurely into vast rooms, clear as windswept skies, where the ladies have space to spread their trains like peacocks, and the lords toy gently with their silver swords. Other couples and groups swim past them, until the floor, as the family portraits look down upon it, is a beautiful pattern of moving colours which never stay or crowd, but circle easily in and out, as though they trod the measure of a stately dance. But there is an inner room, where there are gilt chairs on a polished floor, and one or two brocaded sofas. A wood fire burns clearly, and there are innumerable soft candles. Here, sitting lightly upright, we find some score perhaps of ladies and gentlemen who have no other occupation, it seems, but the use of their tongues. And what talk it is! Each speaks with confidence, and with an indescribable air of ease and dignity commingled, as though, after rolling wisdom for five centuries in the brain, it issued at length in smooth drops, bright as silver, but ponderous with purpose. The Prime Minister, there, unfolds the future of England for the inspection and correction of a certain sagacious dowager with a fan; here a brilliant youth explodes with paradoxes that are to become laws; and here again one pulls a blotted sheet from his shirt frill and reads, while all listen gravely, poems that sound like Keats. A lady quotes Sappho in the Greek, and another flashes with inspired epigram – what was it? for the words escape us. But Lady Dorothy Nevill should be able to repeat them.

It is the only consolation, indeed, of one forced to see Buckingham Palace from the outside and to people it within from the novels of Mrs Humphry Ward,[2] perhaps, that the aristocrat will nowadays grant us a reflection of his privileges by means of his pen. Otherwise the stout walls of their parks, the locked doors of their galleries would be intolerable to any one possessed of pen and ink or dynamite. But memoirs in the past have led us to believe that by refraining from such violence we cherish certain sanctuaries where all that is high-minded and witty and fair can live happily; and for the credit of the race it seems good that a handful of us should grow up with Greek statues round us, Titians on our walls, spacious gardens to walk in, time for reading and music and talk.

Lady Dorothy, as she is proud to tell you, has an indisputable right to all these privileges, for she is the daughter of Lord Orford, and for many generations a Walpole has succeeded a Walpole at the family seat in Norfolk.[3] In her two volumes of memoirs she confirms all that we have imagined of the aristocratic life, but with this qualification: it exists no longer. In the Forties and the Fifties of the last century Society was a real thing, and with melancholy pride she writes of the brilliant days and contrasts them with the ugly, respectable life which has replaced them. Courtesy and good humour distinguish her naturally; she will try to see that there is some good in the change; but, pathetically enough, her native instincts are always asserting themselves.

Society in the old days cannot in any way be compared with the motley crowd that calls itself society today . . . [4] The general level of conversation in the so called society of modern days must, of necessity, be low, for society, or what passes for it, is now very large, whilst wealth is more welcome than intellect. Good conversation, therefore, is practically non-existent.[5]

In the old days society was very small, for birth was the first qualification; then it followed that they all knew each other, 'so that it was more like a large family than anything else',[6] and then though this seems less a matter of human than of divine arrangement, that they were all endowed with powers of intellect as rare as their blood. But if you grant them these gifts and conceive that they have 'no ulterior object beyond intelligent cultured and dignified enjoyment' as Lady Dorothy puts it,[7] you do indeed imagine such a society as that of Athens in the time of Pericles or Paris in the time of Madame Récamier, and our belief in the virtues of our own British aristocracy is splendidly fulfilled. But when we come to read the account of what they said, something – is it time that has done it, or print, or is our taste too plebeian? – something at any rate is not as it should be. For having arranged the whole scene enthusiastically, according to Lady Dorothy's directions, and set noble men and women eating their oysters with knives or toying with a dish of home-grown truffles beneath a shower of prismatic glass in the great dining-room in Berkeley Square, we listen to the talk which, as Lady Dorothy tells us, people could talk then. After 'an awful pause' we hear Miss Gordon Cumming raise her voice. 'I beg to call the attention of the company to the very lucid interval between Novar's waistcoat and his trousers' – Munro of Novar, it must be said, was 'very unconventional in his attire'. 'This utterance naturally provoked uproarious laughter.'[8] Then Bernal Osborne, 'an autocrat of the dinner-table at which his sway was practically unquestioned', utters those brilliant but bitter personalities which delighted a society where all were friends. He nicknames one 'grave and dignified politician' 'the high-stepping hearse horse' 'of a somewhat colourless character' he says. 'He has no affections at all except rheumatic ones.' A political opponent with a slight twist in the neck he calls the man 'with the Tyburn face – a creature who had been imperfectly operated upon'.[9]

This display of wit may continue throughout a meal unchecked, or some unfortunate lady, who is only invited because she is rich, may quote French delightfully badly, and again, perhaps, provoke uproarious laughter. No one, so far as we can discover, of natural rather than hereditary gifts ever found his way into these dining-rooms, although Lady Dorothy assures us that 'the old leisured aristocracy . . .

delighted in gathering together people of conversational power, and for this reason alone certain individuals whose sole credentials were their wit and mental cultivation were accorded a place in society. There were several such men, of whose origin nothing was known or asked'[10] – so that we must lay the blame on the clever men themselves. Did they ask questions then? and if so, what answer would they get?

And with Lady Dorothy's volumes for text we must admit that the answer returned to our anxious questioning is a strange one. It is very natural that, writing of the past, she should write with regret, and wit, as every one knows, is perishable. But there is ample room in the space of two large volumes for something far more illuminating than a dozen obsolete epigrams, nor has she failed to construct round these poor tarnished little scenes a substantial edifice. It is in the strangeness, the audacity, the combined airiness and solidity of this conception that we must find the real value of her book and the answer to our question. For life is not merely a matter of dinner parties; there are the 'lower classes', country houses, politics and the arts. In order that you may have a society such as that which she laments, all these surroundings must be properly arranged in due relation to it. We must begin at the beginning, with the farmer. 'People,' she writes, 'were merry in those days ⟨the Thirties and Forties⟩ . . . Many of my father's tenants had held the same farm for generations, and all of them were imbued with great reverence for the old families.'[11] A robust kind of sympathy existed between the lord and his tenant, bred of dependence on the one side, benevolence on the other, which was comfortable and picturesque. They drew your carriage home for you on occasions of joy, and loaded the hall with cream of their own making on your marriage day. Innumerable customs and crafts still lingered in the pretty old villages, which the great lady loved to encourage, before the board schools came with their 'smatterings of many totally useless subjects' and destroyed the delightful practice, for example, of the art of 'buttony'.[12] There were still old chairs and tables to be picked up, for ridiculously small sums, in the country farms, and 'dignified and spiritual' traditions still flourished in illiterate minds; the whipping of the bounds was continued, and once even, but this was in happier days, an elder sister was 'obliged to dance in a hog's trough should the younger sister marry before her'.[13]

With this superficial rearrangement it is clear that life becomes far more amusing directly. It is so full of charming nooks and corners, in which superstitions and gallantries may lodge themselves, and picturesque inequality breaks up everywhere the monotony of plain human life. But, after all, this is no more than a pleasant disposition of the little village outside the park gates, and the heart of the whole matter is to be found within. How does Lady Dorothy approach her equals?

I have always been much interested in art and artistic people. I do not mean the kind of art which is associated with affectation and oleaginous pedantry, but the cult of what is curious and beautiful and interesting. At different times I have collected all sorts of things and attempted nearly all kinds of amateur work, including book illumination ... leather working, wood carving, and of late years a kind of old-fashioned leather work [...][14]

It is this sublimely insolent disrespect for art that vitiates the whole of the structure, for, surely, it is fatal if you are an aristocrat not to honour the only people who have imagination enough to believe in your beauty. And piecing together one phrase with another, the jests and opinions and habits, what an astonishing erection it is! She has collected watch papers and wedding rings and bills and old buttons, she has surrounded herself with odds and ends of furniture in all styles, she has bred silkworms and imported crayfish, she has visited innumerable picture galleries, and said 'How d'you do' to half the distinguished names in England. Rare dogs and strange birds and 'gifted men'[15] have amused her and paid her compliments. But why does the book, in spite of all these diversions, fill us with depression, as though on a rainy day we had lost ourselves in some dingy and rambling old house, crowded with ornaments, and frivolous in spite of its age? It is partly because it is so solid still in appearance and formidable with all the furniture of life, and partly because whatever genuine test you apply to it, it goes to pieces directly. If you were so rash as to quote Keats there an almost visible struggle would go on for a moment between the words and the atmosphere, alarming as a sudden precipice in a meadow; and afterwards the house is more shabby and less beautiful than ever, as though lightning had singed it. But lightning is rare, and such establishments continue to send their smoke up placidly enough in all the counties of England, and perhaps, melancholy as the conclusion is, do no great harm to anybody.

1 – A signed article in 'The Book on the Table' series in the *Cornhill Magazine*, April 1908, vol. xxiv, (Kp C23) based on *The Reminiscences of Lady Dorothy Nevill*. Edited by her son Ralph Nevill (E. Arnold, 1906); and on *Leaves from the Note-Books of Lady Dorothy Nevill*. Edited by Ralph Nevill (Macmillan & Co., 1907). See also 'Lady Dorothy Nevill' in 'Outlines', *IV VW Essays* and *CR1*.

2 – Mary Augusta Ward (1851–1920), better known as Mrs Humphry Ward, granddaughter of Thomas Arnold, philanthropical social worker, opponent of votes for women, and author. Her works include *Robert Elsmere* (1888), *Eleanor* (1900), *Lady Rose's Daughter* (1903), *Fenwick's Career* (1906) and *The Testing of Diana Mallory* (1908).

3 – Lady Dorothy Nevill (1826–1913), daughter of the 3rd Earl of Orford, author of *Mannington and the Walpoles, Earls of Orford* (1894) and of several volumes of reminiscences.

4 – *Note-Books*, ch. II, p. 22.

5 – *Ibid.*, p. 26.

6 – *Reminiscences*, ch. VIII, p. 103, which has: 'Many years ago, when I first knew London Society, it was more like a large family than anything else.'

7 – *Ibid.*, p. 100: '. . . though not extravagantly dowered with the good things of the world, it had no ulterior object beyond intelligent, cultured and dignified employment, money-making being left to another class which, from time to time, supplied a selected recruit to this corps d'élite.'

8 – For this episode, *Note-Books*, ch. II, p. 26.

9 – For Osborne's name-calling, *Reminiscences*, ch. IX, pp. 107–8.

10 – *Ibid.*, ch. VIII, p. 106.

11 – *Ibid.*, ch. II, p. 19, slightly adapted.

12 – *Ibid.*, ch. III, p. 34; p. 33 for 'buttony', or button-making, a 'very flourishing Dorsetshire village industry in my youth', a subject treated, as Lady Dorothy points out, in Hardy's *Tess of the d'Urbervilles* (1891).

13 – *Note-Books*, ch. XV, p. 312; p. 313.

14 – *Reminiscences*, ch. XVI, p. 217.

15 – Cf. *ibid.*, ch. VII, p. 93: '. . . that exceedingly gifted man Mr Hamilton Aide, whom I am glad to say I can still number amongst my friends.'

Wordsworth Letters

We have at last, in three stout volumes, a collection of Wordsworth's letters, including those already published and scattered in many books, some freshly discovered and a number written by his sister, his wife, and one or two near relatives as well. 'As the work progressed', says Professor Knight, "it became increasingly evident that no new *Life* of Wordsworth was needed.'[2] It might be well, as he suggests, that some one in the future should condense them and compose out of so much fresh matter a fresh picture of the writer, but he fears unfortunately that he must leave that task to a successor. In the meantime lovers of Wordsworth owe him their thanks for his labour, and in default of the arrangement of a master hand, must rejoice in the noble mass of material here given over to them.

But in what sense can it be said, as Professor Knight says, that 'few of his contemporaries, and none of his fellow poets, revealed themselves more fully than ⟨Wordsworth⟩ did'[3] in his letters? He loathed, we know, the labour of penmanship,[4] nor did his mind take naturally to the epistolary form. We never get from him the impression which the great letter-writers, Lamb or FitzGerald or Mrs Carlyle,[5] give us, that the scene which they have in their mind is precisely fit for a sheet of letter paper, and that it is a keen delight to smooth it out there. Wordsworth addressed himself to his task reluctantly, always under other compulsion than his own, and often with audible groans at that which had become a necessity. But the result is that nothing is uttered without urgent need for utterance; there is no frivolity or ornament; and the letters accumulate upon the imagination in a solid mass, and leave there a monument of his mind and nature monotonous and monolithic indeed, but impressive as an authentic building where every stone has been lifted laboriously to its place by the poet's own hand. The letters[6] again cover a long stretch of years, from 1790 to 1849, and must be held therefore to give the amplest possible comment upon his life; the three volumes should illustrate continuously the three periods of effort and achievement and repose. But, though with his poems before us we are able to arrange some such division, there is curiously little in the letters themselves to confirm it. A young man, who is to lead the great poetic revolution of his age, who meets for the first time with other young men of equal genius and with views that correspond with his, should, one conceives, write the most interesting letters in the language. But when we turn to one of the letters, printed here for the first time, written in 1799 and to Coleridge, our expectations are sublimely, if ludicrously, brushed aside. 'Dorothy is now sitting by me, racked with toothache.' The chimney smokes. They have hired a woman to wash the dishes – 'We could have had this attendance for eighteenpence a week, but we added the sixpence for the sake of the poor woman.' 'I feel little disposed to notice what you say of *Lyrical Ballads*.'[7] And when he does deal with matters of prime interest to them both, it is with the judicial discretion of middle age. 'When it is considered what has already been executed in poetry it is strange that a man cannot perceive, particularly when the present tendencies of society . . . are observed, that it is the time when a man of genius may honourably take a station upon different ground.'[8]

Epigram or any unpremeditated utterance which strikes the mind as though red hot, is not to be found in this cautious record of daily life and accumulating experience. And though there are some terse criticisms of writers – Walpole is 'that cold and false-hearted Frenchified coxcomb', Carlyle and Emerson write 'a language which they suppose to be English' – yet we have his own word for it that he 'never felt inclined to write criticism'.[9]

But, although it would be easy enough by quotation to establish the view that Wordsworth, when he was not inspired, had the mind of a country clergyman's wife, that is a piece of impertinence which the succession of the letters completely crushes out of existence. The 'revelation' which they make is so comprehensive that at the very moment when he shows you something petty or commonplace you become aware of the vast outline surrounding it, majestic and indifferent to your sneers. When we expect rhapsody and poetry we find instead careful reckoning of income, or wise plans for the education of the family left, by the death of both parents, in a precarious state. But we get also such words as those which Dorothy uses of her brother, when he was twenty-three. He has, she wrote, a 'violence of affection [. . .] which demonstrates itself every moment of the day [. . .] in a sort of restless watchfulness which I know not how to describe, a tenderness that never sleeps';[10] and their companionship, so equal, so simple, and so sincere, continued throughout their lives, is beautifully apparent; every letter hints at the exquisite relationship. They walk together, notice the same buds and clouds, read at the same table; and Dorothy, when she has given her criticisms, bids him, in fine words, trust the rest to posterity. 'His writing will live,' is her valiant assertion, 'when we and our little cares are all forgotten.'[11] The impression left by the long letters to Mathews, Wrangham, or Sir George Beaumont[12] is of a writer compelled to turn aside for a moment from a sight of absorbing interest; he will concentrate his mind upon his task, give advice, sympathy, or information, but all the while he is engrossed in the country outside the window, and the stern and sufficient life which he has shaped in harmony with it. Again and again he considers the perplexed lives of his friends, Coleridge or De Quincey, and sums up the position with the utmost sagacity. 'Do your duty to yourself immediately' he bids De Quincey. 'Love nature and books; seek these and you will be happy.'[13] He is not blind for a moment to the disastrous weakness underlying the splendid powers of Coleridge, but exposes it with the melancholy insight of a physician. 'I give it you as my deliberate opinion, formed upon proofs that have been strengthening for years, that he neither will nor can execute anything of important benefit to himself, his family, or mankind.'[14] And yet nothing shakes his belief in Coleridge's powers; no one upholds with greater reverence the sanctity of genius, or believes more profoundly in the immeasurable virtue of poetry. This constant faith kindles all these sober judgments, the sheets of political pessimism, the elaborate instructions for the laying out of a garden, the minute description of colours and shapes on the hillside, and, unifying them, proves them all so much fuel for the true fire of poetry. 'To be incapable of a feeling for poetry, in my sense of the word, is to be without love of human nature and reverence for God.'[15]

This, then, is the source of the satisfaction which encompasses us as we read on with little humour or variety of mood to entice us. There is no gulf between the stuff of daily life and the stuff of poetry, save that one is the raw material of the other; and the change is effected constantly, even before our eyes – 'things are lost in each other, and limits vanish, and aspirations are raised'.[16] When he walks in London, melancholy and very thoughtful, he suddenly becomes aware that Fleet Street lies before him, under snow, 'silent, empty, and pure white [. . .] I cannot say how much I was affected . . . and what a blessing I felt there is in habits of exalted imagination. My sorrow was controlled, and . . . seemed at once to receive the gift of an anchor of security.'[17] There is arrogance in that, perhaps, but it is of the kind that makes us ask how we are to distinguish between a reverence for himself and a reverence for nature. The pitch of a common life that permits these transitions is very high; and when, now and again, he speaks of his own beliefs, or his own unhappiness, the words have a poignancy that reaches to the uttermost depths. Beautiful, though we smile, is the sense that comes over him abroad of his own irritability, so that he must ask pardon of his wife at once. 'Dearest Mary, when I have felt how harshly I often demeaned myself to you . . . while correcting the last edition of my poems, I often pray to God . . . that I may make some amends to you . . . You have forgiven me, I know, as you did then; and perhaps that somehow troubles me the more.'[18] Such feelings come frequently to mitigate, with curious pathos, the loneliness and austerity of his figure, and assure us that at no point did he lose his power of living, as he says, 'in the midst of the realities of things'.[19] Metaphors rise constantly to the lips in thinking of him which shall express his majesty, his serenity, in the form of some enduring natural object, a mountain or a river. But it is the merit of the letters that they forbid impersonal abstractions. Noble as his life was, they show it to be made of common stuff, 'transmuted', as he would have said, into a permanent shape by the perfect sincerity of his ambition. His daily life, exposed to us here so largely, and with such indifference to effect, has thus the same quality that moves us in the deepest of his poems; it points unswervingly, through trials and obscurities, to the most exalted end.

1 – A review in the *TLS*, 2 April 1908, (Kp c13) of *Letters of the Wordsworth Family. From 1787 to 1855*. Collected and edited by William Knight (3 vols, Ginn & Co., 1907). See also for William Wordsworth (1770–1850) 'Wordsworth and the Lakes' above; and for Dorothy Wordsworth (1771–1855) see 'Four Figures', *V VW Essays* and *CR2*.

2 – *Letters*, vol. I, Pref., p. v.

3 – *Ibid.*, p. vi.

4 – *Ibid.*, vol. III, App. II, to S. T. Coleridge, Christmas Eve 1799, p. 449: 'Composition I find invariably pernicious to me, and even penmanship, if continued for any length of time at one sitting'; also, vol. II, to Francis Wrangham, January 1816, p. 67: '... my miserable penmanship'.

5 – Charles Lamb (1775–1834); Edward Fitzgerald (1809–83); Jane Welsh Carlyle (1801–66); see 'The Letters of Jane Welsh Carlyle' above, and 'More Carlyle Letters' below.

6 – I.e., those by William Wordsworth.

7 – *Letters*, vol. III, App. II, p. 446; p. 447; p. 449: 'I suspect that it may partly be owing to something like unconscious affectation, but in honest truth I feel little disposed to notice what you say of *Lyrical Ballads*, though the account when I first read it gave me pleasure.'

8 – *Ibid.*, App. II, to S. T. Coleridge, 19 April 1808, p. 467; the ellipsis marks the omission of '(good and bad)'.

9 – *Ibid.*, vol. III, to Alexander Dyce, 20 March 1833, p. 5; to Henry Reed, 16 August 1841, p. 229; to William Rowan Hamilton, 4 January 1838, p. 152: 'Although prevailed upon by Mr Coleridge to write the first *Preface* to my poems ... and induced by my friendship for him to write the *Essay upon Epitaphs* ... I have never felt inclined to write criticism, though I have talked, and am daily talking, a great deal.'

10 – *Ibid.*, vol. I, Dorothy Wordsworth to Jane Pollard, 16 February 1793, pp. 48–9.

11 – *Ibid.*, vol. II, Dorothy Wordsworth to Mrs Clarkson, 15 August 1816, p. 94. 'His writing will live, will comfort the afflicted, and animate the happy to purer happiness; when we, and our little cares, are all forgotten ... '

12 – William Mathews (1769–1801), journalist and barrister, brother of the comic actor Charles Mathews, was a friend and contemporary of Wordsworth at Cambridge. He contracted yellow fever and died a disappointed man shortly after settling in Tobago. Francis Wrangham (1769–1842), classical scholar, clergyman and

author of several works including volumes of verse, both original and translated; he and Wordsworth once considered collaborating in a volume of satirical pieces. Sir George Beaumont (1753–1827), connoisseur, patron, and landscape painter, and his wife Margaret, *née* Willes, of Coleorton Hall, were close friends of the Wordsworths.

13 – *Letters*, vol. I, 6 March 1804, p. 161; 'Do not on any account fail to tell me whether you are satisfied with yourself since your migration to Oxford; if not, do your duty to yourself immediately. Love nature and books; seek these, and you will be happy; for virtuous friendship, and love, and knowledge of mankind must inevitably accompany these, all things thus ripening in their due season.'

14 – *Ibid.*, vol. I, to Thomas Poole, c. May 1809, p. 457, which has 'proofs which', not 'proofs that have been'.

15 – *Ibid.*, vol. I, to Lady Beaumont, 21 May 1807, p. 303: 'This is a truth, and an awful one, because to be incapable of a feeling for poetry . . . '

16 – *Ibid.*, vol. II, to Walter Savage Landor, 21 January 1824, p. 215: 'Even in poetry it is the imaginative only, viz., that which is conversant with, or turns upon infinity that powerfully affects me . . . I mean to say that, unless in those passages where things are lost in each other, and limits vanish, and aspirations are raised, I read with something too much like indifference.'

17 – *Ibid.*, vol. I, to Sir George Beaumont, 8 April ?1808, p. 349, which has: 'My sorrow was controlled, and my uneasiness of mind – not quieted and relieved altogether – seemed at once to receive the gift of an anchor of security.'

18 – *Ibid.*, vol. III, to Mary Wordsworth, 5 July ?1837, p. 136.

19 – *Ibid.*, vol. I, to Sir George Beaumont, 17 October 1805, p. 204: 'The true servants of the Arts pay homage to the human kind as impersonated in unwarped and enlightened minds. / If this be so when we are merely putting together words or colours, how much more ought the feeling to prevail when we are in the midst of the realities of things . . . '

John Delane

If, in the middle days of the last century, you had seen the figure of a certain tall young man, ruddy of complexion and powerful of build, you might have foretold a dozen successful careers for him, as squire, lawyer, or man of business, but perhaps you would not have fitted him at once with his indubitable calling. That spark of genius, for surely it was not less, flashed in the brain of John Walter, proprietor of *The Times*,[2] when he saw the second son of a neighbour of his in the country riding to hounds or conducting a successful election on his behalf. John Thadeus Delane[3] went to Oxford and distinguished himself there rather as a bold rider – 'Mr Delane is part and parcel of his horse,' wrote his tutor[4] – a tennis-player, or a boxer (for the hot Irish blood in him would rise) than as a nice scholar or a mathematician. His letters to his friend George Dasent[5] show him something of a philistine, with a command of vigorous and wholesome English, lending itself happily to such casual remarks as those he had to make about his studies and his sports. He did not know, for instance, 'how I am to cram a sufficient store of divinity into my head. As the premises will only be occupied a short time with the last-named commodity, the trouble of storing it should be slight. [I must] try to secure a patent safety vehicle . . . This is a most glorious country – capital people, excellent horses, prime feeding, and very fair shooting.'[6] Such is the slang of the Forties, which, with its comfortable lapse from the dignity of contemporary prose, reveals a young man lazily conscious of his power, with a capacity for shooting words straight if need be, and for distorting them at will, which is the despair of lady novelists who seek to reproduce it.

Directly he had taken his degree, in 1840, he went to Printing House Square, and was occupied with various duties about the paper. Little is said of their nature, or of the way in which he discharged them, for he had now entered that unnamed world which is crowded but unchecked; there are duties which belong to no profession, nor are the limits of work bounded so long as the brain urges on. He made himself familiar with the House of Commons, we are told, 'summarising the remarks of the principal speakers'.[7] We must imagine how swiftly he took the measure of the world around him, gauging silently the capacity of his machine for reporting and perhaps for directing the turmoil. A year later, at any rate, when Mr Barnes, the editor, died, Mr Walter had no hesitation in choosing 'the youngest member of all the staff', whose age was then twenty-three, to succeed him.[8] Sense and industry and ability were his, but the easy margin of strength, as of a loosely fitting coat, which may be detected in his Oxford letters, marked him, to a discriminating eye, as the man who would put forth greater power than he had yet shown, with a competent tool in his hand, or would so weld himself to his instrument that their joint stroke would be irresistible. But it is one of the mysteries that tempt us and baffle us in this biography that the transition is almost unmarked. We hear Mr Delane exclaim once, in 'tremendous spirits', 'By Jove, John, . . . I am editor of *The Times*,'[9] but in future the editor and *The Times* are one, as in the old days the undergraduate was part of his horse. What the condition of the paper was when he came to it, or what private estimate he had formed of its scope, we are not told. But as all agree that the age of Delane was the great age, and that the paper grew with its editor, we may believe that he undertook the task without articulate reflection, conscious of a power within him that would soon fill all the space permitted it. 'What I dislike about you young men of the present day is that you all shrink from responsibility,'[10] he was wont to laugh, when people wondered.

Much of the paper's industry as chronicler and reporter and simple publisher was merely that of a gigantic natural force, sucking in and casting forth again its daily cloud of print impartially; and the editor was lost in its shade. But almost at once the brain of the monster, which expressed itself daily in the four leading articles, was given cause to show its quality. There was a 'ministerial crisis' and Delane had not only to anticipate the rest of the world in publishing the news, but to express an opinion. No study, were there material for it, could be more fascinating than the analysis of such an opinion. Hawthorne himself might have found scope for all his imagination, all his love of darkness and mystery, in tracing it from its first secret whisper to its final reverberation over the entire land. A great minister sends for the editor to his private room, and speaks to him; a note from someone who has picked up a word at Court is left on him; instantly, with an audacity that may land him in disaster, he fits the parts together, and instructs his leader-writer to embody them in a column of English prose; to-morrow a voice speaks with authority in Court and market and Council Chamber. But whose voice is it? It is not the voice of Mr Delane, the urbane gentleman who rides along Fleet Street on his cob, nor is it the voice of Dr Woodham,[11] the learned Fellow of Jesus. It has the authority of Government and the sting of independence; Downing Street trembles at it and the people of England give ear to it, for such is the voice of *The Times*.

It is easy to submit to the fascination of the idea, and to conceive a monster in Printing House Square without personality but with an infallible knowledge of persons, ruthless as a machine and subtle as a single brain. And there are facts in this book which seem to justify the most extravagant statement that we can make. There is, of course, the romantic story of *The Times* and the repeal of the Corn Laws; we read also how Louise Philippe and Guizot thought it worth their while to impede the paper's correspondence; how the Tsar heard of the Ultimatum of 1854 through *The Times*, and not through the Foreign Office; how it was objected in the House of Lords that Cabinet secrets were made public, and *The Times* answered, 'We are satisfied that it was useful to the public and to Europe';[12] how *The Times* foretold the Indian Mutiny, and was the first to reveal the state of the army in the Crimea; how *The Times* was foremost with the Queen's Speech and with texts and resignations innumerable; making ministries, deciding policies, exalting statesmen, and casting them down. The list might be lengthened, but surely without avail; for already there is some risk lest we grow beyond our strength and forget, what these volumes should recall, the character, the individual will, directing this giant force and placing its blows in such tender quarters. His contemporaries certainly did not forget, for it was the independence of the paper that was chiefly valuable, or dangerous, as fortune chanced, and the spirit that preserved it from the blunt blow and shapeless mass of a machine was of course the spirit of Mr Delane. Together with these triumphs of organisation we read of other triumphs that are no less remarkable. Prime ministers and secretaries of state lay aside (with relief one guesses) their impassive public countenance, and entrust Mr Delane not only with state secrets, but with private prejudices of their own. Here was one with greater knowledge than the best instructed of ministers, with whom no secrecy availed, who was moreover so sequestered from the public eye that you might approach him without reserve, as patients their physician, or penitents their confessor. A letter from Lord Palmerston begins, 'I am told you disapprove ... '[13] and goes on to justify his action with allusions to foreign politics and the gout which, though each had a share in his behaviour, would not have been used to explain it either to the public or to his friends.

The anonymity which Delane took such care to preserve was no doubt of the utmost value in the conduct of the paper, investing it with an impersonal majesty; but there is reason to think that it came from no mere professional policy but was a deep seated instinct in the character of the man. He was infinitely receptive, and so far 'anonymous' by nature that the broad columns of *The Times*, filled with the writing of other men but sharpened and guided by himself, expressed all of him that he chose to express. When he left his rooms in the morning he rode about London, followed by a groom, calling at the House of Commons or at Downing Street, and took his lunch with one great lady and his tea with another. He dined out almost nightly, and met frequently all the great nobles and celebrities of the time. But his demeanour, we are told, was inscrutable; he was of opinion that society should be exclusive; and his attitude generally was one of 'observant silence'. He never mentioned

The Times after he had left the office, though the paper was always in his thoughts. At length, when he had stored his mind with observations, he returned to Printing House Square, and, with his energies at full play and his staff circling round him, shaped the course of the paper in accordance with his own view until it was three or four in the morning and he must rest before the labours of the day. And yet, in spite of his silence – his broad way of looking at tendencies and institutions rather than at individuals – men and women, we read, gave him their confidences. They were sure of able consideration from a man who had infinite experience of men, but, as it appears from his letters, they were sure also of a massive integrity which inspired absolute trust, both that he would respect your secret, and that he would respect, more than you or your secret, what was right. His letters, however, can seldom be said to add anything that the columns of *The Times* have not already supplied; but they are token again of the literal truth of his phrase, when there was talk of his retirement, 'All that was worth having of ⟨my life⟩ has been devoted to the paper.'[14]

There was not sufficient space between his professional life and his private life for any change of view or difference of code. We may find in that fact some clue to the amazing authority which he wielded, for it is easy to see that if you disproved some opinion of his or disparaged some method, you aimed a blow at the nature of the man himself, the two being of one birth. When he travelled abroad and visited towns famous for their beauty or their art he was unconscious of their appeal, but was inclined to adopt on such occasions the attitude of a portly gentleman with pretty children. Perhaps he had noticed some new factory or some stout bridge from the train window, and had found in it the text of a leading article. He travelled much, and visited any place that might become the centre of action; and in time of peace he went on pilgrimage through the great houses of England, where the nerves of the country come nearest to the surface. It was his purpose to know all that could be known of the condition and future of Europe, so far as certain great signs reveal it, and if he ignored much there was no wiser or more discriminating judge of the symptoms he chose to observe.

One quality seems to mark his judgments and to add to their value – they are so dispassionate. The indifference he always showed to what was thought of him came, naturally, from his well-founded trust in himself; but there was another reason for it, once or twice hinted in the course of this book, and once at least outspoken. The paper was more to him than his own fortunes, and, thus divested of personality, he came to take a gigantic and even humorous view of the whole, which sometimes seems to us sublime, sometimes callous, and sometimes, when we read certain phrases near the end, very melancholy. He was the most attentive observer of the political life of his age, but he took no part in it. When he was attacked he gave, with one exception,[15] no answer. His anonymity, his reticence – no man was to take his portrait or to make him look ridiculous – are allied surely with the casual bluntness of speech and indifference to praise or blame which gave his opinion its peculiar weight. 'Something like consternation prevailed at the War Office and at the Horse Guards when it became known that Delane intended to be present upon Salisbury Plain.'[16] But could he have cared so much for the world, for politics, for the welfare of numbers had he not been indifferent to his personal share in it? Or again, would he so soon have tired of the scene had some part of it touched him more nearly? Again and again the phrase recurs, 'The New Year found me, as the last had done, alone at Printing House Square', and the loneliness deepened as life drew on until we find such a sentence as this: 'Nobody now (his mother being dead) cares about me or my success, or my motives, and that weariness of life I had long felt has been gaining on me ever since . . . I have much to be thankful for, [but] I have become so indifferent to life . . . weary both of work and idleness, careless about society and with failing interests.'[17] But it would be unwise to allow such a sentence to set its seal upon the rest, or to colour too sadly that colossal erection of courage and devotion which he called 'the Paper'; his success only was tinged with 'a browner shade' than it might otherwise have worn.

When he was middle-aged he bought himself a tract of common near Ascot, and busied himself in reclaiming the land and in playing the farmer. It is easy to see him there, looking much like a country squire with the interests of his crops at heart, as he rode about and drew in great draughts of the open air. From the clods of earth and the watery English sky he received a passive satisfaction, and came perhaps to enjoy an easier intercourse with these dumb things than with human beings.

1 – A signed article in 'The Book on the Table' series, *Cornhill Magazine*, June 1908, vol. XXIV, (Kp C24) based on *The Life and Letters of John Thadeus Delane* (2 vols, John Murray, 1908) by Arthur Irwin Dasent. The article appeared without revision in the *Living Age*, Boston, 18 July 1908. Reprinted: *B&P*.

VW found the subject distinctly uncongenial. 'I have a long letter of instruction from R. Smith [the *Cornhill*'s editor],' she wrote to Lytton Strachey from St Ives, 22 April 1908 (*I VW Letters*, no. 408). 'He bids me bring out the human side "his unswerving loyalty, alike to subordinates and chief – in a word the high qualities of head and heart which" etc etc.' Smith approved of her finished article – 'it is an ill omen' (*ibid.*, no. 411) – but, to her fury, 'added words to my sentences, cut out others' (*ibid.*, no. 413), until she threatened to resign. See also *I VW Letters*, nos 405, 407, 409.

2 – John Walter (1776–1847), second son of the paper's founder.

3 – John Thadeus Delane (1817–79) edited *The Times*, of which his father was financial manager, from 1841; he graduated from Magdalen Hall, Oxford, in 1839 and was called to the bar at Middle Temple in 1840.

4 – Dr William Jacobson (1803–84), later Bishop of Chester; for his remarks about his pupil's resemblance to 'the Centaurs of old', see Dasent, vol. I, p. 18.

5 – (Sir) George Webbe Dasent (1817–96), a contemporary of Delane at Oxford, was assistant editor of *The Times*, 1845–70, and in 1846 married Delane's sister; he was also an eminent scholar of Norse. Arthur Irwin Dasent was his son, and so Delane's nephew.

6 – Dasent, vol. I, pp. 21–2, letter dated 14 September 1839 and written from Barnet by Le Wold, Lincolnshire.

7 – *Ibid.*, p. 23: 'summarising the remarks of the principal speakers in both Houses'.

8 – *Ibid.*, Thomas Barnes (1785–1841) edited *The Times* from 1817 until his death.

9 – *Ibid.*, p. 26; the exclamation was addressed to his friend John Blackwood with whom he shared lodgings in St James's Square.

10 – *Ibid.*

11 – Dr Henry Annesley Woodham (c. 1813–75), Fellow of Jesus College, Cambridge, 1841–8, honorary fellow, 1862–75, and regular contributor to *The Times*.

12 – Dasent, vol. I, p. 170; this was in February and March 1854 and concerns the political preliminaries to the Crimean War, declared on 27 March.

13 – *Ibid.*, p. 302, letter dated 10 November 1858: 'I am told that you disapprove of the visit of Clarendon and myself to the Emperor at Compiègne, but it seemed to us impolite to avoid going thither. ¶ The invitation was not sought for by us . . . '

14 – *Ibid.*, vol. II, p. 333, to John Walter, 19 March 1877.

15 – VW is possibly referring to Delane's response in 1863 to an attack on him, in his own name rather than as the editor of *The Times*, by Richard Cobden defending John Bright in the correspondence columns of the *Daily News*.

16 – Dasent, vol. II, p. 292, which continues: ' . . . for the military authorities from the Commander-in-chief downwards, stood in wholesome awe of the criticisms of *The Times* and the familiarity possessed by its editor with the minutest details of army organisation.'

17 – *Ibid.*, pp. 255–6, slightly adapted; from the final entry in Delane's diary for 1869 and the last he made for some years.

'The Diary of a Lady-in-Waiting'

Lady Charlotte Bury was the daughter of the fifth Duke of Argyll,[2] and her beauty and her wit made her at once the talk of London when she came up to town in the last years of the eighteenth century. But her head was full of romance, and she preferred a marriage with her kinsman, Jack Campbell, who was handsome, 'a great fellow',[3] but badly off, to an alliance with some rich nobleman in England. They lived in Edinburgh for the most part, and Lady Charlotte was queen of the literary society there, scribbling her own verses, and receiving the compliments of Walter Scott, C. K. Sharpe, and Monk Lewis.[4] Their circumstances, however, were never easy; nine children were born to them, and, when she was thirty-four, her husband died, and left her to bring them up as she might. The natural profession, for a woman with her connexions, was about the Court; and it is characteristic of her that she sought service with the Princess of Wales, with whom she had long sympathised, although the Princess was then in an uncomfortable situation, separated from her husband and estranged from the Royal family. At the same time Lady Charlotte began to keep a diary, and it is this work which is now reprinted, with the omission of certain unnecessary parts, and the addition of a great number of names which the discretion of previous editors thought fit to conceal beneath a dash. As it is, the size of the volumes is sufficiently formidable, and were it not for the watery Georgian atmosphere which they preserve we might wish that Lady Charlotte's sentiments had been curtailed. 'Those evanescent emanations of spirit which are only cognisable to the very few, and which thrive not unless under the influence of congenial feelings'[5] have fallen, to continue her metaphor, upon a barren soil, and are withered by the cold blight of criticism.

The Princess of Wales's court, if it has a right to the name was a comfortless and incongruous place. She kept up all the forms of royalty at Kensington and Blackheath, but she was constantly meeting with some insolence from the great nobles, and flouting them with an irresponsible outburst of wild spirits. She would walk solemnly with her ladies in Kensington Gardens and suddenly 'bolt out at one of the smaller gates and walk all over Bayswater and along the Paddington Canal',[6] asking at every door whether there were any houses to be let, and chuckling at her own ingenuity. Some respectable people stood by her, and gave her parties the semblance of dignity, but as soon as these gentlemen left she 'felt a weight'[7] off her. 'She calls it *dull*' observes Lady Charlotte, or, in her own phrase, '*Mine Gott!* Dat is de dullest person Gott Almighty ever did born!' 'and true enough,' the moralist proceeds, '*good* society is often dull.'[8] Brougham and Whitbread[9] were always coming with documents for her to sign, and good advice for her to follow. There was perpetual talk of policy, whether she should go to the opera, whether she should accept the Regent's terms, or hold out for her own rights; she was always acting on the spur of the moment, and upsetting calculations that were not, as Lady Charlotte guessed, entirely disinterested. They go over the whole story of her wrongs again and again, at these dreary dinner parties; and when that subject becomes intolerable, she chatters about books, or talks scandal, wishes people dead, or sings – 'squall – squall – squall'[10] – with the Sapios, for she loved to imagine herself the centre of a brilliant society. Lady Charlotte had much to deplore from the first, although her kind and sentimental heart was constantly touched by the poor lady's miseries,[11] the cause, she guessed, of much of her levity; and she had sense enough to see that a little good management at this crisis might have invaluable results. The Princess occasionally would act with the utmost dignity, or endure some insult without a word, so that Lady Charlotte herself felt humiliated. A friend reported on one occasion that the Tsar of Russia meant to call upon her, an honour for which she said she would give both her ears, though they are 'very ugly'.[12] She dressed in delight, and waited all the' afternoon, with Lady Charlotte beside her, till it was seven o'clock. For four hours they sat opposite each other keeping up a miserable small talk; and, though the Tsar never came, the Princess would not own that she was disappointed. It was not wonderful, perhaps, that she should relapse after these fruitless efforts into wilder dissipation than ever. When there was no company she would sit over the fire after dinner modelling a little figure of her husband in wax, transfixing it with a pin, and holding it over the flames so that it melted away. Was one to laugh, or was it not unspeakably tragic? Sometimes, says Lady Charlotte, she had the feelings of one who humours a mad woman.

But advice and sentiment had no power to stay the course of the uneasy woman; she was too sensitive to ignore the slights which people who, as she observed, would eat her food thought fit to put upon her, and she was foolish enough to seek redress by making friends of her inferiors. The description which Lady Charlotte gives of 'that incongruous piece of patchwork', the villa at Blackheath – 'It is all glitter and glare and trick; everything is tinsel and trumpery about it; it is altogether like a bad dream'[13] – represents very well the impression which her life makes upon us; it is like Cremorne or Vauxhall by daylight, when the lamps are out, and the pale minarets and pagodas are exposed to the sun, with all their stains and frivolities and their midnight grimace. Lady Charlotte's proprieties were constantly shocked; and, as she could in no way prevent the disaster, she left her mistress in 1814, without offending her, in order, she pretended, to take her children to Geneva. She was little more, however, than a correct and kindly woman, with a diffuse taste for sentiment of all kinds, whether in people, or art, or letters, and, when she had no point to concentrate her mind upon, her observations become insipid. The Princess of Wales, vulgar and flighty as she was, had the quality of making people interested in her, not for her fate alone, but because she had lively feelings and expressed them nakedly. Lady Charlotte when set adrift upon the Continent and exposed now to a picture, now to a church, now to the historical associations of Versailles, floats, with all her sails spread, upon a leaden sea. 'I gazed once more at the undying beauties of the immortal Venus. I felt a spark of inspiration emanate from the divine Apollo . . . Time and circumstance tore me away.' She came at length to Geneva, and settled herself in the midst of the 'literary and scientific republic', smiling and sighing when she remembered the 'great stage of life'[14] upon which she had acted so lately. But she was not to philosophise for long. The rumour spread that the Princess, with a motley court, was upon them, and some of the English ladies hastily made up a ball in her honour. With what an expression Lady Charlotte gazed upon the figure of her late mistress, dressed '*en Venus*', waltzing all night long, we can imagine; it is a delightful picture. 'I was unfeignedly grieved . . . and thought it would be my own fault if she caught me again in a hurry.'[15] But Lady Charlotte was too good-natured to desert any one in difficulties; she had a family to support; and after a few months she joined the Princess at Genoa as her lady-in-waiting. She found that Mr Craven and Mr Gell,[16] her respectable English friends, had left her, and her own position was more odious than ever. Bergami,[17] the tall Italian courier, was now the favourite, and the Princess drove about in a carriage shaped like a sea-shell, lined with blue velvet and drawn by piebald ponies. She protested that she meant to travel on and on, to visit Greece, and never to return to England. Lady

Charlotte had to shut both eyes and ears; but her charity was at length exhausted, and she finally left the Princess in 1815, the last of the English courtiers to stay with her. Lady Charlotte went to Rome, and the Princess wandered about Italy, adding doubtful countesses 'of decayed nobility' to her train, and abbés who could speak forty-four different languages, both living and dead, in perfection – so 'they assure me'.[18] The last sight of her was reported by an English lady living at Florence, who came upon a procession of carriages at some little country village, drawn by the piebald horses, and occupied by a 'rabble rout' of low-looking men and women, dressed like 'itinerant show players' of all nationalities; among them was 'one fat woman', who was said to be the Princess of Wales.[19] Most readers will be tempted to skip the reflections which Lady Charlotte has to record about Rome, for she echoed the taste of her time, and it is not ours; but she corresponded still with the Princess and received from her a number of those odd ungrammatical letters, where all the *t*s are *d*s, which still sound so lively, so absurd, and so unhappy.

All de fine English folk leave me ⟨she writes⟩. I not send them away, though, bye the bye, some of dem not behave as civil as I could like.[20] . . . I detest Rome. It is the burial-place of departed grandeur. It is very well to see it once, like a raree show . . . I shall die of de blue devils, as you English call it . . .[21] Very often we cook our own dinner! What voud de English people say if dey heard dat? Oh, fie! Princess of Wales.[22]

Lady Charlotte returned to London in 1819, in order to introduce an orphan niece to the world. She was forty-four, and the diary, though it is still as profuse as ever, describes merely the respectable life of a lady living in good society, with the remains of beauty, and many memories of happier days. Major Denham described the interior of Africa;[23] Tom Moore sang 'The Parting of the Ships', 'each to sail over the lonely ocean! How very true it is to nature! How thrilling to those who have witnessed the scene!'[24] Once she met Mrs Mee, the miniature painter, and 'another eccentric little artist, by name Blake', who talked to her about his painting, and seemed to her full of imagination and genius. She saw Sir Thomas Lawrence sneer as he watched them.[25] But the diary ends, fitly enough, with the death of Queen Caroline a few days after she had knocked at the door of Westminster Abbey in vain.[26] Many people felt that there was an end to an awkward situation; Lady Charlotte, as one might expect, had a final word of regret for the poor woman, and in this case, at least, we may believe that she meant it, for she had been a good friend.

1 – A review in the *TLS*, 23 July 1908, (Kp C14) of *The Diary of a Lady-in-Waiting by Charlotte Bury* 'being the diary illustrative of the times of George the Fourth interspersed with original letters from the late Queen Caroline and from other distinguished persons'. Edited with an introduction by A. Francis Steuart (2 vols, John Lane, 1908). The *Diary* was originally published anonymously in 1838 and enjoyed an immense *succès de scandale*. Reprinted: *B&P*. See also *I VW Letters*, no. 422.

2 – Lady Charlotte Susan Maria Bury (1775–1861), was the younger daughter of John, 5th Duke of Argyll, and his wife Elizabeth, *née* Gunning; she had married in 1796 Col. John Campbell (d. 1809), eldest of fifteen children of Walter Campbell of Shawfield, and, at the time of his death, M.P. for Ayr. In 1809 she was appointed lady-in-waiting to the Princess of Wales – Caroline Amelia Elizabeth of Brunswick-Wolfenbüttel (1768–1821), the unfortunate wife of George IV (1762–1830), whom Princess Caroline had married in 1795. In 1818 Lady Charlotte married the Rev. Edward John Bury (d. 1832).

3 – Bury, vol. 1, Intro., p. vi.

4 – Sir Walter Scott (1771–1832) to whose *Border Minstrelsy* (1802–3), the antiquary and artist Charles Kirkpatrick Sharpe (1781?–1851) became a contributor, and to Scott a close friend. Matthew Gregory Lewis (1775–1818), author of the lurid romance *Ambrosio, or the Monk* (1796).

5 – Bury, vol. 1, p. 31: 'There is something very interesting in Mr L—... Not that he is devoid of affection for his wife and children; but the finer particles of his nature, those evanescent emanations of spirit which are only cognisable to the very few, and which thrive not unless under the influence of congenial feelings, are dried up and withered within himself; and I should think can hardly be called to life again by any living object.'

6 – *Ibid.*, p. 16; the concluding 'chuckling at her own ingenuity' appears to be an embellishment by VW.

7 – *Ibid.*, p. 107.

8 – *Ibid.*, p. 158.

9 – Henry Peter Brougham (1778–1868), statesman, lawyer and litterateur, created Baron Brougham and Vaux with his appointment in 1830 as Lord Chancellor. According to the *DNB*, he was, from about 1811, 'constantly' consulted by the Princess of Wales. Samuel Whitbread (1758–1815), politician and prosperous brewer.

10 – Bury, vol. 1, p. 103, which has: 'The Princess made many complaints of *La reine des Ostrogoths*, and long histories about the Squallinis, and the G—s. If she likes busying herself with such objects, I do not. The old ourang outang came to dinner, – more free and easy and detestable than ever, – ... Then her Royal Highness sang – squall – squall – squall! Why invite me?'

11 – The text printed in the *TLS* has 'ladies' miseries'.

12 – Bury, vol. 1, p. 212.

13 – *Ibid.*, p. 19, which has: 'The Princess's villa at Blackheath is an incongruous piece of patch-work. It may dazzle for a moment, when lighted up at night; but it is all glitter . . . '

14 – For her sight of Venus in the Louvre and her impressions of Genoa: *ibid.*, vol. I, pp. 251–2; p. 271; p. 270.

15 – *Ibid.*, p. 280; the quotation is drawn from different sentences and paragraphs.

16 – Keppell Richard Craven (1778–1851), traveller and author of books of Italian travel; and Sir William Gell (1777–1836), knighted in 1803, classical archaeologist and traveller – both appointed in 1814 as chamberlains to Princess Caroline.

17 – Bartolomeo Pergami, known in England as Bergami, a former Italian subaltern, now promoted by the Princess from courier to chamberlain and soon to be found a barony in Sicily and to be granted the knighthood of Malta.

18 – 'of decayed nobility' appears to be a paraphrase; *ibid.*, vol. II, p. 29: 'J'ai fait aussi des connaissances très intéressantes pendant mon voyage [illegible] l'Abbé Mezofanti, bibliothécaire à Bologna . . . il possède le grand talent de parler quarante-quatre différentes langues, mortes et vivantes, en perfection, comme on m'assure.'

19 – *Ibid.*, p. 53.

20 – *Ibid.*, p. 152.

21 – *Ibid.*, p. 164.

22 – *Ibid.*, p. 167.

23 – *Ibid.*, pp. 200–1; Dixon Denham (1786–1828), soldier and African traveller.

24 – *Ibid.*, p. 203; the song referred to by Thomas Moore (1779–1852) is possibly 'A Canadian Boat-Song' (1806).

25 – *Ibid.*, pp. 213–14; Anne Mee, *née* Foldsone (1775?–1851), miniature painter, was much patronised by royalty and the aristocracy, as could not be said for William Blake (1757–1827). Sir Thomas Lawrence (1769–1830), knighted in 1815, president of the Royal Academy from 1820, a favourite of both Georges III and IV, and it seems of Princess Caroline whose portrait, together with her daughter Princess Charlotte, he painted; his relations with the Princess of Wales, in particular an alleged 'undue familiarity' in the painting room at Montagu House, Blackheath, were a subject of the famous 'delicate investigation' into the Princess's conduct.

26 – *Ibid.*, p. 274; forbidden to attend her husband's coronation, Queen Caroline was repulsed from the Abbey by soldiers.

The Stranger in London

Every one who writes at all writes a diary of impressions when he travels abroad. The scene is so new, so original, and so charmingly arranged as though on purpose to be looked at and written about, that the fingers curve round a visionary pen, and the lips form words instinctively. It would be pleasant to think that this habit is not altogether vain; and the eagerness with which we read foreign impressions of ourselves gives us good reason to hope. It is not necessary to be profound, to compare situations, or to forecast the future in order to interest; all that is required of you is to see truly, and to describe as closely as may be. The gift is almost obsolete among natives, of a respectable age, for the same reason that you rarely find a middle-aged person who can describe the shape of a coal scuttle. Oxford Street, Kensington Gardens, Piccadilly – the names of these places alone rouse so many echoes, the sight of them is so confused with a multitude of other sights, that a cockney who should sit down to describe them might end with an essay upon party government, or a dissertation upon the immortality of the soul. The impressions of M. Huard and Herr Rutari make excellent reading because they have a certain detachment; we see our surface as though in some spontaneous mirror, and yet the image there is coloured by a number of personal and national idiosyncrasies which make it in another sense full of suggestions for us. The foundation of the picture is much the same in both cases. Each traveller exclaims at the size of London, its uproar, its multitudes, its incongruities. One might think, to hear them, that Paris was a clean country town, and Berlin a centre of provincial culture, like Leeds. Each takes a drive through the streets and is bewildered and exhilarated by the innumerable types which pour through the narrow channels, always moving, always changing, and giving off a perpetual uproar. Each marvels at the dexterity of the newsboys, and at the majesty of the policemen. They visit the City, the Tower, Greenwich, and show themselves sensitive, as only foreigners are, to the imprisonments and executions which have taken place there. Êtes-vous bien sûr,' M. Huard asked the guard at the Tower, 'qu'aucun fantôme n'erre ici la nuit, traînant ses chaînes et murmurant ses plaintes?'[2] 'Quite sure, Sir,' the good man answered; and we should most of us agree with him. They quote their Lambs, and their Spectator, recall what Dr Johnson said about Charing Cross,[3] and imagine how many distinguished people have walked where we walk now.

There is something perhaps a little simple in these reflections, suggestive of a tourist with a Baedeker; but when we have read further we understand that it is no pose, but a genuine impulse. London, they both agree, is immensely old. If Addison and his friends were to come to life again, nay, Richard the Third himself, they would find their haunts unchanged.[4] 'In keinem Lande verändern sich die Zustände so wenig wie in England,' says Herr Rutari, and goes on to insist that it is on account of this conservatism that it has a greater charm than any other town in the world. Both travellers dwell with a kind of humorous tenderness upon the oddities and inconsistencies which are felt even in our streets. They find a perpetual fascination in the sight of the immense town which has gone on growing for so many centuries, absorbing whole worlds and finding space for them, adding impartially, splendid buildings and mean ones, and holding the tumult together by some central heat of its own. The variety of the streets never palls; and owing to the capricious way in which the place has come together, contrasts of the strongest kind are everywhere laid side by side, like strips of different colour. M. Huard, an artist, as his illustrations prove, does not care to seek the causes of sights that make London unlike any other place to look at; he hazards an explanation, breathes a sigh, and then devotes himself to the subtleties of our mysterious atmosphere. We may trace a certain sprightly malice in some of his remarks; the meetings at the Marble Arch tickled him considerably. An old gentleman expounds the Scriptures accompanied by 'une veille lady, sèche, propre, anguleuse, qui ferme les yeux dès qu'elle ouvre la bouche et la bouche dès qu'elle ouvre les yeux',[5] and shoots severe glances at frivolous French strangers. Could we ever do the like in Pais? 'J'en doute, car malins et moqueurs, nous avons à l'excès le sentiment du ridicule, et nous hésitons toujours à publier une conviction forte.'[6] We may even suspect a smile, hidden quickly, when he expatiates upon the 'discrets petits squares silencieux . . . qui ont gardé ce je ne sais quoi d'intime, d'humain, de personnel, qui fait le charme des habitations anglaises';[7] they are charming, but a little shabby and humble after the smart white streets of Paris.

Herr Rutari is as sensitive to the beauty of London as M. Huard, but he prefers the sterner side of it, and cannot stop at æsthetic appreciation but must find a meaning beneath the surface. The City fascinates him more than any other part, because of the tremendous operations which take place there; they excite him so much that he fancies a peculiar dignity in the face of the poorest clerk who earns his living at the centre of the world. It fascinates him, too, because it brings home to him, in the most conclusive way, the reverse of the picture; the innumerable beggars, the horror of the low streets, and the struggle which drives the populace up and down the pavement all day long seeking a living. Like M. Huard, he is amazed by the tokens of intense poverty that meet his eye everywhere, mocking the splendour of Mayfair even, and protests that such sights are only to be seen in London. But then, 'Ist doch

London der Inbegriff aller Widersprüche'; and by weighing one quality with another he comes at a likeness of the English character which is sufficiently agreeable whether we recognise it or not. The English, he says, are a people without nerves, of admirable cleanliness and muscular force. All their virtues are displayed upon the turf at Lord's, when the youth of England play the hereditary game, under the eyes of their parents, and may be summed up in the true English word – 'Gentleman'. Centuries have gone to produce this excellent specimen, endowing him finally with an atmosphere almost of romance; and his sister, with her fresh cheeks, at once suggests that she is the descendant of the long line of illustrious women whose portraits hang in the ancestral home. The rich past underlies all English customs and ideas, and serves, together with their isolated position, to make them almost grotesquely independent of other people. Not only do they hoard all kinds of odd little habits, but they have built up a singular point of view for themselves in art and literature. While Tolstoy, Ibsen, and Nietzsche sent waves of fresh thought across the Continent, the English slept undisturbed or did not raise their eyes from their own affairs. A more serious charge is that a foreigner, accustomed to a free discussion of all subjects upon the Continent, finds no 'frischen lebhaften Streit der Geister' in England. And yet, such is their inconsistency that in spite of this reticence and the complete indifference of the State, a lusty art flourishes, fills an Academy full of pictures every year, and private people are found to line their houses with portraits in a way that is unknown on the Continent. As to the quality of these works, Herr Rutari is not enthusiastic. He finds in them robust thought, humour and a taste for depicting children and dogs; but all English art, he declares, is tinged with sentimentality. The English temperament, however, is on the whole a wonderful compound of humours and oddities; controlled, as the City of London herself, by some profound heat which now and again throws off a Shakespeare or a Dickens. It is characteristic of the Continental view that Dickens is more quoted than any other English writer, and is held to be the type of our national genius.

1 – A review in the *TLS*, 30 July 1908, (Kp C15) of *Londoner Skizzenbuch* (Leipzig, Degener, 19—) by A. von Rutari (Arthur Levi) and of *Londres Comme Je L'ai Vu, texte et dessins par Charles Huard* (Paris, Eugene Rey, Libraire-Editeur, 1908). No copy of Rutari's work has been discovered; extracts from it are therefore unannotated.

2 – Huard, p. 49, extracted from a more extensive sentence.

3 – James Boswell, *Life of Johnson* (1791), Saturday, 2 April 1775: 'Why, Sir, Fleet-street has a very animated appearance; but I think the full tide of human existence is at Charing-cross.'

4 – Joseph Addison (1672–1719), friend of Swift and Steele; Richard III (1452–85).

5 – *Ibid.*, pp. 111–12: 'Un petit harmonium portatif les accompagne, tenu par une veille lady sèche, propre ... '

6 – *Ibid.*, p. 113.

7 – *Ibid.*, p. 118: 'Vous y trouverez, ici et là, de discrets petits squares silencieux, de vénérables et digne maisons d'autre-fois, qui ont gardé ... '

'A Week In The White House'

Dr Hale was invited lately to spend a week at the White House, and during his stay he observed the President 'from morning till night'.[2] He was further allowed to write down these observations, to publish them in a small volume, and to claim for his work that it is 'by all odds the most intimate study of Mr Roosevelt ever made public'. It is not often that distinguished men will submit to such an ordeal, but Dr Hale is surely speaking the truth when he says that if, by such means, one could get an 'accurate and realistic'[3] picture of the President (or of the dustman, we might add) nothing could exceed the interest of it. But prudence, a glance at biographies, a glance at living men and women, make us reflect that it is a perilous undertaking, and suggest a doubt whether Dr Hale's method is really so simple as it seems. His plan, to use his own words, is to give a 'verbal cinematographic study'[4] of the President, to sit with open eyes and let the President print his image a million times upon the retina. Chartran, Sargent, Rouland,[5] and others have tried to secure his likeness in paint; but he is imprisoned on canvas. The only medium that can keep pace with his moods, flowing into them as lead into a mould that is forever recast, is the medium of words. The objection to the method is perhaps that it lays too great a strain upon the reader in the first place; he receives so many shocks, and must understand so much by them; and, in the second, that words were never meant to take the place of eyes, but to interpret what they see. To enlarge upon these peculiarities, however, would be to brand oneself both dullard and pedant – an unenviable reputation, and to escape it let us own immediately that Dr Hale's book leaves a very distinct impression. Whether you are justified in thinking that it is an impression of Mr Roosevelt is another matter, but it should be explained at once that Dr Hale confines himself to the character of the man, and has nothing to say of his politics.

'Get the permanent features of the scene in mind,' Dr Hale commands,[6] in the manner of one who is about to bring off a conjuring trick, and accordingly we imagine a room furnished with a large writing-table, some leather armchairs, a globe, and an 'Art Nouveau' lamp. There is a photograph of a bear, and a framed autograph of a sonnet, by J. J. Ingalls, called 'Opportunity'.[7] The impression which you are to take away from this glance is naturally that the President of the United States enjoys no greater luxury than the ordinary business man, that decrees which change the face of the world are written at a commonplace table, from a substantial armchair. You may moralise as you choose upon the contrast, and if you are happily inspired the figure of the President himself, which is flashed upon the plate directly afterwards, will crown your thoughts appropriately.

'You know his features – the close-clipped brachycephalous head, close-clipped moustache, pince-nez, square and terribly rigid jaw; hair and moustache indeterminate in colour, eyes a clear blue, cheeks and neck ruddy.'[8]

He is, in short, for there must be an end of quotation, a burly man, who prefers comfort and solidity to the refinements of art, and connects the plainness of his furniture, perhaps, with the republican virtues. From ten till half-past one every morning a procession passes through this room, 'a panorama of the national life',[9] composed of men who come from all classes, and represent all professions. They ask questions, give information, lay their plaints, seek advice, receive instructions, discuss policies, or merely crack their jokes and tell their stories. The President receives each, says something, and the man goes away, content, convinced, or at the least, in a better humour because he has seen the President, and some of his illusions have been dispelled. These conversations last but a minute or two; nevertheless, the matter is discussed thoroughly, and in almost every case some phrase is added which enlivens the interview and gives the visitor something to talk about when he gets home. Surely the President was unusually pleased to see him, or delighted to greet a descendant of Jonathan Edwards. 'What was your mother's name? Then you must be descended from Jonathan Edwards ... He was a great man, but he had no sense of humour.'[10]

Italics, capital letters, all the resources of the printer's art are used to give effect to the explosions of the President's speech. Dr Hale, who cannot, of course, reproduce the entire conversation, prints a number of different openings, as Mr Roosevelt sees his visitor, advances upon him, and wrings his hand.

'Senator, I – am GLAD to see you! Senator, this is a – VERY great pleasure! Your daughters? I am, indeed, pleased to have this visit from you! How DARE you introduce yourself to me? A great pleasure – a VERY – GREAT pleasure indeed!'[11]

But the remarkable point about these greetings is, not only that they are discriminating, but that with all their emphasis they are sincere. Contact with another human being seems to ignite some spark in the President, and the shout of laughter, the 'mitrailleuse discharge',[12] the hand-clasp, and thump upon the back represent simply the roar of the necessary explosion. When his visitor is kindled into animation and is conscious of a desire to return the blow, the business of the interview is transacted at lightning speed. Deputations forget their addresses and speak good American; old grievances dissolve; pedants are ashamed; no one can be confused, or subtle, or malicious beneath such a torrent of good humour. Whatever the business may be, the President at once insists that he has personal knowledge of it, that he has driven a train, or run a fire-engine, or lived on a ranche, and is, therefore, fallible and human; moreover, such passions have a part in the sum of civic virtue. While he talks he stands or walks about the room, throws himself on a sofa, or perches on the corner of his table; but now and then you see him write a note, or sign his name, and at intervals a secretary slips in quietly, takes the paper, and disappears. It is tempting, but perhaps inaccurate, to imagine that the great man is thus silently manipulating a thousand strings as he talks, and that the process of government is going on beneath the surface all the time. However this may be, there is no doubt that the interminable conversation fulfils other purposes besides the obvious one of allowing people to state their case to the President in person, and to receive his answer. Every man has in him something that the President does not know, and would like to possess; his talk is often but a rapid search for a fact or a point of view. 'He takes up a new man with a new interest like a machine grabbing a new piece of metal to shape it to the requirement in precisely so many seconds.'[13] One of the results of this habit is that the President has an amazing number of facts in his brain, which have come there with their own little circle of associations round them, such as you get from talking to the actor, rather than from

reading his narrative. His talk, if you listen to it for half an hour, lights
with astonishing precision upon a great number of topics, most of them
as far apart from each other as sport and ethics, literature and politics,
law and food. 'Each subject,' writes Dr Hale, 'gets full attention when it
is up; there is never any hurrying away from it, but there is no loitering
over it.'[14] Such sentences, of course, are meant solely as a tribute to Mr
Roosevelt's excellent qualities, his power, vitality, and industry, but they
come to produce an effect, upon the mind of a stranger, that is little less
than distressing. The notion which this book conveys so vividly, of an
alert machine, efficient in all its parts, from the simplest to the most
private, is impressive, but it also strikes a foreigner with a sense of
suffocation, with a feeling almost as of a gigantic hand laid upon the
windpipe. Business of course must be conducted with the speed of a
machine, but when the whole range of human speculation is made food
for such mechanical measures – 'there is never any hurrying away from
it, but there is no loitering over it' – we ask ourselves what state of
civilisation can make such lives desirable, or anything but depressing to
the beholder. The answer, as Dr Hale gives it, is that America is a
democratic country, and that the President is worshipped by his com-
patriots as the type of their national virtues. It is, indeed, clear from
many touches, from the symbolism of plain furniture and boisterous
welcome, that we are to lay stress upon a particular side of the
President's character, that we are to connect it with something of far
greater importance than the temperament of a single man. The scene
which takes place daily in the President's study when scores of unknown
people shake him by the hand and are greeted as fellow men, makes an
American 'proud of his fellow countrymen', impresses him with a 'sense
of the essential worth of American civilisation', and leads him to assert
that no one 'has ever seen anywhere on earth a scene of such far-reaching
results'.[15] Few people perhaps will be inclined to deny the good sense of
such simplicity in outward ornament and ceremony, but the peculiar
distinction of President Roosevelt is that he has carried it into more
serious matters than any of his predecessors. He asserts that he is
President by virtue of his ability, but that the office, by itself, in no way
separates him from other men; his claim, indeed, is that the greater your
ability the more power you have to sympathise with your fellows, and it
is the main advantage of a high position that it gives you an extraordinary opportunity for such intercourse. No one, judging from Dr Hale's
book, can doubt that the astonishing thing about this daily pilgrimage

through Mr Roosevelt's study lies not at all in any melodramatic contrast between government and leather armchairs, Presidents and farmers, but in the immediate sympathy which at once, so to speak, melts the two men together. There is no need to recapitulate the different types who come to him and at once get into touch with him; it is more interesting to discover what quality this is which most people possess in some degree, and Mr Roosevelt possesses in perfection. The broad explanation is perhaps that which Dr Hale gives. 'Life and the world in every one of innumerable phases, the multitudinous deeds of men, their thoughts and ways, attract him with indescribable fascination.'[16] It is his power of sympathy that distinguishes him from other remarkable men; it is this power, if we may judge from Dr Hale, that stirs American hearts, and makes them recognise in their President the true flower of democracy. Not only does he sympathise perpetually and vigorously, but he sympathises with the common feelings of men, and is as indifferent to the shades of mind and spirit as he is indifferent to degrees of rank or wealth. His natural democracy carries him even further; there are some qualities which, because they can belong only to a few, have no attraction for him. The academic, he says, must give way to the wise and the practical; he does not care for the 'worlds of poetry or romance'; he 'respects sentiment', but himself indulges only in the sentiments that are common to most men; niceties of speculation annoy him; ethical refinements make little appeal to him, 'dreams do not nest in his heart'.[17] But it is unneccessary to point out that even in the most democratic of countries there must be some who dream, who meditate, who enjoy rare and lovely emotions, nor need we insist that to disregard such men is to admit the taint of aristocracy. We need but remark that even the President will not suffer everybody. But the true interest of these limitations is that they serve to define the nature of his sympathy, and show that it is for the simplest form of life, for experiences that are common to all, for humanity in general and not for individuals. He is intoxicated by a crowd; he might do homage to the glow in a dog's eye; the fact that in each of the people who come before him there burns something of the flame, that they are carrying forward the vast onset of life, that he can further it, increase its volume, excites him, and touches him to the quick. His sympathy is with the normal development of this spark; marriage, birth, the upbringing of children, the steady tramp of life through dusty paths to the grave. He is, therefore, understood and loved by the enormous numbers who are occupied with these matters, and they yield to the temptation, to which Dr Hale also falls a victim, of glorifying the man who is so like themselves, who, by his eminence, authorises their contentment.

'After all,' breaks out Dr Hale, in a rhapsody of paradox, 'common humanity is very wonderful and very noble . . . To represent absolutely the average man . . . would be to be great beyond all other greatness . . . to be the possessor of the greatest thoughts that live in the world' to surpass 'any isolated seer or poet whatsoever.'[18]

This is the theme of the book, and it is a familiar doctrine, for it is not only convenient, but it makes a curious appeal to the emotions, so that one who denies it is judged to be both mistaken and morally corrupt – a cynic, and a person of cold imagination.

But however harshly you may judge the embodiment of such a theory – and, to speak honestly, there is nothing lovable in Dr Hale's present-ment of him – you cannot deny him the tribute which a moth perhaps pays to a lighted lamp. It is a coarse flame, fed on the unstrained oil, but at the same time there is a certain rude joy in creeping close to the fire, and in feeling your limbs grow warm and your brain become passive. The American people, however, find a peculiar and a different comfort in such a sensation, if we are to continue the metaphor, or, to change it, in such a reconcilation. People, forced as they are to do without the luxuries of tradition, must find in themselves a raw material and exalt it above the finished form. People, again, set in the midst of vast lands beneath the shadow of forests and seas have need to worship their own force and resent any belittlement of it. In President Roosevelt, who governs and is the peer of kings, they feel at once a muscular strength which is infinitely reassuring to them, and a huge indiscriminate power, equally distributed over the whole of him, which makes him the reconciliation of innumerable qualities, the starting-point of all their energies. Every virtue is possible, no other way of life surpasses theirs, when there is one who recognises in his own person and in the persons of others the sufficiency of their native gifts for all aims that a human being need pursue. They welcome him as the accurate type of their soul, flung off by nature in an impetuous mood, and claim for it that it is made after the original pattern, and fashioned out of the pure clay.

1 – A signed article in 'The Book on the Table' series, *Cornhill Magazine*, August 1908, vol. xxv, (Kp c25) based on *A Week in the White House with Theodore Roosevelt: a study of the President at the nation's business* (G. P. Putnam's & Sons,

1908) by William Bayard Hale (1869–1924), journalist, future biographer of Woodrow Wilson, and propagandist for the German cause in the 1914–18 War.

'I have ... been writing about President Roosevelt, for Smith [Reginald Smith, the *Cornhill*'s editor] at his command. The sublety [*sic*] of the insinuations is so serpentine that no Smith in Europe will see how I jeer the President to derision, seeming to approve the while.' (*I VW Letters*, no. 422, to Violet Dickinson, July 1908.) See also 'Body and Brain', *III VW Essays*.

2 – Theodore Roosevelt (1858–1919) was 25th President of the U.S.A., 1901–9. For the quotation, Hale, p. 115, which has: 'He radiates from morning until night and he is nevertheless always radiant.'

3 – For this and the previous quotation, *ibid.*, Foreword, p. iii.

4 – *Ibid.*, p. 6.

5 – *Ibid.*, p. 5. The portrait of Roosevelt by the American painter Orlando Rouland (1871–1945) has not been identified. That by John Singer Sargent (1856–1925), painted in 1903, is still in the White House. The version by the French painter Theobald Chartran (1849–1907), also executed in 1903, and reproduced in *Harper's Weekly*, 1903, vol. 47, p. 375, was ordered by Mrs Roosevelt to be burned on the family's departure from the White House in 1909; the Roosevelts thought it looked like a mewing cat. (I am indebted to Professor Elizabeth Steele for this information.)

6 – *Ibid.*, p. 14.

7 – J. J. Ingalls (1833–1900); his sonnet 'Opportunity', quoted *ibid.*, p. 10, begins: 'Master of human destinies am I. / Fame, Love, and fortune on my footsteps wait, / Cities and fields I walk.'

8 – Hale, p. 14.

9 – *Ibid.*, pp. 22–3.

10 – *Ibid.*, p. 135; Jonathan Edwards (1703–58), the Calvinist theologian and metaphysician of 'Great Awakening' fame, author of *The Freedom of the Will* (1754).

11 – *Ibid.*, p. 27.

12 – *Ibid.*, p. 57: 'The President's [laugh] is a succession of chuckles – a sort of mitrailleuse discharge of laughs. The fun engulfs his whole face.'

13 – *Ibid.*, p. 47.

14 – *Ibid.*, pp. 124–5.

15 – For these three extracts, *ibid.*, p. 23.

16 – *Ibid.*, p. 130; part of a more extensive sentence.

17 – *Ibid.*, which has 'Dreams do not nest'.

18 – Hale, p. 138, which has: 'After all, common humanity is very wonderful and very noble. To be truly an average man would be to be a part of the mind of millions, to be possessor of the greatest thoughts that live in the world, to have a vision wider and farther-reaching than that of an isolated seer or poet whatsoever.'

Scottish Women

The title of Mr Graham's book suggest that it belongs to a class which is of doubtful reputation. The public, we know, will pay thrice as much for an engraving from Sir Joshua, if the subject is a woman, as it will pay for a picture of equal merit, if the subject is a man. The pious belief seems to be that great grandmothers, when they are dead, crumble to a sweet dust, like the dust of old rose leaves, resembling no substance or fragrance that we can find among the living. In order to gratify the taste the print shops hang their windows with Countess Spencers and Nelly O'Briens,[2] and the book shops are prolific of their memoirs and their love-letters, from which it appears that half the disreputable women of history were ladies of distinguished merit and domestic charm. We are relieved to find that Mr Graham is not among the devout; he will pay his subject the compliment of believing that it has substance enough to stand close examination, and will not vanish even if he sometimes chooses to laugh at it. It has been his object to present 'biographical portraits' of women of different types who have only this in common, that they are Scotswomen, and in some way or other have influenced the history of their country.

When, twenty years ago, the ladies of Scotland raised a sum of money in order to erect a statue to a 'famous and typical Scotswoman' they could settle upon no one who came up to their ideal. There were numbers of interesting women, but no single great one.[3] It would, of course, be too rash to assign a cause for this failure, for we know that nature where genius is concerned will not listen to reason. But these nineteen types serve to show us at any rate some of the facts that made the women of Scotland what they were, and it is perhaps because it furnishes us with this comprehensive view that Mr Graham's book has its interest. The nineteen Scotswomen, at the same time that they reveal themselves, seem to be revealing a view of Scotland from age to age; and, if this is partly because genius never made them independent of their circumstances, it is also because they were in touch with a more permanent state of affairs than the women of England or of France. To understand them, we must know something of the history of their country.

We find the early woman the slave of her husband, a stout labourer in the fields where the thickness of her legs got her the title of 'strong-posted timber' from some English traveller; and, if she misbehaved herself, her husband could have her shut up in a cage.[4] It is not surprising that women of high rank and character should devote themselves to arduous works of a philanthropic nature, such as the establishment of colleges[5] and the building of bridges, when their means permitted it; for the benefits that appealed to them, naturally, were of a practical kind. Later, when their husbands and brothers were fighting with their own countrymen or the stranger, there is scarcely a clan without its story of some heroic lady who hid her husband, outwitted his enemy, or, like Black Agnes of Dunbar, held his fortress for months against the English.[6] Their vigour showed itself also in a peculiar power of coarse witticism, the wit of a woman against men. But they paid dear for their passions, and were burnt, caged, or branded after the brutal custom of the times. In the days of the Covenant women, as one might expect, were the hottest enthusiasts. Lady Hamilton rode against her own son, with golden bullets in her pistol to exorcise his devil;[7] a servant girl would die rather than keep from the meetings and the martyrs of the Solway persisted in their faith until the waves covered them. But what remains of such people? – a rhyme or a legend, unless we can show that their virtues have somehow gone to fortify the race. The lives of women like the Duchess of Lauderdale, Lady Grisell Baillie, and Gay's Duchess of Queensberry,[8] though they differ very much in the way it is applied, show equally a strain of wild vigour running through them, and suggest that it came to them from the blood of such parents. Grisell Baillie displays their qualities at the best; the eldest of eighteen children, she proved herself the most trustworthy, shrewd, and resourceful of daughters, able to plan and carry out some deed of great daring, or to clean a house, or to write one of those melancholy old ballads with which Scottish ladies have so often whiled away their time. She lived to a great age, and who shall limit the influence of her 'dogged and defiant spirit'[9] persisting for more than eighty years in right dealing and passionate care for her kindred? The Duchess of Queensberry had fewer obstacles to fight against, and, accordingly, her high spirits spent themselves in whims and eccentricities that made her notorious in her day. She insisted upon dressing like a Scottish peasant, used to be overcome by 'the humour of the situation' in the Royal dressing-room, and led the peeresses, when their gallery was closed to them, against the House of Lords.[10] At the same time, she was a true friend to Gay, and any one who reads her letters to Swift can judge that she had a mind.

It is clear, however – and with their past it is surely not surprising – that the 'Scotswomen's genius is not of a creative or speculative kind'.[11] If they wrote, they wrote ballads, in their own dialect, to hum over their work or to sing to their children, and were anxious, above all things, not to be 'suspected of writing *anything*', 'perceiving,' as Lady Anne Barnard, the author of 'Auld Robin Gray', said, 'the shyness it created in those who could write nothing.'[12] It is due to this modesty, perhaps, that so many of the beautiful Scottish ballads are without the name of their author; and we may attribute some of them at least to rustic poetesses like Isobel Pagan, the Ayrshire peasant woman, who was entirely illiterate, deformed, and a woman of the wildest morality, but had a strain of rough music in her that set all the gossip of the countryside to song.[13] All that we learn of their literary habits certainly goes to show that writing was a frivolous accompaniment, in their view, to a life that was generally active enough. In the eighteenth century Edinburgh began to be famous for those 'little snug supper parties'[14] which were so homely and so distinguished. Women, of course, collected the guests and saw to their entertainment. Elderly Scotswomen, in particular, seem to have had a genius for a kind of middle-aged hospitality; they are full of breeding, tell innumerable stories in a pleasant accent, and have at the same time a sound literary culture joined to their shrewdness. Such women were Mrs Alison Cockburn, Lady Louisa Stuart,[15] and Mrs Grant of Laggan. But though they could keep a salon – of a kind – the drawing-room, with all its limitations, scarcely seems the proper place for them. We like to think of them on their estates, in the midst of their own people; they deal out medicines, and scold unthrifty housewives; when they are old they become, perhaps, slightly eccentric, and take, like Lady Eglinton,[16] to the taming of rats; but no one dares laugh at them, and in the winter evenings they bethink them of those interminable 'Memoirs for My Grandchildren' which make the raciest reading in the world. Unhappily, their reserve will sometimes forbid them to publish them. Mr Graham tempts us with his story of Lady Anne Barnard, who has left eighteen folio volumes of manuscript, with instructions that they are never to be printed. For Mr Graham's brief portraits, which are so careful, and have at the same time so many happy turns of humour and sympathy, serve to whet our appetite and make us wish for more.

1 – A review in the *TLS*, 3 September 1908, (Kp C16), of *A Group of Scottish*

Women (Methuen & Co., 1908) by Harry Graham. 'I spent this morning toiling over a number of Scotch women', VW wrote to Lytton Strachey on 30 August (*I VW Letters*, no. 445), 'your relative Mrs Grant of Laggan [1755–1838] among them; and had to draw largely upon my imagination.'

2 – Sir Joshua Reynolds painted portraits of two Countess Spencers: Georgiana: (*with Child*) 1759–61, and 1772; Lavinia: 1782, (*with Son*) 1783–4, and 1786. His portrait of the celebrated courtesan Nelly O'Brien (d. 1768) is dated 1764–7.

3 – Graham, Pref., p. ix; this was for a figure to place beside those of Barbour, Raeburn, Knox, Adam Smith etc., in one of the niches at the front of the Scottish National Portrait Gallery, founded, built, and decorated in 1882–1906. There are in fact two women figures on the façade of the building, one representing Mary Queen of Scots and the other Margaret, Queen of Malcolm Canmore.

4 – *Ibid.*, ch. I, 'Scotswomen of Early Times – Dervorguilla (1213–90)', p. 4; the 'discourteous allusion, probably to the thickness of their ankles' is quoted from Thomas Kirke's *A Modern Account of Scotland by an English Gentleman* (1679); and p. 5: 'The merchantis wyves ar lykewayes prisoneres, but not in such strong holdes. They have wooden cages, lyke Englishe borefrankis, through which symtymes peeping to catch the ayre, we ar almost choked with the sight of them' – quoted from *A Perfect Description of the People of Scotland* (1659) by Johnne E. —.

5 – Dervorguilla, wife of John de Baliol (d. 1269) who founded Balliol College, Oxford, continued assiduously the family's patronage of the college after her husband's death.

6 – Black Agnes (1313–69), wife of Patrick, 10th Earl of Dunbar, and an inspired tactician, endured a five-month siege. See Graham, ch. II, 'Some Scottish Amazons . . .', pp. 30–6.

7 – *Ibid.*, ch. V, 'Women of the Covenant', pp. 80–1; Lady Anne Cunningham (1651–1732), wife of the 2nd Marquis of Hamilton, whose son was in command of the king's naval force 'appeared on the seashore with a brace of pistols . . . loaded with balls of gold – it was supposed that lead bullets could not pierce the magic armour of the devil's agents . . .'

8 – Elizabeth, Duchess of Lauderdale (d. 1698). Lady Grisell Baillie (1665–1746), author of the ballad 'Were na my heart light I wad dee', daughter of Patrick Hume, Earl of Marchmont. Catherine, Duchess of Queensbury (d. 1777), sometime collaborator with John Gay in correspondence with Swift; her husband, the 3rd Duke, was Gay's patron.

9 – Graham, ch. VI, p. 101.

10 – *Ibid.*, ch. VIII, p. 131; the phrase 'the humour of the situation' relates not to the Royal dressing-room but to an occasion when the notoriously wilful Duchess, having called a halt to a ball because she had a headache, was run 'violently round the room' in her armchair by her son Lord Drumlanrig who pronounced it 'by far the best treatment' for her condition; for the Duchess and the occupation of the House of Lords Gallery, in 1739, *ibid.*, pp. 137–8 (the incident is recorded in *The Letters and Works of Lady Mary Wortley Montagu*, ed. Lord Wharncliffe, 1861, vol. II, p. 37).

11 – *Ibid.*, ch. VII, 'Anne, Duchess of Buccleuch and Monmouth . . .', p. 113.

12 – *Ibid.*, ch. XVI, 'Lady Anne Barnard . . . (1750–1825)', p. 269; the quotation is from a letter to Sir Walter Scott, July 1823.
13 – *Ibid.*, ch. XII, 'Elspeth Buchan and Isobel Pagan', pp. 225–30; Isobel Pagan (d. 1821), author of a *Collection of Songs and Poems* (1805) and, reputedly, of the famous song transcribed and revised by Burns in 1787, 'Ca' the Yowes to the Knowes'.
14 – *Ibid.*, ch. XI, 'Mrs Alison Cockburn (1713–95)' [author of 'The Flowers of the Forest'], p. 181; the information derives from Lockhart's *Peter's Letters to His Kinsfolk . . .* (1819).
15 – Lady Louisa Stuart (1757–1851).
16 – Susannah, Countess of Eglinton (d. 1780).

Louise de La Vallière

Louise de La Vallière was the daughter of an ancient, though scarcely noble house,[2] with honourable traditions of military service, discharged from one generation to another by father and son. Her own father had taken part in many campaigns with distinction, but his efforts brought him little wealth, and he retired, after the birth of his daughter, to lead the life of a small country gentleman on his estate at Reugny, near Tours. It was from this little property that the family took the name of La Vallière, for the house stands on a gentle hill, and looks over two valleys, a small valley on one side, and on the other the larger valley of the Brenne. A few walls only of the ancient house remained, but within this shell the family of La Vallière had employed some architect, 'se reposant des grands travaux de Chambord ou de Blois' to build them 'un charmant pavillon',[3] ornamented with all the skill of the Renaissance. The windows looked down the slope to flat meadows, where the river circled between rows of tall poplars. There were soft hills all round, covered with woods and vineyards – a charming country indeed, in which a girl might grow up happy in the consciousness of her own beauty. There were painted chimney-pieces in the rooms also, which, with their gentle allegorical scenes – a group of ladies on the grass for instance, and Love hid behind a tree with his bow drawn – might charm her eye; and her father, no doubt, would translate for her the motto that was cut in the stone above. 'Ad Principem ut ad Ignem Amor indissolutus.' 'Au Prince, comme au feu de l'autel, amour indissoluble.'[4] Unhappily the father of Louise died when she was barely ten years old, and she had in future no one to teach her Latin, or to see to it that her translations were correct. Her mother from the first showed herself an indifferent parent, who married, when her husband had been dead scarcely a year, the Marquis de Saint-Remi, first *Maître d'hôtel* in the household of the Duke of Orleans.[5] There were three young princesses for Louise to play with, who also were little controlled by their mother. 'Tenez vous droites, levez la tête'[6] was all the advice she had to give them when they came in to see her. They read romances, romped about the castle of Blois, and wondered which of them should be Queen of France. When their father died[7] the widow moved her household to Paris, the Saint-Remis and Louise going with her, and there, lodged in the Palace of the Luxembourg, they danced and they dreamed with greater zest than ever. The King indeed was married,[8] but there were princes, their cousins, who hunted the woods with them, and Mademoiselle, their half-sister, with her band of violins to set them all dancing. They were gay and extremely young, for the King himself was but twenty-two, and boys and girls of sixteen and seventeen could marry and become at once people of importance. The knowledge that their play was played on the verge of that supreme stage where the King acted in the face of Europe lent it a tragic kind of brilliancy. One or two ladies already had stepped into the full light, and had disappeared again, without applause. The event which decided Louise's fate took place when she was but sixteen, in the spring of 1661. In that year the King's brother married the Princess Henrietta, daughter of Charles I of England, and was endowed at the same time with some of the property of the late Duke of Orleans. The Dowager Duchess, therefore, in whose service the Saint-Remis still continued, was deprived of much of her power, and the future of her dependents seemed doubtful. At this crisis it appeared that Louise had already attracted the notice of an influential woman, Madame de Choisy, who was anxious to be in with the Court, but had neither youth nor beauty of her own to recommend her. With her competent eye she saw that Louise would do what she needed, and suggested that she should be given the post of maid-of-honour in the household of Madame Henriette, which was then being formed.

Madame Henriette was a girl of sixteen also, but, as years were counted at Court, a mature woman, in the flush of her beauty. Indeed, the transformation was surprising; she had been a thin, insignificant child; Louis himself had called her 'les os du cimetière des Innocents'; but the spring of 1661 revealed her suddenly as an exquisite young woman, frail and capricious, perhaps, but of an 'esprit vif, délicat, enjoué'.[9] Louise and her family had good reason to congratulate themselves on the appointment; it was of substantial value, and the maid-of-honour to such a mistress would be in the highest places of the Court.

The summer of 1661 was known in after years for its splendour. June, in spite of some storms, was more lovely even than May; and the Court was at Fontainebleau. To imagine what happened when the sun rose, on a cloudless summer morning, and promised brilliant hours till dusk, and then a warm summer night among the trees, one must conceive the untried vigour of men of twenty and of women of eighteen, set free from all constraint, and inspired by love and fine weather. They drove out to bathe in the morning and came back in the cool of the day on horseback; they wandered in the woods after dinner, at first to the sound of violins, which faded away as the couples drew further and further into the shadows, losing themselves till the dawn had risen. In all these delights Madame Henriette showed the gayest and most passionate. It was seen too that the King enjoyed them best by her side, and took pains to discover fresh ways of amusing her. There were spectacles, and ballets danced on horseback, at night, to the flare of torches. After a month the first check was felt; everyone was saying that they had for each other 'cet agrément qui précède d'ordinaire les grandes passions',[10] and the King's wife and mother perceived it.

It was clear that the intrigue could not go on unless some cover could be found for it. The cover they contrived together was simple, and at the moment neither could see where the fatal danger would lie. Madame Henriette and the Queen had enough maids-of-honour between them to tempt the King's taste. If he professed love to one of them jealousy would be diverted, and he could court his sister-in-law in peace. The plan was adopted. The friends of one girl sent her to Paris; another was quick enough to suspect; there remained the third, Louise de La Vallière, who had no friends and was simple enough to believe. Had she been profoundly astute and wildly ambitious she could have done no more. Neither the courtiers themselves nor observers of her own time ever credited her with much wit, or accused her of ambition. The epithets they apply to her are always soft and honourable; she was 'douce' and 'naïve', 'sincère', and 'sage'. She was not even beautiful; but the portraits and descriptions of her bring before us the image of a tall young woman, supple, her head curled with yellow ringlets; her eyes were blue, and had an expression of great sweetness; an honest look, moreover, simple and claiming nothing. Charm, they all repeat, was her genius – charm in youth that turned before her youth was over to a dignity that had something of melancholy in it. One imagines that she was very silent, and said nothing witty unless she stumbled into it; but her voice for commonplaces was of a 'douceur inexprimable'.[11]

The King had been used to a different kind of love; he had had the flattery of ambitious women, who offered a splendid return for the splendours he could bestow, and never lost consciousness of the bargain. To find himself in possession of an entirely simple and uncalculating affection was a new experience. At first it may have been even embarrassing. When Louise confessed, drawn on by false encouragement, that she loved him, the King tired of the plot, changed his view, and found himself enamoured. The true courtship began carefully, under disguises; but soon, in a fortnight indeed, the love was unconcealed. Madame Henriette had turned elsewhere, and the relationship between Louis and La Vallière was confessed.

It was the etiquette at court that when the King approached all other suitors should withdraw, so that they had solitude when they wished it; but it was pleasant perhaps to come home late from some ride in the woods together, and hours of simple talk, to find their vows confirmed by the flattery of the Court who were waiting for them to act their parts as Shepherd and Shepherdess in one of Benserade's ballets.[12] Louise, when she looked back, could claim that she had spent one happy month. The simplicity that had made her a dupe suffered her to keep a strange innocence all her life, as though she were conscious that the heart of her pleasure had been pure. But she woke by degrees to the fact that her state was no simple one of devotion given and received, but involved relationships with other people which were not happy and reflected harshly upon her passion. The Queen and the Queen Mother, clinging together in their virtuous solitude, had been able to ignore the King's pre-occupation. When he walked with Louise in the garden of an afternoon, followed by a troop of courtiers, they kept indoors with their eyes turned from the windows. But the lovers, growing insolent, triumphed one day over the most sensitive obstacle of all, and sat down to cards together in the Queen Mother's private rooms. Louise, when she became devout, confounded all her sins in one vast crime, needing a lifetime of penitence. Had she distinguished them she might have owned that it was at this season, in the autumn of 1664, that she sinned with the greatest consciousness of sin, and with the greatest confusion of feeling. She was at the height of her beauty, and courtiers who had sneered at her because she had neither rank nor wit were now obsequious. Still, she had but little to count upon, and if she exulted in her splendid moment it was largely because she knew it for a passing one, which she must relish to the full, though half her joy were pain. Her happiness could be disturbed by looking in the glass and finding her face grown thin. People began to remark that she could not stand broad daylight, and then noticed that she had, after all, 'peu d'esprit'.[13] But although she understood what this meant, and suffered acutely, she had a moment of faith in herself and in Louis. She respected their love. 'J'ai perdu presque tout ce qui peut plaire,' she told the King. 'Cependant, ne vous trompez pas, vous ne trouverez jamais ailleurs ce que vous trouvez en moi.'[14] Brave words! In uttering them she seems to return once more to the innocence of the first months of all. The King protested, but the charms of Madame de Montespan[15] were irresistible.

Louise had always kept one resource at the back of her mind, as though she distrusted her happiness; when the King deserted her she would take the veil. But the King found her useful to cover his fresh intrigue, and at the age of twenty-five it seemed best to edify the world by remaining at Court and making public her conversion. She tried to saitsfy herself with scraps of philosophy and a pretence of learning, but what she read served only to disillusion her, and to convince her that peace was to be found in religion alone. At Court she owned to a friend she suffered 'comme une damnée'.[16]

It was not until 1674 that the King allowed her to enter the order of the Carmelites, after having inflicted upon her the most exquisite of punishments. A life where the mind was bent to servile tasks and the body chafed with sackcloth was peace in comparison. She lived to be a rheumatic old woman of sixty-five, whose passions, save for one 'importunate memory', were smoothed away as the expression of a marble face is smoothed by pious kisses; and such was her penitence that her body, when she was dead, was thought by the poor to have divinity enough to bless their offerings. At the time of the Revolution her bones were scattered with the royal bones. Sentiment would like to have it that their dust was mixed.

1 – A signed article in 'The Book on the Table' series, *Cornhill Magazine*, October 1908, vol. xxv, (Kp c26) based on *Louise de La Vallière et la Jeunesse de Louis XIV*.

D'Après des Documents Inédits (1881; the edition referred to here is the 4th, Paris, Plon-Nourrit et Cie, 1907) par J. [Jules Auguste] Lair. (An English translation of this book was published in 1908 by Hutchinson & Co.)

The book appears to have been the reviewer's own choice – ' . . . I dare not tell [Reginald Smith] lest he insists upon a study of Sir Henry Campbell Bannerman' (*I VW Letters*, no. 436, to Lady Robert Cecil, 14 August 1908). See also, concerning the *Cornhill* and the niceties of calling 'a prostitute a prostitute, or a mistress a mistress', nos 428 and 435.

2 – Louise Françoise de la Baume Le Blanc de La Vallière (1644–1710) was the daughter of Laurent de La Vallière (d. 1651) and Françoise Le Provost de la Coutelaye. She was maid-of-honour to Henrietta of England, sister-in-law of Louis XIV, and became Louis's mistress in 1661. She retired in 1674 to lead a life of exemplary piety in a Carmelite monastery.

3 – Lair, p. 5.

4 – *Ibid.*, p. 7.

5 – On the death of La Vallière, her second husband, in 1651, Françoise Le Provost – described by Lair as a proud and mercenary woman – had relinquished the guardianship of her children in order to reclaim her personal estate. She married Jacques de Courtarvel, Marquis of Saint-Remi (1608–60), First Steward to Gaston, duc d'Orleans, in 1654 – i.e., some three years, and not, as VW states, 'scarcely a year', after the death of La Vallière.

6 – Lair, p. 19.

7 – I.e., Gaston d'Orleans (d. 1660), uncle of Louis XIV.

8 – Louis XIV (1638–1715) married Marie Thérèse of Austria in 1660.

9 – *Ibid.*, p. 54; p. 55.

10 – *Ibid.*, p. 58.

11 – *Ibid.*, p. 61.

12 – See, e.g., *ibid.*, p. 111; 'Au surplus, dès le commencement de novembre, elle répétait un rôle de bergère dans le ballet nouveau . . .'; and p. 113: 'Le roi entrait en berger . . . '. Isaac de Benserade (1613–91), poet, and author of several ballets.

13 – *Ibid.*, p. 159.

14 – *Ibid.*, p. 160; the first sentence continues: ' . . . et je crains que, vos yeux n'étant plus satisfaits, vous ne cherchiez dans les beautés de votre cour de quoi les contenter.'

15 – Françoise Athénais, Marquise de Montespan (1641–1707), maid-of-honour to Queen Marie Thérèse, introduced to the King by Louise.

16 – *Ibid.*, p. 241.

'A Room with a View'

Mr E. M. Forster's title *A Room with a View* is symbolical, of course; and to explain the sense which he conveys by it will introduce our comment also. Lucy Honeychurch and her elderly cousin Charlotte go to stay at a pension in Florence; their rooms, they grumble, have no view. A gentleman promptly exclaims, 'I have a view; I have a view',[2] and proceeds to offer them his room and the room of his son George. They are outraged, but they consent; and when cousin Charlotte has insisted that she shall occupy the young man's apartment, because he is a bachelor, she discovers, pinned over the washstand, 'an enormous note of interrogation'. 'What does it mean? she thought . . . Meaningless at first, it gradually became menacing, obnoxious, portentous with evil.'[3] But if we are not cousin Charlotte, in age or temper, if, moreover, we have read what Mr Forster has written in the past, we are amused rather than bewildered. We are more than amused, indeed, for we recognise that odd sense of freedom which books give us when they seem to represent the world as we see it. We are on the side, of course, of Mr Emerson and his son George, who say exactly what they mean. We care very much that Lucy should give up trying to feel what other people feel, and we long for the moment when, inspired by Italy and the Emersons, she shall burst out in all the splendour of her own beliefs. To be able to make one thus a partisan is so much of an achievement, the sense that one sees truth from falsehood is so inspiriting, that it would be right to recommend people to read Mr Forster's book on these accounts alone. If we are honest, we must go on to say that we are not so confident by the time the book is at an end. The story runs simply enough. Lucy is kissed by George Emerson, and the ladies fly to Rome. In Rome they meet Mr Cecil Vyse, a young man who feels in his own accord what other people feel, both about art and about life. When Lucy is back again in her ugly home in Surrey she agrees to marry Mr Vyse. But happily the Emersons take the villa over the way, and Lucy is made to own that she can tell the true from the false before it is too late. To compress the motive of the book into this compass is, of course, to simplify it absurdly, for nothing is said of the cleverness, the sheer fun, and the occasional beauty of the surrounding parts. We sketch the story thus, however, because we believe that it was meant to take this line, and we are conscious of some disappointment when for one reason or another it goes a different way, and the view is smaller than we expected. The disappointment is not due to any change of scene, but to some belittlement, which seems to cramp the souls of the actors. Lucy's conversion becomes a thing of trifling moment, and the views of George and his father no longer spring from the original fountain. But should we complain when we have originality and observation, and a book as clever as the other books that Mr Forster has written already?

1 – A review in the *TLS*, 22 October 1908, (Kp C17) of *A Room with a View* (Edward Arnold, 1908) by E. M. Forster (1879–1970). 'I have read Mr Forster's book –' VW wrote to Madge Vaughan, 'but it repeats what he has said already – However, it is very amusing.' (*I VW Letters*, no. 454, 1 November 1908.) Reprinted: CW.
2 – Forster, pt 1, ch. 1, (Penguin, 1955, p. 8).
3 – *Ibid.*, p. 18.

'Château and Country Life'

Cultivated people grumble at trains, and, if they are old enough, prefer the days of the stage coach. When you crawled over the surface of the earth, and swayed in the ruts, and saw the whole landscape through the steam of four fine horses you knew it face to face, they argue, as one should know one's friends. But surely it is time that someone should sing the praises of express trains. Their comfort, to begin with, sets the mind free, and their speed is the speed of lyric poetry, inarticulate as yet, sweeping rhythm through the brain, regularly, like the wash of great waves. Little fragments of print, picked up by an effort from the book you read, become gigantic, enfolding the earth and disclosing the truth of the scene. The towns you see then are tragic, like the faces of people turned towards you in deep emotion, and the fields with their cottages have profound significance; you imagine the rooms astir and hear the cinders falling on the hearth and the little animals rustling and pausing in the woods. French country, or that space of field and wood which a window frames, has great order and some peculiar distinction. The towns are very compact and the woods themselves seem more definite than in England, as though nature had Latin blood in her veins. Sometimes you see exquisite old houses with a great air of poverty and breeding; sometimes the woods part and there are those ornate country mansions, with their peaked roofs shining like a pigeon's breast with innumerable slates.

Emotions that form, round themselves, break, and disappear, to swell again, are, of course, only to be had in such profusion by exposing oneself to new things, emphatically presented. When a person sits down, as we imagine that Madame Waddington sat down, to describe her life from day to day, she sees none of these outlines; her impression is created by a number of scenes, and some overlap the others. It is not her purpose, although she writes, to treat the matter consciously, conceiving a whole and separating what belongs to it from what does not. Accordingly we take away a pleasant picture from her book, in which somehow the figure of a benevolent country lady is indicated also against a dim landscape. She lived in 'a fine old Château ... a long, perfectly simple, white stone building' close to the forest of Villers Cotterets. The windows overlooked 'the great plains of the Oise – big green fields stretching away to the skyline, broken occasionally by little clumps of wood, with steeples rising out of the green'.[2] Her life was very solitary, for the railway was distant, and French people in the country visit little. The evenings, for instance, were stately, but long and sombre; they sat in the big drawing-room, with one lamp in the middle of the room, so that the corners sank into darkness, and Monsieur A. read Molière or some of the old French memoirs aloud, with discretion. Occasionally Madame A., who wore a green shade over her eyes, played Beethoven and Handel, and as the night drew on 'a mantle of silence seemed to thicken on the house and park'.[3] The roads were all silent, and a branch tapping the pane, or a log shifting, sounded 'like a canon shot echoing through the long corridor'.[4] Madame Waddington, listening for her husband's return, could hear the sound of his horse's hoofs for fifteen minutes before he reached the gate. When she drove out in the daytime to visit some of her neighbours the impression of those lonely nights was confirmed. In the middle of the afternoon you find French ladies seated reposefully at their embroidery frames 'in the embrasures of the windows',[5] while the gentleman of the house reads Musset aloud to them.[6] Cake and wine is brought, and the company all sit round, 'so polite, so stiff', enduring long periods of silence, 'when nobody seemed to have anything to say'.[7] 'Ils ne sont pas de notre monde'[8] was the phrase with which well-bred ladies swept back all that could disturb the serenity of the circle. Something of this silence one may impute to the neighbourhood of a great forest; to visit or to take the train one must drive for miles along the silent forest roads. The only people one meets are of the kind that steal out in dreams; they come shuffling past you, stare furtively, and disappear, wanting you no more than the foxes do. Madame Waddington, as a mistress responsible for her tenants, asked about some people whom she met, heard that they were poachers, and saw the hut in which they lived; but a lame woman at the door prevented her from entering. 'Do they really want one to visit them?' she asks. 'But if you do, you must be prepared to hear a woman say of her father who sits huddled in a corner, "Cela mange comme quatre, et cela n'est plus bon à rien".'⁹ Perhaps, to an imaginative mind, the phrase would not be entirely repulsive – there is too much truth in it.

But, if one is going to construct an image of France from Madame Waddington's book, one will have, undoubtedly, to ignore a great deal of repetition, to make shift with thin material, and to see in a few sentences something more than she sees. Yet there is reason to be grateful when any one will write very simply, both for the sake of the things that are said, and because the writer reveals so much of her own character in her words.

1 – A review in the *TLS*, 29 October 1908, (Kp c18) of *Château and Country Life in France* (Smith, Elder, 1908) by Mary King Waddington.

2 – For both these descriptions of the chateau, Waddington, ch. i, p. 3.

3 – *Ibid.*, p. 10, which has: 'settle', not 'thicken'.

4 – *Ibid.*

5 – *Ibid.*, ch. ii, p. 37: 'The other three ladies were each seated at an embroidery frame in the embrasure of the window.'

6 – *Ibid.*, p. 38: 'The Master of the house . . . having come in from shooting . . . had been reading aloud to the ladies – Alfred de Musset, I think.'

7 – *Ibid.*, pp. 42–3.

8 – *Ibid.*, ch. ix, p. 274.

9 – *Ibid.*, ch. iv, p. 143, which has: 'I only saw the dirt, and smelt [*sic*] all the bad smells, and heard how bad most of the young ones were to all the poor old people. "Cela mange comme quatre . . . " I heard one woman remark casually to her poor old father sitting huddled up in a heap near the fire.'

Letters of Christina Rossetti

Almost all the letters which Mr Rossetti publishes in this volume passed between Christina Rossetti and her brothers.[2] They have therefore certain qualities which interest only if the reader is prepared to take a peculiar interest in the Rossetti family, and they lack almost entirely the obvious qualities which attract us in the letters of distinguished people – they are not remarkable for their wit, nor do they tell us any secrets. But the interest which many readers will feel is surely quite legitimate, for Christina Rossetti was a true artist, and her attitude in private life may well be the same as that which she expressed so exquisitely in her verse. We get it, only, in a different form, obscured of course by all the furniture of existence, but the spirit is the same in both.

She weas, as we are not surprised to learn, 'a highly punctual correspondent',[3] and wrote to her brothers charming letters, the letters that sisters write when they are anxious to keep pace, proud of confidences, and conscious at the same time of gifts that should be recognised. Little family jokes are used frequently, and go to support the half-ludicrous images of themselves which children start in the nursery and continue in private when they are grown up. 'Yesterday I made a dirt pudding in the garden, wherein to plant some slips of currant. The unbusinesslike manner in which the process was gone through affords every prospect of complete failure.[4] We have visited the Z. Gardens. Lizards are in strong force, tortoises active, alligators looking up. The weasel-headed armadillo, as usual, evaded us.'[5] There is nothing profound in it, but it was the same mind that conceived the fantasies of Goblin Market.[6] In one sense the letters contain less than one might expect of the personalities that can make private letters the most intimate form of literature that exists. Unless Mr Rossetti has taken care to omit such passages, there are no disputes, no reflections, no discussion of her own character, or of the characters of other people. But it appears simply enough from what is printed that the reason why Christina Rossetti did not take an interest in these matters was because she had a very clear conception of her own attitude. She knew that she was born with one genuine gift, and that in order to be true to it she must see the world consistently in a certain perspective. 'I am rejoiced,' she wrote when young, 'to feel that my health does really unfit me for miscellaneous governessing.'[7] She withdrew quite deliberately and, so to speak, with a smile upon her face, from the business of life, and felt, though she would not express it, an infinite difference separating herself and her brother, who were poets, from the crowd of people who were not. She was quite secure in her belief, and all the tremulous qualities of the most modest of maiden ladies are composed by it, so that her figure is at once dignified and curiously distinct. There is no need to say that this impression is taken much more from her opinions upon other things and people than from any judgment of her own upon her gifts.

In the family life we see that she played the part of the solicitous maiden sister, the guardian of family traditions, and the conscientious woman who is careful of her relations' susceptibilities. On the death of her grandmother, for example, she found herself without black clothes, and wrote that she had still 'managed to put on nothing contrary to mourning',[8] a sentence typical of something scrupulous and precise in her nature, which only escapes the charge of pettiness because she was never commonplace. Perhaps, after all, that is the remarkable quality in her letters, for though they are slight in manner and trivial in matter she always contrives to give her subject a turn; she writes a language, without affectation, which seems to be the pick of multitudes of words. Remembering her poems again, it is easy to imagine that the writer was naturally downcast and morbidly devout; 'seated', in D. G. Rossetti's phrase, 'by the grave of buried hope'.[9] But her letters show that her usual attitude was detached indeed, but exquisitely playful, as though she had a standard by which to judge events and was not likely to exaggerate their importance. If we talk of a standard we mean, in Christina Rossetti's case above all, an instinctive belief that some things are better than others. But when we have said that she valued most highly an aspect of life that found its only form in poetry, we have said no more than that she was a poet and knew herself for such. She would have added, of course, that she was not a great poet, for did she not answer, when someone urged her to write about 'politics or philanthropy' – 'It is impossible to go on singing out loud to one's one-stringed lyre';[10] if but she was satisfied herself, she was bold to claim her rights. 'It is something of a "lyric cry", and such I will back against all skilled labour,' she wrote to Gabriel, to whom it must have needed courage to write, of one of her poems.[11] When poets sent her their verses again, she could not be made to say that they were good if they were only mediocre; and, considering her tender ways, there is something moving in her decision. The most timid of women will show herself obstinate and heroic though still visibly alarmed in the defence of her children; and Christina Rossetti, one suspects, had that feeling on behalf of her art. The presence of such a feeling is hinted now and again, and it is impossible to mistake the constant presence of her devotion. It dignifies her gentle and rather indolent figure, and suggests irresistibly that to understand what was best in her one must turn to her poems. If the letters have that power, it is surely right that they should have been printed, and we must offer our thanks to Mr Rossetti, for many people would have thought them too slight to be preserved.

1 – A review in the *TLS*, 12 November 1908, (Kp C19) of *The Family Letters of Christina Rossetti*, ed. William Michael Rossetti (Brown, Langham, 1908). See also 'I Am Christina Rossetti', *V VW Essays* and CR2.

2 – Christina Rossetti (1830–94) was the younger daughter of the Italian poet and critic Gabriele Rossetti (1783–1854) and Frances Mary Lavinia Polidori (1800–86); her siblings were: Maria Francesca (1827–76), Dante Gabriel (1828–82) and William Michael (1829–1919).

3 – *Letters*, Pref., p. vii.

4 – *Ibid.*, to William Michael Rossetti, 25 August 1849, p. 6.

5 – *Ibid.*, 18 August 1858, p. 25.

6 – *Goblin Market and Other Poems. With two designs by D. G. Rossetti* (1862).

7 – Letters, to William Michael Rossetti, 13 November 1855, p. 24, extracted from a more extensive sentence.

8 – *Ibid.*, to her mother Frances Rossetti, 28 April 1853, p. 23, on the death of *her* mother Mrs Polidori, aged c. 84.

9 – *Ibid.*, 4 August 1881, p. 95; the phrase is in fact Christina Rossetti's and occurs in a letter to Dante Gabriel: 'If only my figure would shrink somewhat! For a fat poetess is incongruous especially when seated by the grave of buried hope.'

10 – *Ibid.*, to Dante Gabriel Rossetti, April 1870, p. 31; the suggestion that she should extend her range came, it would appear, from W. J. Stillman (1828–1901), American diplomat, correspondent for *The Times*, and author of several books, including *Early Italian Painters* (1892).

11 – *Ibid.*, 1 January 1877, p. 65, which has: 'You shall have one or two pieces more; but the one I sent you is a favourite of my own, and I doubt if you will unearth one to eclipse it: moreover, if I remember the mood in which I wrote it, it is something of a genuine "lyric cry" . . . '

'Blackstick Papers'

Sir Richard Jebb spoke once of Lady Ritchie's 'fairy-like way of viewing life',[2] and fitly enough she invokes the good Fairy Blackstick to preside over the fresh collection of her papers, *Blackstick Papers*. They deal with 'certain things in which she was interested – old books, young people, schools of practical instruction, rings, roses, sentimental affairs, &c.'[3] But the fairy does more than preside; we are convinced, as we read, that she inspires too. Again and again we put the book down, and exclaim that it is impossible to define the charm, or refer it, as the critic should, to some recognised source. It is far simpler to ascribe it to magic, and to leave it to the spirits themselves to say what magic is. It is true that Lady Ritchie makes use of many things that are not in the least supernatural; she picks up an old book about Haydn, or a new book about George Sand;[4] she stays at a place like Brighton, where we may all stay for ourselves if we wish it. We know the kind of treatment which such themes receive generally at the hands of the essayists; they are learned, prosaic, or sentimental. But Lady Ritchie is none of these things. If we try to discover what her method is we must imagine that she looks out of a window, takes somehow the impression of a gay, amusing world, turns over the leaves of her book and seizes a sentence here and there, remembers something that happened forty years ago, and rounds it all into an essay which has the buoyancy and the shifting colours of a bubble in the sun. The genuine nature of her magic is proved by the truth of much that seems almost too good to be true; she snatches a figure from the past, and shows as George Sand 'a sort of sphinx in a black silk dress. Her black hair shone dully in the light as she sat motionless; her eyes were fire; it was a dark face, a dark figure in the front of a theatre box.'[5] Nor is she invariably kind. Comparing modern women with their mothers, she says – 'They may be authors, but they are not such authorities; they may be teachers, but they are no longer mistresses.'[6] We must remember, when we talk of fairies and magic, that the best of them are not purely visionary, but see something more in common things than we do, and have rather a different standard to judge them by. Lady Ritchie will surprise us again and again by her flitting mockery. It is for this reason that we are so little conscious of the fact that by far the greater part of her book is devoted to the past and dead people – Haydn,

Tourgénieff, Bewick, the Misses Berry.[7] There is 'a vivid and innocent brightness',[8] to quote Sir Richard again, in her view, so that the past itself wears cheerful colours. It seems sometimes that she is more at home in the earlier days, when people were upright, smiling, and discreet, than in the present; the words of Horace Walpole[9] lie in perfect harmony upon her page, and we imagine that the great ladies of the eighteenth century had something of the manner of her prose. But to praise good breeding is an impertinence; it will be better to quote one passage, and so to give what analysis fails to give. 'The stately old tree falls, and we miss its spreading shade and comprehending shelter; to the last the birds have sung for us in the branches and the leaves hang on to the end, and old and young gather round still, and find rest and entertainment until the hour comes when all is over. The old branches go, and the ancient stem with so many names and signs carved deep in its bark, and the memories of the storms and sunshines of nearly a century.'[10]

1 – A review in the TLS, 19 November 1908, (Kp C20) of Blackstick Papers (Smith, Elder, 1908) by Lady Ritchie – Anne Isabella (1837–1919), Thackeray's elder daughter and the reviewer's Aunt Annie, who had married in 1877 her cousin Richmond Ritchie (1854–1912). Prolific and profuse, the author of novels and essays, she was to be the model for Mrs Hilbery in VW's second novel Night and Day (1919). See also 'Lady Ritchie' and 'The Enchanted Organ', III VW Essays.
2 – Caroline Jebb, Life and Letters of Sir Richard Claverhouse Jebb (C.U.P., 1907); Jebb (1841–1905) writing to his future wife, Caroline Lane Slemmer, née Reynolds, from Cambridge, 3 December 1872, p. 142.
3 – Ibid., Intro., p. 1.
4 – Ritchie, No. I, 'Haydn'; the book referred to but not identified in Lady Ritchie's text is The Life of Haydn [1732–1809] ... Followed by the Life of Mozart, with observations on Metastasio (John Murray, 1817) by Louis Alexandre César Bombet; no. VI, 'Nohant in 1874'; the book is George Sand. Mes Souvenirs (1893) by Henri Amic (George Sand).
5 – Ibid., no. VI, p. 94.
6 – Ibid., no. VII, 'Links with the Past', pp. 114–15.
7 – Ibid., no. I; no. XII, 'Concerning Tourguénieff' (1818–83; whom Lady Ritchie met, on three occasions); no. XIII 'Concerning Thomas Bewick' (1753–1828; a paper subtitled 'written from a Poultry Farm'); no. VIII, 'Mary and Agnes Berry' (the friends – 'twin wives' as he once called them – of Horace Walpole: Mary, 1763–1852, author and editor of Walpole's Works; and her sister Agnes, b. 1764).
8 – Jebb, p. 142.
9 – As quoted in Ritchie, no. VIII.
10 – Ibid., no. VII, p. 116.

'The Journal of Elizabeth Lady Holland'

Two handsome volumes, with large print and wide margins, portraits, annotations, and introduction, give us after a lapse of almost a century the diary which Lady Holland kept from the year 1791 to the year 1811. At the same time Mr Lloyd Sanders publishes *The Holland House Circle*, a thick volume with many chapters. Each chapter represents a different group of men and women, of all ranks and callings, and is distinguished generally by one important name. But the chief interest of these groups lies in the fact that they were once dispersed about the great drawing-rooms at Holland House, and that the people composing them had been picked out from the tumult of London, and drawn to this one spot by the power of Lady Holland and her husband. Indeed, so much time has passed that it begins to seem strange to us that the imperious-looking lady who sits with her foot displayed in Leslie's picture,[2] as though subjects bowed to her throne, should once have gone upstairs to her room, taken out a sheet of paper, and written down what she thought of the scene. We are told continually how she snubbed people, how she dropped her fan, how she sat at the head of her table and listened to the cleverest talk in England until she was bored, and cried out: 'Enough of this, Macaulay!'[3] But it is hard to remember that she passed through many more experiences than usually fall to the share of women, so that when she sat at her table she may have been thinking of different scenes and marvelling at the accidents that had brought her to this position. Until Lord Ilchester published her diaries there was only material for such a book as that by Mr Lloyd Sanders; we only knew what impression she had made on other people, and had to guess what she had been feeling herself. She was the daughter of a wealthy gentleman of Jamaica, Richard Vassall, and he married her to Sir Godfrey Webster, of Battle Abbey, when she was but fifteen. By her own account she had run wild, picked up her learning where she might, and come by her views without help from anyone else. It was not from lack of care on her parents' part; they were too fond of her to tame her; and it was quite consistent with their affection that when they saw her grown a fine girl with a proud spirit they should think that she deserved to marry. A baronet who was almost twenty-three years her elder, who owned a country seat, was Member of Parliament, and was 'immensely popular in the county, perhaps partly on account of his liberality and extravagance', must have appeared to them mainly in the light of a fine career for their daughter; there could be no question of love.[4] At the time of their marriage Sir Godfrey lived in a small house close to the Abbey; the building itself was tenanted by his aunt. One may gather something of young Lady Webster's temper from the question which she used to send across to the Abbey in the mornings: 'If the old hag was dead yet.'[5] The days in the little Sussex village were dreary enough, for Elizabeth amused herself by rambling over the great house, which had fallen into ruins, and rattling chains, like a naughty child, to frighten her aunt. Her husband was busy with local affairs, and, though he had some of the simple tastes of a country gentleman, was not a husband whom a clever young woman could ignore; he was not merely rough, but his temper was violent; he gambled, and he sank into fits of depression. From all these circumstances Lady Webster conceived such a picture of life in the country that she always shuddered at the thought of it afterwards, and wrote, on leaving a country house, that she felt as though she had 'escaped from some misfortune'.[6] But even as a girl it was not her way to suffer when anything could be done by protesting. She worried her husband with her restlessness until he consented to travel. One must not deny that he had made some effort to see her point of view, and had enough affection to try to satisfy her, for to travel in those days of coaches and to leave his own corner of Sussex must have been a genuine hardship for an important man. Lady Webster, at all events, had her way, and it is likely that she gave her husband fewer thanks for the sacrifice than he deserved. They set off for Italy in 1791, and it was then, being twenty years of age, that Lady Webster began to keep a diary. An English traveller in the eighteenth century could not profit completely by the experience unless he wrote down what he had seen and reflected; something was always left over at the end of the day which had to be disposed of thus, and Lady Webster began her diary from such an impulse. It is written to propitiate her own eye when she reads it later in Sussex; to assure her that she was doing her duty with all her faculties; and that she was going about the world as a sensible young Englishwoman, much like other people. But one imagines that she would never feel on easy terms with this version of herself, and would turn to the pages more and more for a date or a fact, and would soon dissociate herself entirely from her reflections. Her case differs a little, however, from the usual one. From her earliest youth Lady Webster seems to have had a quality which saved her diary from the violent fate of diaries, and spared the writer her blushes; she could be as impersonal as a boy of ten and as intelligent as a politician. How far she really cared to know that flax is grown by the inhabitants of Kempten, and that they must consume their produce themselves, 'for there are no navigable rivers', one cannot tell; but she thought it worth while to observe the fact, and proceeded quite naturally to moralise 'perhaps they are happier without facility of intercourse', for commerce breeds luxury, and luxury leads to a love of gain, and thus 'simplicity of manners' is destroyed, which the moralist felt to be a pity.[7] What strange conversations and what gloomy silences there must have been in the post-chaise! The young lady was indefatigable, and honestly scorned her husband because he had no enthusiasm and no theories.

When they got to Rome the situation was even worse. Lady Webster was beginning to be aware of the fact that she was a remarkable young woman, and all the masterpieces of the world were here to prove it. She set out directly upon her 'course of *virtu*', tramped through galleries, craned her neck back, looked intently where 'old Morrison' bade her look, and wrote stiff sentences of admiration in her diary.[8] When her husband came with her he either hurried her along, so that she could not see the pictures, or flew into such a passion that she could not distinguish them. The pictures, it is clear, threw a disastrous light upon Sir Godfrey. At Rome, too, there were sympathetic married ladies who assured Elizabeth that her husband was a monster, and encouraged her to see herself in a tragic light. She sobbed herself sick, reflected that human miseries must have an end, and pitied herself for thinking so. But there is no doubt that she was unhappy, however one may apportion the blame; for one must pity any young woman of twenty-two who leans out of her window at night, snuffs the air, sees water gleaming, and feels a strange stir in her spirit, and yet must write a few days later that she is now able to laugh at her husband's menaces, although they used to terrify her. It is natural to dread one's own faults, and to feel a peculiar dislike for the circumstances that develop them, for they make you ignoble in your own eyes; and the strain of bitterness which we trace in Lady Webster's diaries points to the presence of this discomfort. She knew that she was disposed to be hard, and she resented treatment which drove her to it, for she was a proud woman, and would have liked to admire herself unreservedly. In Italy, too, she felt often what she had seldom felt in England: hours of confused happiness in which the land was fair and she was young, and wonderful capacities stirred within her. She could not soothe such ecstasies with any of her 'cold maxims of solitary comfort', but admitted the thought of 'another' for her 'heart to open itself into'. Directly that other had shown what he could do in relieving her she dismissed him in agitation, comforting herself with the reflection that there was a 'want of passion' in her nature which would save her from many disasters. 'But what will be my resource if both head and heart accord in their choice?'[9] Her honesty drove her to ask herself that question, but it is evident that it alarmed her still as much as it excited her.

It was in Florence, not a year after the words were written, that she met Lord Holland for the first time. He was a young man of twenty-one, just returning from his travels in Spain. Her first impression is as direct as usual: 'Lord H. is not in the least handsome.'[10] She notes his 'pleasingness of manner and liveliness of conversation'; but it was the 'complex disorder' in his left leg 'called an ossification of the muscles', that interested her most, for, like other practical women, she had a great curiosity about physical disease and loved the society of doctors. She repeats their phrases as though she flattered herself that they meant more to her than to most people.[11] One cannot trace the friendship accurately, for it was not the purpose of her diary to follow her feelings closely, or indeed to record them at all, except to sum them up now and then in a businesslike way, as though she made a note in shorthand for future use. But Lord Holland became one of that singular company of English people, travelling in Italy in the last years of the eighteenth century, whom we come upon later in the first years of the nineteenth when we read the story of Shelley, Byron, and Trelawny. They went about together, like adventurers in a strange land, sharing carriages and admiring statues, had their own little society in Florence and Rome, and were allied generally by birth and wealth and the peculiarity of their taste for the fine arts. Sir Godfrey (it is no wonder) grew restive, and was impatient to put an end to this aimless wandering with a family of small children[12] in a land of foreigners, among picture[s] and ruins which bored him acutely. One entry, made at Rome, shows us what was going on in the spring of 1794: 'Almost the whole of our Neapolitan set was there . . . we all made an excursion to Tivoli. I conveyed Lord Holland, Mr Marsh, and Beauclerk . . . We got back late at night . . . In the course of our evenings Lord H. resolved to make me admire a poet . . . Cowper. [. . .] My evenings were agreeable . . . A sharp fit of gout, brought on by drinking Orvieto wine, did not increase the good temper of [my husband]'.[13] One of the attractive features of those early Italian travels is the leisure that people had, and the instinct, natural in a beautiful land far from all duties, which made them fill it with long hours of aimless reading. Lady Webster says of herself that she 'devoured books',[14] histories, philosophies, serious books for the most part, to increase her knowledge. But Lord Holland made her read poetry; he read Pope's 'Iliad' aloud, besides a translation of Herodotus, 'a good deal of Bayle and a great variety of English poetry'.[15] Her head was conquered, and that, in Lady Webster's case, was the only way to her heart. Sir Godfrey left her alone in Italy for months together; finally, in May 1795, he returned to England without her. The diary is still as sensible as ever; one might imagine her a cultivated British matron with all the natural supports. But, remembering that she had now determined to defy the law and to honour her own passion, there is something more highly strung than usual in the record of her days. She never repents, or analyses her conduct; her diary is still occupied with Correggio and the Medici family and the ruts in the roads. She drove about Italy with her own retinue, spending a few days in one place, a week in another, and settling in Florence for the winter. Lord Holland's name occurs again and again, and always as naturally as another's. But there is a freedom in her manner, a kind of pride in her happiness, which seems to show that she was perfectly confident of her own morality. In April, Lord Holland and Lady Webster travelled back to England together; Sir Godfrey divorced his wife in July 1797, and in the same month she became Lady Holland. Something remarkable might have been expected from such a marriage, for the feeling between a husband and wife who have won each other by such means will not be conventional or easy to explain. One does not know, for instance, how far Lady Holland was led to live the life she did from a sense of gratitude to her husband, and one suspects that Lord Holland was tender and considerate beyond what was natural to him because his wife had made an immense sacrifice on his behalf. He saw, what other people did not see, that she was sometimes made to suffer. One can be sure at least that the oddities were only superficial, and that Lord and Lady Holland, grown old and sedate, never forgot that they had once been in league together against the world, or saw each other without a certain thrill. 'Oh, my beloved friend,' exclaimed Lady Holland, 'how hast thou, by becoming mine, endeared the everyday occurrences of life!'[16]

> I loved you much at twenty-four;
> I love you better at three-score

was, so Lord Holland wrote when they had been married for thirty-four years, the

> One truth which, be it verse or prose,
> From my heart's heart sincerely flows.[17]

If that is so, we must admire them both the more for it, remembering what a reputation Lady Holland won for herself in those years, and how difficult she must have been to live with.

She may well have taken possession of Holland House with a vow to repay herself for wasted time and a determination to make the best of herself and of other people at last. She was determined also to serve Lord Holland in his career; and those unhappy years when she had roamed about the Continent, making her sensible observations, had taught her, at least, habits that were useful to her now, 'to talk the talk of men'[18] and to feel keenly the life in people round her. The house at once, with such a mistress, came to have a character of its own. But who shall say why it is that people agree to meet in one spot, or what qualities go to make a *salon*? In this case the reason why they came seems to have been largely because Lady Holland wished them to come. The presence of someone with a purpose gives shape to shapeless gatherings of people; they take on a character when they meet which serves ever after to stamp the hours so spent. Lady Holland was young and handsome; her past life had given her a decision and a fearlessness which made her go further in one interview than other women in a hundred. She had read a great deal of robust English fiction, histories and travels, Juvenal in a translation, Montaigne and Voltaire and La Rochefoucauld in the French. 'I have no prejudices to combat with,' she wrote;[19] so that the freest thinker could speak his mind in her presence. The reputation of this brilliant and outspoken young woman spread quickly among the politicians, and they came in numbers to dine or sleep or even to watch her dress in the morning. Perhaps they laughed when they discussed her afterwards, but she carried her main point triumphantly – that they should come to see her. Two years after her marriage she notes: 'To-day I had fifty visitors.'[20] Her diary becomes a memorandum-book of anecdotes and political news; and it is very seldom that she raises her eyes for a moment to consider what it is all about. But at one point she gives us a clue, and observes that although she cares for her old friends best she 'seeks new acquaintances with avidity', because 'mixing with a variety of people is an advantage to Lord H'. One must live with one's kind and know them, or 'the mind becomes narrowed to the standard of your own set',[21] as the life of Canning had shown her. There was so much good sense always in what Lady Holland said that it was difficult to protest if her actions, in their excessive vigour, became dangerous. She took up politics for Lord Holland's sake, with the same determination, and became before long a far greater enthusiast than he was; but again, she was able and broad-minded. Such was her success, indeed, that it can be said by a student of the time – nearly a hundred years after it has all faded away – 'Holland House was a political council chamber ... and the value of such a centre to a party under exclusively aristocratic leadership was almost incalculable.'[22] But, however keen she became as a politician, we must not pretend that she inspired ministers, or was the secret author of policies that have changed the world. Her success was of a different nature; for it is possible even now, with her diaries before us, to reconstruct something of her character and to see how, in the course of years, it told upon that portion of the world which came in contact with it.

When we think of her we do not remember witty things that she said; we remember a long series of scenes in which she shows herself insolent, or masterful, or whimsical with the whimsicality of a spoilt great lady who confounds all the conventions as it pleases her. But there is some quality in a scene like the following, trivial as it is, which makes you realise at once the effect of her presence in the room, her way of looking at you, her attitude even, and her tap with her fan. Macaulay describes a breakfast party. 'Lady Holland told us her dreams; how she had dreamed that a mad dog bit her foot, and how she set off to Brodie, and lost her way in St Martin's Lane, and could not find him. She hoped, she said, the dream would not come true.'[23] Lady Holland had her superstitions. We trace it again in her words to Moore, 'This will be a dull book of yours, this *Sheridan*, I fear';[24] or at dinner to her dependent, Mr Allen, 'Mr Allen, there is not enough turtle soup for you. You must take gravy soup or none.'[25] We seem to feel, however dimly, the presence of someone who is large and emphatic, who shows us fearlessly her peculiarities because she does not mind what we think of them, and who has, however peremptory and unsympathetic she may be, an extraordinary force of character. She makes certain things in the world stand up boldly all round her; she calls out certain qualities in other people. While she is there, it is her world; and all the things in the room, the ornaments, the scents, the books that lie on the table, are hers and express her. It is less obvious, but we expect that the whole of the strange society which met round her board owed its flavour to Lady Holland's freaks and passions. It is less obvious, because Lady Holland is far from eccentric in her journal, and adopts more and more as time goes by the attitude of a shrewd man of business who is well used to the world and well content with it. She handles numbers of men and women, rough-hews a portrait of them, and sums up their value. 'His taste is bad; he loves society, but has no selection, and swallows wine for quantity not quality; he is gross in everything . . . [26] He is honourable, just, and true.'[27] These characters are done in a rough style, as though she slashed her clay, now this side, now that. But what numbers of likenesses she struck off, and with what assurance! Indeed, she had seen so much of the world and had such knowledge of families, tempers, and money matters, that with greater concentration she might have shaped a cynical reflection in which a lifetime of observation was compressed. 'Depraved men,' she writes, 'are in a corrupt state of things, but yet they like the names of virtues as much as they abhor the practice.'[28] La Rochefoucauld is often on her lips. But merely to have dealt with so many people and to have kept the mastery over them is in itself the proof of a remarkable mind. Hers was the force that held them together, and showed them in a certain light, and kept them in the places she assigned to them. She took in the whole sweep of the world, and imprinted it with her own broad mark. For not only could she subdue all that happened ordinarily in daily life, but she did not falter when the loftiest heights, which might well have seemed beyond her range, lay across her path. She sent for Wordsworth. 'He came. He is much superior to his writings, and his conversation is even beyond his abilities. I should almost fear he is disposed to apply his talents more towards making himself a vigorous conversationalist . . . than to improve his style of composition [. . .] He holds some opinions upon picturesque subjects with which I completely differ . . . He seems well read in his provincial history.'[29]

Monstrous and absurd as it is, may we not find there some clue to her success? When anyone is able to master all the facts she meets with, so that they fall into some order in her mind, she will present a formidable figure to other people, who will complain that she owes her strength to her lack of perception; but at the same time so smooth a shape of the world appears in her presence that they find peace in contemplating it, and almost love the creator. Her rule was much abused in her lifetime, and even now, we are disposed to make little of it. We need not claim that it was ever of very great importance; but if we recall her at all we cannot, after all these years, pretend that it has not existence. She still sits on her chair as Leslie painted her – a hard woman perhaps, but undoubtedly a strong and courageous one.

1 – A signed article in 'The Book on the Table' series, *Cornhill Magazine*, December 1908, vol. xxv, (Kp c27) based on *The Journal of Elizabeth Lady Holland (1791– 1811)* (2 vols, Longmans, Green & Co., 1908), ed. The Earl of Ilchester; and of *The Holland House Circle* (Methuen & Co., 1908) by Lloyd Sanders. The article appeared without revision in the *Living Age* (Boston), 2 January 1909. Reprinted: *B&P*.

2 – C. R. Leslie (1794–1859), painter and humorous illustrator, notably of literary subjects; the portrait referred to here, and reproduced by Sanders, facing p. 90, is of Lady Holland, John Allen M.D. and Doggett, the librarian.

3 – Sanders, ch. v, p. 64, which has: 'At the fitting moment there came the tap of the fan on the table, and, "Now, Macaulay, we have had enough of this; give us something else."'

4 – For the quotation, *Journal*, vol. I, Intro., p. xii. Sir Godfrey Webster (1748– 1800) was for some years M.P. for Seaford, Sussex.

5 – *Ibid.*, p. xi.

6 – *Ibid.*, p. 195: 'On ye 20th [July 1798] we went with Marsh to see Castle Howard . . . The château is a magnificent pile, surrounded with the appropriate ornaments of woods and gardens, etc., but the sight of a country residence inspires me with gloom. I feel escaped from some misfortune when I get out of its precincts.'

7 – For this account of the inhabitants of Kempten, on the River Iller in Swabia, S.W. Germany, *ibid.*, p. 111.

8 – *Ibid.*, pp. 32ff.

9 – For Lady Webster's 'wonderful capacities', *ibid.*, p. 40, which has: 'About sunset I got out and walked: delicious evening. I partook of the serenity around, tho' my heart felt the want of some object to open itself into; for in spite of my cold maxims of solitary comforts, I often detect my wishes wandering to some imaginary happiness. I strive to repress, but often feel, a strong desire to be dependent upon another for happiness; but circumstanced as I am the thought must be checked and selfish independence alone encouraged. The want of passion in my constitution will always save me from the calamity of letting my heart run away with my reason, but what will be my recourse if both head and heart accord in their choice?'

10 – Henry Richard Vassall Fox, 3rd Baron Holland (1773–1840).

11 – For these references to Lord Holland's appearance, manner, conversation and interesting left leg, *Journal*, vol. I, p. 117.

12 – Lady Holland had three children by her first husband: Godfrey, who succeeded to his father's title, Henry, and Harriet.

13 – *Journal*, vol. I, pp. 124–5, slightly adapted; Lady Webster's other companions

were Matthew Marsh, who took orders in 1799, and was to become Chancellor of the Diocese of Salisbury; Charles George Beauclerk (1774–1846), only son of Topham and Lady Diana Beauclerk.

14 – *Ibid.*, pp. 158–9.

15 – *Ibid.*, p. 140; Pope's 'Illiad', 1715–20; the translation of Herodotus was that by M. Larcher, *Histoire d'Hérodote* (1786); Pierre Bayle (1647–1706), philosopher, author of the *Dictionnaire historique et critique* (1697–1702).

16 – *Ibid.*, p. 183, which has no commas after 'thou' and 'mine'.

17 – *Ibid.*, vol. II, App. A, p. 296; the order of the couplets here is reversed; they are from verses Lord Holland addresses to his wife on the occasion of her sixtieth birthday, 25 March 1831.

18 – The source of this quotation has resisted all efforts at discovery.

19 – *Journal*, vol. I, p. 158: 'I have had so strange an education, that if I speak freely upon sacred subjects it is not from an affectation of being an *esprit fort*, but positively because I have no prejudices to combat with.'

20 – *Ibid.*, p. 236.

21 – For this and the two preceding quotations, *ibid.*, p. 257.

22 – Sanders, ch. IV, p. 56.

23 – George Otto Trevelyan, *The Life and Letters of Lord Macaulay* (2 vols, Longmans, Green, 1877); vol. I, Macaulay writing to Hannah M. Macaulay, 1 June 1831, p. 216. This is not quoted in Sanders.

24 – Sanders, ch. V, p. 63; Thomas Moore, *Memoirs of Sheridan* (1825).

25 – Trevelyan, vol. I, p. 239, Macaulay writing to Hannah M. Macaulay, 25 July 1831, pp. 238–9: 'Her Ladyship is all courtesy and kindness to me: but her demeanour to some others, particularly to poor Allen, is such as it quite pains me to witness. He is really treated like a negro slave ... "Mr Allen there is not enough turtle-soup for you ... "'

26 – *Journal*, vol. II, p. 10; the subject of this sentence is Charles, 11th Duke of Norfolk (1746–1815).

27 – *Ibid.*, p. 87; the subject of this sentence is Francis, 5th Duke of Bedford (1765–1802).

28 – *Ibid.*, p. 18, which has: 'Depraved as men are in a corrupt state of things ... '

29 – *Ibid.*, p. 231; their meeting took place in the summer of 1807.

A Vanished Generation

In Captain Mahan's biography it is said that Nelson insisted that there was a meaning in all written words,[2] and it is surely an admirable text to hang up in a library. We take the great books on trust, or we are happy enough to need no spur; but to deal with the smaller books requires some faith such as Nelson had, lest, in the midst of the downpour, we become dismayed, our eyes closed, our senses numbed, the earth and sky a phantom to us. Yet, if we can but reach the meaning, what a prize awaits us! There are sights, and voices quite audible for a moment; living things behind us and all round; each book peoples some vague region, and instead of a sharp circle of light cast by one pair of eyes on the ground beneath us we walk attended by a whole radiance, as though the sun himself flamed within our heads. A great effort will put that prize within our reach, and a book like *A Vanished Generation* needs this assurance, for it makes, it must be owned, a severe strain upon our sight. Lady St Helier contributes an introduction, in which she asserts that although the writers were neither well known nor brilliant their letters deserve to be published because they give 'a delightfully fresh account of the everyday life of their time'.[3] Mrs Blake, who edits them, claims that they are worth reading because they are written by people with a 'strong sense of duty . . . who did their best'. The 'sacred ties of nature' she fears are loosened in this age, and the present generation may profit by the sight of the 'sweet and wholesome life' which was possible to their parents and grandparents.[4] The book is composed, save for the connecting paragraphs, of the letters and diaries of the Knox family from about the year 1813 to the year 1867. The chief characters are Captain the Hon. E. S. P. Knox, R.N., and his son, Thomas Edmond Knox, a captain in the army; but there are also letters from sisters and cousins, fragments of diaries, journals of travels abroad in the early part of the century – the sweepings of a great many old drawers, in short. The time had come, it is plain, which must come to all people who are too scrupulous to burn their letters, when it was necessary to decide what should be done with them. Were they to be tied up and put away, or burnt, or printed? Different reasons must determine; but we cannot pretend that Mrs Blake's solution – of publication – seems to us in this case entirely the right one. If we look for new lights upon distinguished people we are disappointed; if we look for wit or style we are given something that was never meant to be read outside the schoolroom, and if we dismiss all thoughts of art, and ask simply for human nature in the raw, it must be confessed that the Knox family was in no way extraordinary. But it is still possible to take our stand where, after all, Mrs Blake would have us stand, and to enjoy the spectacle of harmonious family life in the nineteenth century. It is always possible to dub oneself, as she says, 'a student of human nature'.[5]

Captain E. S. P. Knox, after chasing a certain number of French frigates and having the temporary command of the *Eurotas*, left the Navy when peace was proclaimed in 1814. He had married Miss Jane Hope Vere, a lady with a 'slight trim figure, charming hazel eyes, and an expression of great vivacity and sweetness'. He himself was a sturdy man, with a pink and white skin, 'apparently quite impervious to the weather', who was in the habit of saying, 'All for the best.'[6] They travelled in Italy, a family was born to them; they lived much in Paris, and when the only son Tom was old enough he entered the Army and served with his regiment in Canada. Letters were despatched regularly; a gloom was on the breakfast-table if the mail came in without his sheet; but no disasters overtook him. His sisters, on their side, have nothing but cheerful gossip to impart; how they have danced and had a music lesson, seen a cousin, or (if the worst comes to the worst) buried a dog. 'Let the melancholy fate of the Duke of Orleans be a warning to you never to jump out of a carriage,' his mother writes.[7] 'Do not run into debt but apply to your old father and confide all your little misfortunes to him,' writes Captain Knox.[8] Such quotations will explain why it is unnecessary to quote at greater length; with such sentences we must construct our picture. But these pages make a definite impression on the mind when thus read together in the lump. We can distinguish the different people from each other; the mother more plaintive, with daughters to marry; the sisters high-spirited and affectionate, but shapeless as young women are shapeless. They move about among cousins and aunts, dim figures with distinguished names, just distant enough to be old-fashioned, but hardly as yet picturesque. It seems very probable that such people were alive in the year 1840; it is comfortable to imagine that the world before our time was so cheerful a place. Much of our history has to do with the deeds of such men and women in the mass; and to read their trivial family letters is like standing on the hearthrug in the firelight and listening to evening gossip. Captain Knox and his son, although they took part in the campaigns and manoeuvres of the great armies and navies, are among the multitudes who have vanished. There is a certain thrill in the spectacle; we see so bright an image of the family, glowing for a minute, in a compact body; they seem too simple to survive; a kind of pathos is on them, because they must go. But to feel this is to feel also that Mrs Blake might have given us more of what we value and saved us much labour had she been artist as well as editor. The book might have been half the size; she might have brought out a distinct shape, according to her conception, by skilful quotation and comment. But her book is another example of the strange methods of modern English biography; you are presented with a great bundle of papers, and bidden, substantially, to make a book for yourself. To arrange or to criticise, to make people live as they lived, is considered unnecessary, or perhaps disrespectful. We feel that there is a spirit in letters which we must not allow to perish, but we are too timid to set it free.

1 – A review in the *TLS*, 3 December 1908, (Kp C21) of *Memoirs of a Vanished Generation. 1813–35*. Edited by Mrs Warenne Blake. With an introduction by the Lady St Helier (John Lane, 1909).
2 – *The Life of Nelson. The Embodiment of the Sea Power of Great Britain* (1899) by Captain A. T. (Alfred Thayer) Mahan – a copy of which had, incidentally, been awarded seven years previously, as an English essay prize, to VW's brother Thoby Stephen, then in Form VI at Clifton College, Bristol.
3 – *Memoirs*, Intro., p. xxv.
4 – For Mrs Blake's remarks, *ibid.*, Pref., p. xxx, which has: 'they had a strong sense of duty, and they did their best' in the first instance; and 'We realise what a sweet and wholesome thing family life can be . . . ' in the third.
5 – *Ibid.*, p. xxx, which has: 'To the student of human nature – and what study can possibly be more interesting? – these letters will be found worth reading apart from any literary merit they possess.'
6 – For the descriptions of Miss Vere and Captain Knox, *ibid.*, ch. I, p. 17.
7 – *Ibid.*, p. 179, letter 16 July 1842.
8 – *Ibid.*, p. 170, letter 2 April 1842.

1909

'Venice'

The first part of Signor Molmenti's work told the history of Venice from the earliest settlement to the fall of Constantinople. In the four volumes now issued in a translation by Mr Horatio Brown he deals with the Golden Age following the fall of Constantinople, and with the decadence which continued throughout the sixteenth and seventeenth centuries and was completed in the eighteenth. He follows as before the history of the 'individual growth' of the state, ignoring her fortunes abroad and narrowing his gaze upon the nature of her constitution, and, in particular, upon the customs and characteristics of the people in all ranks and upon all occasions.

We take up the story of Venice at the moment of her fullest life. The contest which had occupied the reign of Doge Foscari[2] left her with an empire on the mainland, and not only gave her the ascendency over other Italian states, but established her among the powers of Europe. Her policy of 'wise egoism' and 'self-knowledge',[3] the advantages of her position apart from the world but yet in the centre of it, and the peculiar strength of her constitution set her above her competitors. She had crushed Genoa, she was mistress of the Levant trade, and it seemed as though all these victories were but the prelude to her majestic career as a territorial state. But that, as we know, was not her destiny. She failed to secure her land empire; and, left alone in her struggle against the Turk, she lost her command of the East and spent her strength in vain. The history of Venice after the fifteenth century is the record of foreboding and decay; but at the same time there is no history which so moves us both by its splendour and its tragedy, and the likeness which it bears to the ruin of some great soul. Thanks not only to the learning of Signor Molmenti, but to the vivid way in which he presents his facts, we can make one study supplement the other; we can gaze into streets and workshops and drawing-rooms, and with this insight into the temperament of the people we can understand more clearly their actions abroad.

The first impression no doubt which the reader receives from the opening chapters of *The Golden Age* is one of surprise and paradox. Venice was supreme, but she was exhausted; we pass from the discovery of the Cape route to the League of Cambray, from the Peace of Passarowitz to the conquest by Napoleon.[4] There is a constant demand for wealth and energy and an increasing failure to meet the demand. And yet it was during this time that the private life of the city was most brilliant and luxurious and that her genius in art and learning reached its prime. One part of the paradox at least can be explained; centuries of prosperous trading had endowed the great families with enormous riches; and when the eastern trade diminished they turned bankers or invested their money in estates upon the mainland. For the moment there was no lack of private wealth, and it was possible to maintain the paradox that war and loss outside and an empty exchequer were consistent with a profusion of splendour within. 'After the League of Cambray,' says Mr Brown, 'the Republic resigned herself to the role of magnificent self-presentation.'[5] The city itself was decorated and rebuilt during the sixteenth century by 'a whole army of artists'[6] drawn into her service from all parts of Italy. Palaces were raised along the Grand Canal, wood was turned to stone and bronze, and such masters as Sansovino and Palladio[7] wrought out their prodigious conceptions unhampered. The islands where the grass still grew were laid with stone, and buildings rose upon them; the streets were paved, and bridges crossed the canals everywhere. The gondola succeeded to the horse, and by the end of the sixteenth century a fleet of ten thousand floated in the waterways, not black as yet, but brilliant with green and purple, trimmed with embroideries, and with gilt upon the prow. Venice became, as Signor Molmenti says, 'like one vast dwelling-place where the inhabitants could conduct their lives in the open';[8] the Piazza served for drawing-room, and the great fairs and carnivals were acted in this wonderful apartment with stone for its walls and the sky for ceiling.

The Venetian love of pageantry was stimulated in this age both by the policy of the government, which sought to hide their inner weakness by display, and by that spirit of life which had come to the race, after the austerity of the Middle Ages, later than to the other peoples of Italy. Their houses looked down on spectacles without number; there was a victory to celebrate, or a stone to lay, or some foreign king to entertain. Each crisis in private life, birth, marriage, death, had its formal celebration; processions wound across the Piazza, or there came a great cluster of gondolas down the canal with the Bucentaur[9] in their midst. Signor Molmenti gives the detail of each occasion: we can but compose some picture which shall serve for many. The little black figures of the old prints which cross the Piazza in a narrow file are in truth all cloaked in gold and scarlet; long red staves strike lines across the background; the people crowd and wave like barley in the wind when the coins are flung among them. One imagines a blue sky and the faintest breeze to make the reflections twist in the water. It is easy to conceive the crowd, but not so easy, with one's cramped modern sense, to conceive the surpassing beauty of details and individuals. Glasses were raised that were blown at Murano[10] and had strange golds and opals in them and spiked seahorses for handles; the tables at which they sat were carved with monsters and chimeras; goblets of gold, chased by a master's hand, held the sweetmeats; and the women wore stiff robes of velvet, damask or brocade, of rich or pale colours, with buttons of crystal, hairpins of amber, and a myriad of gems. We must imagine a spirit taking form everywhere and expressing in detail and in mass the beauty of Venice and the joy of life in Venice. The Greek and Latin classics came from the Aldine Press;[11] scholars from Constantinople lived in Venice and taught the wonderful dead languages; private people began to store books in 'cupboards and on shelves of carved walnut'[12] and the State founded the great library in the magnificent building of Sansovino. But the genius of the time is most fully preserved in its paintings. They hang in our galleries like windows into the majestic past, and display both the body of the time and the purest essence of its spirit. The Golden Age in Venice, it is often said, needed the plastic arts to express it, and Signor Molmenti suggests that there is a relationship between the genius of these pictures and the genius of the Venetian constitution. In painting, 'the protagonist of the scene is hardly ever an individual, but the crowd';[13] and in politics 'the individual was absorbed in the State, which refused independent initiative to the individual, and aimed at co-ordinating the action of each member of the community with the movement of the State'.[14] The private houses were built to frame banquets and assemblies of people; the vast rooms did not cherish an intimate family life or shelter talk between men and women. 'Most of the treatises which deal with the family abound in moral maxims",[15] we read. The women led secluded lives of voluptuous calm, and only emerged in their stiff brocades when they were needed as pieces in the pageant. Again and again the State interfered to check extravagance of dress, food, or pageantry, but the nobles preferred in many instances to pay the heavy fines rather than curb their passion for display. Even the tombs of the Renaissance are loaded with the symbols of life; it is rare, says Signor Molmenti, to hear of suicide, and, if so, it is mentioned with a kind of grotesque horror. His remark that 'the profound melancholy of death finds no expression even in Venetian poetry'[16] suggests why it is that the Republic produced painters but no great poet. When we think of our own literature at the same period we think not only of a pageant, but of the sleep that rounds it. The ruin, however, was approaching which distorts before it utterly destroys, and the still virile type of the Renaissance relaxed into the 'fatuous, insolent, servile physiognomy'[17] of the Seicento. Symptoms of decline showed themselves in public and in private life; there was bribery in the rank of the state officials; the aristocracy wasted fortunes in gambling and refused to practise the trades of their fathers; the guilds suffered from competition and their own conservatism, and foreign ships deserted the port. The arts both of painting and architecture showed the same corruption; the stone was carved into florid clusters of ornament, and the lines were waved incongruously; palaces like the Pesaro, churches like the Salute, are typical of this 'grotesque Renaissance', as Ruskin called it.[18]

But as Venice lapsed slowly from her position as a European power, and from her position as the great artist of Europe, she took on another aspect, not less marked than the rest and stamped by a peculiar beauty. She became during the last part of the seventeenth century and throughout the eighteenth, the playground of all that was gay, mysterious, and irresponsible. Her likeness to a great dwelling-place increased, for the people were sociable as one large family, 'with the Doge as grandpapa of all the race',[19] and the fact that they had no political existence united them in their pleasures. A ball that overflowed its room would dance out into the street. The great majority of the nobles were discouraged from taking any interest in the government, and they spent their energies in toying exquisitely with the trifles of life.

They studied the art of deportment and the science of the snuffbox; 'how to blow the nose, how to sneeze, how to beg from a lady "a pinch of her graces"'.[20] The charms of coffee houses were recognised, and in the drawing-rooms there was talk of art and love and letters between men and women, with some light discussion, as time went on, of revolutionary principles. Conversation, wit, scandal, all the intimate relationships of life, flourished with their appropriate parts in perfection. The manners were exquisite, the dress superb, and Venetian art could still adorn a woman or furnish a drawing-room with inimitable taste. But Venice had more to show than this. She was also the city of dark streets and deep waters; there were houses, 'in gloomy and far-off recesses of the city',[21] where one could buy the elixir of life or the philosopher's stone. The crooked waterways, with their sudden angles and shadows, tempted strange wanderers to haunt them and sheltered loves and crimes. One might meet both Casanova and Cagliostro[22] among the crowd of queer people who walked in the piazza. The history of Venice in the eighteenth century has the fascination of extreme distinction and at the same time of a curious unreality. The sounds and sights of the outer world are to be found here, but only in quaint echoes, as though, in passing through the waters, they had suffered some sea change.

But once more, before she fell silent, Venice reflected her image with the utmost decision. The pictures of Canaletto and Guardi, the comedies of Goldoni[23] remain to describe her both within and without. It is no longer a turbulent spectacle; but when we look into these orderly and luminous canvases we can hardly imagine a greater beauty or regret the loss of the old splendour. For who shall say when it was that Venice touched her greatest heights, or deny that we who enjoy her to-day perceive a beauty unimagined by the people of her Golden Age?

1 – A review in the *TLS*, 7 January 1909, (Kp C28) of *Venice. Its Individual Growth from the Earliest Beginnings to the Fall of the Republic* (6 vols, John Murray, 1906–8) by Pompeo Molmenti. Translated by Horatio F. Brown. VW deals with pt II, *The Golden Age* (2 vols, 1907) and pt III, *The Decadence* (2 vols, 1908) of Molmenti's work.

2 – Francesco Foscari (1373–1457), doge from 1423 until his death.

3 – *Golden Age*, vol. I, ch. I, p. 10; p. 11, which has: 'Venetian intelligence was directed solely to the acquisition of that most difficult of all knowledge, knowledge of one's self.'

4 – The League of Cambray, 1508–10, formed by Louis XII of France, the Emperor Maximilian, Pope Julius II, Ferdinand of Spain, the Estensi and the Gonzagas, to check the Republic's territorial ambitions.

The Peace of Passarowitz, 1718, made between, on the one side, Venice and the Holy Roman Emperor and, on the other, the Ottoman Empire, to end a war begun in 1714.

Napoleon Bonaparte declared war on the Republic on 1 May 1797 and on the 12th the Doge capitulated.

5 – Horatio F. Brown, *Venice. An Historical Sketch of the Republic* (Percival & Co., 1893), ch. XXII, p. 420, from a more extensive sentence.

6 – Cf. *Golden Age*, vol. II, ch. V, p. 98: 'A whole army of artists then effected the transition from the caprice of the pointed arch to the gravity of the Latin form . . . '

7 – Jacopo Sansovino (1486–1570) whose masterpiece is the Library of St Mark's in the Piazza San Marco; and Andrea Palladio (1518–80), who built a number of Venetian churches, notably San Giorgio Maggiore.

8 – *Golden Age*, vol. II, ch. XIII, p. 114.

9 – The vast and gilded gondola in which the Doge sailed.

10 – A town on several small islands in the lagoon of Venice, the site of the world-famous glassworks.

11 – Founded by the printer Aldus Manutius (Aldo Manuzio, 1449–1515).

12 – *Golden Age*, vol. I, ch. IX, p. 279.

13 – *Ibid.*, ch. V, p. 119.

14 – *Ibid.*, pp. 119–20, which has: ' . . . with the movement of the whole'.

15 – *Ibid.*, vol. II, ch. XV, p. 174.

16 – *Ibid.*, p. 200, extract.

17 – *Ibid.*, ch. XIV, p. 141.

18 – John Ruskin, *Stones of Venice,* (3 vols, 1851–3), vol. III, ch. I, para. 3: 'Although Renaissance architecture assumes very different forms among different nations, it may be conveniently referred to three heads: – Early Renaissance, consisting of the first corruptions introduced into the Gothic schools; Central or Roman Renaissance, which is the perfectly formed style; and Grotesque Renaissance, which is the corruption of the Renaissance itself.' This is not alluded to in Molmenti.

19 – Brown, ch. XXII, p. 422: 'Goethe likens the Doge to "the grandpapa of all the race"'.

20 – *Decadence*, vol. II, ch. XI, p. 78.

21 – *Ibid.*, ch. XI, p. 97.

22 – Giovanni Giacomo Casanova de Seingalt (1725–98), adventurer and author; arrested in 1755 and placed in the Venetian state prison, he managed to escape the following year and passed the rest of his life in France and Bohemia. Conte Alessandro Cagliostro (1743–95), adventurer and alchemist.

23 – Canaletto (Antonio Canale, 1697–1768); Francesco Guardi (1712–93); and Carlo Goldoni (1707–93).

The Genius of Boswell

The letters which are here reprinted have had an adventurous history. It was in the year 1850 that a gentleman making a purchase at Boulogne found that his parcel was wrapped in sheets of old manuscript. The sheets proved to be letters written by Boswell to the Rev. W. J. Temple,[2] an ancestor of the archbishop,[3] and when the rest of the series had been recovered from the paper merchant they were published in 1857 by Richard Bentley, with an introduction from the hand of an anonymous editor. Mr Seccombe, who introduces the present edition, conjectures that his predecessor was Sir Philip Francis, of the Supreme Consular Court of the Levant.[4] If, as there is reason to think, Boswell never wrote without some thought of posterity, his ghost must have gone through a long time of suspense. The edition of 1857 was greeted with applause by the critics; 'The Times devoted six entire columns to a review of the book';[5] but it was sold out in under two years (a fire, it is thought, helping to destroy it), and there has been no reprint of the book until the present time. There must be many, then, who love their Boswell, but have never read his letters – many, therefore, who will thank Messrs Sidgwick and Jackson for the handsome shape of the volume and Mr Seccombe for the skill and humour with which he has introduced his subject. When a man has had the eyes of Carlyle and Macaulay fixed upon him it may well seem that there is nothing fresh to be said. And yet each of these observers came to a very different conclusion; Carlyle, although he called Boswell 'an ill-assorted, glaring mixture of the highest and the lowest'[6] contrived to make him glow with much of the splendour of the true hero-worshipper; and Macaulay indulged in the famous paradox, which, like the twisted mirror in the fair, shows us the human body with corkscrew legs and an undulating face.[7] Mr Seccombe is not so amusing, but he is far more judicious. He has no theory to parade, and he has had the advantage of studying the letters; he can talk thus of 'a tender-hearted man' in spite of 'ludicrous immoralities'; he can see that Boswell was a 'great artist' as well as a 'freak'.[8] The letters certainly tend to make the usual discrepancies less marked, because they show that Boswell existed independently of Johnson, and had many qualities besides those that we are wont to allow him. To read a man's letters after reading his works has much the same effect as staying with him in his own house after meeting him in full dress at dinner-parties.

The letters begin in 1758, when Boswell was a boy of eighteen; they end a few months only before his death, and though they are scattered with wide gaps over a great many years, the story is continuous – there is a glimpse of Boswell on every page. The Rev. W. J. Temple met Boswell in the Greek class at Edinburgh University; he held the living of Mamhead and then the living of St Gluvias in Cornwall, and Mr Seccombe describes him, judging from published correspondence (unluckily it is not to Boswell), as a 'dissatisfied atrabilious man'.[9] But there is no doubt that he provided Boswell with a perfect audience. He was neither illustrious, like Johnson, not a humorous correspondent, like the Hon. Andrew Erskine;[10] but he was a contemporary, a man with literary ambitions, and a cleric. They shared their loves and their 'hopes of future greatness'; and it was under 'the solemn yew' at Mamhead that Boswell made one of his vows.[11] Temple, who had received the earliest of Boswell's confidences, who had reflected the image of what Boswell would like to be, was used ever after as the person who had a right to know what became of Boswell. During the first years of the correspondence he acted the part of the brilliant but irresponsible young man, whose follies are a proof of his spirit. He was a Newmarket courser yoked to a dung-cart;[12] he was 'a sad dupe – a perfect Don Quixote';[13] his life was 'one of the most romantic that I believe either you or I really know of';[14] his scenes with his 'charmers' were incredible. In short, with such a turmoil of gifts and failings buzzing through his brain, he was often really at a loss to account for himself. There were so many attitudes, and they were all so striking; should he be a Don Juan, or the friend of Johnson and Paoli,[15] or the 'great man at Adamtown'?[16] And then, because he finds himself writing 'in a library forty feet long', these visions fade, and he determines to live like 'the most privileged spirits of antiquity'.[17] He imagines himself with his folios before him the head of a great family and an erudite country gentleman. He was always imagining himself; it is difficult to decide how much of genuine feelings he put into these imaginations. He had affairs with half a dozen ladies before he married; he went through ecstasy and anguish; they failed him or they did not deserve him; but he was never driven from his elegant and half-quizzical attitude, like a man who is conscious that he has the eye of the audience upon him. 'Come, why do I allow myself to be uneasy for a Scots lass? Rouse me, my friend!'[18] I must have an Englishwoman . . .

You cannot say how fine a woman I may marry; perhaps a Howard or some other of the noblest in the kingdom.'[19]

Was it his vanity that made him such good company? For the vanity of Boswell was a rare quality. It kept him alive and it gave a point to him. He was not anxious merely to display all his emotions, but he was anxious to make them tell. He left out much that other people put in, and directly that he had a pen in his hand he became a natural artist. One may go further, indeed, and credit him with a sense that was oddly at variance with his egoism and his garrulity; a sense, as it seems, that something of value lay hidden in other people also beneath the babble of talk. 'I got from my lord a good deal of his life. He says he will put down some particulars of himself if I will put them together and publish them.'[20] In order to get from a man a good deal of his life you must be able to convince him that you see something that he wishes to have seen, so that your curiosity is not impertinent. Boswell was not content, after all, with a view of a 'visible progress through the world'; it was 'a view of the mind in letters and conversation' that he sought, and sought with all the rashness of a hero.[21] He had the gift, which is rare as it is beautiful, of being able 'to contemplate with supreme delight those distinguished spirits by which God is sometimes pleased to honour humanity'.[22] Perhaps that was the reason why most people found something to like in him; it was a part of his wonderful sense of the romance and excitement of life.

His intense consciousness of himself made his progress like a pageant, and every day was a fresh adventure. If he dined out he noticed that there were 'three sorts of ice creams';[23] he noticed the handsome maid; he noticed whether people liked him, and he remembered what clothes he wore. 'It is hardly credible what ground I go over, and what a variety of men and manners I contemplate every day, and all the time I am myself *pars magna*, for my exuberant spirits will not let me listen enough.'[24] But as time went on this same exuberance was his undoing; he could never cease imagining, and settle to what lay before him. He made vows in St Paul's Church and under solemn yews; he vowed to reform and read the classics; he broke them the day after and was carried home drunk; and then 'all the doubts which have ever disturbed thinking men' came over him, and he lay awake at night 'dreading annihilation'.[25] It is characteristic that he helped himself out of his depression by remembering that worthy men like Temple cared for him. He used his friends to reflect his virtues. It is possible, too, that as the years failed to fulfil his hopes he was teased by a suspicion that other people had found something that he had missed. He had conceived too many possibilities to be content to realise one only, and now again he was able to see, as he saw everything, that he had somehow failed in life. 'O Temple, Temple, is this realising any of our towering hopes which have so often been the subject of our conversations and letters?' he exclaimed.[26] Was there, perhaps, as he was wont to hint, some strain of madness in him that made his will shake always before an effort? 'Why should I struggle?' he breaks out. 'I certainly am constitutionally unfit for any employment.'[27] Was it madness or some power allied to genius that let him see in sudden incongruous flashes, as the scene shifted round him, how strange it all was? To get the full impression it would be necessary to quote letters at length; but when we read (for example) the letter upon the death of his wife, with its grief for 'my dear, dear Peggy', and its glory in the nineteen carriages that followed the hearse, and its repentance and its genuine cry of dismay and bewilderment, we feel that Boswell, as he sat and wrote it, had something of the clown in Shakespeare in him.[28] It was granted to this scatter-brained and noisy man with a head full of vanity and grossness to exclaim with the poets and the sages, 'What a motley scene is life!'[29]

It would be more rash in his case than in another's to say what he felt or how strongly he felt it; and yet, whether it was due to his wife's death or whether his system really proved impossible, his fortunes from that time dwindled away. His hopes of preferment were disappointed; he failed at the English bar; and to hearten himself he drank more than ever. But we should underrate the amazing vitality that clung to the shreds of him if we believed that he shuffled out of life, a dejected and disreputable figure, by some back door. There was still a twinkle of curiosity in his eye; the great lips were moist and garrulous as ever. But there is a harsh strain henceforward in his chatter, as though some note had cracked with too much strumming. Someone stole his wig, 'a jest that was very ill-timed to one in my situation',[30] but was probably irresistible. Then he began to finger 'several matrimonial schemes', to plume himself that his classical quotations had not deserted him, and to run after a certain Miss Bagnal.[31] Mr Temple, near the end of their strange correspondence, had to admonish him, for Boswell answers, 'Your suggestion as to my being carried off in a state of intoxication is awful.'[32] How was he 'carried off' in the end? Were his wits fuddled with wine and was his imagination dazed with terror, and did some snatch of an old song come to his lips? It is strange how one wonders with an inquisitive kind of affection, what Boswell felt; it always seems possible with him as with living people that if one watches closely enough one will know. But when we try to say what the secret is, then we understand why Boswell was a genius.

1 – A review in the *TLS*, 21 January 1909, (Kp C29) – 'I think rather good' (*I VW Letters*, no. 465, to Violet Dickinson, 4 January 1909) – of *Letters of James Boswell to the Rev. W. J. Temple. With an introduction by Thomas Seccombe* (Sidgwick & Jackson, 1908). Reprinted: *B&P*. See also *I VW Letters*, nos 443 and 445. (The same work was reviewed by Clive Bell in the *Athenaeum*, 13 February 1909, an article collected in his *Pot-Boilers*, 1918.)

2 – James Boswell (1740–95), the celebrated biographer, and Rev. William Johnstone Temple (1739–96) first formed their intimate friendship as students at Edinburgh University. Temple, an essayist of modest abilities, is remembered chiefly for his friendship with Boswell and with the poet Thomas Gray. He proceeded from Edinburgh to Cambridge, where he was an undergraduate, 1758–61, and fellow commoner, 1763–66, at Trinity Hall, being ordained in 1766. For a few months in 1762–3 he and Boswell had also been law students together in London.

3 – Temple was a grandfather of Frederick Temple (1821–1902), Archbishop of Canterbury from 1896; and, as it has since proved, great-grandfather of yet another eminent prelate, William Temple (1881–1944), Archbishop of Canterbury from 1942.

4 – Sir Philip Francis (1822–76), colonial judge, a grandson of the reputed author of the 'Letters of Junius'.

5 – *Letters*, p. viii n; see also *The Times*, 3–8 January 1857.

6 – See 'Boswell's Life of Johnson', Thomas Carlyle's review of John Wilson Croker's disastrous 5 vol. edition of the *Life* (*Fraser's Magazine*, No. 28) reprinted in vol. IV of *Critical and Miscellaneous Essays*, 45 vols, (James Fraser, 1840), pp. 39–40: 'Thus does poor Bozzy stand out to us an ill-assorted, glaring mixture of the highest and the lowest ... The peculiarity in his case was the unusual defect of amalgamation and subordination: the highest lay side by side with the lowest; not morally combined with it and spiritually transfiguring it, but tumbling in half-mechanical juxtaposition with it, and from time to time, as the mad alternation chanced, irradiating, or eclipsed by it.'

7 – See Lord Macaulay demolishing Croker's edition (n.6 above) in 'Samuel Johnson' (*Edinburgh Review*, September 1831), reprinted in vol. II of *Critical and Historical Essays* (2 vols, 1843).

8 – For all these observations, *Letters*, Intro. p. xxvi.

9 – *Ibid.*, p. xiv; Boswell uses the epithet 'atrabilious' of himself in a letter to Temple, 12 August 1775, p. 174: 'My wife is an admirable companion for a man of my atrabilious temperament . . .'

10 – The Hon. Andrew Erskine (d. 1793), described in the *Life of Johnson* as 'both a good poet and a good critic', some of whose correspondence with Boswell is published at the end of the volume under review.

11 – *Letters*, 28 April 1776, p. 189: 'My promise under the solemn yew at Mamhead was not religiously kept, because a little wine hurried me on too much.'

The source of the preceding phrase 'hopes of future greatness' has eluded discovery.

12 – *Ibid.*, 1 May 1761, p. 12: ' . . . is there any wonder, Sir, that the unlucky dog should be somewhat fretful? Yoke a Newmarket courser to a dung-cart, and I'll lay my life on't he'll either caper and kick most confoundedly, or be as stupid and restive as an old, battered posthorse.'

13 – *Ibid.*, 1 February [4 March] 1767, p. 60.

14 – *Ibid.*, 30 March 1767, p. 63.

15 – General Pasquale Paoli (1725–1807), the Corsican patriot celebrated by Boswell in *An Account of Corsica* (1768).

16 – *Ibid.*, p. 78; from 'Instructions for Mr Temple, on his Tour to Auchinleck and Adamtown'.

17 – For both these quotations, *ibid.*, 30 March 1767, p. 65.

18 – *Ibid.*, 24 December 1767, pp. 103–4.

19 – *Ibid.*, 8 February [11 February] 1768, p. 115.

20 – *Ibid.*, 19 June 1775, p. 166: 'I dined yesterday with the Lord Kames and his Lady *en famille*, and got from my Lord a good deal of his life. He says . . . '

21 – *Ibid.*, 24 February 1788, p. 218, which has: 'I am absolutely certain that my mode of biography, which gives not only a *History* of Johnson's visible progress through the world, and of his publications, but a view of his mind in his letters and conversations, is the most perfect that can be conceived and will be more of a Life than any work that has ever yet appeared.'

22 – *Ibid.*, to the Earl of Chatham, 8 April 1767, p. 66.

23 – *Ibid.*, 19 June 1775, p. 164; the occasion so distinguished was a supper at David Hume's.

24 – *Ibid.*, 17 April 1775, p. 152; 'I try to keep a journal, and shall show you that I have done tolerably; but it is hardly credible what ground I go over . . . '

25 – *Ibid.*, 12 August 1775, p. 174.

26 – *Ibid.*, 28 November 1789, p. 260, which has 'Temple! Temple!' and 'the towering hopes'.

27 – *Ibid.*, 23 August 1789, p. 251.

28 – *Ibid.*, 3 July 1789, p. 247: 'I could hardly bring myself to agree that the body should be removed, for it was still a consolation to me to go and kneel by it, and talk to my dear, dear Peggie. She was much respected by all who knew her, so that her funeral was remarkably well attended. There were nineteen carriages followed by the hearse, and a large body of horsemen and the tenants of all my lands.'

29 – *Ibid.*, 31 March 1789, p. 239.

30 – *Ibid.*, 23 August 1789, pp. 250–1.

31 – For Boswell's 'matrimonial schemes', *ibid.*, 22 August 1791, p. 284; and for Miss Bagnal, p. 279.

32 – *Ibid.*, 21 June 1793, p. 288.

'One Immortality'

There are a certain number of people who share Mr William Watson's feeling about the world:

I have never felt at home,
Never wholly been at ease –[2]

and are for ever musing upon their discomfort and asking themselves what it means. Some such discontent seems to be the natural lot of poets, and, even when it is vague and fruitless, it is at any rate a step in the right direction – the first step perhaps towards making something better. Thus we can imagine an audience to whom Mr Fielding Hall, the author of *One Immortality* brings consolation, and we must be careful in dealing with his words to sympathise with the feeling that prompts them. The need for such a book as this, indeed, is not obvious, unless one bears these considerations in mind. It is cast in the form of a novel, but it has nothing in common with the ordinary novel; it is much taken up with general questions upon life and conduct, but it is neither accurate nor profound; and, finally, although one book is called the West and another the East, there is little of that gentle and charming account of Eastern beliefs that gave Mr Hall's previous books their interest. A number of people travelling to India meet at Venice and become fellow-voyagers for the rest of the journey. Some are happily married, and others unhappily; there are nuns on board the ship, a learned German professor, an Indian girl going home, a certain Mr Holt, and a girl called Miss Ormond. But to supply them with names is to put the picture out of perspective; a name implies substance, passions, and a number of relationships, and Mr Hall's figures have no more flesh than will cover a single point of view. It is, indeed, a modern version of the old allegory; the men and women are brought together solely in order that one may ask a question and another may answer it. There was never a gentler prophet than Mr Hall, but still it is as a prophet, gifted with the sense of what things are not and what things should be, that he comes among us. He feels that the West has forgotten how to live, but it is difficult to say what this means precisely, or how it is to be reformed. The things that he sees and hears suggest to him meditations and explanations. When he sits in the Piazza at Venice, for example, and hears the band play he reflects that 'the nation which first learns how to bring back the music to the battle line will sweep the world'.[3] He goes on to dwell upon the modern doctrine of efficiency, and the mistake of thinking that human beings are machines; and then his train of thought swells into a mystic rhapsody in which it is said that 'all music is a march, a dance, a requiem, or between them . . . All life is love or war, and ends in death . . . The sweetest music is the saddest; the least sad is that which drives to war. That is a truth of life.'[4] If the company in the Piazza had been in the mood for it, these remarks might have led to a prolonged argument, and Mr Hall would have deserved the thanks of the party for setting up a theory to be pulled in pieces. But as it is, the argument must be carried on in silence, and we are hard put to it to find some term which shall express Mr Hall's form of thought without suggesting that it pretends to be more than it is. The greater part of the book is devoted to a discussion of love; and the different standpoints of men and women, East and West, religious people, and learned men are touched upon, illustrated, and so turned that they seem to make parts of a simple whole. Is not this the secret of Mr Hall's popularity? Phrases like 'marriage is the union of man and woman into one organism', or 'the souls of all are part of the World Soul that lives for ever'[5] have an Eastern charm about them, as though they were uttered by some placid philosopher, sitting in the road way, in his rags. And there is virtue surely in the position of one who takes nothing for granted, and is always ready to discuss the universe.

1 – A review in the TLS, 4 February 1909, (Kp C30) of One Immortality (Macmillan, 1909) by H. Fielding Hall. Reprinted: CW. See also 'The Inward Light' above.
2 – The last lines of William Watson's poem 'World-Strangeness' in Selected Poems (John Lane, 1903).
3 – Fielding Hall, Bk I, 'The West', ch. IV, p. 33.
4 – Ibid., pp. 33–4, which begins 'All music' and has no ellipsis between 'or between them' and 'All life is love'.
5 – Ibid., Bk II, 'The East', ch. XVII, p. 171; ch. XIV, p. 138.

More Carlyle Letters

It is impossible to doubt that the feeling with which we regard Mr and Mrs Carlyle has much changed in the last ten or fifteen years. The gauntlet has been thrown down twice at least, for, by the publication of Mr Froude's *My Relations with Carlyle*, and by the introduction which Sir James Crichton-Browne affixed to the *New Letters and Memorials*, we have been urged to declare ourselves upon one side or upon the other.[2] But the public which observes silently and gives the verdict is less and less inclined to read the letters with a view merely to deciding who was in the right and who was in the wrong. As the material for making a judgment increases it becomes more vain to narrow the question to one such issue; it taxes our powers to the utmost to understand; the more we see the less we can label, and both praise and blame become strangely irrelevant.

Carlyle himself forbade the publication of these letters, but Mr Alexander Carlyle urges that as the prohibition has been disregarded already it is his duty to publish the letters in full, so that 'every reader will have the full evidence before him, and be in a position to judge for himself'.[3] It is not hard to see that the editor holds strong views of his own, and allows them once or twice to emphasise a phrase in a way that seems to us unnecessary; but we have nothing but gratitude for his work as a whole. It is true that friends and relations must always shudder when the public is admitted, but if they do as Mr Carlyle has done and 'print practically in full',[4] they kill the most odious form of curiosity. The lives of Mr and Mrs Carlyle are revealed by the additon of these their most private letters on so vast a scale that to confine them to the limits of a drawing-room is no longer possible. We do not deny the truth of those 'revelations' which startled the world when the letters were first published, but when we see them in relation to the rest the facts, if they are still there, are different.

As every one knows, Carlyle was introduced by Edward Irving to Jane Welsh at Haddington in 1821. The letters which fill these volumes were written during the five years that passed between their first meeting and their marriage, Carlyle lent her books; he asked her to write to him, propounding questions such as 'What do you think of the Lady de Staël?'[5] which seem to indicate safe lines for their correspondence. From the first she made it clear that she would not have '*meaning* words underlined'.[6] It was his intellect that she admired, and it was her intellect that she would have him admire. The early letters are full of the delights of fame and genius, of high aspirations, of their hero Byron, of the noble works which they mean to write in time. They are not remarkable letters as yet, and this is partly, we may guess, because the bond was an artificial one. Carlyle when he wrote to a girl of twenty was not sure of himself, and felt his way behind the cover of formal sentences exhorting her to diligence and virtue, which shows that he did not see the facts clearly. He took her genius very seriously, and did his best to draw up a programme for the cultivation of it.

I would familiarise myself with whatever great or noble thing men have done or conceived since the commencment of civilisation – that is, I would study their history, their philosophy, their literature – endeavouring all the while not merely to recollect but to apply, not merely to have in my possession, but to nourish myself with all these accumulated stores of the Past, and to strengthen my hands with them for adding to the stores of the Future.[7]

Their genius, their ambitions, was the one bond which they could recognise. But as they learn to know each other better the tone of the letters becomes bolder. Even though they were never to speak of love, they find that they have much else to speak of, and gradually their first vague raptures give way to a more definite relationship; they discover that they are remarkable people – 'two originals for certain . . . it is very kind in Fortune to have brought us together; otherwise we might have gone on single-handed to the end of time.'[8] She is still 'my dear pupil',[9] who is urged to write a drama upon Boadicea,[10] an essay upon friendship,[11] or to combine in a novel;[12] but the master's care was not for the mind only.

I continue to lament this inordinate love of fame which agitates you so . . . [13] But it is not merely in an intellectual point of view that I congratulate myself upon the progress you are making. As a woman, it strikes me that your improvement is not less marked.[14]

Miss Welsh, as she says herself, was 'powerfully influenced'[15] in life and character from the moment that she knew such a man, and from her letters we can conceive what the nature of the influence was. They are constrained, anxious, sometimes even fretful. She had often, we can imagine, to define to herself the precise nature of this influence – to assure herself that it was 'intellectual' merely, and that one could not allow a man who was lacking in elegance, and was the son of a stonemason, to tyrannise over one's finer feelings. She advanced absurd little fences which were to mark the boundaries; she made him realise her rank and her prospects, and that his manners in the drawing-room were clumsy. She talked of literature until, when he came to know her better, he had to warn her against 'too great an isolation from the everyday interests and enjoyments of life',[16] and to remind her of the 'warm variegated world'[17] and of the 'solid living concerns of our fellow-creatures'[18] which it is not wise to neglect. It is as strange to think that Mrs Carlyle ever needed that warning as to think that her mind was once engrossed with thoughts of her own fame and writings. To some extent, no doubt, she kept to that pose in writing to him because it was the safe one, but it is also clear that she was still unripe and chill. The society of Haddington was not large, and it was easy – too easy, she began to think – to be both genius and beauty there. In taking Carlyle for her friend she was admitting a force that would be checked by no limit save a natural one, and to resist it would compel her to know and to use all her powers. In that lay both the joy and the danger. Lovers she had in plenty, but none that felt her charm as Carlyle felt it, and yet criticised her at the same time. She was discontented and unable to work at home, and his letters, if they increased her discontent, brought her 'consolation'.[19] 'Oh! you have no notion how great a blessing our correspondence is to me! . . . I owe you much! feelings and sentiments that ennoble my character, that give dignity, interest, and enjoyment to my life. In return I can only love you, and that I do, from the bottom of my heart,' she wrote in 1823.[20] To this he answered in words which hint at marriage without (for that would have risked too much) proposing it. Jane Welsh withdrew at once; he had misunderstood her, she said; she loved him, but could love without thought of marriage. 'All the best feelings of my life are concerned in loving you', but the sentiment was 'calm', 'delightful', 'unimpassioned'.[21]

It was clear, however, as Carlyle wrote but a few months later, that 'things cannot stand as they are'.[22] But the quick obvious changes which lead to the union of ordinary people were not possible for them. We may analyse their feeling and trace it to the intellect, or to pride, or to selfishness, but the further we read the less we trust to definitions; in their case love demanded a knowledge as complete as was possible of themselves and of each other. The change, then, that comes over them seems to be not so much in their feeling for each other as in their knowledge of themselves. They were both people of extraordinary capacity, and it seemed again and again, as the process of development and revelation went on, that it was not tending to marriage. The change naturally was more marked in his character than in hers, and the letters which began so respectfully with talk of her genius and future became more and more occupied with his own. The 'genius' which they had both claimed – 'for there *is* a kind of genius in us both'[23] – was beginning to work in him, and not perhaps as she had expected it to work. Indeed, if we are to understand the nature of their alliance, it is necessary to follow his career, for it became obvious that if she ever married him she would have to adapt herself to fit it. Carlyle was never blind to facts, nor did he flinch from speaking them; and he laid before her repeatedly and with vehement insistence what had come to seem to him the truth. He was beginning to realise what was in him, and what would be his fate. The burden of his letters changes. 'Do you know this as it is? Do you dare to front it?'[24] How in the name of wonder *dare* you think of marrying me?'[25] What was it that she was to know, and to dare?

What is my love of you or any one? A wild peal through the desolate chambers of my soul, forcing perhaps a bitter tear into my eyes, and then giving place to silence and death? You know me not; no living mortal knows me . . . seems to know me . . . I can never make you happy. Leave me then![26]

And again, if she thinks of happiness she must know that

Self is a foundation of sand . . . Fools writhe and wriggle and rebel at this; their life is a little waspish battle against all mankind for refusing to take part with them; and their little dole of reputation and sensation, wasting more and more into a shred, is annihilated at the end of a few beggarly years, and they leave the earth without ever feeling that the spirit of man is a child of Heaven and has thoughts and aims in which self and its interests are lost from the eye, and the Eagle is swallowed up in the brightness of the sun, to which it soars.[27]

It is true that she hesitated, said that she was not 'in love'[28] with him, and could imagine a love that swept through her like a torrent. It is here, too, that the reader also hesitates, for even without our knowledge of the future it is clear that two ways were open to her. If she hesitated it was because she realised the sacrifice; if, however, she consented, it was because 'one loves you in proportion to the ideas and sentiments which are in oneself; according as my mind enlarges and my heart improves, I become capable of comprehending the goodness and greatness which are in you, and my affection for you increases'.[29] And then again, 'Are you believing? I could easily convince you with my eyes and my kisses; but ink-words are so ineloquent!'³⁰

How shall we, when 'ink-words' are all that we have, attempt to make them explain the relationship between two such people? She married him, and if it was a tragedy, yet a study of their letters convinces us that it was a noble tragedy. They are not the wittiest or the best letters that their authors wrote, but they are among the most interesting, because they show us (as it seems) why it was necessary that the story should follow the course it followed, and make us respect the man and woman who kept to their parts more profoundly as we understand them better. 'How terrible,' wrote Jane Welsh in the last letter before her marriage, 'and yet full of bliss.'³¹

1 – A review in the *TLS*, 1 April 1909, (Kp c31) of *The Love Letters of Thomas Carlyle* [1795–1881] *and Jane Welsh* [1801–86] ed. Alexander Carlyle (2 vols, John Lane, 1909) – 'The Times, you see, gives me all the subtle and doubtful passions to discuss.' (*I VW Letters*, no. 476, to Violet Dickinson; and see nos 486, 491.) See also 'The Letters of Jane Welsh Carlyle' above and 'Geraldine and Jane', V VW *Essays* and *CR* 2.

2 – The Carlyles' marriage was a topic with which the Stephen family were perhaps more familiar than most: 'I was not as bad as Carlyle, was I?' being part of the rhetoric on Leslie Stephen's remorseful lips after his own wife's death (*Moments of Being*, p. 41). The gauntlet-throwing concerning J. A. Froude (1818–94) and his alleged misrepresentation of the marriage and misuse of source material in his *Life of Carlyle* and in editing *Letters and Memorials*, reached its most frenzied in 1903: that year saw the posthumous publication of his *My Relations With Carlyle*, as well as of *New Letters and Memorials of Jane Welsh Carlyle*, annotated by Thomas Carlyle and edited by Alexander Carlyle, with an introduction by Sir James Crichton-Browne, *Froude and Carlyle* by Crichton-Browne and *The Nemesis of Froude* again by Crichton-Browne, with Alexander Carlyle.

3 – *Love Letters*, vol. I, Preface, p. vii.

4 – *Ibid.*, p. ix.

5 – *Ibid.*, letter 1, 4 June 1821, p. 4.

6 – *Ibid.*, letter 8, January 1822, p. 21: 'Besides this there is about your Letter a *mystery*, which I detest. It is so full of *meaning* words underlined; *meaning* sentences half-finished; *meaning* blanks with notes of admiration; and *meaning* quotations from foreign languages, that really in this abundance of meaning it seems to indicate, I am somewhat at a loss to discover what you would be at.'

7 – *Ibid.*, letter 28, ?October/November 1822, p. 87; the sentence begins: 'I would rigidly set apart some hours of every day for the purposes of study; I would read and think and imagine; I would familiarise myself . . . '

8 – *Ibid.*, letter 49, 6 April 1823, p. 191; the ellipsis marks the omission of ' "in our humble way" '.

9 – *Ibid.*, letter 28, p. 89, and letter 49, p. 192.

10 – *Ibid.*, letter 14, 30 April 1822, p. 39.

11 – *Ibid.*, letter 49, p. 193.

12 – *Ibid.*, letter 28, p. 94, and letter 31, November 1822, p. 107.

13 – *Ibid.*, letter 41, 20 January 1823, p. 156.

14 – *Ibid.*, letter 44, 18 February 1823, p. 166.

15 – *Ibid.*, letter 30, 11 November ?1822, p. 97.

16 – *Ibid.*, letter 49, p. 191.

17 – *Ibid.*, letter 63, 18 July 1823, p. 250: 'There is a world that is not of types and printers: it is a too great abstraction from this warm variegated world that causes most of the misery and many of the faults which deform too frequently the literary life.'

18 – *Ibid.*, letter 49, p. 192.

19 – *Ibid.*, vol. II, letter 102, 17 September 1824, p. 12.

20 – *Ibid.*, vol. I, letter 67, 19 August ?1823, p. 265.

21 – *Ibid.*, letter 69, 16 September ?1823, p. 276.

22 – *Ibid.*, letter 78, 22 December 1823, p. 315.

23 – *Ibid.*, letter 61, 4 July 1823, p. 242.

24 – *Ibid.*, vol. II, letter 130, 10 August 1825, p. 159; which continues: '. . . front it, not decked in the stage-light of the imagination, but in the squalid repulsiveness of the actual world?'

25 – *Ibid.*, letter 125, 4 July 1825, p. 142.

26 – *Ibid.*, letter 128, p. 153.

27 – *Ibid.*, letter 130, 10 August 1825, p. 159; the first sentence here is extracted from a considerably larger one, pp. 158–9; 'and the Eagle' should read 'as the Eagle'.

28 – *Ibid.*, letter 112, 13 January ?1825, p. 69.

29 – *Ibid.*, letter 114, ?29 January 1825, p. 84.

30 – *Ibid.*, letter 166, 28 June ?1826, p. 300.

31 – *Ibid.*, letter 175, ?3 October 1826, p. 334.

'Gentlemen Errant'

The object of Mrs Cust has been to select four narratives from the old German chronicles, relating the adventures of German noblemen, little known to fame, and by 'suppressing or compressing their more "prolixious and Teutonic" divagations to render them agreeable reading'.[2] She speaks modestly of her own work, for not only is it a severe task to extract the pith out of crabbed and verbose writers, but her notes and her long list of contemporary and modern authorities prove how much she has read round her subject before offering the results to her readers. Indeed, were we to complain, we should urge that her modesty has been excessive. 'Of my own part in this book,' she writes, 'not much need be said.'[3] If we had had more of her 'own part', we should not venture the one criticism which the study of her work suggests. We feel occasionally that the adventures of the four gentlemen are not of sufficient interest to be followed so carefully, and that the scrupulous itinerary is sometimes so bald as to be tedious. We should have chosen either that Mrs Cust had furnished us with some richer background of history, or should have allowed herself the liberty which her learning makes a safe one, of interpreting the chronicles instead of piecing them together. A greater freedom might after all have suited the subject better, for each of these four gentlemen had once an extraordinary vitality. It did not, it is true, lift them much above the level of other men, or bring them into contact with any of the great movements of the century; but that they were obscure increases in some respects the interest of their story.

The hundred odd years (1465–1588) during which they lived were momentous years for Europe, and it is curious to see how men could live through them in ignorance of the change, and also how it affected them. There is, for example, the Lord Lev of Rozmital and Blatna, who set forth in the year 1465 on a 'grand expedition throughout the world',[4] his purpose being, it is said, partly political, but also religious and merely inquisitive. He went through France to England, from England to Spain and Portugal, from Spain to Italy, and so home to Bohemia. The mediaeval journey is like the progress of a fly which stops to investigate every knob, every tasssel, every drop of water. On the approach of Rozmital and his company of forty 'knights, nobles, bannerets, and serving men' an escort was sent out to meet them, if the ruler of the town were friendly; they were feasted, served with wine 'both red and white in mighty golden cans',[5] presented with jewels and horses, and invited to display themselves in some great tourney. At each town the process is repeated, until we get the impression that the towns of that period were small but brilliant treasure houses set down in a girdle of stone walls in the midst of a savage country. The 'marvellous rich and busy city of Bruges', for example, housed the 'wares of the known world'. 'Oranges and lemons from Castile . . . wines and fruits from Greece . . . spices and confections from Alexandria and all the East, "even as though one were there"; furs from the Black Sea . . . all Italy with its brocades, its silken stuffs and its armour.'[6] The visitors were generally shown over the treasury where gold and silver and jewels were hoarded; they were shown the parks full of wild beasts, and invited perhaps to choose some precious trinket as token of their visit. They saw the 'great ships, galleons, and cogs'[7] of the English fleet lying at anchor off Sandwich, and in London they were admitted to watch Queen Elizabeth Wood-ville[8] at her dinner. 'And she ate for three hours and many costly meats, whereof it would take too long to write. And all were silent; not a word was spoken.'[9]

This picture of the Queen seated on her golden chair, with her mother and sisters sitting or kneeling far below her, is somehow portentous and compels us to consider. The narrative, we must remember, was written by two scribes who rode in Lord Lev's train for the purpose of recording his adventures. They are not, therefore, concerned with his political mission, nor is it their business to speculate. What interests them mainly is the day's adventure, what they see, what legends, miracles, and strange customs they hear tell of. If we find the scene sometimes dull and curiously flat, we must remember Mrs Cust's claim that we are seeing the age as the writers saw it, and that we have first-hand material for whatever judgment we may pass. We find, then, that the mediaeval chronicler was a simple, matter-of-fact man, who was almost entirely occupied with the things he saw, and recorded the solemn ceremonies of the age (as we have seen) with perfect faith. Whenever something appears to be out of the way, a legend is invented to account for it; the mind seems content to register and never to inquire. The result, then, is a curious mixture of literal catalogue and vague credulity. The genuine charm which the chronicles possess is surely the result of the contrast. The passions and joys of the travellers are simple and coarse; their reflections are childlike; their eyes are drawn like a child's to bright colours and strange objects; but, on the other hand, they are able to widen their horizons and flood the world with mystery until all things – the romance of the Faerie Queen, the romance of the early Shakespeare plays – seem possible. Standing on the cliff at Finisterre, they look out to sea and tell each other tales of the phantom islands that have sprung out there, where the houses are of gold and silver and the roofs of flowers, and of ships that had sailed away with vigorous young men and returned in two years' time with a crew of withered grey beards. In addition, there is for the modern reader a charm in these narratives which presumably the chroniclers neither felt nor attempted to convey. The land which they describe (the land, say, between London and Poole) is empty and unfamiliar to us; the adventures of a man on horseback in an age when the roads were few and dangerous have a wonderful sincerity of detail that convinces us, like a story by Defoe.

But it is more interesting perhaps when the chronicler becomes biographer and attempts to describe a hero. There is the life of Wilwolt von Schaumburg, written by Eyb in 1507, 'the oldest biography of a German nobleman and commander of Landsknechts at present known'.[10] He was a page in the train of the Emperor Frederick the Third; he learnt the art of war under Duke Charles of Burgundy; finally, he became a professional soldier, ready to serve any master who had need of him. It is not necessary to follow the story of the innumerable 'battles, sieges, jousts, and courses', which he carried through so triumphantly that his biographer likens him to one of the 'ancient knights of the Round Table'.[11] The impression that one gets after all these years, is not of a man but of a type, once held admirable and once no doubt necessary. The forests of Germany swarmed with cut-throats; the town walls were besieged with ponderous castles of wood; moats separated knights from their ladies; and ropes weighted with a great knob of wax were let down to them; steep walls, storms that drive the ship on to the enemies' lands, clouds dropping over the moon at the critical moment take part in the struggle of man with man; they seem to get between any rational human relationship, to distort it, and make it picturesque. Eyb's 'perfect knight' then was versed in all the crafts which do battle with these obstacles, and we must endow him further with a kind of simple heroic beauty both of person and of nature. The death of Count William of Henneberg, who died in a village inn on his way to Italy, shows us at once the beauty and the barbarity of this ideal. He called for a candle and seized it 'even as though it were a lance' and defied death in these words, 'Thou evil enemy, thou hast no hold upon me, and I will overcome thee with this spear;' he then drank deep, clasped his crucifix, and prayed to God; those who stood round said they had never beheld a 'more reasonable ending by any man in all our time'.[12] There is beauty in that; we feel, for an instant, what kind of faith drove men on, like people in a mist, through that dreary age of bloodshed and brutality. But when all is said this hero of Eyb's remains a mythical personage; the ideal which the chronicler has in his mind implies a world so crude, so barbarous, and so inhuman that we must look upon it as a spectacle in which we have no part. 'Few things', writes Mrs Cust, 'are more astonishing . . . than the strange blend of penury and splendour that constantly appears in the annals of fifteenth-century knighthood.'[13] She refers, of course, to their dress and furniture, but it is also true of their point of view. They have a certain greatness of soul and are incredibly callous at the same time. They travel with a company of gorgeous knights, and seven of them use the water in a wine jar for a bath; they excel in courage and have such blunt perceptions that the spectacle of bloodshed is a treat to which men and women flock greedily. In their love affairs they were either frankly animal, or, if the diplomatic courtship of the Palsgrave Frederick[14] is to be taken as an example, made them an excuse for indulging in forms and ceremonies that are unspeakably tedious to us.

The last of Mrs Cust's studies, 'An Epic of Debts', is in some ways the most interesting of the four. It is taken from the memoirs of Hans von Schweinichen, who served six dukes of Liegnitz and brought his story from the last half of the sixteenth century down to the year 1602. The ducal court of Liegnitz was the home of a strange race, sprung from the Piasts of Poland, who only ruled the land in order to scrape money from it, and by the time that Hans entered their service had laid their house heavily in debt. It was his duty to travel round with his master, begging money, pacifying creditors, and trying to preserve still some show of princely state. Whenever they managed to raise a few crowns they were lavished at once upon fresh trappings or a splendid feast. But there is a note in this chronicle which we have not heard before. It is a note of ridicule and comedy; the portentous ceremonies of an earlier age seem to be burlesqued in this one. There are still the old embassies, the banquetings, and the sieges; but 'three hundred and twenty-five aged rams, so old that none other would buy them',[15] serve the ducal feast; and the great 'butter war' of Liegnitz, when the town was besieged by the Imperial army, harmed only the cows upon the ramparts.[16] Do we trace here the rude echo of that spirit of joy which, according to a famous historian, characterises the great men of a great age? At any rate, the attitude of the world has changed, even in small German courts, since Lord Lev of Bohemia set out on his travels; the Renaissance has come to its full splendour, and these obscure lives have somehow flitted on the verge of it. To combine the two stories, the story of a country and the story of an individual, throws a new light on each of them, and it is the great charm of Mrs Cust's book that it not only excites a thousand speculations, but gives us sound matter to make them of.

1 – A review in the TLS, 15 April 1909, (Kp c32) of *Gentlemen Errant. Being the Journeys and Adventures of Four Noblemen in Europe during the Fifteenth and Sixteenth Centuries* (John Murray, 1909) by Mrs Henry Cust – Emmeline (Nina)

Mary Elizabeth Cust: ' . . . a woman who had a child before she was married . . . and atones for it by studying mediaeval Germany profoundly. My review,' continued VW to Violet Dickinson, 'is going to deal with the subject of the illicit passions in a masterly way – and to suggest better means of penitence.' (*I VW Letters*, no. 476.)

2 – Cust, Intro., p. xiv.
3 – *Ibid.*, p. xiii.
4 – *Ibid.*, 'The Bohemian Ulysses: The Wanderings of Lev, Lord of Rozmital and Blatna, round the Courts of Europe', p. 8.
5 – *Ibid.*, p. 10; p. 18.
6 – For the account of Bruges, *ibid.*, p. 27, which has 'armour' in the plural.
7 – *Ibid.*, p. 30.
8 – Elizabeth Woodville (c.1437–92), Queen Consort of Edward IV of England.
9 – *Ibid.*, p. 39, which concludes: ' . . . not a word was spoken. And my Lord with his company stood ever in his corner and looked on.'
10 – *Ibid.*, 'A Master of War: The Exploits and Hazards of Wilwolt of Schaumburg, Soldier of Fortune', p. 124, on Eyb's *Stories and Deeds of Wilwolt of Schaumberg*.
11 – *Ibid.*, p. 155.
12 – For the account of Count William of Henneberg's death, *ibid.*, pp. 172–3.
13 – *Ibid.*, p. 166: 'For few things are more astonishing even in that astonishing age, than the strange blend . . . '
14 – See Cust's third study: 'The Adventures of a Palsgrave: The Early Life and Vicissitudes of Frederick II, Elector Palatine of the Rhine'.
15 – *Ibid.*, 'An Epic of Debts: The Curious Fortunes of Hans von Schweinichen at the Court of Duke Heinrich XI of Liegnitz in Silesia', p. 464.
16 – *Ibid.*, p. 483: 'Three persons came by their death in it, concludes Hans: "Whether they died of fright or other causes is not known to me, but no man was shot. The cows on the ramparts had the worst of it, since they had nothing to eat and were hourly in fear of their necks."'

Caroline Emelia Stephen

The death of Caroline Emelia Stephen will grieve many who knew her only from her writing. Her life had for years been that of an invalid, but she was wonderfully active in certain directions – she wrote, she saw her friends, she was able occasionally to read a paper to a religious society, until her final illness began some six weeks ago. Her books are known to a great number of readers, and it is not necessary here to dwell upon their contents. The *Service of the Poor* was published in 1871, *Quaker Strongholds* in 1890, *The First Sir James Stephen* in 1906, and *Light Arising* in 1908. A few words as to her life and character may interest those who had not the happiness of knowing her personally. She was born in 1834, and was the daughter of Sir James Stephen, Under-Secretary for the Colonies, and of his wife, Jane Catherine Venn, daughter of the Rector of Clapham.[2] She was educated, after the fashion of the time, by masters and governesses, but the influence which affected her most, no doubt, was that of her father, always revered by her, and of her home, with its strong Evangelical traditions. Attendance upon her mother during her last long illness injured her health so seriously that she never fully recovered. From that date (1875) she was often on the sofa, and was never again able to lead a perfectly active life. But those who have read her *Quaker Strongholds* will remember that the great change of her life took place at about this time, when, after feeling that she 'could not conscientiously join in the Church of England Service'[3] she found herself 'one never-to-be-forgotten Sunday morning . . . one of a small company of silent worshippers'.[4] In the preface to that book she has described something of what the change meant to her; her written and spoken words, her entire life in after-years, were testimony to the complete satisfaction it brought her.

Her life was marked by little outward change. She lived at Malvern for some time, but moved in 1895 to Cambridge, where she spent the last years of her life in a little cottage surrounded by a garden. But the secret of her influence and of the deep impression she made even upon those who did not think as she did was that her faith inspired all that she did and said. One could not be with her without feeling that after suffering and thought she had come to dwell apart, among the 'things which are unseen and eternal'[5] and that it was her perpetual wish to make others share her peace. But she was no solitary mystic. She was one of the few to whom the gift of expression is given together with the need of it, and in addition to a wonderful command of language she had a scrupulous wish to use it accurately. Thus her effect upon people is scarcely yet to be decided, and must have reached many to whom her books are unknown. Together with her profound belief she had a robust common sense and a practical ability which seemed to show that with health and opportunity she might have ruled and organised. She had all her life enjoyed many intimate friendships, and the dignity and charm of her presence, the quaint humour which played over her talk, drew to her during her last years many to whom her relationship was almost maternal. Indeed, many of those who mourn her to-day will remember her in that aspect, remembering the long hours of talk in her room with the windows opening on to the garden, her interest in their lives and in her own;

remembering, too, something tender and almost pathetic about her which drew their love as well as their respect. The last years of her life among her flowers and with young people round her seemed to end fittingly a life which had about it the harmony of a large design.

1 – An obituary published in the *Guardian*, 21 April 1909, (Kp c32.1) of VW's Quaker aunt who died at Cambridge on 7 April. 'If one could only say what one thinks ... ,' she wrote to Nelly Cecil, 'I can't see the need for respectful lamentations.' (*I VW Letters*, no. 480.) VW's comic life of 'the Quaker' or 'Nun', written in 1904, has not survived; but for an indication of her true regard for her aunt – banter and the narrow strait of the obituary column apart – see the account of 'a very wise and witty old lady' in *I VW Letters*, no. 275, to Madge Vaughan, July 1906. The Quaker aunt's regard for her niece was made tangible by her will, in which she left to Virginia £2500; and, by contrast, to Vanessa and Adrian Stephen £100 each (see *I VW Letters*, no. 481).
2 – Sir James Stephen (1789–1859); his wife Jane, who died in 1875, was the daughter of John Venn (1759–1813), rector of Clapham from 1792 until his death.
3 – *Quaker Strongholds* (Kegan Paul, 1890), Intro., p. 2.
4 – *Ibid.*, pp. 3–4.
5 – Cf. *Light Arising. Thoughts on the Central Radiance* (Heffer & Sons, 1908), ch. v, p. 75, where those who make a distinction between the inner and the outer life are said to 'all agree in regarding as "inward" the more permanent and important elements of our life – the "things unseen and eternal" – and in the feeling that these unchanging inner realities must dominate the outward ... '

The Opera

The Opera season is upon us, and for some weeks the programme from which a selection will be made has lain under discussion. No one, of course, is satisfied; but then universal satisfaction could only be obtained if we all thought alike. As it is, the Grand Opera Syndicate has to consider a variety of tastes, and the ambiguous state of mind which their list indicates hints at the varieties of the public taste. We shall have *Armide* and *La Traviata, Die Walküre* and *Pelléas et Mélisande* to choose between.[2] From these hints we may arrange the public in groups, something after this fashion. There are numbers who prefer *Traviata* to *Walküre*; there are some who disapprove of opera altogether, but, go, cynically enough, for the sake of what they term its bastard merits; and there is a third party which opposes Gluck to Wagner.

This last is the difference of opinion most worthy of discussion, because each side takes the Opera seriously, and finds fault with its rivals' theory of the art. It is an old dispute, of course; but its survival shows that the difference is profound, and a glance at the views expressed may throw light upon other divisions in the public mind. Certain differences lie on the surface: thus, the lover of Gluck will point out that his master deals with emotions that are far from ordinary experience; they express themselves more fittingly in movement and colour than in speech. It is true that his music is in close relation with the emotions of the actors, but these emotions are not essentially dramatic, and the music raises in us emotions of a general character which cannot be referred to the experiences of a particular person. So nice is the correspondence between the music and the emotions which it expresses that they seem to be caused by the music itself, and only to be reinforced by the men and women on the stage. In short, the mysterious shapes, dances, and exquisite melody which here come miraculously together produce a perfect whole of which the parts seem to embody a beauty which we could realise by no other means. But with Wagner it is very different: not only does he express human emotions with far greater closeness than Gluck, but these emotions are of the most pronounced character; they flash out in men and women, as the story winds and knots itself, under the stress of sharp conflict. The music which follows them and expresses them excites the strongest sympathy in us. And yet, swept away as we are at some moments, there are others when we seem to be dropped again. It is that there is some cleavage between the drama and the music? Music (it may be) raises associations in the mind which are incongruous with the associations raised by another art; the effort to resolve them into one clear conception is painful, and the mind is constantly woken and disillusioned. Something like this, we imagine, is the meaning of the gentleman who leaves the opera-house on Wagner nights protesting, 'This is not music.'

But then there can be no doubt that Wagner is incomparably the more popular of the two, and for this among other reasons: his story and his characters appeal to people who would never listen to music in a concert-room. They find a Wagner opera much the same as a play, but easier to follow, because the emotions are emphasised by the music. They find the men and women much like themselves, only with a wonderful capacity for feeling things. How many, as the opera goes on, see themselves in the place of Tristan and Iseult, are delighted with the depth of their own capacities, but feel little sympathy with the passages where they cannot undertake the parts? Strange men and women are to be found in the cheap seats on a Wagner night; there is something primitive in the look of them, as though they did their best to live in forests, upon the elemental emotions, and were quick to suspect their fellows of a lack of 'reality', as they call it. They find a philosophy of life in the operas, hum 'motives' to symbolise stages in their thought, and walk off their fervour on the Embankment, wrapped in great black cloaks. There are further the scholarly Wagnerians, detecting 'motives' by the flash of their electric lamps, and instructing humble female relatives in the intricacies of the score. And finally there is the true enthusiast, who may include or reject all these reasons for admiring his master, but declares that the opera as he wrote it is the last and highest development of musical art.

If it is true that the reason which attracts most people to the Wagner operas is that they find there real men and women with passions like our own, it is also true that this very quality repels others. Mme Tetrazzini[3] in the mad scene in *Lucia* is an ideal to great numbers. To begin with, it is impossible to conceive how she does it; and then her notes are flawless; but, above all, the combination of exquisite clothing, madness, melody, and death is irresistible. It is just the world for men and women who are by nature or calling of a shrewd practical disposition in the daytime. The ideas are simple but highly romantic, and they are set out with the utmost luxury. There is more than one opinion, however, about Italian opera; and among the audience no doubt one could find some elderly old-fashioned gentlemen recalling the days of Malibran and Mario,[4] 'when singing was an art'. The Opera to them is merely the occasion for a number of beautiful airs, without any dramatic connexion, upon which the prima donna lavishes all her skill.

These are but a few points of view, but the variety seems to show that there is, at any rate, no general idea as to the true nature of the Opera, and that those who believe it to be a serious artistic form are much in the minority. The words 'The Opera' alone call up a complex vision. We see the immense house, with its vast curved sides, its soft depths of rose colour and cream, the laces hanging down in loops from the boxes, and the twinkle of diamonds within. We think of this: of the hum and animation when the pyramid of light blazes out and all the colours move; and of the strange hush and dimness when the vistas of the stage are revealed and the voices mingle with the violins. Undoubtedly the great dome which has risen so pompously among the cabbages and slums shelters one of the oddest of all worlds – brilliant, beautiful, and absurd.

1 – An article published in *The Times*, 24 April 1909, (Kp c32.2) marking the forthcoming opening, as announced by the Directors of the Grand Opera Syndicate, of the Royal Opera Season at Covent Garden, on Monday 26 April. See also 'Impressions at Bayreuth' below.

2 – Neither Gluck's *Armide* (1772) nor Debussy's *Pelléas et Mélisande* (1902) were among the works performed in the opening week of the season. Verdi's *La Traviata* (1853), 'with Mr McCormack and Mme Tetrazzini' was performed on Saturday 1 March; *Die Walküre* (1870), 'under Dr Hans Richter, with Mr Walter Hyde, Herr Schützendorf, and Mmes Saltzmann-Stevens and Kirkby Lunn', on Thursday 29 April. The remainder of the week's programme consisted of: Saint-Saens's *Samson et Dalila* (1877), 27 April; Gounod's *Faust* (1859), 28 April; Mascagni's *Cavalleria Rusticana* (1890) and Leoncavallo's *Pagliaci* (1892) on 30 April.

3 – Luisa Tetrazzini (1871–1940), the celebrated Italian coloratura soprano, a member of the Manhattan Opera Company, 1908–10, had made her London debut in 1907 with a series of concerts. During one of these, *The Times* reported on 9 December, 'The Mad Scene from *Lucia [di Lammermoor,* 1835, by Donizetti] was interrupted by so much applause that a good many of the hearers thought the singer was obliging with an encore when she was only finishing her song.'

4 – Maria Felicita Malibran (1808–36), contralto, famous for the great range of her voice; her first London appearance was in 1825 as Rosina in *The Barber of Seville*; and Giovanni Matteo Mario (1810–83), tenor, made his London debut in 1839 as Gennaro in Donizetti's *Lucrezia Borgia*.

A Friend of Johnson

A great book, like a great nature, may have disastrous effects upon other people. It robs them of their character and substitutes its own. No one, for instance, who has read what Carlyle has to say about Lamb[2] ever rids his mind completely of the impression, in spite of the fact that we judge the writer of it far more than his victim. Some deposit remains with us. It is strange to reflect what numbers of men and women live in our minds merely because Boswell took a note of their talk. Two or three such lines have a generating power; a body grows from the seed. The ordinary English reader knows Baretti[3] solely through Johnson. 'His account of Italy', said Johnson, 'is a very entertaining book; and, Sir, I know no man who carries his head higher in conversation than Baretti. There are strong powers in his mind. He has not, indeed, many hooks, but with what hooks he has he grapples very forcibly.'[4] This may be, as Mr Collison-Morley says, 'a very good summary',[5] and yet his character is scarcely to be summarised thus; his vitality is too great for that. Mr Collison-Morley, further, has the advantage of knowing the Italian side of the story.

The Barettis came from Piedmont, and Giuseppe boasted romantically of his noble birth. He could not live at home, where they wished to train him for a lawyer, but ran away to see the world. He lived at Milan, Venice, and Turin by his pen, turning out ceremonial verses to order. His qualities, however, were not those that bring success. He was susceptible, but so importunate that a certain Mrs Paradise[6] had to snub him with boiling water from her tea urn. Great animal vigour and a powerful mind made him insolent and overbearing in manner before his fame authorised it. Thus he took it upon himself as a young writer to denounce Goldoni, the Arcadians, and Italian blank verse, when they were in fashion; later, when archaeology was the rage, he declared that antiquaries should be clapped into lunatic asylums, seeing merely the pedantic side of the pursuit and failing from some lack of imagination to foretell its future. To succeed in letters needed in that age the utmost tact. Then as now France supplied Italy with her reading to a great extent, for every province had its own dialect; authors were miserably paid, and their manuscripts had to be passed by two censors. Italy afforded no place for a man whose intellect led him to despise mere grace and scholarship, and whose temper urged him to speak out.

He decided to try his fortune in England. He was amazed by London: Lincoln's Inn, he wrote home, was three times the size of St Mark's Square; 'a great street, hung with painted signs and clamorous with droves of oxen and of sheep, carriages and foot passengers, ran right through the city; the wheels splash you with mud black as ink; there are women of "perfect beauty" mixing with horrid cripples';[7] Fielding told him that a thousand or even two thousand die every year from want and hunger, 'but London is so large it is hardly noticed';[8] a din of whips and curses lasts all day long, and at night the watchmen cry the hours hoarsely, 'vile hounds'[9] ring bells as they collect the letters; sweeps, milk-women, oyster-sellers vociferate perpetually. In spite of this London gradually ousted all other places in his affections. To begin with he found that the Italian language was in fashion, for an Italian tour was essential; and the Italian opera was so popular that the audience followed the words by the light of private candles. He could thus keep himself by teaching – one of his pupils being the famous Mrs Lennox,[10] by whom he was introduced to Johnson. The merits of the society which Johnson ruled were precisely to the taste of Baretti. He loved to stretch his legs, to talk enormously, to mix with men of all callings, to ramble the streets at night with a companion, and the booksellers with their vast and indiscriminate greed for copy suited his powers admirably. His mind, we know, had strong hooks and having set himself to learn English he made extraordinary progress in 'that strange and most irregular tongue'.[11] He could speak street slang even, and soon could carry on a controversy in vigorous English prose. It is typical of him that he could acquire any living language with enthusiasm, but the dead languages bored him. He turned out dictionaries, and translations and travels, with the printer's devil waiting at the door, until a lump grew on his finger where the pen rested. His struggle to live by his brains is, for us, full of picturesque adventures. A dissertation upon the Italian poets introduced him to a wealthy English gentleman who had been engaged on a translation of Ariosto for twenty years. For the sake of Baretti's advice and conversation he offered him a house and garden in his park, a gold watch worth forty guineas, and a wife. But the friendship ended in bitterness; it was said that the watch was only lent. Whether it was that Baretti had a drop of hot southern blood in him, or whether the society of scholars was in truth a rough and hasty world, we certainly find matter, even in a slight memoir like the present, for comparisons between that age and this. One cannot imagine, for instance, that writers then retired to their studies or worked by the clock. They seem to have learnt by talk; their friendships thus were important and outspoken. Conversation was a kind of strife, and the jealousies and contradictions which attended the display gave it at least an eager excitement. Goldsmith found Baretti 'insolent and overbearing', Baretti thought Goldsmith 'an unpolished man, and an absurd companion'.[12] Mrs Lennox, having complained that Baretti paid more attention to her child than to herself, he retorted: 'You are a child in stature and a child in understanding',[13] being generally provoking, where opportunity offered. Indeed a society of clever people whose witticisms, jealousies, and emotions circulate is much like a society of children. Reticence and ceremony seem to mark middle age.

The life of Baretti reminds us, too, in a singular way of the rudeness that lay outside the coffee houses and the clubs. One afternoon in October 1769, he walked from Soho to the Orange coffee house in the Haymarket. On his way back a woman sitting on a doorstep jumped up and struck him. In the darkness he returned the blow, whereupon three bullies set upon him, and he was chased along Oxenden Street, shouting 'Murder' with a crowd at his heels, who reviled him for a Frenchman. One man made dashes for his pigtail, and to save himself Baretti drew a silver-bladed fruit knife, and stabbed him twice. As the only means of escape, for he was stout, near-sighted and the road swam with puddles, he burst into a shop and gave himself up to the police. Goldsmith, we notice, drove with him to the prison and offered him 'every shilling' in his purse. The man died from the blow; Baretti was acquitted, and the fruit knife used to be shown at dessert.[14] The same kind of roughness marks the famous friendship with the Thrales, of which Mr Collison-Morley gives a very lively account. He lived in the family, not as a regular tutor with a salary, but as a hired friend who must talk in return for board and lodging, and might hope for an occasional present. The good-natured Mrs Thrale stood it for nearly three years, and then, finding him intolerable with his airs and arrogances, treated him 'with some cold-ness'; whereupon he set down his dish of tea, 'not half drunk', went 'for my hat and stick that lay in the corner of the room', and walked off to London without saying goodbye.[15] Johnson pleaded for him. 'Forgive him, dearest lady, the rather because of his misbehaviour; I am afraid he has learned part of me.'[16] It was true, no doubt, that he traded upon a certain likeness to the doctor, and expected the same consideration, but he learnt much from him that was wholly admirable. When he went back to Italy in 1763 he found that the old abuses at which he had tilted as a boy were still rampant. He decided to bring out a review, on the model of the *Rambler*, in which he could lash the Arcadians freely. In the person of Aristarco he delivered himself of his views upon the state of Italian literature, upon black verse, Goldoni and the antiquaries, retail-ing at the same time some of Johnson's peculiarities — that the Scotch are inferior, and that Milton is sometimes dull. Nevertheless, his satire told, and his controversies raised such an outcry that the *Frustra letteraria* was suspended. But 'no such criticism had as yet appeared in Italy'[17] and it is to-day a classic among his countrymen. But he 'could not enjoy his own country'.[18] England rewarded him with a secretaryship at the Royal Academy, and added a pension in his later years. For, industrious as he was, and in receipt sometimes of huge profits, his earnings never stuck to him. A strange kind of clumsiness united to a passionate nature seemed to make a child of him. What, for instance, could be more childish than the quarrel with Johnson as to whether Omai, an Otaheitan, had beaten him at chess or not? 'Do you think I should be conquered at chess by a savage?' 'I know you were', says Johnson.[19] The two men, who respected each other, parted and never met again. English people now scarcely read his books, unless it be the Italian dictionary, but his life is worth reading, because he exhibits so curious a mixture of power and weakness; he is in many ways so true a type of the man who lived by his pen in the eighteenth century; and Mr Collison-Morley fills in the old story as Boswell and Mrs Thrale told it with new matter from Italian sources. His life was full and vigorous; as for his works, he wished that every page lay at the bottom of the sea.

1 – A review in the *TLS*, 29 July 1909, (Kp C33) of *Giuseppe Baretti and His Friends. With an account of his Literary Friendships and Feuds in Italy and England in the Days of Dr Johnson* (John Murray, 1909) by Lacy Collison-Morley. With an introduction by the late F. Marion Crawford. VW clearly derived some of the material in her article from another source, but what this was has not been discovered. Reprinted: *G&R, CE.*

2 – Thomas Carlyle, *Reminiscences*, ed. J. A. Froude (2 vols, Longmans, Green, 1881), p. 232: 'At his own house I saw him once; once I gradually felt to have been enough for me. Poor Lamb! such a "divine genius" you could find in the London world only.'

3 – Giuseppe Marc' Antonio Baretti (1719–89), author of the classic *A Dictionary of English and Italian Languages* (1760), for which Dr Johnson wrote a dedication. Baretti came to England in 1751 and opened a school for teaching Italian. He returned to Italy in 1760, established *La Frustra letteraria* ('The Literary Scourge') in 1763, and when this controversial periodical was suppressed by the authorities in 1765, made his way back to London again, arriving in 1766 to publish *An Account of the Manners and Customs of Italy.*

4 – Collison-Morley, ch. VIII, p. 188; quoted from Boswell's *Life.*

5 – *Ibid.*

6 – *Ibid.*, ch. II, p. 33; Mrs Paradise, the American wife, otherwise unidentified, of Johnson's friend the linguist, John Paradise.

7 – Cf. *ibid.*, ch. IV, pp. 64–5 and 65–6.

8 – *Ibid.*, p. 67.

9 – *Ibid.*, p. 68.

10 – Mrs Charlotte Lennox (1720–1804), author of *The Female Quixote* (1752).

11 – Collison-Morley, ch. IV, p. 63.

12 – *Ibid.*, ch. III, p. 193; p. 194.
13 – *Ibid.*, ch. IV, p. 82.
14 – For 'The Stabbing Affair in the Haymarket', *ibid.*, ch. IX.
15 – For this incident cf. *ibid.*, ch. XII, pp. 297–301.
16 – *Ibid.*, p. 294, Johnson writing on 15 July 1775 in answer to general complaints by Mrs Thrale about Baretti's treatment of her.
17 – *Ibid.*, ch. VII, p. 165.
18 – *Ibid.*, ch. X, p. 229.
19 – *Ibid.*, ch. XIV, pp. 332–3.

Art and Life

There is in everything that Vernon Lee writes an emotional quality which makes it particularly hard to criticise her work. Again, in the present book, we feel her enthusiasm; and that somewhat vague sensation is perhaps the most definite thing that we take away from her writing. On this occasion she wishes to lay stress upon three 'coincidences', as she calls them – 'that between development of the aesthetic faculties and the development of the altruistic instincts; that between development of a sense of the higher harmonies of universal life; and, before everything else, the coincidence between the preference for aesthetic pleasures and the nobler growth of the individual'.[2]

In the main few people will deny that these coincidences exist, but difficulties begin when we have to define our meaning. In the first place, who is going to say what aesthetic beauty is? Here, at any rate, is Vernon Lee's definition: 'Beauty is that mode of existence of visible, audible, or thinkable things which imposes on our contemplating energies rhythms and patterns of unity, harmony, and completeness; and thereby gives us the foretaste and the habit of higher and more perfect forms of life.'[3] If we accept this definition, we may find fault with the application. As Vernon Lee applies it, for example, the works of Wagner are said to have less of this quality than the works of Handel. But, setting aside applications for the moment, we must agree in our definition if we are to agree in our estimate of the influence of beauty and art upon life, and to define this, after all, is the main purpose of Vernon Lee's work. If aesthetic beauty is to affect other qualities in the human being the emotion which we get from beauty must in some way induce us (for example) to do right. She establishes the connection by conceiving that there is a power outside ourselves, which is, as Plato has it in the *Symposium*, 'the essence of beauty'.[4] The effect of this 'real beauty' is to make us aware of some of 'the immense harmonies of which all beauty is the product, of which all separate beautiful things are, so to speak, the single patterns happening to be in our line of vision, while all around other patterns connect with them, meshes and meshes of harmonies spread out, outside our narrow field of momentary vision, an endless web like the constellations which, strung on their threads of mutual dependence, cover and fill up infinitude'.[5] We cannot perceive beauty through the senses without its awakening other harmonies within us, which are a part of the Divine harmony outside of us. A man who loves beauty in painting, therefore, will be more alive to moral beauty also; he will be a better citizen than a man without the aesthetic sense.

Further, as whatever is in harmony with the absolute harmony satisfies our innate sense of harmony more completely, it also fulfils our needs more completely, for 'attention is rendered difficult by lack of harmony',[6] and therefore a beautiful object is also more useful to us, by reason of its beauty. A Greek pot which 'embodies the same visible rhythm of being'[7] as a Greek temple was more useful because it was more harmonious than a modern jug turned off by a machine; and, following this train of reasoning, it is easy to see how the degeneracy of the moderns is both proved and accounted for. But these theories, which bring into force a power outside ourselves, are not to be disputed because one has to deal with intuitions. As far as we can judge, the qualities that constitute a 'harmony' and 'real beauty' may be different to different people, and it is only when we come to apply these theories that we are upon sure ground. Thus it is said that a love of beauty will bring about a love of simplicity and usefulness, because the beauty 'of people working in a field . . . is enhanced by their being common and useful'.[8] But the fact that they are common and useful may not increase their beauty at all; and, if this is so, then we can appreciate their beauty to the full without any love of the qualities that accompany it. The school which Vernon Lee would attack, therefore, is the school which has for its catchword 'Art for art's sake,'[9] and allows no connection between aesthetic beauty and beauty of other kinds. The vagueness and occasional inconsistency of Vernon Lee's arguments seem to arise from a desire to account for things logically without defining her terms sufficiently, and at the same time to prove that they are all pieces in a Divine system which the reason cannot appreciate. It will be remembered how, when one is reading Plato, there comes a moment, after pages of question and answer, when the constructive part of the dialogue is given us, very often in a myth or in the words of some wise woman. The device makes us realise that we are no longer arguing, but that we are listening to something beyond the reach of argument, now that we have gone as far as reason will take us. That is the point where Vernon Lee begins, with very little attempt to make the long ascent which leads to the view; and the result is that her statements have none of the Divine imper-sonality which stamps the myths and visions of Plato, but they are expressions of individual opinion. The very qualities of her style get in the way of any clear sight of the matter which she discusses; images and symbols, unless they spring from a profound understanding, illustrate not the object but the writer.

But if Vernon Lee lacks the temper of the great aesthetic critic, she has many of the gifts of a first-rate disciple. She has read Plato and Ruskin and Pater with enthusiasm because she cares passionately for the subjects they deal with. Moreover, although we may doubt her conclu-sions or admit that they bewilder us, her exposition is full of ingenuity, and has often the suggestive power of brilliant talk. One may not make things more clear by talking about them, but one can infect others with the same desire.

1 – A review in the *TLS*, 5 August 1909, (Kp c34) of *Laurus Nobilis: Chapters on Art and Life* (John Lane, 1909) by Vernon Lee (Violet Paget, 1856–1935). 'My head spins with Vernon Lee . . . ' VW wrote to Violet Dickinson in early July, 'What a woman! Like a garrulous baby. However, I suppose she has a sense of beauty, in a vague way – but such a watery mind.' (*I VW Letters*, no. 495.) See '*The Sentimental Traveller*' above.
2 – Lee, 'The Use of Beauty', p. 11.
3 – *Ibid.*, 'Art and Usefulness', p. 279, which has: 'For beauty is that mode of existence . . . ' and no comma after 'audible' or after 'harmony'. The next, also the chapter's concluding sentence reads: 'Art is born of the utilities of life; and art is in itself one of life's greatest utilities.'
4 – *Ibid.*, 'Higher Harmonies', p. 79; the words, in an unattributed translation, are those of Diotima, the prophetess of Mantineia.
5 – *Ibid.*, p. 107: 'Whenever we come in contact with real beauty, we become aware, in an unformulated but overwhelming manner, of some of the immense harmonies . . . '
6 – *Ibid.*, 'Art and Usefulness', p. 250: 'Beauty is born of attention, as happiness is born of life, because attention is rendered difficult and painful by lack of harmony, even as life is clogged or destroyed by pain.'
7 – *Ibid.*, p. 246.

8 – *Ibid.*, 'Nisi Citharam', p. 68.

9 – See, e.g., *ibid.*, 'Art and Usefulness', p. 260: 'Art for art's sake! We see it nowhere revealed so clearly as in the Exhibition, where it masks as "Decorative Art". Art is answering no claim of practical life and obeying no law of contemplative preference, art without root, without organism, without logical reason or moral decorum, art for mere buying and selling, art which expresses only self-assertion on the part of the seller, and self-satisfaction on the part of the buyer.'

Sterne

It is the custom to draw a distinction between a man and his works and to add that, although the world has a claim to read every line of his writing, it must not ask questions about the author. The distinction has arisen, we may believe, because the art of biography has fallen very low, and people of good taste infer that a 'life' will merely gratify a base curiosity, or will set up a respectable figure of sawdust. It is therefore a wise precaution to limit one's study of a writer to the study of his works; but, like other precautions, it implies some loss. We sacrifice an aesthetic pleasure, possibly of first-rate value – a life of Johnson, for example – and we raise boundaries where there should be none. A writer is a writer from his cradle; in his dealings with the world, in his affections, in his attitude to the thousand small things that happen between dawn and sunset, he shows the same point of view as that which he elaborates afterwards with a pen in his hand. It is more fragmentary and incoherent, but it is also more intense. To this, which one may call the aesthetic interest of his character, there are added the various interests of circumstance – where and how he was born and bred and educated – which all men share, but which are of greater interest as they affect a more original talent. The weakness of modern biographers seems to lie not in their failure to realise that both elements are present in the life of a writer, but in their determination to separate them. It is easier for them to draw distinctions than to see things whole. There is a common formula, in which, having delivered judgment upon his work, they state that 'a few facts about his life' may not be inappropriate, or, writing from the opposite standpoint, proclaim that their concern is 'with the man and not with his works'. A distinction is made in this way which we do not find in the original, and from this reason mainly arises the common complaint against a biography, that it is 'not like'. We have lives that are all ceremony and work; and lives that are all chatter and scandal. A certain stigma is attached to the biography which deals mainly with a man's personal history, and the writer who sees him most clearly in that light is driven to represent him under the cover of fiction. The fascination of novel writing lies in its freedom; the dull parts can be skipped, and the excitements intensifed; but above all the character can be placed artistically, set, that is, in fitting surroundings and composed so as to give whatever impression you choose. The traditional form is far less definite in the case of novels than in the case of biographies, because (one may guess) the sensibilities of conventional people have much less say in the matter. One of the objects of biography is to make men appear as they ought to be, for they are husbands and brothers; but no one takes a character in fiction quite seriously. It is there, indeed, that the main disadvantage of novel writing lies, for the aesthetic effect of truth is only to be equalled by the imagination of genius. There are a thousand incidents in a second-rate novel which might have happened in a dozen different ways, and the least consciousness of indecision blurs the effect; but the bare statement of facts has an indisputable power, if we have reason to think them true. The knowledge that they are true, it may be, leads us to connect them with other ideas; but if we know that they never happened at all, and doubt that they could have happened in this way, they suggest nothing distinct, because they are not distinct themselves. Again, a real life is wonderfully prolific; it passes through such strange places and draws along with it a train of adventures that no novelist can better them, if only he can deal with them as with his own inventions.

Certainly, no novelist could wish for finer material than the life of Sterne affords him. His story was 'like a romance'[2] and his genius was of the rarest. There is a trace of the usual apology in Professor Cross's preface, to the effect that he is not going to pass judgment on the writings, but merely to give the facts of the life. In his opinion such facts would be dull enough, if it did not 'turn out', as he remarks, that the writings are in part autobiographical, so that one may consider his life without irrelevance. But Professor Cross has surely underrated the value of his material, or the use he has made of it, for the book makes excellent reading from start to finish, and persuades us that we know Sterne better than we did before.

There are certain scenes upon which, were one writing a novel, one would like to dwell. The story of his youth is one; he was dragged about

England and Ireland in the train of the regiment which his father served. His mother was a vulgar woman, daughter of a sutler, and his father was a 'little smart man'[3] who got the wound that killed him in a quarrel over a goose. The family trailed about, always in staits for money, from one garrison town to another. Sometimes they were taken in by a rich cousin, for the Sternes were of old descent; sometimes in crossing the Channel they were 'nearly cast away by a leak springing up on board ship'.[4] Little brothers and sisters were born on their wanderings, and died, 'being of a fine delicate frame not made to last long'.[5] Sterne, after the death of his father, was taken in charge by his cousin, Richard Sterne of Elvington, and sent to Cambridge. He sat with John Hall-Stevenson[6] under a great walnut tree in the court of Jesus College, reading Rabelais, Rochester, and Aphra Behn, Homer, Virgil, and Theocritus, evil books and good books, so that they called the tree the tree of knowledge. Sterne, further, railed at 'rhetoric, logic, and metaphysics ... amused that intellect should employ itself in that way'.[7]

But it is at Sutton, eight miles from York, that we should like to pause and draw the portrait of the vicar. 'So slovenly was his dress and strange his gait, that the little boys used to flock round him and walk by his side.'[8] He would stop on his way to church, if his pointer started a covey of partridges, and leave his flock without a sermon while he shot. Once, when his wife was out of her mind for a while and thought herself Queen of Bohemia, Sterne drove her through the stubble fields with bladders fastened to the wheels of her chaise to make a noise 'and then I told her this is the way they course in Bohemia'.[9] He farmed his own land, played the violin, took lessons in painting and drawing, and drove into York for the races. In addition he was a violent partisan in the ecclesiastical disputes and drew Dr Slop from the life.[10] Then, when he was tired of parochial life he could drive over to the great stone house with the moat of stagnant water round it where John Hall-Stevenson lived, in retreat from the world, humouring his fancies. If the weathercock which he saw from his bed pointed to the north-east, for example, Mr Hall-Stevenson would lie all day in bed. If he could be induced to rise, he spent his time in writing indecent rhymes and in reading with his friend among the old and obscene books in the library. Then, in October, the brotherhood of the Demoniacs met at the Hall, in imitation of the monks of Medmenham Abbey; but it was a rustic copy, for they were 'noisy Yorkshire squires and gentlemen',[11] who hunted by day, drank deep into the night, and told rude stories over their burgundy. Their spirit and their oddity (for they were the freaks of the countryside) rejoiced Sterne hugely, just as he loved the immense freedom of the old writers. When he was back in his parsonage again he had books all round him to take the place of talk. York was full of books, for the sales of the county took place there. Sterne's love of books reminds us sometimes of Charles Lamb. He loved the vast forgotten folios, where a lifetime of learning and fancy has been poured into the notes; he loved Burton and Bouchet and Bruscambille;[12] Montaigne, Rabelais, and Cervantes he loved of course; but one may believe that he delighted most in his wild researches into medicine, midwifery, and military engineering. He was only brought to a stop by the difficulty of understanding in what way a cannon ball travels, for the 'laws of the parabola'[13] were not to his mind.

He was forty-five before it occurred to him that these vivid experiences among the parsons, the country peasants, and the wits of Crazy Castle had given him a view of the world which it would be possible to put into shape. The first books of *Tristram Shandy* were written at fever heat, 'quaint demons grinning and clawing at his head',[14] ideas striking him as he walked, and sending him back home at a run to secure them. It is in this way that the first books still impress us; a wonderful conception, long imprisoned in the brain and delicately formed, seems to leap out, surprising and intoxicating the writer himself. He had found a key to the world. He thought he could go on like this, at the rate of two volumes a year for ever, for a miracle had happened which turned all his experiences to words; to write about them was to be master of all that was in him and all that was to come. A slight knowledge of his life is enough to identify many of the characters with real people and to trace the humours of Uncle Toby and Mr Shandy to the oddities of Crazy Castle and to the studies of the writer himself. But these are merely marks on the surface, and the source from which they sprang lies very deep. Wilfully strange and whimsical of course Sterne was, but the spirit which inspires his humours and connects them is the spirit of the humorist; the world is an absurd place, and to prove it he invents absurdities which he shows to be as sensible as the views by which the world is governed. The stranger's nose, it will be remembered, 'just served as a frigate to launch them into a gulf of school divinity, and then they all sailed before the wind'.[15] Whichever way the story winds it is accompanied by a jibing at 'great wigs, grave faces, and other implements of deceit',[16] and thus the innumerable darts and spurts of fancy, in spite of their variety, have a certain likeness. Shandy Hall, the home of cranks and eccentricities, nevertheless contrives to make the whole of the outer world appear heavy, and dull and brutal, and teased by innumerable imps. But it is probable that this effect is given quite as much by indirect means as by direct satire and parody. The form of the book, which seems to allow the writer to put down at once the first thought that comes into his head, suggests freedom; and then the thoughts themselves are so informal, so small, private, and far-fetched, that the reader is amazed and delighted to think how easy it must be to write. Even his indecency impresses one as an odd kind of honesty. In comparison other novels seem intolerably portly and platitudinous and remote from life. At the same time, what kind of life is it that Sterne can show us? It is easy to see that it has nothing in common with what, in the shorthand of speech, one calls 'real life'. Sterne skips immense tracts of living in order to concentrate upon the little whim or the oddity which most delighted him. His people are always at high pressure, with their brains in a state of abnormal activity. Their wills and their affections can make small way against their intellects. Uncle Toby, it will be remembered, picks up a Bible directly he has made his offer of marriage, and becomes so much engrossed by the siege of Jericho that he leaves his proposal 'to work with her after its own way'.[17] When the news of his son's death reaches Mr Shandy, his mind at once fills with the fine sayings of the philosophers, and in spouting them his private sorrow is completely forgotten. Nevertheless, although such reversals of ordinary experience startle us, they do not seem to us unnatural – they do not turn to chill conceits – because Sterne, the first of 'motive-mongers'[18] has observed the humours of man with an exquisite subtlety. His sphere is in the most exalted regions, where the thought and not the act is the thing criticised; where the thought, moreover, is almost completely severed from ordinary associations and the support of facts. Uncle Toby, with his simple questionings and avowals – 'You puzzle me to death'[19] – plays a most important part by bringing his brother's flights to earth and giving them that contrast with normal human thought in which the essence of humour lies.

Yet there are moments, especially in the later books of *Tristram Shandy*, where the hobby-horse is ridden to death, and Mr Shandy's invariable eccentricity tries our patience. The truth is that we cannot live happily in such fine air for long, and that we begin to become conscious of limitations; moreover, this astonishing vivacity has something a little chill about it. The same qualities that were so exhilarating at first – the malice, the wit, and the irresponsibility – are less pleasing when they seem less spontaneous, like the grin on a weary face; or, it may be, when one has had enough of them. A writer who feels his responsibility to his characters tries to give vent to portentous groans at intervals; he does his best to insist that he is a showman merely, that his judgments are fallible, and that a great mystery lies round us all. But Sterne's sense of humour will suffer no mystery to settle on his page; he is never sublime like Meredith, but on the other hand he is never ridiculous like Thackeray. When he wished to get some relief from his fantastic brilliancy, he sought it in the portrayal of exquisite instants and pangs of emotion. The famous account of Uncle Toby and the fly – '"Go," says he, lifting up the sash, and opening his hand as he spoke, to let it escape; "go, poor devil; get thee gone, why should I hurt thee? This world surely is wide enough to hold both thee and me"' – is followed by a description of the effect which such words had upon Sterne himself. They 'instantly set my whole frame into one vibration of most pleasurable sensation'.[20] It is this strange contradiction, as it seems, between feeling pain and joy acutely, and at the same time, observing and admiring his own power to do so, that has thrown so much discredit upon the famous 'sentimentality', and has so much perplexed his admirers. The amazing truth of these observations is the best proof that he felt them; but when it becomes obvious that he has now time to think of himself our attention strays also, and we ask irrelevant questions – whether, for instance, Sterne was a good man. Sometimes – the incident of the donkey in *Tristram Shandy* is a good example[21] – his method is brilliantly successful, for he touches upon the emotion, and passes on to show us how it travels through his mind, and what associations cling to it; different ideas meet and disperse, naturally as it seems; and the whole scene is lit for the moment with air and colour. In the *Sentimental Journey*, however, Sterne seems anxious to suppress his natural curiosity, and to have a double intention in his sentiment – to convey a feeling to the reader, but with the object of winning admiration for his own simple virtues. It is when his unmixed sentiment falls very flat that we begin to ask ourselves whether we like the writer, and to call him hypocrite. 'The *pauvre honteux* ⟨to whom Sterne had given alms⟩ could say nothing; he pull'd out a little handkerchief, and wiped his face as he turned away – and I thought he thanked me more than them all.'[22] The last words, with their affectation of simplicity, are like eyes turned unctuously to Heaven.

There is abundant evidence in the story of his life to show how strange and complicated was the state of mind that produced such works of art. Sterne was a man of many passions, driven 'according as the fly stings';[23] but the most serious was said to have been inspired by Mrs Draper, the Eliza of the letters.[24] Nevertheless, sentiments that had done duty for his wife in 1740 were copied out, with a change of name, and made to serve again for Eliza, in the year 1767; and again if he had turned a phrase happily in writing to Eliza, Lydia, his daughter, was given the benefit of it. Shall we infer from this that Sterne cared nothing for wife or mistress or daughter, or shall we believe that he was, before everything else, and with all the failing of his kind, a great artist? If he had been among the greatest, no doubt these little economies would not have been necessary; but with his exquisite and penetrating but not very exuberant genius it was essential to make shifts and to eke out as best he might. Accordingly, we have, as Professor Cross demonstrates, the strange spectacle of a man who uses his emotions twice over, for different purposes. The journal to Eliza in which the most secret passions of his heart are laid bare is but the notebook for passages in the *Sentimental Journey* which all the world may read. Sterne himself, no doubt, scarcely knew at what point his own pain was dissolved in the joy of an artist. We at this distance of time, might speculate indefinitely.

Indeed, however we may test it, there is no life which it is harder to judge; its eccentricities are often genuine, and its impulses are often premeditated. In the same way the final impression is twofold in its nature, for we must combine a life of extraordinary flightiness and oddity with the infinite painstaking and self-consciousness of an artist. This thin, excitable man, who was devoured by consumption, who said of himself that he generally acted on the first impulse, and was a bundle of sensations scarcely checked by reason, not only kept a record of all that he felt, but could sit close at his table, arranging and rearranging, adding and altering, until every scene was clear, every tone was felt, and each word was fit and in its place. 'How do the slight touches of the chisel,' he exclaimed in *Tristram Shandy*, 'the pencil, the pen, the fiddle stick, et cetera, give the true swell, which gives the true pleasure! O, my fellow countrymen! – be nice; be cautious of your language – and never, O! never let it be forgotten upon what small particles your eloquence and your fame depend.'[25] His fame depends partly upon that inimitable style, but rests most safely upon the extraordinary zest with which he lived, and upon the joy with which his mind worked ceaselessly upon the world.

1 – A review in the *TLS*, 12 August 1909, (Kp c35) of *The Life and Times of Laurence Sterne* [1713–68] (Macmillan Co., 1909) by Wilbur L. Cross. Reprinted: *G&R, CE*. Reading Notes (Berg xxix). See also 'Sterne's Ghost', *IV VW Essays*, and 'The *Sentimental Journey*', *V VW Essays* and CR2.

2 – Cross, pp. 194–5, concerning Sterne's reception in London following the publication in 1759–60 of the first two volumes of *The Life and Opinions of Tristram Shandy*.

3 – *Ibid.*, p. 16, from the memoir Sterne wrote for his daughter Lydia. Roger Sterne (c. 1692–1731), the author's father, an ensign in the army, married in 1711 Agnes Herbert, widow of an army captain; he received his wound duelling at Gibraltar and died of it some months later, still serving his regiment at Port Antonio in Jamaica.

4 – *Ibid.*, p. 14.

5 – *Ibid.*

6 – John Hall-Stevenson (1718–85), country gentleman and author of licentious verse, Sterne's intimate friend, from whom he drew the character of Eugenius in *Tristram Shandy* and *A Sentimental Journey* (1768). Hall-Stevenson was admitted to Jesus College, Cambridge, in June 1735, where Sterne was then completing his second year.

7 – Cross, pp. 29–30.

8 – *Ibid.*, p. 60, which has 'around him'.

9 – *Ibid.*, p. 521, which has 'tell' not 'told'. See also *ibid.*, p. 185, for extracts from John Croft's *Scrapeana* (1792) recounting the episode.

10 – The original of Dr Slop was Dr John Burton (1710–71), antiquary and physician, author of *A Treatise of the Non-Naturals* (1738), and *An Essay toward a Complete New System of Midwifery* (1751), known to his, chiefly political, enemies (among whom Sterne was eminent) as 'Hippocrates Obstetricius'; he was a staunch Tory but not, as Dr Slop is, a 'Papist'.

11 – Cross, p. 123.

12 – Robert Burton (1577–1640) author of *The Anatomy of Melancholy* (1621); see *ibid.*, pp. 132–3, for Guillaume Bouchet, magistrate at Poitiers, author of volumes of *Serées. Or Evening Conferences* (1584–); also for Bruscambille, stage name of Deslauiers, a comedian, who wrote *Fantasies* or *Pensées Facétieuses* (1612).

13 – Cross, p. 143: ' . . . and the search ended with Galileo and Torricelli, whose infallible laws of the parabola he could not understand. There Sterne stopped, hopelessly bewildered.'

14 – *Ibid.*, p. 236.

15 – *Tristram Shandy*, vol. IV, 'Slawkenbergius's Tale' (ed. Christopher Ricks, Penguin, 1967, p. 266).

16 – *Ibid.*, vol. III, ch. 20, p. 210, concerning 'The Author's PREFACE'.

17 – *Ibid.*, vol. IX, 'The Eighteenth Chapter', p. 603, which has: 'When he had told Mrs Wadman once that he loved her, he let it alone, and left the matter to work after its own way.'

18 – Cf. *ibid.*, vol. VI, ch. 31, p. 440: 'My father, who was a great MOTIVE-MONGER, and consequently a very dangerous person for a man to sit by . . . '

19 – *Ibid.*, vol. III, ch. 18, p. 200; the source of puzzlement here is Walter Shandy's metaphysical dissertation on 'the succession of our ideas'.

20 – For this account of Uncle Toby and the fly, *ibid.*, vol. II, ch. 12, p. 131.
21 – *Ibid.*, vol. VII, ch. 32.
22 – *A Sentimental Journey through France and Italy*, vol. I, 'Montriul' (ed. Graham Petrie, Penguin, 1967, p. 60). (The same passage is quoted in 'The Sentimental Journey', see V VW Essays.)
23 – *Tristram Shandy*, vol. I, ch. 8, p. 43: 'De gustibus non est disputandum; that is, there is no disputing against HOBBY-HORSES; and, for my part, I seldom do ... happening, at certain intervals and changes of the Moon, to be both fiddler and painter, according as the fly stings ... '
24 – Mrs Eliza Draper (1744–78), the wife of an East India Company official, whom Sterne met in London in 1766; the course of their sentimental affair is traced in the *Journal to Eliza*, which was first published in 1904.
25 – *Tristram Shandy*, vol. II, ch. 6, p. 120.

Impressions at Bayreuth

The commonplace remark that music is in its infancy is best borne out by the ambiguous state of musical criticism. It has few traditions behind it, and the art itself is so much alive that it fairly suffocates those who try to deal with it. A critic of writing is hardly to be taken by surprise, for he can compare almost every literary form with some earlier form and can measure the achievement by some familiar standard. But who in music has tried to do what Strauss[2] is doing, or Debussy? Before we have made up our minds as to the nature of the operatic form we have to value very different and very emphatic examples of it. This lack of tradition and of current standards is of course the freest and happiest state that a critic can wish for: it offers some one the chance of doing now for music what Aristotle did 2000 years ago for poetry. The fact however that so little has yet been done to lay bare the principles of the art accounts for the indecision which marks our attempts to judge new music. As for the old, we take it for granted, or concentrate our minds upon the *prima donna*'s cold. It is criticism of a single hour, in a particular day, and tomorrow the mark has faded.

There is only one way open thus for a writer who is not disposed to go to the root of the matter and is yet dissatisfied with the old evasions – he may try to give his impressions as an amateur. The seats in the great bare house in Bayreuth are packed with them; they have a secret belief that they understand as well as other people, although they seldom venture an opinion; and, at any rate, there is no doubt that they love music. If they hesitate to criticise, it is perhaps that they have not sufficient technical knowledge to fasten upon details; a criticism of the whole resolves itself into vague formulas, comparisons, and adjectives. Nevertheless, no one can doubt that the audience at Bayreuth, pilgrims many of them from distant lands, attend with all their power. As the lights sink, they rustle into their seats, and scarcely stir till the last wave of sound has ceased; when a stick falls, there is a nervous shudder, like a ripple in water, through the entire house. During the intervals between the acts, when they come out into the sun, they seem oppressed with a desire to disburden themselves somehow of the impression which they have received. *Parsifal*, in particular, lays such a weight upon the mind that it is not until one has heard it many times over that one can begin, as it were, to move it to and fro. The unfamiliarity of the ideas hinders one at the outset from bringing the different parts together. One feels vaguely for a crisis that never comes, for, accustomed as one is to find the explanation of a drama in the love of man and woman, or in battle, one is bewildered by a music that continues with the utmost calm and intensity independently of them. Further, the change from the Temple of the Grail to the magic garden, with its swarms of flower-maidens and its hot red blossoms, is too violent a break to be bridged conveniently.

Nevertheless, although they are great, these difficulties scarcely do more than disturb the surface of a very deep and perhaps indescribable impression. Puzzled we may be, but it is primarily because the music has reached a place not yet visited by sound. An anthem sung with perfect skill in some great church will suggest a part of the scene in the vast hall, with its green distances, and yet a part only. Ecclesiastical music is too rigidly serene and too final in its spirit to penetrate as the music of *Parsifal* penetrates. Somehow Wagner has conveyed the desire of the Knights for the Grail in such a way that the intense emotion of human beings is combined with the unearthly nature of the things they seek. It tears us, as we hear it, as though its wings were sharply edged. Again, feelings of this kind that are equally diffused and felt for one object in common create an impression of largeness and, when the music is played as it was played on the night of the 11th, of an overwhelming unity. The Grail seems to burn through all superincumbences; the music is intimate in a sense that none other is; one is fired with emotion and yet possessed with tranquillity at the same time, for the words are continued by the music so that we hardly notice the transition.

It may be that these exalted emotions, which belong to the essence of our being, and are rarely expressed, are those that are best translated by music; so that a satisfaction, or whatever one may call that sense of answer which the finest art supplies to its own question, is constantly conveyed here. Like Shakespeare, Wagner seems to have attained in the end to such a mastery of technique that he could float and soar in regions where in the beginning he could scarcely breathe; the stubborn matter of his art dissolves in his fingers, and he shapes it as he chooses. When the opera is over, it is surely the completeness of the work that remains with us. The earlier operas have always their awkward moments, when the illusion breaks; but *Parsifal* seems poured out in a smooth stream at white heat; its shape is solid and entire. How much of the singular atmosphere which surrounds the opera in one's mind springs from other sources than the music itself it would be hard to say. It is the only work which has no incongruous associations.[3]

It has been possible, during these last performances, to step out of the opera house and find oneself in the midst of a warm summer evening. From the hill above the theatre you look over a wide land, smooth and without hedges; it is not beautiful, but it is very large and tranquil. One may sit among rows of turnips and watch a gigantic old woman, with a blue cotton bonnet on her head and a figure like one of Dürer's, swinging her hoe. The sun draws out strong scents from the hay and the pine trees, and if one thinks at all, it is to combine the simple landscape with the landscape of the stage. When the music is silent the mind insensibly slackens and expands, among happy surroundings: heat and the yellow light, and the intermittent but not unmusical noises of insects and leaves smooth out the folds. In the next interval, between seven and eight, there is another act out here also: it is now dusky and perceptibly fresher; the light is thinner, and the roads are no longer crossed by regular bars of shade. The figures in light dresses moving between the trees of the avenue, with depths of blue air behind them, have a curiously decorative effect. Finally, when the opera is over, it is quite late; and half way down the hill one looks back upon a dark torrent of carriages descending, their lamps wavering one above another, like irregular torches.

These strange intervals in the open air, as though a curtain were regularly drawn and shut again, have no disturbing effect, upon *Parsifal* at least. A bat from the woods circled Kundry's[4] head in the meadow, and little white moths dance incessantly over the footlights. It was curious, although scarcely fair, to test *Lohengrin* two days after one had heard *Parsifal*.[5] The difference which a chorus, alive in all its parts so that eyes and arms are moving when the voice is silent, can make to a work in which the chorus means so much is surprising certainly; and yet, recognising the admirable performance, other reflections were suggested by it. The same surroundings that were so congenial to *Parsifal* turn much of *Lohengrin* to tinsel and sham armour; one thinks of gorgeous skirts and the mantles of knights trailed along the dusty paths and pricked by the stubble. An opera house which shelters such a troop should be hemmed in by streets with great shop windows; their splendour somehow dwindles away and falls flat in the empty country.

But although this was one of the impressions that *Lohengrin* gave rise to, can it be held to be any reflection upon the music? No one, perhaps, save a writer properly versed in the science, can decide which impressions are relevant and which impertinent, and it is here that the amateur is apt to incur the contempt of the professional. We know the critic who, in painting, prefers the art of Fra Angelico because that painter worked upon his knees; others choose books because they teach one to rise early; and one has only to read the descriptive notes in a concert programme to be led hopelessly astray. Apart from the difficulty of changing a musical impression into a literary one, and the tendency to appeal to the literary sense because of the associations of words, there is the further difficulty in the case of music that its scope is much less clearly defined than the scope of the other arts. The more beautiful a phrase of music is the richer its burden of suggestion, and if we understand the form but slightly, we are little restrained in our interpretation. We are led on to connect the beautiful sound with some experience of our own, or to make it symbolise some conception of a general nature. Perhaps music owes something of its astonishing power over us to this lack of definite articulation; its statements have all the majesty of a generalisation, and yet contain our private emotions. Something of the same effect is given by Shakespeare, when he makes an old nurse the type of all the old nurses in the world, while she keeps her identity as a particular old woman. The comparative weakness of *Lohengrin* urges one to such speculations, for there are many passages which fit loosely to the singer's mood, and yet carry one's mind out with a beauty of their own.

In the meantime, we are miserably aware how little words can do to render music. When the moment of suspense is over, and the bows actually move across the strings, our definitions are relinquished, and words disappear in our minds. Enormous is the relief, and yet, when the spell is over, how great is the joy with which we turn to our old tools again! These definitions indeed, which would limit the bounds of an art and regulate our emotions, are arbitrary enough; and here at Bayreuth, where the music fades into the open air, and we wander with *Parsifal* in our heads through empty streets at night, where the gardens of the Hermitage glow with flowers like those other magic blossoms, and sound melts into colour, and colour calls out for words, where, in short, we are lifted out of the ordinary world and allowed merely to breathe and see – it is here that we realise how thin are the walls between one emotion and another; and how fused our impressions are with elements which we may not attempt to separate. Thus, in the final impression of Bayreuth this year, beauty is still triumphant, although the actual performances (if we except *Götterdämmerung*, which remains to be heard)[6] have been below the level of many that have been given in London. Details which have contributed to this disappointment – that the orchestra was weak, that there were few great singers, and that the prompter whispered incessantly – might be furnished; but to refrain seems better, since they must cross the Channel.

1 – An article in *The Times*, 21 August 1909, (Kp c36); 'From a correspondent. Bayreuth, Aug. 17', written during VW's visit that month to the Bayreuth Festival. Reprinted: *B&P*, in which the concluding passage from 'Thus, in the final impression ... ' is omitted. VW's companions to the Festival were her brother Adrian Stephen and the eccentric Saxon Sydney-Turner, a devoted and microscopically informed Wagnerian. As her letters reveal, she found their company less than ideal. See *I VW Letters*, no. 499 *et seq.*; see also 'The Opera' above.
2 – After Bayreuth the party travelled to Dresden for more opera and to visit the galleries. While there, whether by chance or by prior arrangement it is not known, they attended a performance of Richard Strauss's *Salome* (1905) – 'I was very much excited, and believe that it is a new discovery. He gets great emotion into his music, without any beauty.' (*I VW Letters*, no. 505, to Vanessa Bell.)
3 – VW saw *Parsifal* (1877–82) twice during her visit on 7 and then on 11 August. After the first occasion she wrote to Vanessa Bell: 'We heard Parsifal yesterday – a very mysterious emotional work, unlike any of the others I thought. There is no love in it; it is more religious than anything. People dress in half mourning and you are hissed if you try to clap. As the emotions are all abstract – I mean not between men and women – the effect is very diffused; and peaceful on the whole. However, Saxon and Adrian say that it was not a good performance, and that I shant know anything about it until I have heard it 4 times. Between the acts, one goes and sits in a field, and watches a man hoeing turnips.' (*I VW Letters*, no. 500.) The second performance, she wrote again to Vanessa, ' ... was much better done, and I felt within a space of

tears. I expect it is the most remarkable of the operas; it slides from music to words almost imperceptibly. However, I have been niggling at the effect all the morning, without much success. It is very hard to write in ones bedroom, without any books to look at, or my especial rabbit path, into the next room. I have balanced my box on my commode, and made a shaky desk.' (*I VW Letters*, no. 502.)

By 1913, VW's view of Wagner had shifted so considerably that it is worth noting here. 'We came up here 10 days ago to attend the Ring' – she wrote from London to Katherine Cox, ' – and I hereby state that I will never go again, and you must help us both to keep to that. My eyes are bruised, my ears dulled, my brain a mere pudding of pulp – O the noise and the heat, and the bawling sentimentality, which used once to carry me away, and now leaves me sitting perfectly still. Everyone seems to have come to this opinion, though some pretend to believe still.' (*II VW Letters*, no. 668, 16 May 1913).

4 – In the full programme for the Bühnenfestspiele Bayreuth 1909 the following casting is given for Kundry: Martha Leffler-Burckard, Wiesbaden; Marie Wittich, Dresden. (Parsifal: Alois Burgstaller, Holzkirchen; Fritz Vogelstrom, Mannheim.)
5 – It is known from VW's letters that the party went to hear *Lohengrin* (1846–8) on 19 August, Dr Alfred v. Bary of Dresden in the title role. According to the festival programme, the opera was also performed on 1, 5 and 12 August. VW presumably refers here to the performance on the 12th, just one day after she had heard *Parsifal*.
6 – *Die Götterdämmerung* (1874) was performed on 17 August, whether VW saw it on this occasion has not been established.

'Oliver Wendell Holmes'

A hundred years ago one might talk more glibly of American literature than it is safe to do at present. The ships that pass each other on the Atlantic do more than lift a handful of Americans and Englishmen from one shore to another; they have dulled our national self-consciousness. Save for the voice and certain small differences of manner which give them a flavour of their own, Americans sink into us, over here, like raindrops into the sea. On their side they have lost much of that nervous desire to assert their own independence and maturity in opposition to a mother country which was always reminding them of their tender age. Such questions as Lowell conceived – 'A country of *parvenus*, with a horrible consciousness of shoddy running through politics, manners, art, literature, nay, religion itself?'[2] and answered as we may guess, no longer fret them; the old adjectives which Hawthorne rapped out – 'the boorishness, the solidity, the self-sufficiency, the contemptuous jealousy, the half-sagacity ⟨etc., etc.⟩ that characterise this strange people'³ – are left for their daily press in moments of panic; for international criticism, as Mr Henry James has proved, has become a very delicate and serious matter. The truth is that time and the steam-boats have rubbed out these crudities; and if we wish to understand American art, or politics, or literature, we must look as closely as we look when blood and speech are strange to us.

The men who were most outspoken against us brought about this reasonable relationship partly because we read their books as our own, and partly because literature is able to suggest the surroundings in which it is produced. We are now able to think of Boston or Cambridge as places with a life of their own as distinct and as different from ours as the London of Pope is different from the London of Edward VII. The man who contributed to this intimacy, which is founded upon an understand-ing that we differ in many ways, as much as any of the rest, was undoubtedly Oliver Wendell Holmes, although he did it by means that were very different from theirs. He was, in some respects, the most complete American of them all.

He was born in 1809 of the best blood in the country, for his father, the Rev. Abiel Holmes, came from an old Puritan stock which might be traced to a lawyer of Gray's Inn in the sixteenth century, and his mother, Sarah Wendell, had distinguished blood from many sources, Dutch and Norman and good American. His father was stern and handsome, and taught 'the old-fashioned Calvinism, with all its horrors';⁴ his mother was a little sprightly woman, inquisitive and emotional. People who knew them said that the son inherited more from her than from his father. It was one of the charming characteristics of the mature man that he was always looking back to his childhood, and steeping it in such shade and quaintness as a 'gambrel-roofed house'⁵ built in 1730 will provide; like Hawthorne he had a pathetic desire to mix his childish memories with something old, mysterious, and beautiful in itself. There were dents in the floor where the soldiers had dropped their muskets during the Revolution; the family portraits had been slashed by British rapiers; and there was a chair where Lord Percy⁶ had sat to have his hair dressed. From the vague memories that hang about his early years, and inspire some of the pleasantest pages in his books, one may choose two for their importance. 'I might have been a minister myself, for aught I know, if — had not looked and talked so like an undertaker.'⁷ It was not until much later that he could analyse what had happened to him as a child. When he could read he was taught that 'We were a set of little fallen wretches, exposed to the wrath of God by the fact of that existence which we could not help.'[8] He was roused in revolt against what he called 'the inherited servitude of my ancestors',[9] and not only decided against the ministry as a calling, but never ceased to preach the beliefs which his early revolt had taught him. These beliefs were started in him, or at any rate his old views were shaken for ever, by a peep through a telescope on the common at the transit of Venus. He looked, and the thought came to him, like a shock, that the earth too was no bigger than a marble; he went on to think how this planet is 'equipped and provisioned for a long voyage in space'. The shock seems to have shown him both that we are part of a great system, and also that our world will last for a period 'transcending all our ordinary measures of time'. If it is true that we are to continue indefinitely, then it is possible, he found, to consider that 'this colony of the universe is an educational institution' and this is 'the only theory which can "justify the way of God to man"'. We may disbelieve in the Garden of Eden and in the fall of man; and we may believe that 'this so-called evil to which I cannot close my eyes' is a passing condition from which we shall emerge.[10] He had found a basis for that optimism which inspired his teaching, and, if the reasons which he gave seem insufficient, his conclusions and the way they came to him – looking through a telescope for ten cents at the transit of Venus – bear out much that we think when we know him better. The practical result of the conflict was that he became a doctor instead of a clergyman, spent two years in Paris studying his profesion, visited England and Italy on his way, and returned to practise in Boston, living there and at Cambridge, with the exception of his hundred days in Europe, for the rest of his life.

The most diligent of biographers – and Mr Morse was among them – can find little to add to such a record, nor did Dr Holmes come to the rescue. His letters are not intimate; like other people who write much about themselves in public, he has little to say in private. As a doctor he never won a large practice, for he not only collected a volume of poetry from time to time, but smiled when the door was opened and made jokes upon the staircase. When someone asked him what part of anatomy he liked best, he answered: 'The bones; they are cleanest.'[11] The answer shows us the 'plain little dapper man',[12] who could never bear the sights of a sick-room, who laughed to relieve the tension, who would run away when a rabbit was to be chloroformed, who was clean and scrupulous in all respects, and inclined, as a young man, to satirise the world with a somewhat acrid humour. Two friends have put together a picture of him. 'A small, compact, little man ... buzzing about like a bee, or fluttering like a humming bird, exceedingly difficult to catch unless he be really wanted for some kind act, and then you are sure of him.'[13] The other adds that he has a 'powerful jaw and a thick strong under-lip, that gives decision to his look, with a dash of pertness. In conversation he is animated and cordial – sharp, too, taking the words out of one's mouth.'[14]

At this time, before the publication of *The Autocrat*,[15] he was famous for his talk and for his verses. The verses were for the most part inspired by dinners and 'occasions'[16] they light up for us the circle of American men of letters who met and talked at Parker's Hotel,[17] as men had talked at Will's Coffee House; they are addressed to people who know each other well. His reputation, therefore, independently of his medical works, was very intense, but very local. He was almost fifty when the first of the *Autocrat* papers 'came from my mind almost with an explosion'.[18] *The Professor*[19] and *The Poet* followed; then there were the two novels;[20] he became, in short, a man of letters from whom the public expects a regular statement of opinion. Even at this distance it is easy to imagine the rush with which *The Autocrat* came into the world. Every breakfast-table in Boston knew the writer by repute, knew of his birth and traditions, and read his views in print with a kind of personal pride, as though he were the mouthpiece of a family. Those associations are no longer ours; but, as the manner of beauty clings when beauty is gone, so we can still relish the gusto with which Dr Holmes addressed himself to his fellow-citizens.

This is true, and yet is it possible that we should not dwell upon such considerations if we were altogether beneath *The Autocrat*'s spell? There is, we must own it, a little temptation to try to account for our ancestors' tastes, and so to avoid formulating our own. The chief interest, however, of these centenary celebrations is that they provide an opportunity for one generation to speak its mind of another with a candour and perhaps with an insight which contemporaries may hardly possess. The trial is sharp, for the books that live to such an age will live to a much greater age, and raise the standard of merit very high. Let us own at once that Dr Holmes's works can hardly be said to survive in the sense that they still play any part in our lives; nor is he among the writers who live on without any message to deliver because of the sheer delight that we take in their art. The fact that there is someone – Mr Townsend to wit – who will write a centenary biography for a public that reads *The*

Autocrat cannot be set down to either of these causes; and yet, if we seek it on a lower plane, we shall surely find reason enough. There is, to begin with, the reason that our own experience affords us. When we take it up at a tender age – for it is one of the first books that one reads for oneself – it tastes like champagne after breakfast-cups of weak tea. The miraculous ease with which the talk flows on, the richness of simile and anecdote, the humour and the pathos, the astonishing maturity of the style, and, above all, some quality less easy to define, as though fruits just beyond our reach were being dropped plump into our hands and proving deliciously firm and bright – these sensations make it impossible to think of the Autocrat save as an elderly relative who has pressed half-sovereigns into one's palm and at the same time flattered one's self-esteem. Later, if some of the charm is gone, one is able to appraise these virtues more soberly. They have, curiously enough, far more of the useful than of the ornamental in their composition. We are more impressed, that is, by the honesty and the common sense of the Autocrat's remarks, and by the fact that they are the fruit of wide observation, than by the devices with which they are decked out.

The pages of the book abound with passages like the following:

Two men are walking by the polyphloesboean ocean, one of them having a small tin cup with which he can scoop up a gill of sea-water when he will, and the other nothing but his hands, which will hardly hold water at all – and you call the tin cup a miraculous possession! It is the ocean that is the miracle, my infant apostle! Nothing is clearer than that all things are in all things, and that just according to the intensity and extension of our mental being we shall see the many in the one and the one in the many. Did Sir Isaac think what he was saying when he made *his* speech about the ocean – the child and the pebbles, you know? Did he mean to speak slightingly of a pebble? Of a spherical solid which stood sentinel over its compartment of space before the stone that became the pyramids had grown solid, and has watched it until now! A body which knows all the currents of force that traverse the globe; which holds by invisible threads to the ring of Saturn and the belt of Orion! A body from the contemplation of which an archangel could infer the entire inorganic universe as the simplest of corollaries! A throne of the all-pervading Deity, who has guided its every atom since the rosary of heaven was strung with beaded stars![21]

This is sufficiently plausible and yet light in weight; the style shares what we are apt to think the typical American defect of over-ingenuity and an uneasy love of decoration; as though they had not yet learnt the art of sitting still. The universe to him, as he says, 'swam in an ocean of similitudes and analogies';[22] but the imaginative power which is thus implied is often more simply and more happily displayed. The sight of old things inspires him, or memories of boyhood.

Now, the sloop-of-war the *Wasp*, Captain Blakely, after gloriously capturing the *Reindeer* and the *Avon*, had disappeared from the face of the ocean, and was supposed to be lost. But there was no proof of it, and, of course, for a time, hopes were entertained that she might be heard from. Long after the last real chance had utterly vanished, I pleased myself with the fond illusion that somewhere on the waste of waters she was still floating, and there were *years* during which I never heard the sound of the great gun booming inland from the Navy-yard without saying to myself, 'The *Wasp* has come!' and almost thinking I could see her, as she rolled in, crumbling the water before her, weather-beaten, barnacled, with shattered spars and threadbare canvas, welcomed by the shouts and tears of thousands. This was one of those dreams that I nursed and never told. Let me make a clean breast of it now, and say that, so late as to have outgrown childhood, perhaps to have got far on towards manhood, when the roar of the cannon has struck suddenly on my ear, I have started with a thrill of vague expectation and tremulous delight, and the long-unspoken words have articulated themselves in the mind's dumb whisper, *The* Wasp *has come!*[23]

The useful virtues are there, nevertheless. The love of joy, in the first place, which raced in his blood from the cradle was even more of a virtue when *The Autocrat* was published than it is now. There were strict parents who forbade their children to read the book because it made free with the gloomy morality of the time. His sincerity, too, which would show itself in an acrid humour as a young man, gives an air of pugnacity to the kindly pages of *The Autocrat*. He hated pomp, and stupidity, and disease. It may not be due to the presence of high virtues, and yet how briskly his writing moves along! We can almost hear him talk, 'taking the words out of one's mouth,'[24] in his eagerness to get them said. Much of this animation is due to the easy and almost incessant play of the Autocrat's humour; and yet we doubt whether Dr Holmes can be called a humorist in the true sense of the word. There is something that paralyses the will in humour, and Dr Holmes was primarily a medical man who valued sanity above all things. Laughter is good, as fresh air is good, but he retracts instinctively if there is any fear that he has gone too deep:

> I know it is a sin
> For me to sit and grin —[25]

that is the kindly spirit that gives his humour its lightness, and, it must be added, its shallowness. For, when the range is so scrupulously limited, only a superficial insight is possible; if the world is only moderately ridiculous it can never be very sublime. But it is easy enough to account for the fact that his characters have little hold upon our sympathies by reflecting that Dr Holmes did not write in order to create men and women, but in order to state the opinions which a lifetime of observation had taught him. We feel this even in the book which has at least the form of a novel. In *Elsie Venner* he wished to answer the question which he had asked as a child; can we be justly punished for an hereditary sin? The result is that we watch a skilful experiment; all Dr Holmes's humour and learning (he kept a live rattlesnake for months, and read 'all printed knowledge'[26] about poison) play round the subject, and he makes us perceive how curious and interesting the case is. But – for this is the sum of our objections – we are not interested in the heroine; and the novel so far as it seeks to convince us emotionally is a failure. Even so, Dr Holmes succeeds, as he nearly always does succeed, in making us think; he presents so many facts about rattlesnakes and provincial life, so many reflections upon human life in general, with such briskness and such a lively interest in his own ideas, that the portentous 'physiological conception, fertilised by a theological idea',[27] is as fresh and almost as amusing as *The Autocrat* or *The Professor*. The likeness to these works, which no disguise of fiction will obscure, proves again that he could not, as he puts it, 'get out of his personality',[28] but by that we only mean to define his powers in certain respects, for 'personality' limits Shakespeare himself. We mean that he is one of those writers who do not see much more than other people see, and yet they see it with some indescribable turn of vision, which reveals their own character and serves to form their views into a coherent creed. Thus it is that his readers always talk of their 'intimacy' with Dr Holmes; they know what kind of person he was as well as what he taught. They know that he loved rowing and horses and great trees; that he was full of sentiment for his childhood; that he liked men to be strong and sanguine, and honoured the weakness of women; that he loathed all gloom and unhealthiness; that charity and tolerance were the virtues he loved, and if one could combine them with wit it was so much to the good. Above all, one must enjoy life and live to the utmost of one's powers. It reads something like a medical prescription, and one does not want health alone. Nevertheless, when the obvious objections are made, we need not doubt that it will benefit thousands in the future, and they will love the man who lived as he wrote.

1 – A review in the *TLS*, 26 August 1909, (Kp C37) of *Oliver Wendell Holmes* [1809–94] (Headley Brothers, 1909), a 'Centenary Biography', by Lewis W. Townsend. VW's father, Leslie Stephen, also wrote on Holmes: see *Studies of a*

Biographer (Duckworth & Co.; vol. II, 1898), for his review of the *Life and Letters of Oliver Wendell Holmes* (2 vols, Sampson Low, Marston & Co. Ltd, 1896) by John T. Morse, Jr, a book VW also used in writing her article. Reprinted: *G&R, CE*. Reading Notes (Berg XXIX).

2 – James Russell Lowell, *My Study Windows* (Sampson Low, 1871), 'On a Certain Condescension in Foreigners', p. 43, which has: 'A country without traditions, without ennobling associations, a scramble of *parvenus*, with a horrible consciousness of shoddy . . . '

3 – Nathaniel Hawthorne, writing about the English in *Our Old Home* (Smith, Elder, 1863), p. 23: 'It has required nothing less than the boorishness, the stolidity, the self-sufficiency, the contemptuous jealousy, the half-sagacity, invariably blind of one eye and often distorted of the other, that characterise this strange people, to compel us to be a great nation in our own right, instead of continuing virtually, if not in name, a province of their small island.'

4 – The origin of this quotation has not been traced.

5 – Townsend, ch. I, p. 1, quoting Holmes on 'the life of a house'. See also O. W. Holmes, *The Poet at the Breakfast-Table* (G. Routledge and Sons, 1872), Paper I, which has a passage entitled 'The Gambrel-Roofed House and Its Outlook. A Panorama, with side-shows'; and see Leslie Stephen, p. 169: 'Holmes loved the old "gambrel-roofed house" in which he was born, all the more because a house which existed at the time of Washington represented exceptional antiquity in America.'

6 – *Ibid.*, ch. I, p. 3. General Hugh Percy, 2nd Duke of Northumberland (1742–1817), had commanded the British in and around Boston, 1774–60.

7 – *The Poet*, Paper I, p. 20, which has: ' . . . if this clergyman had not looked and . . .'

8 – Morse, vol. I, p. 38.

9 – Townsend, ch. I, p. 14: ' . . . we must not forget that the spirit of the times and the growing impatience of many with New England Calvinism, rather than his reading Bunyan and Scott, account for his revolt from what he calls "the inherited servitude of my ancestors".'

10 – For the preceding extracts, Morse, vol. I, p. 46; which has 'the so-called evil'. Townsend, p. 17, also quotes 'this colony of the universe . . . '

11 – Townsend, ch. III, p. 58.

12 – *Ibid.*, p. 56; the description is by Holmes's friend David Macrae.

13 – *Ibid.*, quoting Miss Mitford.

14 – *Ibid.*, quoting Macrae.

15 – O. W. Holmes, *The Autocrat of the Breakfast-Table* (Phillips, Sampson & Co. 1858), papers collected from the *Atlantic Monthly*.

16 – Morse, vol. I, ch. VIII, p. 203.

17 – I.e., members of the Saturday Club, an informal literary dining club founded in 1857, among whom were: Emerson, J. R. Lowell, Longfellow, Holmes, John Greenleaf Whittier, C. E. Norton, W. D. Howells and Henry James.

18 – The source of this quotation has escaped detection.

19 – O. W. Holmes, *The Professor at the Breakfast-Table* (S. Low, Son & Co., 1860).

20 – Holmes wrote three novels: *Elsie Venner* (1861), *The Guardian Angel* (1867) and *A Mortal Antipathy* (1885).

21 – *The Autocrat of the Breakfast-Table*: see the edition introduced by Leslie Stephen (Macmillan & Co., 1903), ch. IV, p. 84.
22 – *Ibid.*, p. 85, repeated on p. 97.
23 – *Ibid.*, ch. IX, p. 211.
24 – Townsend, ch. III, p. 56; from David Macrae's description of Holmes.
25 – From Holmes's poem 'The Last Leaf', an autograph facsimile of which is reproduced in Morse, vol. II, beteen pp. 98–9. The verse continues: 'At him here/ But the old three-cornered hat/ And the breeches and all that/ Are so queer!'
26 – Townsend, ch. VIII., p. 135.
27 – *Ibid.*, ch. VII, p. 131.
28 – This quotation remains unidentified.

A Cookery Book

Independently of the knowledge they convey, cookery books such as *The Cookery Book of Lady Clark of Tillypronie*, arranged and edited by Catherine Frances Frere, are delightful to read. A charming directness stamps them, with their imperative, 'Take an uncooked fowl, and split its skin from end to end';[1] and their massive common sense which stares frivolity out of countenance. Then, apart from the wonderful suggestive power of the words they deal in – Southdown mutton, hares, jugged venison, fresh strawberries – it is pleasant to think of herbs growing on moors, hares running in the stubble, spices brought, with bales of embroidery, from the Indies; and the strings of words themselves often have a beauty such as poets aim at. 'Strain it and sweeten to taste with sugar honey or candied Eringo root[3] . . . add a few cloves, whole pepper, salt, a bay-leaf, a sprig of thyme, one of marjoram, and some parsley . . .[4] Then a finger-glass and rose and orange water poured over the guests' hands.'[5] Not only are the furs and fruits beautiful in themselves, as they lie heaped together on a Dutch canvas, with a thin Venetian glass among them and a necklace of silver balls drooping over the corner of the table, but it is a relief to think of anything so practical as cookery. The cook gets something done every day; she has no time to ask why she cooks, or to question the ultimate effect upon the world; the plainest cooks are happier than most artists in that they have one dish which they do to perfection – a work of genius in its way. Sir John Clark's anxiety lest the reader should infer that because his wife was interested in cookery, she was a 'mere housewife' seems to us misplaced.[6] It is a genuine art after all, calling not only for skill, but for virtues of character; and the fact that one is interested in any subject, whatever it may be, makes it all the more likely that one is interested in others. From a glance at those 'three thousand pages of manuscript', scored 'like a shepherd's plaid',[7] from which Miss Frere has compiled the present book, we can see that to Lady Clark the kitchen was only one 'department' of life; the library was another. Anecdotes, rhymes, names of French plays, and new books to be read, quotations like the quotation from Voltaire – 'Tout est perdu quand on digère mal; c'est l'estomac qui fait les heureux'[8] – crowd into the corners of the recipes. Then, too, she was cosmopolitan, for, when her husband was in the Diplomatic Service, she had the chance of knowing many people and of sampling the cookery of Europe. 'When any dish interested her' she made inquiries of the artist, who, touched by her intelligence, told her what she wanted; if this was impossible, she 'sketched' her impressions in a notebook.[9] Thus, as Miss Frere says, Lady Clark 'may be said to have focussed much of the best cookery of Europe in her collection';[10] India and Turkey each yielded her something. Royal ladies and ambassadors contributed to the book. There is a poet's pudding – the poet Rogers' pudding – otherwise called lemon pudding.[11] ' . . . brown it with browning, Lady Clark commands cryptically on one occasion.[12] 'Do not scruple to add rabbits if it suits a somewhat empty larder' is an aside under goose pie;[13] and then there is a sentence which reads like an aphorism, 'When a pig is sacrificed for future bacon, there is still a good deal for present consumption.'[14] But the housekeeper confronted in the chill early hours with the formidable 'What shall we have to-day, Ma'am?' will rather be assured that Lady Clark's book is full of suggestions for small houses and simple tables, which the ordinary cook will accept gratefully and can carry out triumphantly. In saying this we shall have the support of a number of witnesses, for Lady Clarke's wisdom, copied and passed from hand to hand (like the songs of the early minstrels), lies in many a kitchen drawer already. Even for those who know them, this handsome volume, in which references to the recipes are made as easy as possible, is a far more convenient shape in which to possess them; and a much larger public will thank Sir John Clark for putting his wife's collection at their disposal. When tired or dispirited the cook should read the introduction by Miss Frere, and the description which is given there of a Scottish household will put energy into her at once.

1 – A review in the *TLS*, 25 November 1909, (Kp c38) of *The Cookery Book of*

Lady Clark of Tillypronie. Arranged and edited by Catherine Frances Frere
(Constable & Co., 1909).
2 – Frere, p. 261, from the recipe for 'Chicken Galantine No. 1 (Cataldi)'.
3 – *Ibid.*, p. 163, the recipe for 'Carragheen or Irish Pearl Moss' in the chapter
'Invalid Cookery'.
4 – *Ibid.*, p. 183, the recipe for 'Beefsteak Pickled'.
5 – *Ibid.*, Pref., p. x, from an entry quoted by the editor describing 'Bishop Alet's
Dinner'.
6 – Lady Clark, daughter of Mr Justice Coltman, married in 1851 Sir John Clark, a
diplomat, who described her in a letter to Miss Frere (Pref., p. vii) as 'not the mere
"housewife" on culinary things intent, but an exceptionally widely-read woman,
gifted with fine and accurate memory and great conversational powers, never
degraded to mere culinary talk – which she particularly disliked.'
7 – Frere, Pref., p. ix.
8 – From the epigraph to this book, an unidentified passage from Voltaire originally
copied by Lady Clark into one of her recipe books: 'Madame, songez à la santé
surtout. C'est là ce qu'il faut souhaiter – la beauté, la grandeur, l'esprit, le don de
plaire, tout est perdu quand on digère mal; c'est l'estomac qui fait les heureux.'
9 – Frere, Pref., p. vii, Sir John Clark to Miss Frere describing his travels with Lady
Clark to Turin and her method of gathering recipes.
10 – *Ibid.*, p. xiv.
11 – *Ibid.*, p. 485; Samuel Rogers (1763–1855).
12 – *Ibid.*, p. 282, on 'Roux, Browning, and Glaze'.
13 – *Ibid.*, p. 234, under 'Goose Pie. A Yorkshire Dish': 'A fine goose is selected, carefully boned and laid out flat; on it are laid fowl, pheasant or any convenient game, i.e.
birds only; hares are too strong in flavour . . . Do not scruple to add rabbits . . . '
14 – *Ibid.*, p. 209, from the instructions on 'How to use a whole Pig (Mrs Thomas)'.

'Sheridan'

At first sight there may seem some incongruity between one's idea of
Sheridan[2] and the size of Mr Sichel's volumes. Nine people out of ten, if
asked to give you their impression of Sheridan, would tell you that he
wrote three standard plays, was famous for his debts, his wit, and his
speech at the trial of Warren Hastings;[3] they would add that he had
played a distinguished but not a commanding part as a statesman, and
flitted through the society of the Georgian era, a brilliant but slightly
intoxicated insect, with gorgeous wings but an erratic flight. The
important aspect of two stout volumes, numbering some 1100 pages
between them, seems strangely at variance with such a figure. How

completely Mr Sichel corrects the popular view we shall attempt to show; but let us insist at once that the heaviness of the volumes is true in a literal sense only, and that, after reading from cover to cover, the importance of his subject seems to demand an even fuller treatment than it was possible to bestow. We should like more about the Linleys, more of Sheridan's own letters, and more of Mrs Tickell and her sister.[4]

If only to enlighten the reader as to the extreme interest and complexity of his task, and to point out its true nature, it is best to read the 'Overture' first, in which Mr Sichel seeks to 'psychologise a temperament and a time'.[5] At first (let us own) the clash of contrasts, urged with unusual sharpness and precision, blinds our eyes to the form which they would reveal; simplicity and extravagance, generosity and meanness, rash confidence and moderation, passion and coldness – how are we to compose them all into one human shape? But later, when we begin to understand, it appears that the clue to Sheridan's baffling career must be sought among these contradictory fragments. For, looked at from the outside, the inconsistencies of his life fill us with a sense of dissatisfaction. Before he was thirty he had written three plays that are classics in our literature; then, once in Parliament,[6] he turned to reform and finance and gave up writing altogether; 'the Muses of Love and Satire beckoned to him from Parnassus, and to the last he persisted in declaring that they, and not politics, were his true vocation';[7] yet 'his heart stayed in the Assembly of the nation, and to the last, like Congreve, he slighted his theatrical triumphs';[8] his married life, which began with two duels on his wife's behalf, and ended in an agony of grief as she lay dying in his arms, would present a perfect example of devotion were it not that he had been unfaithful while she lived, and married again, a girl of twenty, three years after her death;[9] finally, his political career is as incomprehensible as the rest, for, with gifts as orator and statesman that made him famous over Europe, he never held high office;[10] with a character of singular independence he acted 'equivocally', and with a record of devotion to his Prince he lost his favour completely,[11] and died, without a seat, dishonoured and in debt. Nothing tends to make us lose interest in a character so much as the suspicion that there is something monstrous about it, and the achievement of Mr Sichel's biography is that it restores Sheridan to human size and brings him to life again.

The first gift that makes itself felt is the gift that is always present and at work, but is yet the hardest to recapture – the gift of charm. 'There has been nothing like it since the days of Orpheus,' wrote Byron;[12] it made the boys at Harrow love him; Sumner, the headmaster,[13] overlooked his mischief because of it; it drew the bailiffs in later days to stand behind his chair; as for his sister, she confessed that she 'admired – I almost adored him'.[14] In early days his face expressed only the finer part of him; 'its half-heaviness was lit up by the comedy of his smile, the audacity of his air', and the brilliance of those eyes that were to outshine the rest of him, and to 'look up at the coffin lid as brightly as ever'[15] when the mouth and chin had grown coarse as a Satyr's.[16] There are only two letters from Sheridan at Harrow; and they are both about dress. In one he complains that his clothes are so shabby that he 'is almost ashamed to wear them on Sunday'; in the other he is anxious to have the proper mourning sent him on his mother's death.[17] Most schoolboys are conventional, but in addition to conforming to its laws, Sheridan liked the world to know that he grieved. A year or two later, when we come to Miss Linley and the famous elopement and the duels, the romance of Sheridan's nature blossoms out, with curious qualifications. He discovered that the beautiful Miss Linley, who sang like an angel, was tormented by a man called Mathews, who was married;[18] she had flirted with him as a child and he now pressed her dishonourably. Sheridan became her knight; he snatched her away to France without her parents' knowledge, and placed her in a convent. It is probable that they went through 'some form of marriage' near Calais.[19] Mathews, meanwhile, proclaimed his rival a liar and a scoundrel in the *Bath Chronicle*,[20] and Sheridan vowed that he 'would never sleep in England till he had thanked him as he deserved'.[21] He left Miss Linley in her father's hands, fought with Mathews twice, and obliged him to fly the country. It is a tale no doubt that might be matched by others of that age, but in the romantic arrangement of the plot, in the delicate respect with which he treated his charge, and in the extravagance of the vow which constrained him to spend the night out of bed at Canterbury and to reach his rival starved for want of sleep, there are signs of something out of the ordinary. Nor was his behaviour ordinary in the months of separation that followed. In his letters and his lyrics he luxuriated – for the passion that finds words has pleasure about it – in the shades of his emotion.

But love also started his brain into activity.[22] Not only did he work at mathematics, make an abstract of the history of England, and comment upon Blackstone,[23] but he thought about the principles upon which the world is run. It seemed to him that 'all the nobler feelings of man', which he began to perceive in himself, were blunted by civilisation, and sighed for the early days when the ties of friendship and of love 'could with some safety be formed at the first instigation of our hearts'.[24] Now and perhaps throughout his life he believed that one's emotions are supreme, and that one should rate the obstacles that thwart them as tokens of bondage. He was fond of dreaming about the enchanted world of the *Arcadia* and of the *Faerie Queen*, liking rather to dwell upon 'the characters of life as I would wish that they *were* than as they *are*',[25] and persuading himself that his wish was really a desire to pierce beneath the corruptions of society to the true face of man beneath. Perhaps he felt that a world so simplified would be easier to live in than ours – but can one believe in it? He wished to replace all Fielding and Smollett[26] with knights and ladies, but he did not believe in them either. The true romantic makes his past out of an intense joy in the present; it is the best of what he sees, caught up and set beyond the reach of change; Sheridan's vague rapture with the glamour of life was only sufficient to make him discontented, sentimental, and chivalrous. The strange admixture is shown in his behaviour when he was asked to allow his wife – for they had married with the consent of her father, but to the rage of his – to sing publicly for money. He refused to agree, although they were very poor and large sums were offered. It was said that the sight of George III ogling her decided him, and Johnson declared, 'He resolved wisely and nobly, to be sure.'[27] But later, when he was struggling for a position in London drawing-rooms he allowed her to advertise concerts 'to the Nobility and Gentry'[28] at which she was to sing without taking money. He gained a reputation for chivalry, for it implied that he cared for his wife's honour more than for gold, and spurned a friendship that was brought; but then he valued the favour of the great very highly, and if it is true that he never cared for money, he seldom paid his debts.

Sheridan would do anything to make the world think well of him; he would wear intense mourning; he would keep a fine establishment; he would faint if people wished it; he could anticipate the popular desires, and exaggerate them brilliantly. The actor's blood in him, which rises on applause like a ship on the waves, was responsible for the touch of melodrama; but the finer perceptions of artists were his too, and these, trained to discover emotions beneath small talk and domesticity, threw him off his balance in the uproar of the world. There is certainly a strange discrepancy between Sheridan in private and Sheridan in public – between his written words and his spoken. The three famous plays were written before he took to public life, and represent more of him than tradition or the imperfect reports of his speeches can now preserve. They show what Sheridan thought when there was no public to send the blood to his head. The way in which he takes the word 'honour' in *The Rivals* and makes it the jewel of a frightened country bumpkin and the sport of his shrewd serving-man assures us that he fought his own duels with a full sense of their absurdity. 'Odds blades! David,' cries Acres, 'no gentleman will ever risk the loss of his honour!' 'I say, then,' answers David, 'it would be but civil in *honour* never to risk the loss of a *gentleman*. Look'ee, master, this *honour* seems to me to be a marvellous false friend; ay truly, a very courtier-like servant',[29] and so on, until honour and the valiant man of honour are laughed out of court together.

Then again we have some reason to believe that Sheridan was an unthinking sentimentalist, and so slipshod in his morality that he acted upon no reasoned view, but used the current conventions. If that were so, he would have been the last to see the humour of Charles Surface in *The School for Scandal*. The good qualities of this character are lovable only because we know them to be slightly ridiculous; we are meant to think it a weak but endearing trait in him that he refuses to sell his uncle's picture. 'No, hang it; I'll not part with poor Noll; the old fellow has been very good to me, and, egad, I'll keep his picture while I've a room to put it in.'[30] And Sheridan satirises his own system of generosity by adding to Charles's offer of a hundred pounds to poor Stanley, 'If you don't make haste, we shall have some one call that has a better right to the money.'[31] These are details, but they keep us in mind of the acutely sensible side of Sheridan's temperament. He laughs at the vapours of his age – at old women sending out for novels from the library, at bombastic Irishmen, picking quarrels for the glory of it, at romantic young ladies sighing for the joys of 'sentimental elopements – ladder of ropes! – conscious moon – four horses – Scotch parson . . . paragraphs in the newspapers'.[32] The pity is that his Irish gift of hyperbole made it so easy for him to heap one absurdity on another, to accumulate superlatives and smother everything in laughter. Mrs Malaprop would be more to the point if she could stay her tongue from deranging epitaphs; and the play scene in *The Critic* suffers from the same voluble buffoonery – but that it has such a rapture of fun in it that we can never cease to laugh.

> The wind whistles – the moon rises – see
> They have kill'd my squirrel in his cage!
> Is this a grasshopper? – Ha! no; it is my
> Whiskerandos – you shall not keep him –

I know you have him in your pocket –
An oyster may be cross'd in love! – Who says
A whale's a bird? –[33]

His humour makes one remember that he liked practical jokes. It is absolutely free from coarseness. The most profound humour is not fit reading for a girls' school, because innocence is supposed to ignore half the facts of life, and, however we may define humour, it is the most honest of the gifts.

Among other reasons for the morality of the stage in Sheridan's day may be found the reason that it lacked vigour of every kind. Sheridan, the first of the playwrights, was prevented, partly by the fact that his audience would not like it, and partly by an innate prudery of his own – a touch of that sentimentality which led him to prefer unreal characters to real ones – from giving a candid account of life. He took some thought of appearances, even in the study. His own view of the stage may be gathered in the first act of *The Critic*. Having regard to the limitations of an audience which could not brook Vanbrugh and Congreve, one should not 'dramatise the penal laws' or make the stage the school of morality, but find the proper sphere for the comic muse in 'the follies and foibles of society'.[34] That was Sheridan's natural province, in spite of a fitful longing to write a romantic Italian tragedy. If we grant that he had not the power which moves us so keenly in Congreve of showing how witty people love, and lacked the coarse vigour which still keeps *The Rehearsal*[35] alive, we are conscious that he has another power of his own; Sir Henry Irving found it in his 'play of human nature';[36] Mr Sichel speaks of his sympathy – 'a sympathy that Congreve lacked'.[37] It is that surely that gives his comedy its peculiar glow. It does not spring from insight, or from any unusual profundity. It lies rather in his power to get on with ordinary people – to come into a room full of men and women who know him for the cleverest man of his time, and to set them at once at their ease. Other dramatists would treat such a character as Charles Surface with condescension, for a blockhead, or with uneasy respect, because of his courage and muscle; but Sheridan liked him heartily; he was his 'ideal of a good fellow'.[38] This humanity – it was part of his charm as a man – still warms his writing; and it has another quality which also appeals to us. He reminds us sometimes of our modern dramatists in his power to see accepted conventions in a fresh light. He tests the current view of honour; he derides the education that was given to women; he was for reforming the conventions of the stage. His interest in ideas was only a faint forecast of our own obsession; and he was too true an artist to make any character the slave of a theory. A great fastidiousness was one of the many gifts that were half-failings, and the more he wrote the less possible it became to make the drama an instrument of reform. *The School for Scandal* was polished and polished again; 'after nineteen years he had been unable to satisfy himself'[39] with his style. The excessive care was fatal; it helped to dry up his vein before he had fully explored it, and his last comedy *Affectation*[40] has dwindled to a few careful sentences, very neatly written in a small copy-book.

An acute sense of comedy does not seem compatible with a reformer's zeal; and, when the success of his plays and the charm of his wife brought him into touch with the rulers of the country, the chance of acting among them proved irresistible. His success with the great ladies who came to his wife's drawing-room showed him what kind of power might be his – he might lead human beings. From the first, too, he had had the political instinct – a sense of distress among the people and a desire to make their lives better by improving the laws of the land. 'Government for the people, through the people, and by the people'[41] was the creed with which he started his career under the guidance of Fox. A boyish essay shows how natural it was to him to think of man as a free being oppressed by the laws. '. . . all laws at present are Tyranny. . . . All Liberty consists in the Probability of not being oppressed. What assurance have we that we shall not be taxed at eight shillings in the pound? No more than the colonies have.'[42] One of the first causes that attracted him was the cause of the American colonies, and he urged passionately their right to independence. He resolved to 'sacrifice every other object' to politics, and to 'force myself into business, punctuality, and information'.[43]

But it is not necessary to trace Sheridan's parliamentary career. Mr Sichel proves, if one can separate them, that it was more important than his career as a man of letters, and for this reason his second volume is even more interesting than his first. What is interesting, of course, is the spectacle of a man who tries to give some shape to his beliefs, and has great opportunities. He had to do what he could with questions like that of the American colonists, of the Irish Union, of Indian government, of the French Revolution, which sprang up one after the other. They have come to be facts now, lying sunk beneath a heap of results; but they were then in the making, composed of the united wills of individuals and shaped by the wills of individuals. This is one source of interest; but it happens very often that we lose sight of the aim in amazement at the spectacle. When Sheridan entered Parliament, Burke and Pitt and Fox, to take the leaders only, gave every question an extraordinary depth and complexity. It seems that we are not tracing ideas, but watching a gigantic drama, like those old Homeric combats where the motive may be the sack of Troy, but in which the episodes represent every phase of human life. Sometimes the vast range of the fight narrows itself to the will of one man; the central figure is undraped; and we have to contemplate the absurd or touching spectacle of a gentleman afflicted with the gout – 'a poor, bare, forked animal',[44] touched in his mind, too, who for the moment represents humanity. There are strange anecdotes in the Duchess of Devonshire's diary. The King began to go mad, and said 'the Prince of Wales was dead, so women may be honest'.[45] He made Sir George Baker go down on his knees to look at the stars; he ordered a 'tye wig, and danc'd with Dr Reynolds';[46] the courtiers had to pretend that he could play chess when he could only play draughts, and that they had all been a little mad and worn strait waistcoats themselves. Such contrasts abound, but if we know enough there appears to be some order in the tumult; it is shaped something after a human form. We need only observe out of what elements the conduct of a public man is made.

Sheridan, in spite of his vanity and irresponsibility, had an unwavering sense of something more stable than any private advantage. He could look beyond his own life, and judge clearly of things to come. Again and again we find him on the side of reform, courageous and 'unpurchaseable',[47] a statesman whose views grew wider as he aged. And yet, how strangely little traits of character, small vices unchecked since boyhood, assert themselves and corrupt his actions! The speech upon the Begums of Oude,[48] which made great men tremble and women cry with ecstasy, lacks something essential, for all its thunder of eloquence. Years afterwards he met Warren Hastings, shook his hand, and begged him to believe that 'political necessity' had inspired some of his rage. When Hastings 'with great gravity' asked him to make that sentence public, he could only 'mutter', and get out of it as best he might.[49] It is the same with his friendship for the Regent; he could not care for anything for its own sake. The man was a Prince, girt about with romance, and hung with stars and ribbons; Mrs Fitzherbert was a woman, beautiful and in distress; his sympathies were volatile, and he moved in a world of gems and decorations, which might be had for the asking. Yet gold was too gross to tempt him; he craved for love, confidence, and demonstrative affection in the face of the world. What he asked he could not get, or perhaps he asked it of the wrong people. From the first an uneasy note sounds beneath the rest. The beautiful Mrs Sheridan implored him, when they began to rise, to let his friends know of their poverty. He had not the courage to do it, and she was led on to bet and to flirt. 'Oh, my own,' she wrote him, ''ee can't think how they beat me every night.'[50] He condoned her frailties with the tact of a perfect gentleman. But once in the race there was no standing still. The Duchess of Devonshire, Lady Bessborough, Lady Elizabeth Foster[51] – all the great ladies and the brilliant young men were there to egg him on. At their pressure such a fountain of wit and satire and imagery sprang from his lips as no one else could rival. His face might grow fiery and his nose purple, but his voice kept its melody to the end. Yet, in spite of all this, he was never at his ease, and always conscious of a certain misfit. When he stood on the Down where, twenty years before, he had fought and lain wounded, he considered his situation:

What an interval had passed since, and scarcely one promise that I then made to my own soul have I attempted to fulfil . . . The irregularity of all my life and pursuits, the restless, contriving temper with which I have persevered in wrong pursuits and passions makes [some words erased, of which 'errors' is legible] reflexion worse to me than even to those who have acted worse.[52]

He thought he could foresee the 'too probable conclusion',[53] but even his imagination, though made intense by sorrow, could hardly have foreseen the end. Perhaps it was the humour of it that he could not have foreseen. He became 'Old Sherry' to the younger generation, and was to be met 'half seas over',[54] a disreputable figure, but still talking divinely, a battered Orpheus, but still a very polite gentleman, a little bewildered by the course of events, and somewhat disappointed by his lot. He fell into sponging houses, escaped ingeniously from the 'two strange men'[55] who had followed him all his life, and begged as eloquently as ever, with a touch of Irish brogue in his voice. 'They are going to put the carpets out of window, and break into Mrs Sheridan's room, and take me'[56] he wrote, but was sanguine on the morrow. Then he lay dying, and the prescriptions were unopened in the bare parlour, and 'there were strange people in the hall'.[57] But so long as life promised adventures Sheridan had a part to act, and could welcome a future. It is not in any event that his tragedy lay, for there is something ludicrous in the stupidity of fate which never fits the fortune to the desert and blunts our pain in wonder.

The tragedy lies in making promises, and seeing possibilities, and in the sense of failure. There at least the pain is without mixture. But one does not fail so long as one sees possibilities still, and the judgment on our failure is that which Byron murmured when he heard that Sheridan was dead, and praised his gifts and greatness – 'But alas, poor human nature!'[58]

1 – A review in the TLS, 2 December 1909, (Kp C39) of *Sheridan. From new and original material; including a manuscript diary by Georgiana, Duchess of Devonshire* (2 vols, Constable & Co., 1909) by Walter Sichel. Reprinted: *B&P*.

2 – Richard Brinsley Sheridan (1751–1816), dramatist and politician, whose plays include the classics *The Rivals* (1775), *The School for Scandal* (1777), and *The Critic; or, a tragedy rehearsed* (1779).

3 – Warren Hastings (1732–1818), first governor-general of British India, 1774–84, was impeached in 1787 on charges of corruption and cruelty in the conduct of his office. He was acquitted, but only in 1795, after a trial lasting 145 days, during which his prosecutors were Edmund Burke, Sir Philip Francis, Charles James Fox, and Sheridan.

4 – The gifted and 'charming' (Sichel, vol. I, p. x) family of Thomas Linley (1732–95), composer, sometime director of provincial oratorios and of the Bath concerts, whose musical offspring included: Thomas (1756–78), a prodigy, admired and befriended by Mozart; the celebrated vocalist Elizabeth Ann (1754–92), whom Sheridan married in 1773; and Mary (1758–87), Elizabeth's successor in the concert room from 1773, and, from 1780, wife of the pamphleteer and commissioner of stamps, Richard Tickell.

5 – Sichel, vol. I, Pref., p. x.

6 – Sheridan's parliamentary career began in 1780, when he was returned as a member for Stafford in the Whig interest, and ran its illustrious and spiritedly independent course down to 1812. See n. 7 and n. 8 below.

7 – Sichel, vol. I, ch. III, p. 271.

8 – *Ibid.*, ch. XIV, p. 376.

9 – Sheridan's second wife, whom he married in 1795, was Esther (or Hester) Jane, *née* Ogle, daughter of the Dean of Winchester.

10 – Sheridan served as under-secretary for foreign affairs in Rockingham's ministry (1782), secretary to the treasury in the coalition under the Duke of Portland (1783), and treasurer of the navy in the ministry of 'all the talents' (1806).

11 – Having lent the Prince of Wales ardent (not to say unconstitutional) support in the matter of the establishment of the Regency, Sheridan found himself adjudged to have acted equivocally in the political *fiasco* of 1812 concerning the government's insistence upon the dismissal of the Regent's household, upon which 'a storm of obloquy, public and private, burst over Sheridan's head ... and the Regent turned his back' (Sichel, vol. II, p. 362).

12 – Sichel, vol. I, 'Overture', p. 56; Byron's sentence continues: 'he could soften the heart of an attorney'.

13 – Charles Sumner, headmaster of Harrow School, 1760–71, and a friend of the Sheridan family.

14 – Sichel, vol. I, ch. II, pp. 263–4; Sheridan's eldest sister Alicia (Mrs Joseph Le Fanu) writing to her brother's widow.

15 – *Ibid.*, vol. I, 'Overture', p. 14, which has: 'Contrasts like these showed in a countenance by turns listless and lambent. Its half-heaviness was lit up by the comedy of his smile, the audacity of his air, and the fire of eye abnormally brilliant, as Reynolds noted in Sheridan's youth, Byron in his age, and he himself on his deathbed, when he sent the message to Lady Bessborough that they would "look up to the coffin-lid as brightly as ever"; of eyes so lustrous that tutor Smyth remembered to have seen them by night "glowing through the bars and outshining the lamps of the carriage".'

16 – *Ibid.*, p. 11; the description is again Byron's.

17 – *Ibid.*, vol. I, ch. II, p. 259; the letters are both addressed to Sheridan's uncle, Dr Richard Chamberlaine.

18 – 'Captain' (or 'Major') Thomas Mathews (b. 1744), a retired army ensign, had married c. 1770 Diana Jones, an heiress of Glamorgan; his duels with Sheridan took place in May–July 1772.

19 – Sichel, vol. I, ch. IV, p. 344.

20 – *Ibid.*, p. 353; Mathews's advertisement appeared in the *Bath Chronicle*, 9 April 1772.

21 – *Ibid.*

22 – Cf. *ibid.*, vol. I, ch. VI, pp. 400–1; 'Monotony was an avowed incentive to study, but his main stimulus was the diversion of his thoughts from Bath, with all its connected and continued vexations.'

23 – Sir William Blackstone (1723–80), author of *Commentaries on the Laws of England* (1765–9). From Sheridan's remarks on Blackstone, see Sichel, vol. I, ch. VI, p. 414.

24 – *Ibid.*, p. 406; from a letter by Sheridan, 30 October 1772, to his friend Thomas Grenville.

25 – *Ibid.*, vol. I, 'Overture', pp. 95–6; from an early letter to Thomas Grenville.

26 – Henry Fielding (1707–54), author of *Tom Jones* (1749), also *Tom Thumb, A Tragedy* (1730); Tobias George Smollett (1721–71), author of *Roderick Random* (1748), *Peregrine Pickle* (1751), *Humphrey Clinker* (1771).

27 – *Ibid.*, vol. I, ch. VI, p. 429: 'Two years later, Dr Johnson exclaimed of the quixotic bridegroom, "He resolved wisely and nobly to be sure. He is a brave man. Would not a gentleman be disgraced by having his wife singing publicly for hire? No, Sir, there can be no doubt here."'

28 – *Ibid.*, vol. I, ch. VIII, p. 462; notice of these twice-weekly 'Orchard Street Concerts' appeared in the *Morning Post*, 4 February 1774.

29 – *The Rivals*, act IV, i, l. 14ff. (*Sheridan. Plays*. Ed. Cecil Price; O.U.P., 1975.)

30 – *The School for Scandal*, act IV, i, l. 97ff.; Charles Surface to Sir Oliver Surface (disguised as 'Mr Premium').

31 – *Ibid.*, act IV, i, ll. 161–2; Charles Surface to Rowley.

32 – *The Rivals*, act V, i, l. 130ff.; Lydia Languish to Julia: 'There had I projected one of the most sentimental elopements! – so becoming a disguise! – so amiable a ladder

of Ropes! – Conscious Moon – four horses – Scotch parson – with such surprise to Mrs Malaprop – and such paragraphs in the News-papers! – O, I shall die with disappointment.'

33 – *The Critic*, act III, i, ll. 292 ff., the play scene ('... Tilburnia *and* Confidant mad, according to custom').

34 – Sir John Vanbrugh (1664–1726); William Congreve (1670–1729); the quotations are from *The Critic*, act I, i, ll. 134, 148 respectively.

35 – *The Rehearsal* (1671) by George Villiers, Duke of Buckingham (1628–87).

36 – Sichel, vol. I, ch. XI, p. 552: 'The sunshine dances across ... [his wit], and the play of human nature lies, as Sir Henry Irving [1838–1905] insisted, at the root of his charm.'

37 – *Ibid.*, p. 553.

38 – *Ibid.*, p. 556.

39 – *Ibid.*, p. 551.

40 – *Ibid.*, p. 611.

41 – *Ibid.*, vol. II, ch. I, pp. 3–4.

42 – *Ibid.*, vol. I, ch. VI, p. 414; from Sheridan's remarks on Blackstone (see n.23 above).

43 – *Ibid.*, vol. II, ch. I, p. 17; Sheridan writing to his brother Charles upon his appointment as under-secretary of state.

44 – *King Lear*, III, IV, l.105ff.; if this line is quoted in Sichel it has not been discovered there.

45 – Sichel, vol. II, App. III, 'Georgiana, Duchess of Devonshire's Diary', p. 403.

46 – *Ibid.*, ch. VIII, pp. 173–4, also App. III, p. 404; Sir George Baker (1722–1809), the King's physician; *ibid.*, App. III, p. 408; Dr Henry Reynolds (1745–1811), physician to the King at Kew.

47 – *Ibid.*, vol. I, 'Overture', p. 39: '... Addington, who had begged him to enter his Cabinet, would gladly have conferred a peerage and a pension, but Sheridan disdained to "hide his head in a coronet". He left the premier in no doubt that he refused the slightest requital for his "unpurchaseable mind".'

48 – *Ibid.*, vol. II, pp. 128ff.; this famous speech during Sheridan's protracted prosecution of Warren Hastings took place on 7 February 1787.

49 – *Ibid.*, p. 145, and n.

50 – *Ibid.*, ch. IV, p. 97; Mrs Sheridan writing from Crewe Hall about 'the abominable whist they make me play – twenty-one guineas last night and fifteen before ...'

51 – The 'Whig sybarites', as Sichel calls them (vol. II, p. 73), were: Georgiana, Duchess of Devonshire, *née* Spencer; her sister Henrietta Frances, wife of the 4th Earl of Bessborough; and the enigmatical Lady Elizabeth Foster, who later married the 5th Duke of Devonshire.

52 – Sichel, vol. II, App. IV, 'Letters from Sheridan to the Duchess of Devonshire and her sister Lady Bessborough', p. 437; Sheridan's thoughts were prompted by recollections of his second duel, in July 1772, for the sake of his future wife, who was now, in 1792, dying.

53 – *Ibid.*

54 – See *ibid.*, ch. XIII, p. 350. (The expression 'Old Sherry' occurs at several points in Sichel's narrative.)

55 – *Ibid.*, ch. XIV, pp. 373–4.

56 – *Ibid.*, p. 379; Sheridan writing to the poet Samuel Rogers (1763–1855), c. 15 May 1816; the words 'take me' should be italicised.

57 – *Ibid.*, p. 380; from a memoir by Professor Smyth, tutor to Sheridan's son Tom.

58 – *Ibid.*, p. 388; Byron writing from Venice to Thomas Moore (whose *Memoir of Sheridan* was published in 1825).

'Maria Edgeworth and Her Circle'

So far as we can remember, Miss Hill does not ask herself once in the volume before us whether people now read Miss Edgeworth's novels.[2] Perhaps she takes it for granted that they do, or perhaps she thinks that it does not matter. The past has an immense charm of its own; and if one can show how people lived a hundred years ago – one means by that, how they powdered their hair, and drove in yellow chariots, and passed Lord Byron in the street – one need not trouble oneself with minds and emotions. Indeed, we can know very little of the dead; when we talk of the different ages of the past we are really thinking of different fashions of dress and different styles of architecture. We have an enormous supply of such properties in our minds, deposited there by a library of books like this book of Miss Hill's. She stamps the figure of a chariot in gold upon her boards, as though it helped us to understand Miss Edgeworth. We persuade ourselves that it does, and yet we should think it strange if the future biographer of 'Mrs Humphry Ward[3] and her Circle' illustrated his meaning by a hansom cab. To Miss Edgeworth herself, we may be sure, Miss Hill's account of her would seem a little irrelevant and perhaps not very amusing; nevertheless, we are under the illusion that this enumeration of trifles and names helps us somehow to see her more clearly than before, as certainly it produces in us a mild feeling of benevolence and pleasure. To Miss Hill undoubtedly belongs the credit of choosing her illustrations happily, so that they excite in us the curious illusion that we are peopling the past. For the moment it seems very much alive, and yet it is nothing like the life we know. The chief difference is that it makes us laugh much more consistently than the present does, and that it is composed to a much greater extent of visual impressions – of turbans and chariots with nothing inside them.

Miss Edgeworth, although she lived in Ireland, sometimes visited London and Paris. She crossed the Channel for the first time in 1802, the voyage taking three hours and a half, 'a comparatively quick passage for those days of sailing packets', Miss Hill points out,[4] invoking the spell of the past. Something, after all, must be invoked when one has a heroine who, brought face to face with Mme Récamier, merely remarks, 'Mme Récamier is of quite an opposite sort, though in the first fashion a graceful and *decent* beauty of excellent character.'[5] To solidify the chapter one can also quote at length what the poet Rogers said about the famous bath and how Miss Berry admired the famous bed.[6] At the same time, we cannot believe that Maria would have included Mme Récamier among her circle. In common with all the women writers of the eighteenth century, Miss Edgeworth was strikingly modest. Her habits were such that no one would have taken her for a remarkable person, but it is scarcely necessary to be at such pains to prove it. She was diminutive in figure, plain in feature, and wrote demurely at her desk in the family living-room. Nevertheless, she observed everything, and in congenial company talked well upon 'old French classic literature'[7] and listened sympathetically to stories of the Revolution. Moreover, she was so sprightly and sensible that young men of fashion both of 'the light, easy, enjoying-the-world style' and of the 'melancholy and Byronic' were fascinated and let her twit them with impunity.[8] She turned the conversation adroitly from politics to wit, and ridiculed the fashion for the 'triste' in manner and 'le vague' in poetry.[9] One love affair she had with a Swedish gentleman called Edelcrantz, whose understanding was superior and whose manners were mild. But, on ascertaining that she would have to leave her family and live in Sweden if she married him, she refused, although, 'being exceedingly in love with him',[10] she suffered much at the time and long afterwards. In May 1813, Maria Edgeworth, with her father and stepmother, spent some weeks in London. The town ran mad to see her; at parties the crowd turned and twisted to discover her, and, as she was very small, almost closed above her head. She bore it with composure and amusement; the general verdict seems to have been Lord Byron's: – 'One would never have guessed that she could write *her name*; whereas her father talked, *not* as if he could write nothing else, but as if nothing else was worth writing.'[11] On the other hand, we have

Miss Edgeworth: — 'Of Lord Byron I can tell you only that his appearance is nothing that you would remark.'[12]

The obvious thing happened; people stared, were disappointed, laughed good-humouredly, and began to talk of other things. Her biographer is in the same predicament. She has recourse, with the rest of the world, to Mme de Staël. That lady was lavishing her eloquence upon London; report said that when she was silent – that is while her hair was dressed and while she breakfasted – she continued to scribble. She extorted four words from that Duke of Marlborough, who was scarcely known to speak. 'Let me go away,' he cried, on hearing her announced.[13] Unfortunately, Napoleon escaped from Elba and Miss Edgeworth withdrew to Ireland, and for some reason we hear much more of Mme d'Arblay's impressions of the battle of Waterloo[14] than of a much more interesting subject – Miss Edgeworth herself. Maria took no part in the campaign, save that she describes (from hearsay) a banquet given at Drogheda by the Lord Mayor, at which the victorious generals were represented in sugared paste. Perverse although it may seem, Drogheda and the opinion of Drogheda upon the victory interests us far more than the account of Wellington's reception in Paris; possibly if we were told what Miss Edgeworth saw among the peasants on her estate we should realise far better what Waterloo meant than by reading the faded exclamations of Mme d'Arblay upon the spot.

Europe settled down again, however, and Maria was able to visit Hampstead in 1818, and to stay with Miss Joanna Baillie, the author of *Plays on the Passions*, and the lyric, 'The chough and crow to roost are gone',[15] admired by Scott. In spite of her fame she, too, was modest: 'No one could have taken her for a married woman. An innocent maiden grace hovered over her to the end of old age.'[16] She walked discreetly behind her elder sister when the two old ladies, dressed in grey silk and lace caps alike, were present at the reading of one of Joanna's *Plays on the Passions* in the Assembly Rooms. On hearing of it some of her friends were shocked and wrote, 'Have ye heard that Jocky Baillie has taken to the *public line*?'[17] There was Mrs Barbauld also, who sometimes stayed at Hampstead, and was severely reproved by the *Quarterly Review* for her ode,'1811', by which she depressed the spirits of the nation.[18] There was Lady Breadalbane, who fell asleep in her carriage and was locked up in the coach house; nobody missing her for a considerable time, several carriages were rolled in after hers, and then, 'she wakened'[19] – but what she said Maria has no time to report. There was Mr Standish, 'the tip-top dandy', who stayed at Trentham and displayed such a toilet-table that all the ladies' maids were invited to a private view of his dressing-case, 'which, I assure you, my lady, is the thing best worth seeing in this house, all of gilt plate, and I wish, my lady, you had such a dressing-box'.[20] How charming out ancestors were! – so simple in their manners, so humorous in their behaviour, so strange in their expressions! Thus, as we run through Miss Hill's book, we pick up straws everywhere, and dull must be our fancy if we fail in the end to furnish all the Georgian houses in existence with tables and chairs and ladies and gentlemen. There is no need to tease ourselves with the suspicion that they were quite different in the flesh, and as ugly, as complex, and as emotional as we are, for their simplicity is more amusing to believe in and much easier to write about. Nevertheless, there are moments when we bewail the opportunity that Miss Hill seems to have missed – the opportunity of getting at the truth at the risk of being dull.

1 – A review in the *TLS*, 9 December 1909, (Kp C40) of *Maria Edgeworth and her Circle in the days of Buonaparte and Bourbon. With numerous illustrations by Ellen G. Hill and reproductions of contemporary portraits* (John Lane, 1909) by Constance Hill. Reprinted: *B&P*. See also, *The Lives of the Obscure', IV VW Essays* and *CR1*.

2 – Maria Edgeworth (1767–1849) wrote many novels, most set in Ireland, among them: *Castle Rackrent* (1800), *Belinda* (1801), *The Absentee* (1812) and *Ormond* (1817).

3 – Mrs Humphry (Mary Augusta) Ward (1851–1920), novelist and philanthropical social worker; her most recent novel, *The Testing of Diana Mallory*, had appeared in 1908.

4 – Hill, ch. I, pp. 2–3.

5 – *Ibid.*, ch. III, pp. 16–17; Juliette Récamier (1777–1849), besides being a great beauty, was the friend of Chateaubriand, Mme de Staël, Sainte-Beuve, Benjamin Constant and other important literary and political figures.

6 – *Ibid.*, p. 19: '"Mme Récamier," writes the poet [Samuel] Rogers [1763–1855], "outshines the consul himself! Her bath and bedchamber are hung with silks of many colours and lighted with aromatic lamps and alabaster vases."' And: '"Her bed is reckoned the most beautiful in Paris," writes Miss [Mary] Berry [1763–1852, the friend of Horace Walpole].'

7 – *Ibid.*, ch. V, p. 45.

8 – *Ibid.*, ch. XXVIII, p. 258.

9 – *Ibid.*

10 – *Ibid.* ch. IV, p. 36; M. Edelcrantz was a Swedish courtier.

11 – *Ibid.*, ch. XII, p. 107; quoting Byron's Journal, 19 January 1821.

12 – *Ibid.*, p. 100.

13 – *Ibid.*, ch. XXV, p. 220; for the Duke of Marlborough's 'four words' upon the announcement of Mme (Germaine) de Staël (1766–1817).

14 – *Ibid.*, ch. XIX, devoted entirely to accounts of the battle of Waterloo.

15 – *Ibid.*, ch. XXIII, p. 198; the line is from the 'Outlaws' Chorus' in the play *Orra* (1811) by the Scottish author Joanna Baillie (1762–1851), who published three volumes of *Plays on the Passions* (1798, 1802, 1812).

16 – *Ibid.*, p. 202.

17 – *Ibid.*, p. 205.

18 – *Ibid.*, ch. XXXIV, p. 213; Mrs (Anna Letitia) Barbauld (1743–1825) whose ode, according to the *DNB*, 'at a time of the deepest national gloom', prophesied that 'on some future day a traveller from the antipodes will, from a broken arch of Blackfriars Bridge, contemplate the ruin of St. Paul's.'

19 – *Ibid.*, ch. XXV, pp. 220–1.

20 For the '*exquisite*' Mr Standish and his gilt dressing-box, *ibid.*, pp. 217–18.

'The Girlhood of Queen Elizabeth'

There is a memorable passage at the end of Froude's *History*, in which, before summing up the qualities of the great Queen and delivering judgment, he bids us consider what it is to be a Sovereign. Their mean thoughts 'rise like accusing spirits ... out of the private drawers of statesmen's cabinets'.[2] They may not stand aside, but must always act. Their duties cling to them as their shadows. Their words and deeds live after them, and must bear a scrutiny to which few could look forward without dismay. Having pronounced this warning, he goes on to strip Elizabeth of every virtue that was claimed for her, save the virtue of her supreme bravery. In some degree such seems to be the fate of the majority of rulers of whom we can form a judgment. Human nature when set upon a throne seems unable to sustain the enormous enlargement. The very early kings alone, in whom courage was the essential virtue, are dubbed 'the good'. The later ones, grown subtle, are deformed by vice, stupidity, or bigotry. And yet, partly because it is extraordinary, the spectacle of royalty never fails to surprise us. To see the pageant is strange enough, but it is far stranger to look into the mind of one of the great actors themselves and to watch the normal human being struggling, an ant laden with a pebble, beneath the superhuman burden laid upon it by its fellows. The difficulty of framing an opinion arises from the necessity that such a person is under of conforming to an unnatural standard, so that it is only at rare moments that one can see how he behaves as an individual. For the rest, one must use one's imagination. Mr Rait, in introducing the present volume of Queen Elizabeth's private letters, enumerates other difficulties that must beset the student of early documents. With their formalities and encumbrances, the very language they write is different from ours; they have a thousand inducements to tell lies, nor can they always tell the truth if they wish it. But, allowing for all obstacles, 'it remains true,' he proceeds, 'that in such letters as are contained in this book we have the very marrow of history'.[3] By the very marrow in this case we mean the temperament of the woman who ruled England from the time she was twenty-five, and whose whims and qualities lay at the centre of the vast expansion of the Elizabethan age. If we can arrive at some knowledge of her nature and of the circumstances that formed it, we shall read our history with a greater understanding; and Mr Mumby's collection gives us a splendid chance at least, by laying the original matter out of which history is fashioned before us. He has restricted himself to supply the necessary links as briefly and as lucidly as possible.

The story from the first is strange and violent. Her birth made enemies of her own kinsmen, for on that account her half-sister was degraded of her title and shorn of her household. Then three years later Elizabeth was deposed in her turn, without a mother, and left in the hands of a governess who confessed that she did not know what to do with her. The Princess, she wrote, had scarcely any clothes, and it was not good for a child of three who had 'great pain with her great teeth and they come very slowly forth'[4] to sup every day at the board of estate. 'For there she shall see divers meats, and fruits, and wine, which it would be hard for me to restrain her Grace from.'[5] It was the third stepmother, Catherine Parr, who first noticed her, and encouraged her to learn. Elizabeth, aged eleven, recognising her 'fervent zeal . . . towards all goodly learning',[6] dedicated to her a translation which she had made of 'The Mirror, or Glass, of the sinful soul'.[7] Making allowance for the constraint put upon her, one may infer that Elizabeth was a very precocious and somewhat priggish child, whose precocity was sometimes disagreeable. At the age of fourteen she was ripe for a serious flirtation with her stepmother's husband, Thomas Seymour,[8] and was so outspoken in this precocious love-making as to bring all those concerned into trouble and herself, finally, to disgrace. Yet, though Elizabeth was forward enough according to her governess, it seems pitiable that a girl of that age should have her feelings made the subject of inquisition by a council of noblemen. She subdued her passions, and in the retreat at Hatfield vanity drove her to excel in the only direction now open to her. Grave scholars like William Grindal and Roger Ascham had been her tutors from the first, and had predicted great things of 'that noble imp'.[9] At the end of her sixteenth year Ascham reckoned up her accomplishments, and stated that she could speak French and Italian like English; Latin and Greek she could speak with fluency; she had read some of Cicero, Livy, and Sophocles; she liked a style that was 'chaste in its propriety and beautiful in perspicuity', but 'greatly admired metaphors';[10] at that age (her tutor says) she preferred simple dress to 'show and splendour'.[11] This was one stage in her development. Such an educational one was enough to isolate her from her sex, save for the half-dozen noble ladies, the Greys and the Cecils, who were also prodigies.

Then, when Mary came to the throne she had to summon all her ability and the composure which learning gives in order to devise a policy and steer 'like a ship in tempestuous weather'[12] between the two parties. The Protestant party endangered her by their favouritism and made her the Queen's most serious rival. Every movement was watched; after Wyatt's conspiracy the Queen's nerve was so much shaken that she dared the people's rage and sent Elizabeth to the Tower.[13] The three years that followed were sufficient to give her the habit of telling lies all her life. But the memory of her unhappiness was bitter enough also to rouse in her the one 'sustained and generous feeling'[14] of her life; she showed, Mr Froude thinks, true pity for the Queen of Scots when, years afterwards, she too lay in prison. To be 'cold and unemotional',[15] the faults with which Elizabeth is oftenest charged, was the natural refuge for a woman of powerful intellect in the midst of spies. To think perpetually and never to act without a motive was the one safe policy. But it makes it unusually difficult to arrive at her genuine feeling. Thus, some one wishing to endow the magnificent young woman with human tenderness suggests that she was really fond of children, because when she walked in the Tower Garden she liked to play with a child of four who gave her flowers. Yet it was at once suspected that her motive was not tender after all, but that letters from Courtenay[16] lay hid among the leaves. Perhaps it is a trifle, yet it is our certain knowledge of the incidents of life that inspires our conception of character, for there is much less individuality in the way great acts are done. It would be interesting to know how far we still make use of tradition in giving colour to the great figures of the past when we are without details. But there are more definite statements about her appearance: she was tall, with a swarthy skin, and fine eyes – 'above all a beautiful hand, of which she makes display'.[17] She liked to have it said that she resembled her father, for 'she prides herself on her father and glories in him'.[18] In manner it is probable that she was overbearing and argumentative, insisting, 'from vanity',[19] in talking Italian to Italians, and because she spoke it better than Mary.

Thus, at the age of twenty-three she was a remarkable personage, impressing the Venetian Ambassador by her intellect and by her 'astute and judicious'[20] behaviour, and a perpetual menace to her sister. Some of the most interesting letters in the collection are the Bedingfeld papers concerning her imprisonment at Woodstock, which Froude, it seems, had never read. They show that Sir Henry Bedingfeld,[21] far from ill-treating her as is commonly said, very much disliked his task and did what he could to help her. But Elizabeth was a formidable prisoner, very observant, silent if crossed, capable of a 'most unpleasant'[22] manner, and so royal in her demeanour that it seemed impertinent to restrain her. There was nothing for her to do save to embroider the covers of a Bible and scratch plaintive verses on the window panes; she asked for books, a Cicero and an English Bible; she wanted to walk freely and demanded to write her complaints to the Council. Sir Henry had to check her in every way; he was made uneasy if a servant bringing presents of 'freshwater fish . . . and two dead pheasant cocks'[23] stayed too long gossiping with the servants. But such was the tone in which she issued 'an importunate command' that in spite of all injunctions Sir Henry not only gave her pen and paper, but wrote at her dictation, although he spelt very badly, the Princess 'saying that she never wrote to your Lordships but by a secretary'.[24] He pointed out the inconveniences of Woodstock as a residence in winter – how the wind and rain would come through the chinks, and how the villagers grumbled already at the soldiers who were quartered upon them. It is clear that he only wished to be rid of her.

When Mary died three years later no more seasoned woman of her age could be found in Europe than Elizabeth. She had known love, and seen death very close; she had learnt to suspect almost every one, and to let men struggle and plot before her without taking part. Her intellect was trained to wrestle with intricate arguments and to delight in flourishes of ornament. Her poverty had taught her to hoard money and to hint for gifts. In short, her education and her adventures had equipped her with a complete armour of cold and harsh feelings, under the control of a perfectly dauntless bravery. Thus, splendid and inscrutable, she rode through London on the day of her Coronation; arches, pyramids, and fountains stood in her way, from which boys sang greeting; a fine snow kept falling over her, but the gems and the golden collars shone clearly through the whiteness.

1 – A review in the *TLS*, 30 December 1909 (Kp C41) of *The Girlhood of Queen Elizabeth* [1533–1603]. *A narrative in contemporary letters* (Constable & Co., 1909) by Frank A. Mumby, with an introduction by R. S. Rait. Reprinted: *B&P*.

2 – J. A. Froude, *History of England. From the Fall of Wolsey to the Defeat of the Spanish Armada* (12 vols, Longmans, Green, 1870), vol. XII, 'The Reign of Elizabeth', p. 556.

3 – Mumby, Intro., p. xviii. Robert Sangster Rait (1874–1936), at this time a Fellow of New College, Oxford.

4 – *Ibid.*, ch. I, p. 17; Lady Bryan in a letter to Lord Cromwell, 1536.

5 – *Ibid.*

6 – *Ibid.*, Princess Elizabeth to Catherine Parr, 31 December 1544, p. 24, which has: 'Not only knowing the effectuous will and fervent zeal, the which your highness hath towards all godly learning . . . '

7 – A devotional treatise translated by Elizabeth from the French.

8 – Thomas Seymour, Baron Seymour of Sudeley (b. 1508?), Lord High Admiral, married Catherine Parr, the dowager queen, in 1647, and on her death that same year he renewed an earlier suit for Elizabeth's hand. This conduct aroused suspicion in the Council and Seymour was duly convicted of high treason and executed in 1549.

9 – Mumby, ch. I, p. 27; Roger Ascham (1515–68) in a letter to Mrs Ashley. Ascham succeeded William Grindal, upon the latter's death in 1548, as tutor to Princess Elizabeth, and remained her tutor when, in 1558, she became Queen.

10 – *Ibid.*, ch. III, p. 71; Ascham on 'Elizabeth's learning' to John Sturmius, 1550.

11 – *Ibid.*, p. 70.

12 – *Ibid.*, ch. V, p. 185; quoting William Camden. Mary I (1516–58) came to the throne in 1553.

13 – Sir Thomas Wyatt (d. 1554), son of the poet, whose conspiracy and insurrection against the proposed Spanish marriage of Queen Mary led to his execution and Elizabeth's detention in the Tower.

14 – Froude, vol. XII, p. 560.

15 – Mumby, ch. IV, p. 124.

16 – Edward Courtenay, Earl of Devonshire (d. 1556), also detained in the Tower after Wyatt's insurrection; see Mumby, pp. 123–4.

17 – Mumby, ch. VII, p. 228; Giovanni Michiel writing to the Venetian Senate, 13 May 1557.

18 – *Ibid.*, p. 229.

19 – *Ibid.*

20 – *Ibid.*

21 – Sir Henry Bedingfield (1511–83) in whose charge Elizabeth was placed while imprisoned in the Tower and at Woodstock, March 1554–June 1555.

22 – Mumby, ch. V, p. 147; Sir Henry Bedingfield to the Council, 12 June 1554, describing Elizabeth's anger at not being allowed an English Bible.

23 – *Ibid.*, p. 149; the ellipsis should come after 'and', according to the text.

24 – For these two quotations, *ibid.*, p. 169, Sir Henry Bedingfield to the Council, 20 September 1554, which has 'saying she never wrote . . . '

1910

'Lady Hester Stanhope'

The writers in the *Dictionary of National Biography* have a pleasant habit of summing up a life, before they write it, in one word, thus – 'Stanhope, Lady Hester Lucy (1770–1839), eccentric'.[2] The reason why her life is written at all is that she differed from other people, but never converted them to her own way of thinking. Mrs Roundell, who has written the latest account of her, is sympathetic and respectful, but she is clearly no convert. One feels that she is smoothing over eccentricities, as though we were all at a tea-party together. It would be polite there to remark, 'Lady Hester is very fond of cats,' but in private, and writing is private, one should allow oneself to luxuriate in the fact that she kept forty-eight of them,[3] choosing them for the harmony of their stars with her own, joining in a deep bass voice with their music at night, and accusing her doctor of a lumpish, cold, effeminate disposition if he found the noise intolerable. But the merit of Mrs Roundell's work, together with its simplicity and its quotations from later writers, is that it brings or recalls to our notice a most entertaining book, *The Memoirs and Travels of Lady Hester Stanhope*, by Dr Meryon, in six volumes. The charm of Dr Meryon's work lies in its comprehensiveness. He lived with her off and on for twenty-eight years, and the people we live with are the last we seek to define in one word. Dr Meryon never attempted it. To him she was not an eccentric by profession, but a lady of exalted birth, who condescended when she shook hands with him, a woman of political greatness, inspired at times, with a spell like Circe. As a middle-class Englishman, as a doctor, as a man respecting woman's courage but a little touched by the need for it, he felt her charm. She treated him like a servant, but the 'magical illusion which she ever contrived to throw around herself in the commonest circumstances of life'[4] kept its glamour. Happily the conditions of life on Mount Lebanon in the Thirties of the last century allowed him to write profusely, and gave him only the one subject to treat. When he got back at dawn from those long audiences, by the end of which the lady was hidden in smoke, he tried to put down the stories and to express the kind of stupefaction with which she overwhelmed him.

Very little, unfortunately, is known of Lady's Hester's early life. When she kept house for William Pitt[5] she made herself disliked, presumably, from the account that she gives of her triumphs. With a scanty education but great natural force, she despised people without troubling to give them a reason for it. Intuition took the place of argument, and her penetration was great. 'Fort grande, fort maigre, fort décidée, fort independante'[6] a French lady describes her as girl in the ball-room; she herself recalled her complexion of alabaster and her lips of carnation. Further, she had a conviction of the rights of the aristocracy, and ordered her life from an eminence which made her conduct almost sublime. 'Principle!' she exclaimed; 'what do you mean by principle? – I am a Pitt.'[7] Unluckily her sex closed the proper channels. 'If you were a man, Hester,' Mr Pitt would say, 'I would send you on the Continent with 60,000 men, and give you *carte blanche*; and I am sure that not one of my plans would fail, and not one soldier would go with his shoes unblacked.'[8] But, as it was, her powers fermented within her; she detested her sex, as though in revenge for the limitations with which ordinary women cramp remarkable ones; and drove herself as near madness as one can go by feeding a measureless ambition upon phantoms.

When her uncle died she had a pension of fifteen hundred a year and a house in Montague Square; but she pointed out in a remarkable conversation how these conditions are precisely the most intolerable if you are a person of rank. They condemn you to nothing less than imprisonment in your own drawing-room, for you cannot do yourself justice in the streets upon such a pittance. She preferred to sacrifice her health rather than lower her standards, until it occurred to her that simplicity, so extreme that no one can connect it with necessity, is the other way of being distinguished. Accordingly she retired to a cottage at

Builth, in Wales, where she lived in a room 'not more than a dozen feet square', 'curing the poor' and keeping a dairy.[9] She was then thirty-two. With a mixture of true greatness and grandiloquence, she determined that English ways of life are made to suit timid herds, and that a remarkable person must seek a land less corrupted by hypocrisy, where nature prevails. With what expectations she set sail for the East we know not, but she emerged in Syria, astride her horse, in the trousers of a Turkish gentleman. For the rest of her life she did nothing but shake her fist at England, where the people had forgotten their great men.

As usual, her sublimity was accompanied by a touch of the ridiculous. It is impossible not to feel that the presence of Mrs Fry, the respectable English maid, impaired the romance of the cavalcade. Dressed in men's clothes, she was expected to ride like a man, but with the heroism of her class she persisted in sitting 'in the decorous posture customary with women in England', and was thus 'often exposed to the danger of falling from her ass'.[10] Then, how pathetic were her attempts to redeem the wild Eastern names to the semblance at least of Christianity – Philippaki became Philip Parker and Mustapha Mr Farr. Lady Hester and Dr Meryon saw nothing in this but the feebleness of a womanish disposition. A convent on the slopes of Mount Lebanon was bought, and there Lady Hester settled down to exert her mysterious spells. All round the house, which was perched on the top of a hill, she dug an elaborate garden, from whose terraces one could see the Mediterranean between the hills. Her influence at one time was vast, though vague; the children for twenty miles round Constantinople had heard her name. The apparition of this Englishwoman, with her large frame and her cadaverous face and her connection with august personages in England, was in itself a miracle; the natives thought her neither man nor woman, but a being apart. The chiefs came to her for counsel, because she was absolutely without fear and loved to intrigue. The English consuls all along the coast held her in horror. Sitting on her hilltop, she thought that she arranged the affairs of the countryside and overheard the faintest whispers. A sponge diver called Logmagi was sent to pick up news in the seaports and the bazaars of Constantinople, and in particular to report the first tidings of unrest among the people. At once new rooms and secret tunnels were added to the house, till it was shaped like a labyrinth, for she believed that 'events and catastrophes'[11] would come to pass, when people of all nations would fly to her, and she would lead them forth to Jerusalem itself, mounted upon one of the two sacred mares which now fattened in her stalls. Upon the other 'a boy without a father' would ride, who was none other than the Messiah Himself. For some time the Duke of Reichstadt was the boy of the prophecy, but when he died she 'fixed on another'.[12]

Talk, since nothing ever happened, became the solace of her life. The memoirs are made out of talk. Wrapped in a white cloak, with a great turban on her head, she sat in the dusk, so that you might not notice how her skin was wrinkled 'like the network which we see on the rind of some species of melons',[13] picking spoonfuls of meat and sweetstuff from saucers, and pouring forth her soliloquy. Nothing that had happened in the years she lived with Mr Pitt was forgotten: she remembered how she had snubbed Admiral —, what the Duchess of D. had worn, what a leg had Sir W— R—; in particular, how Mr Pitt had praised her, and how he liked his food. She gossiped as though she were talking over the events of the night before, although she sat among broken crockery, in the Syrian mountains, smoking pipes with her doctor, twenty years or more after it had all faded away. Thus she rambled on:

What can be the reason? I am now always thinking of Sir G. H—. I have been thinking how well he would do for Master of the Horse to the Queen, and I have a good way of giving a hint of it through the Buckleys; for I always said that, next to Lord Chatham, nobody ever had such handsome equipages as Sir G.; nobody's coaches and horses were so neatly picked out as theirs. Sir G. is a man, Doctor, from what you tell me, that would have just suited Mr Pitt. That polished and quiet manner which Sir G. has was what Mr Pitt found so agreeable in Mr Long. It is very odd – Mr Pitt always would dress for dinner, even if we were alone. One day I said to him, 'You are tired, and there is no one but ourselves; why need you dress?' He replied, 'Why, I don't know, Hester; but if one omits to do it to-day, we neglect it to-morrow, and so on, until one grows a pig.'[14]

Her spirits fell, and she went on:

To look at me now, what a lesson against vanity! Look at this arm, all skin and bone, so thin, so thin that you may see through it; and once, without exaggeration, so rounded that you could not pinch the skin up. My neck was once so fair that a pearl necklace scarcely showed on it; and men – no fools, but sensible men – would say to me, 'God has given you a neck you really may be proud of; you are one of Nature's favourites, and one may be excused for admiring that beautiful skin.' If they could behold me now, with my teeth all gone and with long lines in my face – not wrinkles, for I have no wrinkles when I am left quiet and not made angry; but my face is drawn out of composure by these wretches. I thank God that old age has come upon me unperceived. When I used to see the painted Lady H., dressed in pink and silver, with her head shaking, and jumped by her footman into her sociable, attempting to appear young, I felt a kind of horror and disgust I can't describe. I wonder how Lady Stafford dresses now she is no longer young; but I can't fancy her grown old.[15]

Fierce storms of rage possessed her, and then she would weep with a wild howl painful to hear, as though Bellona should weep. More and more, as time passed without any revolution and her influence waned, and debts crushed her, did she seek the support of magic. Although she had failed to subdue the forces of this world, and the Queen and Lord Palmerston were against her, she was mistress of arts that the vulgar knew nothing of. She saw the sylphs perched on her chest of drawers and clumsy fellows tripped up for ignoring them; seated in the convent at Dar Djoun, she could look into the heart of Paris or of London; she knew the cavern where the King of the Serpents lived, with the head of a man; she knew where to find the lost book of Adam and Eve's language written in letters a span high; 'I believe in vampires, but the people in England know not how to distinguish them.'[16]

After a time she never left her hilltop; then she scarcely went beyond her room, but sat in bed, arguing, scolding and ringing bells perpetually, the floor littered with pipes and bits of string; she was never to ride into Jerusalem upon her mare, and the aristocratic ideal remained high. She would let no European come near her, and at last she turned even Dr Meryon away. In June 1839, the news came to Beirut that she had died with only native servants round her. Rooms were found full of mouldy stores hoarded for the great emergency, but her valuables had been stolen while she lay helpless. The dead lady looked 'composed and placid',[17] but she was so much in the habit of hiding her feelings that her expression told nothing. She was buried in a corner of her rose garden in the grave of a certain prophet, where she had not wished to be buried. Ten years later the place was a thicket of brambles and roses; now there are lines of mulberry trees. But Lady Hester, the last of the great English aristocrats, lives on in despite of the plough.

---

1 – A review in the TLS, 20 January 1910, (Kp C42) of 'a silly new book' (I VW Letters, no. 514, to Violet Dickinson, 27 December 1909) Lady Hester Stanhope (John Murray, 1909) by Mrs Charles Roundell, but largely based on a reading of Memoirs of the Lady Hester Stanhope, as related by herself in conversations with her physician (3 vols, Henry Colburn, 1845) and Travels of Lady Hester Stanhope; forming the completion of her memoirs. Narrated by her physician. (3 vols, Henry Colburn, 1846) by Charles (Lewis) Meryon (1783–1877.) 'One reads like an express train – from tea to bed time,' VW wrote to Clive Bell, on 26 December 1909 (I VW

Letters, no. 513); 'It makes me rock with delight – thinking what a number of wonderful things I shall dig out of it in my article. One gradually sees shapes and thinks oneself in the middle of a world.' Reprinted: *B&P*.

2 – A contribution by Thomas Seccombe (1866–1923), critic and biographer.

3 – See Roundell, ch. VIII, p. 132: 'The discomfort was increased by the large number of cats which Lady Hester kept.' Roundell then quotes *Memoirs*, vol. III, p. 146: 'I have counted as many as thirty old cats and kittens, without including those that haunted the store-rooms, the granaries, the outhouses, and gardens, and it was forbidden to molest them.'

4 – Roundell, ch. VIII, p. 172, quoting *Memoirs*, vol. III, p. 4.

5 – Lady Hester kept house for William Pitt (1759–1806), the statesman and her uncle, from 1803 until his death, during which period, from May 1804, Pitt was Prime Minister.

6 – Roundell, ch. I, p. 9, quoting from *Mémoires de la Duchesse de Gontaut*: 'Je la voyais pour la première fois; elle me parut . . . '

7 – *Memoirs*, vol. II, p. 360.

8 – *Ibid.*, which concludes: ' . . . meaning, that my attention would embrace every duty that belongs to a general and a corporal – and so it would, doctor.'

9 – Roundell, ch. I, p. 16, quoting *Memoirs*, vol. II, p. 7.

10 – Roundell, ch. V, p. 53–4, quoting *Travels*, vol. I, p. 299.

11 – *Memoirs*, vol. I, p. 89: ' . . . her servants were taught to look forward, with a sort of awe and religious expectation, to events and catastrophes, where their services and energies would be tasked to the utmost.'

12 – For the fatherless boy and the Duke's unidentified successor, *ibid.*, p. 206.

13 – *Ibid.*, vol. I, p. 98, which has: 'But age will, without furrowing the brow or the cheeks, bring that sort of network which we see . . . '

14 – *Ibid.*, vol. II, pp. 164–5, which has 'horses and carriages', not 'coaches and horses'.

15 – *Ibid.*, pp. 166–7: 'She here began to cry and wring her hands, presenting a most melancholy picture of despair. When she had recovered a little, she went on . . . '

16 – *Ibid.*, p. 279.

17 – Roundell, ch. X, p. 228.

'Modes and Manners of
the Nineteenth Century'

When one has read no history for a time the sad-coloured volumes are really surprising. That so much energy should have been wasted in the effort to believe in something spectral fills one with pity. Wars and ministries and legislation – unexampled prosperity and unbridled corruption tumbling the nation headlong to decay – what a strange delusion it all is! – invented presumably by gentlemen in tall hats in the Forties who wished to dignify mankind. Our point of view they ignore entirely: we have never felt the pressure of a single law; our passions and despairs have nothing to do with trade; our virtues and vices flourish under all governments impartially. The machine they describe; they succeed to some extent in making us believe in it; but the heart of it they leave untouched – is it because they cannot understand it? At any rate, we are left out, and history, in our opinion, lacks an eye. It is with unusual hope that we open the three volumes in which a nameless author has dealt with the *Modes and Manners of the Nineteenth Century*. Thin and green, with innumerable coloured pictures and a fair type, they are less like a mausoleum than usual; and modes and manners – how we feel and dress – are precisely what the other historian ignores.

The connection between dress and character has been pointed out often enough. Because dress represents some part of a man picturesquely it lends itself happily to the satirist. He can exaggerate it without losing touch with the object of his satire. Like a shadow, it walks beside the truth and apes it. The device of making the smaller ridicule the greater by representing it recommended itself to Swift and Carlyle. But to discover soberly how far thought has expressed itself in clothes, and manners as we call them, is far more difficult. There is the temptation to hook the two together by the most airy conjectures. A gentleman had the habit, for example, of walking in the streets of Berlin with tame deer;[2] that was characteristic, we are told, of a certain middle-class section of German society, in the Twenties, Thirties and Forties, which was learned, pedantic, philistine, and vulgar; for to make oneself conspicuous is a mark of the vulgarian, and to walk with tame deer is to make oneself conspicuous. But there are more solid links. The French Revolution, of course, sundered the traditions of ages. It decreed that man in future must be mainly black, and should wear trousers instead of breeches. The waistcoat alone remained aristocratic, and drew to itself all the reds and oranges of the other garments, and, as they became cotton, turned to plush and brocade. At length this rich territory was conquered, and sparks of colour only burnt in the cravat and on the fob. The different garments moved up and down, swelled and shrank at intervals, but after 1815 a man's clothes were 'essentially the same as they are now'.[3] Men wished to obliterate classes, and a dress that could be worn became necessary. Women, on the other hand, were exposed to fewer influences, so that it may be easier to trace one idea in their clothes. The effect of the Revolution seems to be definite enough. Rousseau had bidden them return to nature; the Revolution had left them poor; the Greeks were ancient, and therefore natural; and their dress was cheap enough for a democracy. Accordingly, they dressed in pure white cottons and calicoes, without a frill or an exuberance; nature alone was to shape the lines; nature was to suffer not more than eight ounces of artificial concealment. The effect of these tapering nymphs, dancing on a hilltop among slim trees, is exquisite but chill. Because Greek temples were white, they whitewashed their walls; the bedroom was the Temple of Sleep; the tables were altars; the chair legs were grooved into columns; reticules were shaped like funeral urns, and classical cameos were worn at the neck. The absolute consistency of their attitude may be ridiculous, but it is also remarkable. In fact, the society of the Empire is the last to 'boast a style of its own, owing to the perfect correspondence between its aims, ideas, and character, and their outward manifestations'.[4] Any unanimity is overwhelming; it is one of the great gifts we bestow upon the Greeks; and, although there were many beautiful episodes in the nineteenth century, no single style was again strong enough to make everything consistent. Before the Revolution some sort of order was stamped upon fashion by the will of the Queen, who could afford to make beauty the prime virtue; but in 1792 Mlle Bertin, Marie Antoinette's modiste, fled from Paris, and although she touched at other courts, eventually settling in England, her rule was over; shops for ready-made clothing opened as she left. For ten years, 1794–1804, the didactic classic spirit served instead of the royal will; and then a confusion set in which threatens never to grow calm. Still the author does his best to make one change account for another, at the risk of wide generalisations. 'Feeling and sensibility took the place in this generation ⟨the generation of the Napoleonic wars⟩ of religion . . . [5] During the First Empire love and passion had been but the passing gratification of the moment, but now love was to be the one lasting object of life and being'[6] – therefore puffs and ruffs were worn; the furniture became rococo, and Gothic cathedrals influenced the chairs and the clocks.

A woman's clothes are so sensitive that, far from seeking one influence to account for their changes, we must seek a thousand. The opening of a railway line, the marriage of a princess, the trapping of a skunk – such external events tell upon them; then there is the 'relationship between the sexes';[7] in 1867 the Empress Eugénie, wearing a short skirt for the first time, went for a drive with the Emperor and Empress of Austria. As the ladies stepped into the carriage, the Emperor turned to his wife and said, 'Take care, or some one may catch sight of your feet.'[8] The influences of beauty and of reason are always fighting in a woman's clothes; reason has won some remarkable triumphs, in Germany for the most part, but generally submits to a weak compromise. When we talk of fashion, however, we mean something definite though hard to define. It comes from without; we wake in the morning and find the shops alive with it; soon it is abroad in the streets. As we turn over the pictures in these volumes we see the spirit at work. It travels all over the body ceaselessly. Now the skirt begins to grow, until it trails for six feet upon the ground; suddenly the spirit leaps to the throat, and creates a gigantic ruff there, while the skirt shrinks to the knees; then it enters the hair, which immediately rises in the pinnacles of Salisbury Cathedral; a slight swelling appears beneath the skirt; it grows, alarmingly; at last a frame has to support the flounces; next the arms are attacked; they imitate Chinese pagodas; steel hoops do what they can to relieve them. The hair, meanwhile, has subsided. The lady has outgrown all cloaks, and only a vast shawl can encompass her. Suddenly, without warning, the entire fabric is pricked; the spirit moves the Empress Eugénie one night (January 1859) to reject her crinoline. In an instant the skirts of Europe melt away, and with pursed lips and acrimonious manners the ladies mince about the streets clasped tightly round the knees, instead of swimming. It is from the crinoline, no doubt, that Meredith got his favourite 'she swam'.[9]

Fashion dealt more discreetly with men, and chiefly haunted their legs. Nevertheless, there was a sympathy between the sexes. When her skirts ballooned, his trousers swelled; when she dwindled away, he wore stays; when her hair was Gothic, his was romantic; when she dragged a train, his cloak swept the ground. About 1820 his waistcoat was more uncontrollable than any garment of hers; five times within eight months it changed its shape; for a long time the cravat preserved a space for jewellery where the necklaces were rivalled. The only parts of men that survived the stark years of the Thirties and Forties were the hat and the beard; they still felt the sway of political changes. The democratic spirit required felt hats that drooped; in 1848 they dissolved about the ears; stiffening again as reaction set in. The same principle ruled the beard; to be clean shaven was a sign of unflinching respectability; a ragged beard, or even a beard alone, showed that one's opinions were out of control.

At the present time 'Only at home does the gentleman indulge in coloured gold-laced velvet, silk, or cashmere; when he appears in public he may only venture by the superior cut of his garments to aim at any distinction; if the male attire thereby loses in effect, it gains in tone.'[10]

With furniture we find the same thing. Quite slowly every chair and table round us changes its form; if one had fallen asleep in an early Victorian drawing-room, among the patterns and plush, one would wake up this year with a horrid start. The room would seem little better than an attic. Yet, if one had sat there open-eyed, one would scarcely have seen the things change. Dress and furniture are always moving, but, having done his utmost to make them depend upon 'the spirit of the time', the author declares himself baffled. 'The longer we study the question, the more certain do we become that though we know the how, we shall never know the wherefore.'[11] Are we truly in the grip of a spirit that makes us dance to its measure, or can it be laid without recourse to magic? When one compromises one delivers no clear message. Throughout the nineteenth century both dress and furniture were at the mercy of a dozen different aims, and the original meaning was further blunted by the intervention of machines. Only great artists, giving their minds to nothing else, represent their age; dressmakers and cabinet-makers generally caricature it or say nothing about it. As for manners, the term is so vague that it is difficult to test it; but it is probable that they too only approximate, and that people's behaviour is the roughest guide to what they mean. If manners are not rubbed smooth by a machine, the comfort of society depends upon using a common language, and only saying what can be misunderstood without disaster. For this reason a history of modes and manners must use phrases which are as empty as any in the language, and the history is not a history of ourselves, but of our disguises. The poets and the novelists are the only people from whom we cannot hide.

---

1 – A review in the *TLS*, 24 February 1910, (Kp C43) of *Modes and Manners of the Nineteenth Century. As represented in the Pictures and Engravings of the time.* Translated by Marian Edwardes. With an introduction by Grace Rhys (3 vols, J. M. Dent & Co., 1909) [by Max Ulrich von Boehn]. Reprinted: *B&P*.

2 – Boehn, vol. II, p. 76: 'The love of making one's self conspicuous is a mark of the vulgarian; and yet in what other way can we explain the conduct of Prince Pückler, who walked about Berlin with tame deer . . .'

3 – *Ibid.*, vol. I, p. 136.

4 – *Ibid.*, p. 32.
5 – *Ibid.*, p. 42.
6 – *Ibid.*, vol. II, p. 57.
7 – *Ibid.*, vol. I, p. 41, which has: 'This affected sensibility expressed itself in still more peculiar ways in the intercourse between the sexes.'
8 – *Ibid.*, vol. III, p. 96.
9 – George Meredith's favourite expression remains untraced.
10 – Boehn, vol. III, p. 105.
11 – For these two quotations, *ibid.*, p. 42; p. 43.

Emerson's Journals

Emerson's *Journals* have little in common with other journals. They might have been written by starlight in a cave if the sides of the rock had been lined with books. In reality they cover twelve most important years – when he was at college, when he was a clergyman, and when he was married for the first time. But circumstances as well as nature made him peculiar. The Emerson family was now threadbare, but it had noble traditions in the past. His widowed mother and his eccentric aunt were possessed with the fierce Puritan pride of family which insisted upon intellectual distinction and coveted with a pride that was not wholly of the other world a high place for their name among the select families of Boston. They stinted themselves and stinted the boys that they might afford learning. The creed of the enthusiastic women was but too acceptable to children 'born to be educated'.[2] They chopped the fire-wood, read classics in their spare time, and lay bare in all their sensitiveness to the 'pressure of I know not how many literary influences'[3] with which the Emerson household was charged. The influence of Aunt Mary, their father's sister, was clearly the most powerful. There are general rough sketches of men of genius in the family, and Miss Emerson rudely represented her nephew. She possessed the intense faith of the first Americans, together with a poetic imagination which made her doubt it. Her soul was always in conflict. She did not know whether she could suffer her nephews to reform the precious fabric, and yet was so full of new ideas herself that she could not help imparting them. But, unlike them, she was only self-taught, and her fervour boiled within her, scalding those she loved best. 'I love to be a vessel of cumbersomeness to society,' she remarked.[4] But the strange correspondence which she kept up with Ralph, although it is but half intelligible from difficulty of thought and inadequacy of language, shows us what an intense and crabbed business life was to a serious American.

With such voices urging him on Emerson went to school fully impressed with the importance of the intellect. But his journals do not show vanity so much as a painful desire to get the most out of himself and a precocious recognition of ends to be aimed at. His first object was to learn how to write. The early pages are written to the echo of great prose long before he could fit words that gave his meaning into the rhythm. 'He studied nature with a classical enthusiasm, and the constant activity of his mind endowed him with an energy of thought little short of inspiration.'[5] Then he began to collect rare words out of the books he read: 'Ill conditioned, Cameleon, Zeal, Whortleberry'.[6] The frigid exercises upon 'The Drama', 'Death', 'Providence'[7] were useful also to decide the anxious question whether he belonged to the society of distinguished men or not. But it was the responsibility and the labour of being great and not the joy that impressed him. His upbringing had early made him conscious that he was exceptional, and school no doubt confirmed him. At any rate he could not share his thoughts with friends. Their arguments and views are never quoted beside his own in the diary. The face of one Freshman attracted him, but 'it would seem that this was an imaginary friendship. There is no evidence that the elder student ever brought himself to risk disenchantment by active advances.'[8] To make up for the absence of human interest we have the annals of the Pythologian Club.[9] But although they show that Emerson occasionally read and listened to papers comparing love and ambition, marriage and celibacy, town life and country life, they give no impression of intimacy. Compared with the contemporary life of an Englishman at Oxford or Cambridge, the life of an American undergraduate seems unfortunately raw. Shelley took the world seriously enough, but Oxford was so full of prejudices that he could never settle into complacent self-improvement; Cambridge made even Wordsworth drunk. But the great bare building at Harvard, which looks (in an engraving of 1823)[10] like a reformatory in the middle of a desert, had no such traditions; its pupils were profoundly conscious that they had to make them. Several volumes of the *Journals* are dedicated to 'America', as though to a cause.[11]

A weaker mind, shut up with its finger on its pulse, would have used a diary to revile its own unworthiness. But Emerson's diary merely confirms the impression he made on his friends; he appeared 'kindly, affable, but self-contained . . . apart, as if in a tower';[12] nor was he more emotional writing at midnight for his own eye; but we can guess the reason. It was because he had convictions. His indefatigable brain raised a problem out of every sight and incident; but they could be solved if he applied his intellect. Safe in this knowledge, which time assured, he could live alone, registering the development, relying more and more on his sufficiency, and coming to believe that by close scrutiny he could devise a system. Life at twenty-one made him ponder thoughts like these: 'Books and Men; Civilisation; Society and Solitude; Time; God within'.[13] Novels, romances, and plays seemed for the most part written for 'coxcombs and deficient persons'.[14] The only voice that reached him from without was the voice of his Aunt Mary, tumultuous in fear lest he should lose his belief in original sin. Before he had developed his theory of compensation, he was sometimes harassed by the existence of evil; occasionally he accused himself of wasting time. But his composure is best proved by an elaborate essay headed 'Myself'.[15] There one quality is weighed with another, so that the character seems to balance scrupulously. Yet he was conscious of a 'signal defect', which troubled him because it could destroy this balance more completely than its importance seemed to justify. Either he was without 'address', or there was a 'levity of understanding' or there was an 'absence of common sympathies'.[16] At any rate, he felt a 'sore uneasiness in the company of most men and women . . . [17] even before women and children I am compelled to remember the poor boy who cried, "I told you, Father, they would find me out."'[18] To be a sage in one's study, and a stumbling schoolboy out of it – that was the irony he had to face.

Instead, however, of slipping into easier views, he went on with his speculations; nor was he bitter against the world because it puzzled him. What he did was to assert that he could not be rejected because he held the universe within him. Each man, by finding out what he feels, discovers the laws of the universe; the essential thing, therefore, is to be as conscious of yourself as possible.

He that explores the principles of architecture and detects the beauty of the proportions of a column, what doth he but ascertain one of the laws of his own mind? . . . The Kingdom of God is within you . . . [19] I hold fast to my old faith: that to each soul is a solitary law, a several universe.[20]

Every man is a new creation: can do something best, has some intellectual modes or forms, or a character the general result of all, such as no other in the universe has.[21]

But this is different from selfishness; praise or blame or a reflection in the face of society – anything that made him remember himself discomfited him; a solitude as empty as possible, in which he could feel most acutely his contact with the universe, rejoiced him. 'The more exclusively idiosyncratic man is, the more general and infinite he is'²² – that was the justification of solitude, but the fruits depend upon the worth of the man. Small minds, imbibing this doctrine, turn their possessors into cranks and egoists, and a delicate mind is strained until it is too pure to act: there was Mr Bradford, for example, who, 'too modest and sensitive' to be a clergyman, became a 'teacher of classes for young ladies', and was a 'devoted gardener'.²³ In Emerson the reason was strong enough to lift him beyond the temptation of purifying his own soul. Yet it did not free him, in youth at least, from an interest in the distempers of his spirit which is unpleasantly professional. Often in company and in solitude he was absorbed in regulating his sensations. 'When I stamp through the mud in dirty boots, I hug myself with the feeling of my immortality.'²⁴ Only the bland and impersonal spirit which never left him makes such reflections other than smug; they are often dismal enough. But the wonder is that, treating as he does of platitudes and expounding them for our good, he yet contrives to make them glow so frequently, as if, next minute, they would illumine the world. He had the poet's gift of turning far, abstract thoughts, if not into flesh and blood, at least into something firm and glittering. In the pages of his diary one can see how his style slowly emerged from its wrappings, and became more definite and so strong that we can still read it even when the thought is too remote to hold us. He discovered that 'No man can write well who thinks there is any choice of words for him . . . In good writing, every word means something. In good writing, words become one with things.'²⁵ But the theory has something priggish about it. All good writing is honest in the sense that it says what the writer means; but Emerson did not see that one can write with phrases as well as with words. His sentences are made up of hard fragments each of which has been matched separately with the vision in his head. It is far rarer to find sentences which, lacking emphasis because the joins are perfect and the words common, yet grow together so that you cannot dismember them, and are steeped in meaning and suggestion.

But what is true of his style is true of his mind. An austere life, spent in generalising from one's own emotions and in keeping their edges sharp, will not yield rich romantic pages, so deep that the more you gaze into them the more you see. Isolated, one loses the power of understanding why men and women do not live by rule, and the confusion of their feelings merely distresses one. Emerson, born among half-taught people, in a new land, kept always the immature habit of conceiving that man is made up of separate qualities, which can be separately developed and praised. It is a belief necessary to schoolmasters; and to some extent Emerson is always a schoolmaster, making the world very simple for his scholars, a place of discipline and reward. But this simplicity, which is in his diaries as well as in his finished works – for he was not to be 'found out' – is the result not only of ignoring so much, but of such concentration upon a few things. By means of it he can produce an extraordinary effect of exaltation, as though the disembodied mind were staring at the truth. He takes us to a peak above the world, and all familiar things have shrunk into pinheads and faint greys and pinks upon the flat. There, with beating hearts, we enjoy the sensation of our own dizziness; there he is natural and benign. But these exaltations are not practicable; they will not stand interruption. Where shall we lay the blame? Is he too simple, or are we too worn? But the beauty of his view is great, because it can rebuke us, even while we feel that he does not understand.

1 – A review in the *TLS*, 3 March 1910, (Kp C44) of the *Journals of Ralph Waldo Emerson. With annotations*. Ed. Edward Waldo Emerson and Waldo Emerson Forbes (vols I and II, 1820–32; Constable & Co., 1909, 1910), for which VW also read *A Memoir of Ralph Waldo Emerson* (2 vols, Macmillan & Co., 1887) by James Elliot Cabot. Reprinted: *B&P*. Reading Notes (Berg XXIX).

Leslie Stephen, during one of his visits to America, was taken by his friend James Russell Lowell to meet Ralph Waldo Emerson (1803–82) in his house at Concord, Massachusetts, and afterwards also wrote about him in 'Emerson' (*Studies of a Biographer*, 2nd Series, vol. IV; Duckworth & Co., 1902).

2 – Cabot, vol. I, ch. I, p. 28: '... "they were born to be educated", their aunt Mary said.' This was their father's sister, Aunt Mary Moody Emerson.

3 – *Ibid.*, p. 34, which has 'literary atmospheres'.

4 – *Ibid.*, p. 31.

5 – *Journals*, vol. I, p. 6, which has: 'He studied Nature with a chastised enthusiasm ...'

6 – *Ibid.*, p. 7.

7 – *Ibid.*, for 'Drama', see pp. 54ff., 106ff., 127ff., 147ff.; for 'Death', pp. 126ff.; for 'Providence', pp. 112ff.

8 – *Ibid.*, p. 28n., referring to Martin Gay of Hingham, which concludes: '... active advances, and the younger boy could not understand why he was watched and even followed afar by this strange upper-class man.'

9 – This was 'a small literary (and, when fines permitted, mildly convivial,) club' of which Emerson was secretary, *ibid.*, p. 31 and n., and pp. 33ff.; also Cabot, vol. i, p. 65.

10 – *Journals*, vol. i, 'South View of Harvard College Yard from Craigie Road, 1823', facing p. 264.

11 – E.g., *ibid.*, p. 160: 'I dedicate my book to the Spirit of America. I dedicate it to that living soul, which doth exist somewhere beyond the Fancy, to whom the Divinity hath assigned the care of this bright corner of the Universe.'

12 – Cabot, vol. i, ch. ii, p. 54.

13 – *Journals*, vol. ii, p. 13 for 'Books and Men'; p. 18 for 'Civilisation, Moral'; p. 19 for 'Society or Solitude?'; p. 21 for 'Time'; and p. 22–3 for 'Fragment for a Sermon. God Within'.

14 – *Ibid.*, p. 13: 'In so great a mass of works, doubtless every appetite must be suited, and so we find a portion which seems specially intended for coxcombs and deficient persons. To this department belong the **greatest** parts of Novels and Romances, and all that part of the English Drama which is called Living Plays . . . '

15 – *Ibid.*, vol. i, p. 360.

16 – For the 'signal defect' and in what it consisted, *ibid.*, pp. 361–2; the words 'address' and 'sympathies' are italicised in the original.

17 – *Ibid.*, p. 362.

18 – *Ibid.*, p. 365.

19 – *Ibid.*, vol. ii, p. 251, which has no ellipsis between 'mind?' and 'The Kingdom'.

20 – *Ibid.*, p. 77.

21 – *Ibid.*, pp. 214–15, which has: '. . . such as no other **agent** in the universe has'; the sentence concludes: 'if he would exhibit that, it must needs be engaging, a curious study to every inquisitive mind.'

22 – *Ibid.*, p. 310, extracted.

23 – *Ibid.*, p. 444n., concerning Emerson's close friend George Partridge Bradford of Duxbury, which has: 'so modest and sensitive' and ' . . . classes of young ladies'.

24 – *Ibid.*, p. 387, which the editors of the *Journals* annotate: 'The image was borrowed from Mme de Staël, quoted by Mr Emerson in the beginning of the chapter "Literature" in *English Traits*: "I tramp in the mire with wooden shoes whenever they would force me into the clouds."'

25 – *Ibid.*, p. 401, on 'The Right Word'.

'Mrs Gaskell'

From what one can gather of Mrs Gaskell's[2] nature, she would not have liked Mrs Chadwick's book. A cultivated woman, for whom publicity had no glamour, with a keen sense of humour and a quick temper, she would have opened it with a shiver and dropped it with a laugh. It is delightful to see how cleverly she vanishes. There are no letters to be had; no gossip; people remember her, but they seem to have forgotten what she was like. At least, cries Mrs Chadwick, she must have lived somewhere; houses can be described. 'There is a long, glass-covered porch, forming a conservatory, which is the main entrance . . . On the ground-floor, to the right, is a large drawing-room. On the left are a billiard-room . . . a large kitchen . . . and a scullery . . . There are ten bedrooms . . . and a kitchen garden sufficiently large to supply vegetables for a large family.'[3] The ghost would feel grateful to the houses; it might give her a twinge to hear that she had 'got into the best literary set of the day', but on the other hand it would please her to read of how Charles Darwin was 'the well-known naturalist'.[4]

The surprising thing is that there should be a public who wishes to know where Mrs Gaskell lived. Curiosity about the houses, the coats, and the pens of Shelley, Peacock, Charlotte Brontë,[5] and George Meredith seems lawful. One imagines that these people did everything in a way of their own; and in such cases a trifle will start the imagination when the whole body of their published writings fails to thrill. But Mrs Gaskell would be the last person to have that peculiarity. One can believe that she prided herself upon doing things as other women did them, only better – that she swept manuscripts off the table lest a visitor should think her odd. She was, we know, the best of housekeepers, 'her standard of comfort', writes Mrs Chadwick being 'expensive, but her tastes were always refined';[6] and she kept a cow in her back garden to remind her of the country.

For a moment it seems surprising that we should still be reading her books. The novels of to-day are so much terser, intenser, and more scientific. Compare the strike in *North and South*, for example, with the *Strife* of Mr Galsworthy.[7] She seems a sympathetic amateur beside a professional in earnest. But this is partly due to a kind of irritation with the methods of mid-Victorian novelists. Nothing would persuade them to concentrate. Able by nature to spin sentence after sentence melodiously, they seem to have left out nothing that they knew how to say. Our ambition, on the other hand, is to put in nothing that need not be there. What we want to be there is the brain and the view of life; the autumnal woods, the history of the whale fishery, and the decline of stage coaching we omit entirely. But by means of comment, dialogues that depart from truth by their wit and not by their pomposity, descriptions fused into a metaphor, we get a world carved out arbitrarily enough by one dominant brain. Every page supplies a little heap of reflections, which, so to speak, we sweep aside from the story and keep to build a philosophy with. There is really nothing to stimulate such industry in the pages of Thackeray, Dickens, Trollope, and Mrs Gaskell. A further deficiency (in modern eyes) is that they lack 'personality'. Cut out a passage and set it apart and it lies unclaimed, unless a trick of rhythm mark it. Yet it may be a merit that personality, the effect not of depth of thought but of the manner of it, should be absent. The tuft of heather that Charlotte Brontë saw was her tuft; Mrs Gaskell's world was a large place, but it was everybody's world.

She waited to begin her first novel until she was thirty-four, driven to write by the death of her baby. A mother, a woman who had seen much of life, her instinct in writing was to sympathise with others. Loving men and women, she seems to have done her best, like a wise parent, to keep her own eccentricities in the background. She would devote the whole of her large mind to understanding. That is why, when one begins to read her, one is dismayed by the lack of cleverness.

Carriages still roll along the streets, concerts are still crowded by subscribers, the shops for expensive luxuries still find daily customers, while the workman loiters away his unemployed time in watching these things, and thinking of the pale, uncomplaining wife at home, and the wailing children asking in vain for enough of food – of the sinking health, of the dying life of those near and dear to him. The contrast is too great. Why should he alone suffer from bad times? I know that this is not really the case; and I know what is the truth in such matters; but what I wish to impress is what the workman feels and thinks.[8]

So she misses the contrast. But by adding detail after detail in this profuse impersonal way she nearly achieves what has not been achieved by all our science. Because they are strange and terrible to us, we always see the poor in stress of some kind, so that the violence of their feeling may break through conventions, and, bringing them rudely into touch with us, do away with the need of subtle understanding. But Mrs Gaskell knows how the poor enjoy themselves; how they visit and gossip and fry bacon and lend each other bits of finery and show off their sores. This is the more remarkable because she was hampered by a refined upbringing and traditions of culture. Her working men and women, her outspoken and crabbed old family domestics, are generally more vigorous than her ladies and gentlemen, as though a touch of coarseness did her good. How admirable, for instance, is the scene when Mrs Boucher is told of her husband's death.

'Hoo mun be told because of th' inquest. See! hoo's coming round; shall you or I do it? Or m'appen your father would be best?'

'No; you, you,' said Margaret.

They awaited her perfect recovery in silence. Then the neighbour woman sat down on the floor, and took Mrs Boucher's head and shoulders on her lap.

'Neighbour,' said she, 'your man is ded. Guess yo' how he died?'

'He were drowned,' said Mrs. Boucher feebly, beginning to cry for the first time at this rough probing of her sorrow.

'He were found drowned. He were coming home very hopeless o' aught on earth . . . I'm not saying he did right, and I'm not saying he did wrong. All I say is, may neither me nor mine ever have his sore heart, or we may do like things.'

'He has left me alone w' a' these children!' moaned the widow, less distressed at the manner of the death than Margaret expected; but it was of a piece with her helpless character to feel his loss as principally affecting herself and her children.[9]

Too great a refinement gives *Cranford*[10] that prettiness which is the weakest thing about it, making it, superficially at least, the favourite copy for gentle writers who have hired rooms over the village post-office.

When she was a girl, Mrs Gaskell was famous for her ghost stories. A great story-teller she remained to the end, able always in the middle of the thickest book to make us ask 'What happens next?' Keeping a diary to catch the overflow of life, observing clouds and trees moving about among numbers of very articulate men and women, high-spirited, observant, and free from bitterness and bigotry, it seems as though the art of writing came to her as easily as an instinct. She had only to let her pen run to shape a novel. When we look at her work in the mass we remember her world, not her individuals. In spite of Lady Ritchie, who hails Molly Gibson 'dearest of heroines, a born lady, unconsciously noble and generous in every thought',[11] in spite of the critic's praise of her 'psychological subtlety',[12] her heroes and heroines remain solid rather than interesting. With all her humour she was seldom witty, and the lack of wit in her character-drawing leaves the edges blunt. These pure heroines, having no such foibles as she loved to draw, no coarseness and no violent passions, depress one like an old acquaintance. One will never get to know them; and that is profoundly sad. One reads her most perhaps because one wishes to have the run of her world. Melt them together, and her books compose a large, bright, country town, widely paved, with a great stir of life in the streets and a decorous row of old Georgian houses standing back from the road. 'Leaving behind your husband, children, and civilisation, you must come out to barbarism, loneliness, and liberty.'[13] Thus Charlotte Brontë, inviting her to Haworth, compared their lives, and Mrs Gaskell's comment was 'Poor Miss Brontë'.[14] We who never saw her, with her manner 'gay but definite',[15] her beautiful face, and her 'almost perfect arm',[16] find something of the same delight in her books. What a pleasure it is to read them![17]

1 – A review in the *TLS*, 29 September 1910, (Kp C45) of *Mrs Gaskell. Haunts, Homes, and Stories* (Pitman & Sons, Ltd, 1910) by Mrs Ellis H. Chadwick. Reprinted: *B&P*, *W&W*.

2 – Elizabeth Cleghorn Gaskell (1810–65).

3 – Chadwick, ch. XX, pp. 436–7; the description is of Mrs Gaskell's home, The Lawn, at Holybourne, near Alton, Hampshire.

4 – *Ibid.*, ch. XII, p. 251; having established Mrs Gaskell's acquaintance with Dickens, the Carlyles, Thackeray, Samuel Rogers, the Macreadys, Monckton Milnes, Guizot, Archdeacon Hare, F. D. Maurice and Chevalier Bunsen, Mrs Chadwick observes: 'All these invitations show that Mrs Gaskell had got into the best literary set of the day. Having got there, she never let herself slip out of it . . .'; and *ibid.*, ch. I, p. 14, where we are also told that 'Darwin was the model for Roger Hamley in *Wives and Daughters*'.

5 – See 'Haworth, November, 1904' and 'Literary Geography' above, and 'Great Men's Houses', *V VW Essays* and *The London Scene* (1982).

6 – Chadwick, ch. XX, p. 431.

7 – *North and South* (1854–5); John Galsworthy's play *Strife* (1909).

8 – *Mary Barton. A Tale of Manchester Life* (1848), vol. I, ch. 3; (Penguin, 1970), pp. 59–60.

9 – *North and South* (1854–5), Ch. 36; (Penguin, 1970, pp. 372–3).

10 – *Cranford* (1851–3).

11 – Chadwick, ch. IV, p. 63, quoting Lady Ritchie's praise of the heroine of *Wives and Daughters* (1864–6) in *Blackstick Papers* (Smith, Elder, 1908), no. XI, 'Mrs Gaskell', pp. 229–30.

12 – This criticism has not been identified.

13 – Chadwick, ch. XIV, p. 285; Charlotte Brontë writing to Mrs Gaskell on 1 June 1853, a letter incorporated into the third edition, 'Revised and Corrected', of *Gaskell's Life of Charlotte Brontë* (1857).

14 – Chadwick, ch. XIII, p. 259.

15 – *Ibid.*, ch. XIX, pp. 402–3: Lady Ritchie describing Mrs Gaskell on a visit to the Thackerays at Palace Green.

16 – The source of this phrase has not been discovered.

17 – Beneath this article there appeared the following paragraph: 'Miss Gaskell writes from Manchester, September 24: – "Would you most kindly allow me to correct in your columns a false impression that I have 'co-operated' with Mrs Ellis Chadwick in her recent book about my mother, Mrs Gaskell?"'

1911

The Duke and Duchess of
Newcastle-Upon-Tyne

Some one has probably written a story in which the hero is for ever thinking about the dead. It troubles him that people think of them so little. He is always wondering what he ought to do for them. Then he wonders whether it really needs more imagination to believe in the present or in the past. Becoming obsessed by the idea, he spends his life in reading, volume after volume. He discovers that great men had uncles and aunts and cousins. He dives after them, so to speak, and rescues them by the hair of their heads. It is another form of philanthropy. After all, when he comes to think of it, he cares much more genuinely for the late Duchess of Newcastle[2] than for the old woman who cleans his stairs; he thinks about her all day. What else is affection? Indeed, affection for the living is generally a far more hazardous business than this; the living change and lie and drop one; all the arguments, in short, are on his side; and finally, outraged by contact with unreal fugitive flesh-encumbered live people, he draws his razor and departs.

That there is some truth in this unhappy story no one who owns a library will deny. The anonymous author of this book is evidently touched by the feeling. It is that which keeps his narrative so fresh. One can imagine that it makes him uneasy to sit beside books for long; he hears people talking in them, and must let them out. To do this one must get at them, see them, make them talk sense; a fascinating employment, although not without its risks. Fortunately there is generally some obstacle to prevent us from crashing through the little plank on which we stand into the immense abyss; there is the difficulty of language. When the Duke of Newcastle was in exile[3] he was very deeply in debt, but wished to leave Paris. 'That day,' writes the Duchess, 'when we left Paris, the creditors, coming to take their farewell of my Lord, expressed so great a love and kindness for him, accompanied with so many prayers and wishes, that he could not but prosper on his journey.' 'No wonder!' the editor exclaims. 'It is easy to understand that they would be anxious to have a few words with him – perhaps a good many words – and to come to a very clear understanding before losing sight of him. Love and kindness, indeed!'[4] Yet our impression is that the Duchess was subtle in her language, and that the editor is polishing the bloom off. They were formal obsequious citizens, abashed by nobility in distress, and not seedy-looking men in black coats, ready to whip one off in a four-wheeler to the police court. That is the kind of difficulty that makes it heartbreaking sometimes to read of the ancient dead. With all our knowledge of literary history, we do not know what our ancestors thought about writing. Far more direct of speech than we are, not one of their written sentences could have been spoken by the lips. It may be that writing was always connected in their minds with legal business; certainly the style survives in the letters one receives from solicitors, banks, and men of business in general. But, where our formal style is purely vicious, theirs is often beautiful and characteristic, as though the soul were different and not the manner.

Looking about for a modern figure to compare with the first Duke of Newcastle, we find no one who will do. If we could find a rich nobleman, 'amorous in poetry, music, and art',[5] a bit of a poet, though not much of a scholar, we should not find him in command of the army in time of war. He would finance an opera house. But to be born about the year 1592, and to be the fruit of a succession of fortunate marriages, put one in a position which we can barely conceive. Cavendish, going to Cambridge at fourteen, learnt there how to manage horses and weapons; he left at eighteen, finding the food bad and the 'disputations' of the hungry scholars 'wracking' to the brain.[6] Next he visited Savoy, in the suite of Sir Henry Wotton, and began to write verses, like his master;[7] although he 'entirely concealed the scholar under the more taking appearance of the fine gentleman'.[8] His father's death left him very wealthy and a personage at Court. If, for instance, King Charles was making a progress, and passed near Welbeck, Newcastle would invite him to dinner. Ben Jonson would be sent for to write a masque;[9] the country gentry would be called in, and four or five thousand pounds would be spent upon the feasting. In this way he mounted the steps of the peerage, and bought the post of Governor to the King's son. Money, it may be, could do as much for a nobleman now, but he would, surely, have to specialise. Possibly that is where we differ. Owing to the scarcity of rich men and the subjection of the poor, a fortunate human being had space to grow in. We see how gorgeously Newcastle's tastes were fed. With a taste for poetry and art, he had Vandyke, Suckling,[10] and Ben Jonson for friends; with a taste for diplomacy, he served under Wotton, and was in the counsels of his King; with a taste for riding, he became commander of the army in the north against Cromwell. With sublime confidence in the virtues of gentle birth, he made those qualities go as far as they could. 'In acts of courtesy, affability, bounty, and generosity he abounded . . . but the substantial part and fatigue of a general, he did not in any degree understand (being utterly unacquainted with war) nor could submit to.'[11] Having risked his life like a gentleman, he retired like a gentleman to enjoy his music. He chose poets for captains. Davenant was his General of Artillery, 'because he was a poet';[12] the Church was represented by the 'Rev Mr Hudson', who, being 'a very able Divine', became 'Scout Master General of the Army'.[13] Duty to royalty made him waive his own opinion and fight at Marston Moor. '"Happen what may," he declared, "I will not shun to fight; for I have no other ambition than to live and die a loyal subject of his Majesty."'[14] Accordingly, he drove behind the army to Marston Moor, in his state coach and six; having reached the field, he lit his pipe, sank upon the cushions and slept until the attack should begin. Directly he heard the pistols and the shouting, he sprang up, and with a little 'half-leaden sword'[15] belonging to his page, ran three Scots through the body himself. He stayed on the field to the end, and then escaped to Holland. In excuse for his flight, it must be said that he had spent all his fortune, save ninety pounds, upon the cause, and that he had proved that this kind of war wanted a different sort of general. 'His edge, a friend said, had too much razor in it; for he had a tincture of a romantic spirit, and had the misfortune to have somewhat of the poet in him.'[16] It may have been the poet, the comic poet, that fell in love, in Paris, with that eccentric Maid of Honour,[17] Margaret Lucas. It may have been, as the author is inclined to think, his inherited instinct for a good match; why the dead loved and how is one of those points that we finger but leave unsolved. They cannot explain it. Only, so soon after Shakespeare wrote, there must have been people who fell in love for no reason whatever.

Margaret Lucas was not happy at Court. She was often lost in thought. Have snails got teeth? Do hogs have the measles? Why do dogs that rejoice swing their tails? It was a bad habit in the eyes of the French ladies. One of the pleasant things about Newcastle is that he seems to have allowed her to go on with these investigations without bullying her, although she brought him no children. His 'manage' it may be took up all his thoughts. Enraged too, with his great work *A New Method and Extraordinary Invention to Dress Horses, &c.*,[18] he may not have noticed that his wife was making a name for herself with her folios. They are to be seen at the British Museum, but one would be a 'Mountebank in learning',[19] as she has it, to pretend that one has read them. Now and then adventurous editors extract a slim volume, and, lured on by Lamb's praises,[20] a few people in every generation will take them off the shelves. The Duchess had what is called an active mind. It was a dangerous possession if you were a woman and a Duchess and lived in the time of Charles the Second. It was not trained; its gambols were received with explosions of flattery; it could have the run of all the sciences. If a clever Duchess chanced to be vain into the bargain, there was nothing to stop her. '*Ipse dixit*,' the Duke remarked, 'will not serve my turn';[21] the Duchess prided herself upon a still more perfect ignorance. She had only seen Descartes and Hobbes,[22] not questioned them; she did ask Mr Hobbes to dinner once, but he would not come; she knew no French, though she had lived abroad five years; she seldom listened to what was said to her; in short her genius was her own. If she found a spider's web, she did her best to explain it; her maid brought her a chrysalis and she pinched its tail; ideas upon the destiny of mankind came over her in bed; 'John,' she cried, 'I conceive!'[23] and a servant came running with a pen. She was like a child picking a watch to pieces. Sir Thomas Browne[24] had the same kind of curiosity. But she had the misfortune to live either too late or too soon. In Elizabeth's time she might have been one of the select band of learned ladies who were taught Greek; if she were alive now, we should turn her energy on to a thousand committees. Our ancestors were wittier but more cruel than we are. The Society of the Restoration was as intolerant of eccentricity as the society of boys at a public school. The Duchess, with her folio volumes, her odd manner of dress and behaviour, was a laughing stock in London. They called her 'That fool

Madge Newcastle.'[25] The children ran after her coach, so that Mr Pepys, puffing behind them, could only see that it was painted silver where it is usually painted gold.[26]

As I was getting out of my chair ⟨said Count Grammont⟩, I was stopped by the devil of a phantom in masquerade . . . It is worth while to see her dress; for she must have at least sixty ells of gauze and silver tissue about her, not to mention a sort of pyramid upon her head, adorned with a hundred thousand baubles. 'I bet,' said the King, 'that it is the Duchess of Newcastle.'[27]

Thus baited, the Duchess withdrew to contemplate alone in the gardens at Welbeck. She was still full of ideas, but there was no one to listen to her; the Duke was teaching a horse to dance, or at work on a play of his own. If there had been any kind of discussion – a literary society such as we have now in the provinces – something might have come of her ideas. Some practical woman might have educated her daughter. 'The best bred women,' she said, 'are those whose minds are civilest.'[28] 'Women live like Bats or Owls, labour like Beasts, and die like Worms.'[29] Again it is better to be an atheist than a superstitious man. Hunting, she declared, was a cruel sport. But what did it matter if she thought sanely, or chattered about the affections of the loadstone? Nobody listened to her. 'I shall not rashly go there again,'[30] she declared, commenting upon a scene, no doubt a real one, in which she had told certain wives that they were no better than they should be. Easily bored – 'I hate your Fools'[31] – she dismissed dull guests by 'bragging of myself'[32] which so frightened them that they went, calling her heartless and a pedant. Left alone she worked herself into a glow by telling over the praises of posterity.

All this being over, the Duke and Duchess lie beneath their tomb in Westminster Abbey; when we look upon them, we think not of them, but of ourselves, and the mystery of the past. Tombs are milestones to show us how far we have travelled along the invisible way.

1 – A review in the TLS, 2 February 1911, (Kp C46) of The First Duke and Duchess of Newcastle-upon-Tyne (Longmans, Green, & Co., 1910) by 'the Author of A Life of Kenelm Digby' (Thomas Longueville). VW appears also to have used another source, which remains untraced. See also 'The Duchess of Newcastle', IV VW Essays and CR1.

2 – Margaret Cavendish, née Lucas (1624?–74), author of poems, plays and other miscellaneous writings, including The Life of William Cavendish [1592–1676] Duke of Newcastle (1667), the royalist general and authority on horsemanship, whom she had married, as his second wife, in Paris in 1645.

3 – Newcastle left England in 1644, after the battle of Marston Moor, in which he had fought with distinguished courage at the head of 'a troop of gentlemen' (*DNB*), and, as 'the greatest traitor of England' (*ibid.*), was not able to return until the Restoration.

4 – Longueville, ch. XVI, p. 192.

5 – *Ibid.*, ch. III, p. 22, quoting Clarendon's *The True Historical Narrative of the Rebellion and Civil War in England* (1702–4).

6 – *Ibid.*, p. 6; Newcastle was a scholar of St John's College, Cambridge.

7 – Sir Henry Wotton (1568–1639), ambassador and poet.

8 – Longueville, ch. I, p. 7, quoting *Biographia Britannica* (1748).

9 – Ben Jonson (1572–1637) wrote two masques for Newcastle in honour of King Charles: 'Love's Welcome at Welbeck' (1633) and 'Love's Welcome at Bolsover' (1634).

10 – Sir Anthony van Dyck (1599–1641), painter and etcher; and Sir John Suckling (1609–42), poet.

11 – Longueville, ch. VI., p. 73, quoting Clarendon; slightly adapted.

12 – *Ibid.*, ch. VII, p. 77; Sir William D'Avenant (1606–68), created poet laureate in 1638; he was imprisoned in the Tower in 1650–2, gaining his release by the reputed intervention of Milton.

13 – *Ibid.*, p. 78; Michael Hudson D.D. (1605–48), who, having been imprisoned in the Tower in 1647, escaped early the following year to raise a Royalist force in Lincolnshire, Norfolk and Suffolk. This was swiftly defeated by the Parliamentarians at Woodcroft House, Northamptonshire, and Hudson killed.

14 – *Ibid.*, ch. XII, p. 142.

15 – *Ibid.*, ch. XIII, p. 150.

16 – *Ibid.*, ch. VI, p. 74, quoting *Memoires of the Reign of King Charles I* (1701) by Sir Philip Warwick.

17 – To Henrietta-Maria, Queen Consort of Charles I, during 1643–5.

18 – *A New Method and Extraordinary Invention to Dress Horses, and work them, According to Nature by the Subtlety of Art* (1667), not to be confused with Newcastle's first book on this subject, *La Méthode et Invention Nouvelle de dresser les Chevaux* (1657).

19 – The source of this quotation has not been discovered.

20 – Charles Lamb (1775–1834) makes several references to Margaret Cavendish, notably in *Elia*, 1823: in 'A Complaint of the Decay of Beggars in the Metropolis', where he speaks of 'Dear Margaret Newcastle'; in 'Mackery End, in Hertfordshire' where he calls her 'a dear favourite of mine'; and in 'The Two Races of Men', where she is 'that princely woman, the thrice noble Margaret Newcastle'. She is also mentioned in 'Detached Thoughts on Books and Reading' (*Elia*, 1828).

21 – This reference remains undiscovered.

22 – The Duke of Newcastle was a patron of both Descartes (1596–1650) and Hobbes (1588–1670), both of whom are reputed to have dined with him during his stay in Paris (see *The Life of William Cavendish*, ed. C. H. Frith; John C. Nimmo, 1886, p. 197n.).

23 – This quotation remains unidentified.

24 – Sir Thomas Browne (1605–82), on whom VW later wrote; see *III VW Essays*.

25 – Longueville, ch. XXXI, p. 267.

26 – *Ibid.*, p. 270, quoting Pepys's diary entry for 1 May 1667.

27 – *Ibid.*, p. 271, quoting *Memoirs of the Life of Count Grammont* (1714).

28 – Duchess of Newcastle, *CCXI Sociable Letters* (London, 1644), no. XXVI, p. 51, which has: ' . . . wherefore those Women are best bred, whose Minds are Civilest . . . '

29 – The source of this quotation has resisted discovery.

30 – *Sociable Letters*, no. CIII, p. 208, which has: ' . . . and it hath so Frighted me, as I shall not hastily go to a gossiping meeting again'.

31 – Duchess of Newcastle, *Poems and Fancies* (1653), 'Of a Foole': 'I hate your Fooles, for they my Braines do crack, / And when they speak, my Patience's on the Rack'.

32 – *Sociable Letters*, no. CXXII, pp. 243–4, apparently an adaptation.

'Rachel'

According to Mr Gribble the manse and the rectory are under illusions about the stage. Innocent girls and innocent parents dream of a beautiful place in London where genius displays its treasures and virtue is adored. Possibly Mr Gribble, who knows all about France and the stage, is under illusions about England and the rectory. However this may be, it seems hard upon the world that clergymen's daughters should have to be educated publicly. They are responsible for the only fault we find with Mr Gribble's book. The vices are made very plain; the melancholy very dark. 'It was borne in upon her at last, indeed, that she was a shadow pursuing shadows, but the habit of the chase had hold of her, and she could not desist . . . *La pauvre Rachel*! That is the *Leit-motif*.'[2] We can imagine a country clergyman's daughter reading this exclaiming, 'Poor thing! But I'm not a bit like that,' and going up to town as gay as ever.

Leaving the rectory out of the question, however, how far is this fair to Rachel? Was she so vicious and so melancholy? What did her genius mean to her? To make up one's mind about an actress is, of course, the most troublesome of tasks. Mr Gribble is bold – he talks of her 'stage life and her real life'. 'The real individual is only to be discovered after the curtain has fallen and the applause has ceased.'[3] When the curtain fell it is clear that Rachel was generally to be found reckless and demoralised. She went off to supper, and spent the night in dissipation. She scattered rings about the table. She used Musset's swordstick to pick her teeth.[4]

Dipping her lace sleeves in the sauce, she confided to the company that she could not remember a time when she was 'what the world calls innocent'.[5] She drank punch from a spoon already sticky with soup. With one supper for sample we can imagine the rest. We can imagine Grand Dukes jumping on to the dinner-table to stare at her, and Empresses tossing diamonds on to the stage. We can imagine Queen Victoria remarking to her lady-in-waiting, 'Such a nice modest girl'[6] and the great Duke of Wellington paying compliments in broken French![7] We can take all this for granted. But her acting? Can we imagine that?

Upon her acting Mr Gribble has some interesting remarks to make. An actress, he says, does not create; she interprets; and although 'interpretation affords scope for genius as well as talent',[8] it only leaves a little room for the expression of personality. The personality asserts itself when the curtain falls. Here we have the secret of Rachel's sadness; that was why she wept and cried, 'It is because I have to live the life of others and not my own.'[9] But what, after all, is one's 'own life'? Why should we draw these distinctions between real life and stage life? It is when we feel most that we live most; and we cannot believe that Rachel, married to a real man, bearing real children, and adding up real butcher's bills, would have lived more truly than Rachel imagining the passions of women who never existed.

We are taking it for granted, with Mr Gribble, that Rachel had genius as but two or three actresses have ever had it. But even so, it is hard to decide about an actress. Did she mean more when she cried, 'I have lived the life of others' than a poet or a novelist would have meant? In one sense, of course, she did. 'I was thinking,' she said, 'that time would soon carry away every trace of my talent, and that nothing would remain of what had once been Rachel.'[10] But besides the transiency of great acting compared with other forms of art, there is another reason for discontent, we must believe. A great deal that is not felt comes into the life; there is a great deal of pose and bad art. Rachel was a Jewess, the daughter of a pedlar and an old-clothes woman. As a child she jolted about France in the back of her father's cart, and sang at street corners. With his trained eye for business he saw that there was money in her talent. She was taught enough to learn her parts, rinsing the carrots as she read, but for a long time she never read a play through, and when she was famous, she could not answer her own invitations.

Scarcely any one could be less trained or supported to stand the blaze of sudden and violent celebrity. But that was her fate before she was twenty. Her career makes one think of a very ingenious debtor, always finding means at the last moment to pay his creditors. Manners that served very tolerably in the Faubourg St Germain she acquired. She coaxed a great lawyer to spell for her; to those who liked virtue she pretended that she was modesty besieged. She could persuade authors who gave her their books that what she liked best was a quiet hour with the classics. Then she had her supper parties and defined the state of her innocence. Was she real at such times, or was she real when Charlotte Brontë saw her?

I had seen acting before, but never anything like this; never anything which astonished Hope and hushed Desire; which outstripped Impulse and paled Conception; which, instead of merely irritating Imagination with the thought of what *might* be done, at the same time fevering the nerves because it was *not* done, disclosed power like a deep swollen winter river, thundering in cataract, and bearing the soul, like a leaf, on the steep and steel sweep of its descent.[11]

The truth seems to be that one does not stop acting or painting or writing just because one happens to be dining or driving in the Park; only trying to combine the two things often ends disastrously. Perhaps disaster is more common among actresses than among other artists, because the body plays so large a part upon the stage. At any rate, Rachel's experiment ended in something like ruin, if we consider that she died of exhaustion at the age of thirty-seven, having kicked her body round the world, secured no permanent happiness, and outlived her success. Melancholy indeed she was. But surely the seed of that melancholy lay in the thought, not that she had been an actress, leading an unreal life, but that she might have been a greater actress, leading a still more real life. 'I have not been one quarter as great as I might have been. I have talent, but I might have had genius. Ah, if only I had been brought up differently! If I had had different friends around me! If I had lived a better life! What an artist I should have been in that case!'[12] There, surely, is the true cry of sorrow. Her life was so hurried, so mixed; there was so much trash in it, and such enormous ecstasy.

1 – A review in the TLS, 20 April 1911, (Kp C47) of Rachel. Her Stage Life and Her Real Life (Chapman and Hall, 1911) by Francis Gribble.

Rachel, stage-name of Elisa Felix (1820–58), was born in Munf in the Swiss canton of Aargau, daughter of a pedlar, Jacques (or Jacob) Felix and his wife Esther Haya Felix.

2 – Gribble, ch. 1, 'The *Leit-motif*', p. 7.

3 – *Ibid.*, ch. XIII, p. 122.

4 – *Ibid.*, ch. VI, p. 50; Rachel had one of her typically tempestuous and short-lived liaisons with the poet and dramatist Alfred de Musset (1810–57).

5 – *Ibid.*, ch. I, p. 4.

6 – *Ibid.*, ch. VIII, p. 73; see also p. 62 for Rachel's reaction to her encounter with English royalty: 'O, mes amis, que j'ai besoin de m'encanailler!'

7 – *Ibid.*, p. 77: 'Le maréchal duc de Wellington présente ses hommages à Mlle Rachel; il a fait prévenir au théâtre qu'il désirait y retenir sa loge enfin de pouvoir y assister à la représentation pour le bénéfice de Mlle Rachel . . . '

8 – *Ibid.*, ch. XIII, p. 121.

9 – *Ibid.*, ch. I, p. 6.

10 – *Ibid.*, ch. XXI, p. 211; Rachel's thoughts, recorded by the dramatist Ernest Legouve (1807–1903), concern her interpretation of the title role in *Adrienne Lecouvreur* (performed 1849) by Legouve and Eugène Scribe (1791–1861).

11 – *Ibid.*, ch. XIV, p. 133; from the description in *Villette* (1853), vol. II, ch. 23, of Vashti ('Hate and Murder and Madness incarnate, she stood').

12 – *Ibid.*, ch. XXI, p. 213.

1912

The Novels of George Gissing

Let any one who has spent his life in writing novels consider the day which has now arrived for George Gissing. The fruit of his life stands before us – a row of red volumes. If they were biographies, histories, books about books even, or speculations upon money or the course of the world, there would be no need for the peculiar shudder. But they bear titles like these – *Denzil Quarrier, Born in Exile, New Grub Street*;[2] places and people that have never existed save in one brain now cold. They are only novels. It seems that there is genuine cause for shuddering when one's work takes this form. Dead leaves cannot be more brittle or more worthless than things faintly imagined – and that the fruit of one's life should be twelve volumes of dead leaves! We have one moment of such panic before the novels of George Gissing, and then we rise again. Not in our time will they be found worthless.

An interesting letter to Mr Clodd was printed the other day. In it Gissing wrote:

By the bye, Pinker has suggested to me that he should try to get all my works into the hands of some one publisher. I should like this, but I have a doubt whether the time has come yet. There is a curious blending of respect and contempt in the publishers' minds towards me, and I should like to see which sentiment will prevail. If the contempt, one must relinquish ambitions proved to be idle, and so attain a certain tranquillity – even if it be that of the workhouse. I was always envious of workhouse folk; they are the most independent of all.[3]

Respect has prevailed; Messrs Sidgwick and Jackson reprint the eight later works both well and cheaply. One, *Born in Exile*, is to be bought upon railway bookstalls for sevenpence. Nevertheless it is his own word 'respect' that seems to describe the attitude of the public towards him; he is certainly not popular: he is not really famous. If we may guess at the destiny of this new edition, we can imagine that it will find its way to houses where very few novels are kept. Ordinary cultivated people will buy them of course: but also governesses who scarcely ever read; mechanics; working men who despise novels; dons who place him high among writers of English prose; professional men; the daughters of farmers in the North. We can imagine that he is the favourite novelist of a great many middle-aged, sceptical, rather depressed men and women who when they read want thought and understanding of life as it is, not wit or romance. In saying this we are saying also that Gissing does not appeal to a great multitude; the phrase 'life as it is' is always the phrase of people who try to see life honestly and find it hard and dreary. Other versions of life they reject. They are not, perhaps, in the majority, but they form a minority that is very respectable, and perhaps increasing.

If this is at all true of his readers, what shall we say of the writer himself? There is a great difference between writing and reading, and Gissing was a born writer. When a novelist has been dead for some years and his books are gathered together we want as far as possible to stand where he stood; not to be moved by one character or one idea, but to grasp his point of view. His books are very sad; that is the first thing that strikes the reader. The ordinary excitement of guessing the end is scarcely to be indulged in. Conceive the most gloomy, yet natural, conclusion to every complexity, and you are likely to be right. He had, as most novelists have, one great theme. It is the life of a man of fine character and intelligence who is absolutely penniless and is therefore the sport of all that is most sordid and brutal in modern life. He earns, perhaps, a pound a week. He has thrown up his job in an office because an editor has accepted one of his stories. He marries a woman of some refinement; they live in a couple of rooms somewhere off the Tottenham Court Road. In a short time they cannot pay the rent; they move; they sell pieces of furniture; they live off tea and bread and butter; then his books go; all day long, in spite of headache and sore throat, in bitter fog and clinging mist, the wretched man has to spin imaginary loves and imaginary jests from his exhausted brain. He has the additional agony of loving good writing; he can lose himself still in dreams of the Acropolis or in argument about Euripides. His wife leaves him, for the dirt repels her; at last his stuff has become too poor even to sell, and he dies knowing himself beaten on every hand.

Many readers, happily, rebound from their depression when the end is reached, exclaiming, 'After all, this is only one side.' There are quantities of people who have enough money to avoid these horrors; a few who can command luxury. But what Gissing proves is the terrible importance of money, and, if you slip, how you fall and fall and fall. With learning, sensitive feelings, a love of beauty both in art and in human nature – all the qualities that generally (one hopes) keep their possessor somehow afloat – he descended to the depths where men and women live in vast shoals without light or freedom. What a strange place it is – this Nether World![4] There are women as brutal as savages, men who are half animals, women still preserving some ghost of love and pity, men turning a stunted brain upon the problems of their lot. All the things that grow fine and large up here are starved and twisted down there; just as the squares and parks, and the houses standing separate with rooms measured off for different occupations, are shrivelled into black alleys, sooty patches of green, and sordid lodging houses, where there is shelter, but only the shelter that pigs or cows have, not room for the soul. Without money you cannot have space or leisure; worse than that, the chances are very much against your having either love or intelligence.

Many writers before and after Gissing have written with both knowledge and sympathy of the poor. What, after all, is more stimulating to the imagination than the sight of great poverty or great wealth? There was Mrs Gaskell, for instance, and Dickens; a score of writers in our own day have studied the conditions of their lives. But the impressive part about Gissing is that knowing them as he did he makes no secret of the fact that he hated them. That is the reason why his voice is so harsh, so penetrating, so little grateful to the ears. Can any one hate poverty with all their soul who does not hate the poor? 'Some great and noble sorrow,' he writes, 'may have the effect of drawing hearts together, but to struggle against destitution, to be crushed by care about shillings and sixpences ... that must always degrade.'[5] There is no sentimentalism about the fundamental equality of men in his works. Adela Mutimer in *Demos*, gazing at her husband's face opposite her, ponders thus; Gissing must often have thought the same:

> It was the face of a man by birth and breeding altogether beneath her.
> Never had she understood that as now; never had she conceived so forcibly the reason which made him and her husband and wife only in name. Suppose that

apparent sleep of his to be the sleep of death; he would pass from her consciousness like a shadow from the field, leaving no trace behind. Their life of union was a mockery; their married intimacy was an unnatural horror. He was not of her class, not of her world; only by violent wrenching of the laws of nature had they come together. She had spent years in trying to convince herself that there were no such distinctions, that only an unworthy prejudice parted class from class. One moment of true insight was worth more than all her theorising on abstract principles. To be her equal this man must be born again, of other parents, in other conditions of life . . . She had no claims to aristocratic descent, but her parents were gentlefolk; that is to say, they were both born in a position which encouraged personal refinement rather than the contrary, which expected of them a certain education in excess of life's barest need, which authorised them to use the service of ruder men and women in order to secure to themselves a margin of life for life's sake. Perhaps for three generations her ancestors could claim so much gentility; it was more than enough to put a vast gulf between her and the Mutimers. Favourable circumstances of upbringing had endowed her with delicacy of heart and mind not inferior to that of any woman living; mated with an equal husband, the children born of her might hope to take their place among the most beautiful and the most intelligent. And her husband was a man incapable of understanding her idlest thought.[6]

It would have been so much easier to lessen the gulf; so much more graceful to waive the advantages of three generations of gentle birth. But to have the vices of the poor is the way to incite the best kind of pity. The measure of his bitterness is the measure of his love of good.

But there is nothing surprising in the fact that Gissing was never popular. However harsh and censorious people are in their daily actions, they do it unofficially as it were; they shrink from any statement of the creed that makes them act thus. In fiction particularly, which is a relaxation, like golf, they detest anything severe. It is part of their enjoyment to see others looking rosy and thus to feel somewhat rosier themselves. Gissing had no sympathy whatever with this common weakness. 'No, no,' he makes Biffen say in New Grub Street, 'let us copy life. When the man and woman are to meet for the great scene of passion, let it all be frustrated by one or other of them having a bad cold in the head, and so on. Let the pretty girl get a disfiguring pimple on her nose just before the ball at which she is going to shine. Show the numberless repulsive features of common decent life. Seriously, coldly; not a hint of facetiousness, or the thing becomes different.'[7] The novel that Biffen wrote on these lines is, of course, a failure, and eventually he takes his own life upon Putney Heath.

The reader, then, whose pleasure it is to identify himself with the hero or heroine, and to feel in some strange way that he shares their virtues, is completely baffled. His natural instinct is to find fault with the cynicism of the writer. But Gissing is no cynic; the real cynics are the writers who have a trivial merry view of life, and make people easily content and drugged with cheap happiness. What good Gissing finds in human beings is absolutely genuine, for it has stood such tests; and the pleasures he allows them, the pleasures of reading, companionship, and a few comfortable evenings, glow with a warmth as of red-hot coals. His work has another quality that does not make for popularity either. His men and women think. When we seek the cause of his gloom is it not most truly to be found there? Each of the people who from one cause or another has to suffer the worst bruises in the Nether World is a thinking creature, capable not only of feeling, but of making that feeling part of a view of life. It is not gone when the pain is over, but persists in the form of melancholy questionings. What is to be said for a world in which there is so much suffering? By itself this peculiarity is enough to distinguish Gissing's characters from those of other novelists. There are characters who feel violently; characters who are true types; witty characters, bad ones, good ones, eccentric ones, buffoons; but the thinking man has seldom had justice done to him. The great advantage of making people think is that you can describe other relationships besides the great one between the lover and the beloved. There is friendship, for instance; the relationship that is founded on liking the same books, or sharing the same enthusiasms; there is a relationship between one man and men in general. All these, it seems to us, Gissing has described with extraordinary fineness. It is out of these relationships that he makes the texture of his works. Loves have exploded; tragedies have fired up and sunk to ashes; these quiet, undemonstrative feelings between one man and another, one woman and another, persist; they spin some kind of thread across the ravages; they are the noblest things he has found in the world.

Naturally Gissing practised what is generally called the English method of writing fiction. Instead of leaping from one high pinnacle of emotion to the next, he filled in all the adjoining parts most carefully. It is sometimes very dull. The general effect is very low in tone. You have to read from the first page to the last to get the full benefit of his art. But if you read steadily the low almost insignificant chapters gather weight and impetus; they accumulate upon the imagination; they are building up a world from which there seems to be no escape; violence would have the effect of an escape. But thus it comes about that it is difficult to point to any scene or passage and demand admiration. Do we even single out one character among all his men and women to be remembered? He has no Jane Eyres, no Uncle Tobys. But here is a passage that is characteristic of his terse workmanlike prose, glowing at the heart with a kind of flameless fire:

Manor Park Cemetery lies in the remote East End, and gives sleeping places to the inhabitants of a vast district . . . The regions around were then being built upon for the first time; the familiar streets of pale, damp brick were stretching here and there, continuing London, much like the spreading of a disease. Epping Forest is near at hand, and nearer the dreary expanse of Wanstead Flats.

Not grief, but chill desolation makes this cemetery its abode. A country church-yard touches the tenderest memories, and softens the heart with longing for the eternal rest. The cemeteries of wealthy London abound in dear and great associations, or at worst preach homilies which connect themselves with human dignity and pride. Here on the waste limits of that dread East, to wander among tombs is to go hand in hand with the stark and eyeless emblem of mortality; the spirit fails beneath the cold burden of ignoble destiny. Here lie those who were born for toil; who, when toil has worn them to the uttermost, have but to yield their useless breath and pass into oblivion. For them is no day, only the brief twilight of a winter sky between the former and the latter night. For them no aspiration; for them no hope of memory in the dust; their very children are wearied into forgetfulness. Indistinguishable units in the vast throng that labours but to support life, the name of each, father, mother, child, is as a dumb cry for the warmth and love of which Fate so stinted them. The wind wails above their narrow tenements; the sandy soil, soaking in the rain as soon as it has fallen, is a symbol of the great world which absorbs their toil and straightway blots their being.[8]

We are in the habit of throwing faults upon the public as though it were a general rubbish heap, for it cannot bring an action for libel. But to be unpopular is a sign that there is something wrong, or how have the classics come to be the classics? Gissing's public we believe to be a very good public, but it leaves out much that is good in the great public. The reason is that he wrote his best only when he was describing struggles and miseries and noble sufferings like those we have dwelt upon above. Directly he dealt with men and women living at ease he lost his grip; he did not see; directly he changed his sober prosaic prose for a loftier style he was without merit. He had a world of his own as real, as hard, as convincing as though it were made of earth and stone – nay, far more so – but it was a small world. There is no such place as 'the' world; no such life as 'life as it is'. We need only consider the result of reading too much Gissing; we want another world; we take down *Evan Harrington*.[9] Which is true – that misery, or this magnificence? They are both true; everything is true that can make us believe it to be true. Beauty beyond all other beauty, horror beyond all other horror still lie hidden about us, waiting for some one to see them. The thing that really matters, that makes a writer a true writer and his work permanent, is that he should really see. Then we believe, then there arise those passionate feelings that true books inspire. Is it possible to mistake books that have this life for books without it, hard though it is to explain where the difference lies? Two figures suggest themselves in default of reasons. You clasp a bird in your hands; it is so frightened that it lies perfectly still; yet somehow it is a living body, there is a heart in it and the breast is warm. You feel a fish on your line; the line hangs straight as before down into the sea, but there is a strain on it; it thrills and quivers. That is something like the feeling which live books give and dead ones cannot give; they strain and quiver. But satisfactory works of art have a quality that is no less important. It is that they are complete. A good novelist, it seems, goes about the world seeing squares and circles where the ordinary person sees mere storm-drift. The wildest extravagance of life in the moon can be complete, or the most shattered fragment. When a book has this quality it seems unsinkable. Here is a little world for us to walk in with all that a human being needs. Gissing's novels seem to us to possess both these essential qualities – life and completeness – and for these reasons we cannot imagine that they will perish. There will always be one or two people to exclaim, 'This man understood!'

1 – An article in the TLS, 11 January 1912, (Kp C48) marking the publication by Sidgwick & Jackson of a new edition of the works of George Gissing (1857–1903), listing these titles in the following order: *The Odd Women* (1893), *Eve's Ransom* (1895), *The Whirlpool* (1897), *The Unclassed* (1884), *The Emancipated* (1890), *In the Year of Jubilee* (1894), *Denzil Quarrier* (1892) and *Human Odds and Ends* (1898). See also 'The Private Papers of Henry Ryecroft' above; 'The Private Life of Henry Maitland', *III VW Essays*; and 'George Gissing', *V VW Essays* and CR2.
2 – *Born in Exile* (1892); *New Grub Street* (1891).
3 – Gissing to Edward Clodd (1840–1930), banker and author, writing from 13 rue de Siam, Passy, Paris, 7 November 1899; the place of publication referred to has not been discovered. The version of the letter published in *The Letters of George Gissing to Edward Clodd* (Enitharmon Press, 1973), ed. Pierre Coustillas, has: '. . . whether the time has come yet; there is a curious blending . . . ' and 'which sentiment will prevail. If the respect, one ought to be able to make decent terms with a good house; if the contempt . . . '
4 – *The Nether World* (1889).
5 – *New Grub Street*, ch. XXVII; (Penguin, 1968, p. 418): Edwin Reardon's letter to Amy.
6 – *Demos: A Story of English Socialism* (1886), ch. XXVI (Harvester Press, 1972,

pp. 350–1); the ellipsis marks the omission of: '"I go back to London a mechanical engineer in search of employment." They were the truest words he had ever uttered; they characterised him, classed him.'

7 – *New Grub Street*, ch. X; (Penguin, 1968, p. 176).
8 – *Demos*,. ch. XVI, pp. 220–1.
9 – George Meredith, *Evan Harrington* (1861).

Appendices

APPENDIX I

'The English Mail Coach'

'The English Mail Coach', *Guardian*, 29 August 1906, identified too late for inclusion in the main text, is clearly the article for which VW made brief notes, headed 'Auto. of De Quincey', on the last page of MHP, B 1a. In these she records: 'ideas reverberate through his mind | like a person staggering about [the] world. | profoundly garrulous | rather awful & impressive tumultuous words. | death in summer. | [undeciphered word] | words like anthems.' There is, in addition, a distinct similarity between the view of De Quincey expressed here and that in VW's later writings: 'Impassioned Prose', *IV VW Essays*; and 'De Quincey's Autobiography', *V VW Essays* and *CR2*. The works by De Quincey referred to in the present article were periodical publications collected for the first time in *Selections Grave and Gay* (14 vols, James Hogg, 1853–60).

'The English Mail Coach'

That a true book dictates the mood and season in which it shall be read is certainly as simple-minded a statement as that mustard demands to be eaten with beef. The only reason for dragging in such a platitude is that there are certain cases in which we find it somewhat altered or embellished, and then it is possible that it may make the starting point for some reflections radiating in very different directions.

The writings of Thomas De Quincey, for instance, if we may make a selection from that formidable row which shall include the *Autobiography*, and the *Lake Poets*, and *The English Mail Coach*, have the quality of suggesting quite forcibly to each individual reader the circumstances which set them off to the best advantage. Take us out of doors, they seem to plead, read us in a leisurely mood when time is more than usually irrelevant, and supplement the printed page with draughts of generous sunlight. Then we will do our best for you. In a chill atmosphere indoors, certainly, with a clock ticking on the mantelpiece, De Quincey is far from looking his best; and the opinion of the age seems to be – meaning by that, of course, the opinions of two or three elderly people – that the writings of De Quincey are best suited to the taste of the young. But that verdict can be interpreted in more ways than one; and at the present moment the reading that seems most suggestive is that which indicates a youthfulness not of years but of generation. Men who were old in the early days of the nineteenth century enjoyed De Quincey and gave him his fame because their taste in prose was, as we should call it now, 'immature' – that is, it was considerably different from our own. Indeed, to read a page of De Quincey beside a page of Walter Pater or of Stevenson is like picking out of the waste-paper basked some rapid, exuberant sketch which either of these writers might have made in order to get their ecstasies disposed of before setting to work in earnest. We can almost see upon the printed page the stroke that would have run not only through lines and epithets but through whole paragraphs; each sentence, surely, would have been clipped and combed, and the architecture of the whole thing would have been freshly ordered and established. It is sufficiently easy to see all this scored on the page before you; but the fact that it is not easy to read any addition there hints that, after all, the older writer had a great deal of his own to say, although nowadays, maybe, we could teach him how to say it better. Or did not his fault of speech result from causes far too deeply-seated and too intimately connected with his virtues to be drilled into good behaviour by Stevenson and his art of writing?

De Quincey's chief fault at least is one that under other circumstances becomes his chief virtue. He suffers from the gift of seeing everything a size too large, and of reproducing his vision in words which are also a size too large, unless indeed, they are applied as, happily, is so often the case, to emotions which cannot be magnified. But when the nature of his narrative compels him to state certain ordinary facts they become gigantically ridiculous, like boots seen in an elongated mirror; when he laughs you see a pre-historic monster on its hind legs. And it is one of the weaknesses of this copious mind, a sensitive spot in its splendid equipment, that it cannot pass by an allusion or a statement that is capable of further explanation without setting down the whole burden of the story and proceeding to remove the imperceptible pebble, elaborately, from the reader's path. Thus the casual mention of 'my sister Mary's governess' requires three-quarters of a page of small print to explain it, because she was, unfortunately a niece of John Wesley, and De Quincey has views of his own upon the connection between Wesleys and Wellesleys and the evolution of family names in general, and this, to his thinking, is as good a place as another in which to expound them. Different readers may have different standards of morality concerning the faithful reading of notes, but the most lax can scarcely help feeling an uncomfortable twinge at the complete neglect of a star. But it is well worth while to be callous in reading De Quincey, or in the midst of some rushing sentence like that upon the mail coach – 'A fiery arrow seems to be let loose, which from that moment is destined to travel, without intermission, westwards for three hundred miles' – you are suddenly pulled up by the necessity of considering minutely what the effect of such a statement would be upon the mind of a thoughtless American. And the same habit of giving precise and unnecessary information creeps into the text and neutralises all its splendour; as, in the eloquent passage upon the emotions of the young man and woman in the pony-carriage when they see the Royal Mail thundering down upon them, he states that if the man is found wanting the girl 'must, by the fiercest of translations – must, without time for a prayer – must, within seventy seconds, stand before the judgment-seat of God.'

But if his mind is thus painfully contracted by the action of certain foreign substances upon it, the conditions in which it dwells habitually allow it to expand to its naturally majestic circumference. Indeed, De Quincey's writing at its best has the effect of rings of sound which break into each other and widen out and out till the brain can hardly expand far enough to realise the last remote vibrations which spend themselves on the verge of everything where speech melts into silence. The image which affixes itself most easily to his writing is that of an organ booming down the vast and intricate spaces of a cathedral, because there is an obvious relation between De Quincey's use of language and a musician's use of sound; and the sounds which he delights in most are those that suggest vast dimly lighted places, solemn and mysterious, like those ancient cathedrals where the organ speaks with appropriate voice. That beautiful sights and strange emotions created waves of sound in his brain before they shaped themselves into articulate words, and thus

367

suggested words that reproduced sound as well as meaning seems likely, among other reasons, from the frequent and peculiar use that he makes of the word 'orchestral'. Thus to his ear, 'the sea, the atmosphere, the light, bore each an orchestral part in the universal lull'. And his favourite images are those which combine the two ideas of sound and infinite space; as when he stands by the dead body of his sister and hears the 'solemn wind that might have swept the fields of mortality for a thousand centuries', and 'a vault seemed to open in the zenith of the far blue sky, a shaft which ran up for ever'.

His mind seems naturally to haunt the region of clouds and glories; and his voice travels down to us from great heights, reverberating with strange thunders. Such experiments must often fail; and a more self-conscious age will hesitate to run the risk; for a man who looks for stars in broad daylight, and stumbles over a pail, is held, rightly or wrongly, to be an object of ridicule. Still, the generous reader, reading luxuriously in some sheltered garden where the view between hedges is of a vast plain sunk beneath an ocean of air, will find that a page of De Quincey is no mere sheet of bald signs, but part of the pageant itself. It will carry on the air and the sky, and, as words do, invest them with a finer meaning.

APPENDIX II

Apocrypha

The articles in this appendix are listed by Kirkpatrick as 'Doubtful contributions'. They are reprinted here, with summary annotations, for the convenience of readers who may wish to assess for themselves the evidence for and against attributing them to VW. For discussion of those articles also listed as 'Doubtful' by Kirkpatrick but now firmly attributed to VW and incorporated in the main text of this volume, see Editorial Note, pp. xxi–xxiii.

'Social England'

The first volume of the illustrated edition of this excellent work was noticed in the *Guardian* in the autumn of 1902. It carried us from the earliest times of English history to the end of the reign of Henry III. Dealing with so early a period, there was naturally little scope for the illustrations which were to form so great a feature in the complete work. We could not from it give a definite opinion on the plan of the editor or judge of the practical utility of the work. The magnificent volumes before us show clearly the nature of the effort. It is certainly the most successful attempt that has yet been made to popularise English history. In its original form the book was to some extent a pioneer effort. Special periods and subjects were undertaken by special scholars. The old landmarks were discarded. The crises in the growth and development of the people became the dividing lines of the history. The late Mr J. R. Green had set the example. In the present work we have, however, not a mere reproduction of the original volumes increased by a promiscuous collection of pictures. It is an entirely new edition. The list of subjects is enlarged, many new specialists have taken up fresh sections, improvements have been introduced and earlier errors corrected. With the exception of the last volume, which deals with the period from 1815 to 1885, the reigns of kings mark the contents of the volumes, though the chapters in each are independent of royal dynasties.

While enough is told us in a series of most valuable historical sketches by Mr A. L. Smith and Mr A. Hassall to keep us in touch with the ordinary history, the design of the book to show us the social growth of the people is never once lost sight of. It is impossible, however, to describe, much less to criticise, the various chapters in these volumes. The illustrations are no mere adjuncts of the history, but enter into and form part of each era and chapter. It is thus that the work differs from its predecessors. This vast series of illustrations, chosen evidently with infinite pains and excellent judgment, is meant to tell a story, and is of the highest educational value. The editors have also, as in the earlier edition, varied the sections in accordance with the leading features of each era. We have a perfect gallery of portraits of British authors. The literature of each age is dealt with by Professor Saintsbury, who, with Mr Heath, writes also on the development of the English language and of ideas of education. In the earlier volumes, which deal with the period before the age of printing, we have exquisite reproductions of miniatures and scenery from Early English MSS., and in later times Mr Gordon Duff writes most lucidly on the art of printing. We have, too, a long series of pictures which show the steady improvement in printing and the art of woodcutting and engraving. Not the least important, as showing the interest the people took in current politics, is a series of reproductions of contemporary caricatures. Professor Rockstro and Mr Sutherland Edwards write on the history of English music, and through each of the volumes there are numerous illustrations of musical instruments. Dr Charles Creighton writes on Epidemics and Public Health for the earlier period, and Dr D'Arcy Power takes up the narrative in later times. Art, Science, Agriculture, Commerce, Colonial Enterprise, Navigation, the Army and the Navy, and many other sides of the life of a nation are all in their turn dealt with and illustrated, and the result is that we have here a series of volumes which cannot but appeal to all classes of people, since they concern every side of human interest. The volumes are, in addition, embellished with a goodly number of coloured reproductions of famous historical pictures or of celebrated works of art. Messrs Cassell, as well as the editor, are to be congratulated on the completion of the work, which, in our opinion, supplies a universal need.

1 – *Social England: a Record of the Progress of the People. . . . By various writers.* Ed. H. D. Traill and J. S. Mann, illustrated edition. (6 vols, Cassell & Co., 1901–4), reviewed in the *Guardian*, 7 December 1904, and referred to in the Diary, Christmas 1904–31 May 1905, Berg Collection, New York Public Library.

The Story of the Mutiny

Although the form of Mr Forrest's narrative of the Indian Mutiny is new, the substance of it has been known to students for some time in the three substantial volumes of *Selections from State Papers preserved in the Military Department 1857–8*, which he has edited during the last ten years. Those volumes contain selections from despatches, reports, evidence taken at inquiries, and other records of the Government of India; and to them Mr Forrest prefaced two lengthy introductions, in which he told, in the form of a consecutive narrative, the story which was scattered up and down the official records, at the same time supplementing it from many unofficial sources. These introductions he now republishes in a separate form, with many new illustrations, and copious indices which enable the reader to run any of his statements to earth among the *pièces justificatives* of the *State Papers*. They were an excellent piece of work, and their reproduction in a form more accessible to the general public is entirely justified. The narrative given in the text is a collation of practically all the sources of information, official and private, available, many of which (such as the diaries of Captain Fulton and Sir J. Fayter) have never been published before, while the notes either set forth at length, or give sufficient references to, the evidence (often conflicting) on which the narrative is based.

Mr Forrest has spared no pains to secure – by search among published writings, by inquiry among the survivors of the Mutiny, and by topographical examination of the various localities – the highest possible degree of accuracy. He tells his story – which is one of the most thrilling in English history – in a plain and straightforward manner; and if his style lacks distinction, it is not marred by any inartistic attempts to paint in words pictures to which no words can do justice. He tells it, moreover, with good sense and impartiality. The time has now come when it is possible to write a history of the Mutiny without bitterness and personal recriminations. It has not always been possible; nor can it be altogether denied that the events of 1857–8 afforded ground for them. Grave mistakes were undoubtedly made by both civil and military authorities. But, however gravely the Government of India may in some respects have erred, they surely did not deserve so severe a punishment as to be pilloried by persons to whom Sir Charles Napier was an ideal Commander-in-Chief and Lord Ellenborough an ideal Viceroy. Yet that was the retribution which overtook them; and the poisoned pen of the author of the famous 'red pamphlet', and other similar works are responsible for almost as many misapprehensions in the public mind regarding the policy of Lord Canning's Government as the irresponsible rhetoric of Macaulay raised about the administration of Warren Hastings. Of all these disagreeable controversies Mr Forrest allows but faint echoes to be heard. He does not hesitate to criticise where he thinks criticism is due, as in his remarks on the tone of Sir Colin Campbell's instructions to Outram regarding the occupation of the Alum Bagh (which he attributes to the Chief of the Staff, but for which the Commander-in-Chief must be held responsible), or on his refusal to cross the river after the capture of the Kaiser Bagh on 14 March 1858. But his general attitude is one of great reserve, as is natural in a work which, though not official, was originally dated from the India Office.

But while Mr Forrest's work in its original form was entirely praiseworthy, it is open to certain criticisms in the form in which it now appears. For it is not in fact a 'History of the Indian Mutiny' at all. In the first place, Mr Forrest lacks – or, at all events, in these volumes makes no pretension to – those qualities of mind, that power of grasping and laying bare before the reader the deep-lying principles inherent in human events, which are an essential part of the equipment of the historian properly so called. He chronicles and narrates admirably, and when he indulges in comments they are always to the point, but nothing more. And, secondly, he gives almost no account of the all-important political and administrative history of the Mutiny. The book is thus reduced to a chronicle of the military operations. But even as such it is incomplete, for it ends abruptly with the capture of Lucknow in March 1858, and Sir Hugh Rose's campaign in Central India, and the subsequent course of events down to the capture of Tantia Topee in April 1859 (which marked the close of the war), are not even hinted at. Moreover, as a military historian Mr Forrest has certain conspicuous defects, of which the chief is an inability to give a clear general view of the operations as a whole which he is describing. This is doubtless to some extent due to the nature of these particular operations, which, being dominated throughout by considerations not purely strategical – the political necessity of capturing first Delhi and then Lucknow, and the moral necessity of relieving Cawnpore and the Lucknow Residency – interfered with the organic development of the campaign. Mr Forrest rightly concentrates his attention upon Delhi, Cawnpore, and Lucknow; but he fails to impart an air of unity to the *disiecta membra* of the various operations. His narrative, too, is too overladen with details to serve the purpose of a history in the higher sense of the term. But here, again, in dealing with a period in which every day was a tragedy and every man a hero, the narrator is at a disadvantage which only very uncommon gifts could enable him to surmount.

We have made these remarks with no desire to disparage Mr Forrest's achievement. It is within its limitations (which are partly self-imposed) an admirable piece of work, and a storehouse of accurate information regarding deeds and sufferings which will ever remain the pride of our countrymen. And Mr Forrest deserves our hearty thanks for the skill and industry with which he has constructed it.

1 – *A History of the Indian Mutiny, reviewed and illustrated from original documents . . . with maps, plans, and portraits* (3 vols, Blackwood, 1904–12) by Sir George William Forrest (1845–1926); vols I and II were reviewed in the *Guardian*, 22 February 1905; the work is referred to in the Diary, Christmas 1904–31 May 1905, Berg Collection, New York Public Library.

'The Oxford History of Music'

The fifth volume of the *Oxford History of Music* covers the period from C. P. E. Bach to Schubert, a period which is chiefly notable for the revolution in operatic methods effected by Gluck, and the development of purely instrumental forms in the hands of the three great masters, Haydn, Mozart, and Beethoven. Mr Hadow's method is to trace in succession the progress of opera, oratorio, instrumental music, and song. In a work which prides itself on being a history of music rather than of musicians this is clearly the right method, and indeed the only one that can give a continuous view of art forms so widely different in function. It is, perhaps, to be regretted that the history of music is still so largely a history of form. What we should all like to see is a history rather of musical expression, of the sources, and conditions which render possible the 'inspiration' of a noble melody or a striking progression. It may be his attention to the formal side of music which makes Mr Hadow, as it seems to us, understate the immense advance made by Beethoven in musical expression. When once he was out of leading-strings he never repeated himself, but was ever going forward. The earlier masters seem to reach a certain stage of maturity and then to vary but little from the level, high though it may be, to which they have attained. But with Beethoven each fresh composition reflects a fresh emotional mood, and the mood in itself gives a new kind of unity to each composition. Especially is this true of the nine great symphonies. Mr Hadow writes in a scholarly and epigrammatic style, and his criticism is always sane and well balanced.

1 – *The Oxford History of Music*, ed. W. H. Hadow (6 vols, Clarendon Press, 1901–5), vol. v, *The Viennese Period*, noticed in the *Guardian*, 14 June 1905, and referred to in the Diary, Christmas 1904–31 May 1905, Berg Collection, New York Public Library.

'Fenwick's Career'

We have grown accustomed to look to Mrs Humphry Ward for studies of modern life and thought. She has treated, *inter alia*, of religious unsettlement, of social reform, of politics and politicians; and now, true to her reputation, she gives us a study of art and the artistic temperament. *Fenwick's Career* owes something to George Romney. Mrs Ward justifies this – that, and not 'defends', is the word – in a brief preface. Romney's story is well known. The son of a Lake Country carpenter, and himself for some years of his father's trade, he turned to his true vocation. For five years he painted in Westmoreland, and then went to push his fortunes in London, leaving behind him a wife and two children. For the next thirty-five years he saw his wife only twice; the object to which he gave such devotion as was his to give is recorded for all time in the many portraits of Lady Hamilton that testify to his artistic powers. At the end of these years of neglect he returned, an old and stricken man, to the wife he had deserted; she received him, forgave him, and tended him until the end came. To this story Fenwick's presents obvious resemblances and no less obvious differences. He, too, pursues his bent in the face of difficulties; leaves Westmoreland for London; goes there alone while his wife and child remain behind; has a genius for portraiture, which is the foundation on which is built an intimacy between him and his Lady Hamilton. But with him the separation is for only a third of the period of Romney's desertion, and it is involuntary on his part. At most he had prepared the way for it – it was his wife who brought it about. His position with regard to Madame de Pastourelles is as unlike Romney's to Lady Hamilton as Lady Hamilton is to Madame de Pastourelles; and, to add no more, at the end of his twelve years he comes back home, ill and worn indeed, but to be nursed back to vigour and renewed success. It goes without saying that these disjointed bones we have roughly sketched are put each in its proper place, that the skeleton is completed and clothed with flesh with consummate literary skill. Here, as elsewhere, there is no slipshod work, no fine writing; the pen is a servant, never for one instant allowed either to shirk or to domineer, and, further, it is the servant of a remarkably fine, acute, and observant mind. Its chief work is to depict Fenwick. Phoebe, his wife, figures only in the opening and the closing scenes; Lord Findon, the patron of art, and Eugénie de Pastourelle's father, is a subordinate character; Eugénie herself is in conception Fenwick's complementary, and in execution so tenuous and so remote as to be just a little tedious. The rest are cogs to make the story move or padding to round it off, though cogs and padding of the best kind. Mrs Ward may not thank us for finding morals in Fenwick, but, nevertheless, we have found them, and nowhere else do we remember to have seen more strikingly sketched the ease with which a man slips into lying when the truth is inconvenient, the way in which conceit and arrogance make a man his own worst enemy, and the dislocation and confusion which the something wrong in fundamentals brings into a man's whole life and powers, even into those very powers for the sake of which the something wrong has been allowed to arise. For the rest, the book is the creation of Mrs Humphry Ward, which is to say that it is the work of an unquestionably able and accomplished writer, who would be greater if she could convince us that her pictures of what life should be were founded on a deeper and truer grasp of what in the average it is.

1 – *Fenwick's Career* (Smith, Elder, 1906) by Mrs Humphry Ward (1851–1920), reviewed in the *Guardian*, 16 May 1906. Cf. Reading Notes (MHP, B 1a): dated 3 May, with which, however, the article shares neither coincidental phrases nor the damning final judgment: 'a flimsy book: held together by the spun web of words'.

The Last Days of Marie Antoinette

In *The Last Days of Marie Antoinette* which has been translated by Mrs Rodolph Stawell, M. Lenotre has collected a bundle of old pamphlets written by the gaolers, valets, and chambermaids who served Louis and Marie Antoinette during their imprisonments. Such pamphlets, written sometimes in coarse language and lacking form and arrangement, have been dressed by every historian of the time to suit his theory or colour his picture, till one who reads the original sheet finds it 'absolutely unrecognisable'. But 'facts – let us have facts!' cries M. Lenotre; and he has therefore performed a task needing not only research, but restraint, so that every reader can know the truth and be his own interpreter. M. Lenotre takes upon himself only the duty of introducing the speaker, adding notes, and, when it is needed, providing such careful instruction as that conveyed in the plans of the Temple, one of which is constructed for the first time. The testimony of the different witnesses varies very much in value; some wish to illustrate their own virtues, others will not be denied their reflections; but, as a rule, the report they give has about it an unmistakable air of something seen, though seen according to the capacity of the observer. In such a chronicle the only sights are very minute and very homely. We read how Louis found his warders playing dominoes, took them into his own hands, and built little houses with them very skilfully; how he watched the destruction of a wall, and 'broke into a roar of hearty laughter' as each piece fell; how he kept a Tacitus in his bedroom, in which he made his own comment. There are many details, too, of the five schemes that were contributed so patiently by the Queen and Madame Elizabeth to bring them news of the world outside, possibly to arrange an escape; of the dexterous signalling that went on at table beneath the eyes of the officers; of messages written on the paper stoppers of decanters, or pressed into the crumb of bread. But the simplest words and gestures have significance; they are signs of hope or affection or despair, in an atmosphere of such stillness and tension.

Perhaps the most striking of the documents are those of Daujon and of Rosalie Larmorlière; the first was a member of the Commune, and his account is here published in full for the first time; the second was the servant-maid in the conciergerie who attended on Marie Antoinette till the end. From Daujon's tale we realise more than from the others the nature of the storm that raged outside; for it was he who encountered the incredible obscenity of the Parisian mob when they came to the walls of the Temple with scraps of the flesh of the Princess de Lamballe which, they threatened, the Queen was to kiss. Rosalie's history, on the other hand, is perhaps the most vivid of those sordid little chronicles that repeat so carefully the story of dinners and dressings and goings to bed. For over two months Marie Antoinette was so closely imprisoned that it is possible to watch every movement, to judge the effect of every hardship. Her cell was a little low room of about fourteen feet square. The Queen sat by her bed. Two gendarmes with swords and muskets were in the opposite corner and a woman of the people sat between the Queen's chair and the door. She was not allowed to work, and the only occupation she could make for herself was to pull coarse threads from the canvas that served as wall paper and to plait them into a kind of braid. Flowers were forbidden her; she had to beg for linen and for a carboard box in which to keep it – the detail is almost insufferable. And then the poor woman was tormented by sightseers, who forced themselves into her cell, and by the efforts of priest and lady for the good of her soul. Mademoiselle Fouché's account is as piteous as any. 'The Queen had been so long surrounded by snares that she could not yield her confidence so soon.' She would not answer save by a 'look of dignity'. When she was pressed to say whether her visitor might come again she murmured 'As you will.' The good woman came, of course, and brought with her in time the Abbé Magnin. People were astonished by what they called her composure, a vestment of calm left her, relic of queenship perhaps, when the surface show of feeling had been worn away. It was time that such a scene should end.

1 – The work discussed is in fact entitled *The Flight of Marie Antoinette. From the French ... by Mrs Rodolph Stawell* (Heinemann, 1906) by G. Lenotre, and was

reviewed in the *TLS*, 7 November 1907; see *I VW Letters*, no. 389, to Violet Dickinson, 15? October 1907: 'I have got to review a book on Marie Antoinette.'

'Somehow Good'

Mr William De Morgan is becoming a national institution, and, as such, beyond criticism. We do not criticise Somerset House, or Madame Tussaud's, or the Bank. We accept them. And so it is getting to be with the author of *Joseph Vance* and *Alice-for-Short*, and now *Somehow Good*. He is here, and we cannot do without him. The fastidious stranger gazing upon Somerset House for the first time might hint that it had a certain monotony and was undoubtedly long; he might suggest of Madame Tussaud's that her flesh tints were too uniformly happy, or of the Bank that it is richer than any other building. But such remarks would not matter; these historic and necessary institutions would remain to fulfil their functions. Mr De Morgan similarly remains; and, short though the time is since he first appeared, it is difficult to remember what life was like before that advent. What did we read in that dark period? How did we manage at all? Was there not once talk of 'art for art's sake'? Did not the priests and prophets have such catchwords as 'reticence' and 'form'? Well, they are all discredited, and Mr De Morgan reigns instead, and we are at his feet. He has no form and no reticence, and no care for art. He is simply an elderly, wise, humorous, loving observer of life, with a sense of character and a fluent pen, who apparently can reel off a novel of five hundred crowded pages as easily as not. He cares so little for plot that he takes just as it comes the most threadbare commonplace of the melodramatic stage; so little for veracity that he covers the floor of a Twopenny Tube carriage with live wires and makes the train stop at a station that does not exist. But what of that? It does not matter a pin. The only thing that matters is the mind of Mr De Morgan, and that is entirely right and delightful, so that you care nothing for his story, but everything for his puppets and his kindliness and shrewdness and incorrigibly charming mannerisms. He invites you to his comfortably-furnished novel for a weekend among the most conversable entertaining people, and you accept and are enchanted. You would be an idiot if you did not, for Professor Sales-Wilson is there, and Sally too.

1 – *Somehow Good* (Heinemann, 1908) by William (Friend) De Morgan (1839–1917) reviewed in the *TLS*, 2 June 1908. Innovatory ceramic artist, friend of and collaborator with William Morris, Morgan began to write stories shortly before his retirement, in 1905, and the following year published the immediately successful novel *Joseph Vance*, after which he produced, at an almost annual rate, a series of books similarly humorous and leisurely. The review is possibly that alluded to by VW in a letter, albeit dated April 1908, to Lady Robert Cecil: 'I hope De Morgan is done to our liking. I am so sick of writing at this moment!' (*I VW Letters*, no. 405.)

'The Post-Impressionists'

In many ways, Mr Hind is the ideal writer for a book that aims at spreading the underlying idea of Post-Impressionism among a wider public than has hitherto tried to grasp it. He has the light touch and the persuasive manner. His sincerity is undoubted; at the same time he preserves, at any rate, the semblance of impartiality. To doubting Thomases he holds out the hand of the sweetly reasonable Cicerone. 'Just come with me a moment,' he says, in effect, 'and I will tell you a little story of how the Post-Impressionists affected me, and why.' Then gently, almost apologetically, he explains that while the now historic exhibition at the Grafton Gallery came as a shock to most people, his own nerves withstood the strain, because he had had previous experience of the cult in Paris and Berlin. His conversion to Cézanne, Gauguin, and Van Gogh – the leaders of the movement – appears to have come fairly quickly once he was convinced that the appreciation of their art was reconcilable with that of old favourites among the masters; that to Henri Matisse took longer, but he at length learned to understand, if not to love, him; and it follows that the understanding had to be extended to the sculptures of Jacob Epstein and Eric Gill. So the book progresses vivaciously in its plea for the open mind and for recognition of the possibility that Art has still a future before it. Perhaps Mr Hind's best point is concerned with the reconcilability of a taste for Post-Impressionism with that for more conventional forms of artistic expression. He found it possible to reconcile Puvis de Chavannes and Matisse by the simple expedient of altering his point of view. This sounds – and is – simple and sane enough; but it is unfortunately a fact that very few critics of Art have thought it worth while to try it, and we are afraid that the lay opponents of Post-Impressionism never will. Human nature is perverse where preferences in Art are concerned. Nevertheless, this book is eloquent enough to give pause to the most rabid opponent – to make him consider whether he cannot respect even where he cannot like; and it is refreshingly lucid after the confused masses of ethics, mysticism, aestheticism, and Art that have hitherto served, for the most part, for the serious literary criticism of the movement.

1 – *The Post Impressionists* (Methuen, 1911) by C. (Charles) Lewis Hind (1862–1927; editor of the *Academy & Literature*, 1896–1903), noticed in the *Nation*, 14 October 1911. This is almost certainly the piece in the *Nation* alluded to by Vanessa Bell in a letter to VW, dated 20 October 1911 (Berg Collection, New York Public Library), and said to have the approval of both Roger Fry and Ducan Grant. See p. xxiii.

APPENDIX III

'The Golden Bowl' Reading Notes

The following notes are those which VW made while reading Henry James's *The Golden Bowl* (Methuen, 1905) in preparation for her review 'Mr Henry James's Latest Novel' (see p. 22). This was published in the *Guardian* of 22 February 1905, but not at all to the reviewer's satisfaction. ' . . . I want a little base popularity at this moment – ' she began, warming to her discontent in a letter to Violet Dickinson, 'I spend 5 days of precious time toiling through Henry James's subleties [*sic*] for Mrs Lyttelton, and write a very hardworking review for her; then come orders to cut out quite half of it – *at once* – as it has to go into next week's Guardian, and the Parsonesses, I suppose prefer midwifery, to literature. So I gave up 10 minutes, all I had, to laying about me with a pair of scissors: literally I cut two sheets to pieces, wrote a scrawl to mend them together, and so sent the maimed thing off – with a curse. I never hope to see it again. It was quite good before the official eye fell upon it; now it is worthless, and doesn't in the least represent all the toil I put into it – and the book deserved a good and careful review.' (*I VW Letters*, no. 217).

The notes are transcribed from the Reading Notebook B 1a in the Monks House Papers. They begin on folio 10 of the notebook and end on folio 22 and are faced on the verso of folio 9 by the following note: 'Henry James the master of a point of view. Typical Americans & Italians'. The transcription retains the original and, as might be expected in notes of this kind, fairly erratic punctuation. But quotation marks, occasionally opened but not closed (and vice versa), have been provided wherever these are incomplete, with the aid of James's text. The author's cancellations are marked through with a fine line. Square brackets are used to enclose and incorporate into the text of the notes those page references from James's text that VW sometimes leaves in isolation at the start of a new page in her notebook.

The Golden Bowl. Guardian
Henry James.
Methuen: 6/-   7th Feb:

Chap. 1: Roman Prince in Bond Street. Engaged to an American girl. Roman prince poor, noble, with ancestors with romantic names. American girl with a Father who is the 'best man I've ever seen in my life'. 'Americans incredibly romantic.' Father has a city in America wh. he worships. Intends to endow it with a museum – the Prince an object of beauty for the Museum. The Prince conscious of his family history: wishes to contradict if ~~possible~~ need be flatly dishonour the old, by means of Mr Verver's millions & fresh American blood. Goes to see Mrs Assingham who made the match. treats him like some old embossed coin; useless, but priceless.

Chap. 2.17
~~How~~ Why did Mrs A: take the risk of such a marriage? What is there in him that makes her confident? Must always have her with to guide him in case he doesn't see right. English have a moral sense that 'sends you up like a rocket'. Roman without this 'life was multitudinous detail'.
26
Charlotte Stant in London. 'a handsome clever odd girl' coming to stay with Mrs A:
Chap 3/3 1/ wonderful subtlety of description; words quite simple at the end of it ~~but~~ mainly without words, which issue in quite commonplace speech. 33. explains why people say the things they do – which is always a mystery even to the speaker. Prince agrees to go and buy a wedding present with Miss Stant.
Chap. 4. 45
She wants to see the Prince again. But 'what does she want it for?' Ch. Stant come from America? Ch.St. & the Prince had been in love, but had to give it up, because neither had money: had the courage to look the facts in the face: every move like a move on the chess board, which changes the whole course of the game, & we are shown why & how. talk a little impossibly literary. Mrs A. at once recognises 5 different 'cases' deriving from the fact that Ch. Stant is staying with her. Mrs A concludes that Ch: came over to show her heroism in helping her friend through her marriage with the man whom she hoped to marry. Mrs A: determines to matchmake.

Chap. 5
'It was one of those for which you had to be, [63] blessedly, an American
– as indeed you had to be blessedly, an American, for all sorts of things:
so long as you hadn't, blessedly or not, to remain in America;' accumu-
lates touches; 'rubbed with her palm the polished mahogany of the
balustrade, which was mounted on fine iron-work, 18th century
English' sort of refinements wh. an overtired and sleepless hour might
weave, but which daylight shows to have no foundation. Question of
buying a wedding present assumes gigantic proportions. One asks
what's it all about? Maggie 'not selfish enough'. M. Does everything for
herself: Spoils people: believes in them:
6.75. Suave & subtle Italians. Shopman produces the 'Golden Bowl'. a
present for Maggie; lined with crystal, which, possibly, has a flaw,
'might break if one should *want* to smash it!' Prince sees the crack
from the street. result of the morning shopping is that they can give
each other nothing. 'You *must* marry' 'To make you feel better?' 'Well –
it will – '

Part Second VII.87.
Mr Verver at Fawns; entirely modest & and unselfish man attacked in
his billiard room, during a rare 15 minutes of egoism, by a lady who may
wish to marry him.
98.
When Mr V. felt the spirit of the connoisseur quicken in him in one single
magnificent night, he had been a Cortez in Keats Sonnet; a world was left
to him to conquer & that he might conquer if he tried. Sketch of Mrs
Verver, dead, thrown in –
8. 101
Mr Vs. Museum 'a receptacle of treasures sifted to positive sanctity'
carries connoisseurship to genius 'his freedom to see' 'this perception
expanded on the spot, as a flower, one of the strangest, might, at a
breath, have suddenly opened' H.Js. curious overburdened sentences.
Mr V:s re-marriage makes itself felt.
109.9
'So much mute communication was doubtless, all this time, marvellous,
& we may confess to having perhaps read into the scene, prematurely, a
critical character that took longer to develop' The looking a Henry
James paper: all close print, like a serious discourse: Mrs Assingham a
kind of official explainer. Prince's liking for beauty.

119. X.
Henry James like the velvet depths of an engraving compared to the exquisite descriptions of people's faces.
132 invite Ch: to stay.
XI. 135
All talk used for purposes of analysis & self revelation; no epigrams of the ordinary kind. It follows that the talkers must be as subtle as H.J. himself. Mr V. considers the possibility of marrying Ch. not so much for herself, as in order to set M: free from any compunction about him.
12. 148
The proposal; Ch: 'interested' by the refinements of the case apparently: wont decide till she has found out what M. feels.
13. 161
The Prince telegraphs his approval; upon which Ch: consents.
Part 3.172. Chap. 14
At a grand party alone – with the Prince. M. apparently glad to be with her Father. 'Maggie thinks more of Fathers than of husbands' in a crowded evening party they find time to discuss the delicacies of husband & wife Mr Vs. affection for his daughter the greatest of which he is capable. M: *thinks* of him – not of her husband.

15. 187
Mr V: a common benefactor – both to [189] Ch. & the Prince: all in the same boat, which boat is anchored, so that one has to jump out of her occasionally & splash about. this evening is one of those splashes. 'You Ch. 16. 195
'You have to do it all as if you were playing some game with its rules drawn up.' A single HJ sentence enough to illustrate a whole page in an ordinary novel; the effect of the whole accumulation is almost too rich. Mrs A. has to bury her mistake.
17. 203
Ch. & the Prince passive in the hands of Mr V. & M. They had been brought together by American wealth & benevolence against their will. Ch. come Prince waits for M. & Ch. comes in.
Chap. 18. 213
Ch. & Prince both slightly bored with the perfect ease & goodness of their lives. Mr V. & M. spend the day together, wh. naturally sends Ch. to visit the Prince. Ch. & the Prince both 'personages' to the humble Vs. who are proud to possess them. They agree to act in concert. Prince can't

understand his wife – M. & Mr V. are happy: why shouldn't he & Ch. be happy? Agree [222] with a kiss, to take care of Mr Vs & Ms interests. They are so simple.

19. 222.

This development is too delicate even for Mrs A. They must manage it for themselves. Ch. has to represent the family in public. Ch. did the 'worldly' wh. left M. & her father still more together.

20.233

'fine embroidery of thought' M. & Mr V. 'good children' two chapters of solid explanation always follows on any conversation or action.

21. 239

Ch. & the Prince 'we' now, even to Mrs A.

22. 249

Great landscape painter. Loves the rich light colour & harmony. the day, they feel, is 'like a great gold cup' has it a flaw? – Make an expedition to Gloucester together.

23. 259

Always has to sum up his results very cautiously. Is Maggie unhappy? Does Ch. complain?

24. 276.

M. beginning to realise. She misses – has always missed, her husband.

292

'She'll triumph' She never really *had* the Prince; now she's awake, & will have him. She will have to keep her father from her own knowledge. Mr V. really young. Ch. really old. 'Its their mutual consideration all round that has made it the bottomless gulf.' M. began it: wished to be with her father – had to provide her husband with a companion. Pr. didn't really care for Ch. because he had her too easily. M. watching her father for the first faint sign of her noticing. He *won't* notice – She'll die first.

Book. 2. The Princess. 290

Maggie goes home to wait her husband's arrival. This a definite step on her part.

26. 303

M. & Mr V. had sat at home in peace because the others had held the field & braved the weather. All 'very nice' people.

More A greater artist would suggest more without so much analysis. The whole thing an arrangement for Ms peace & happiness.

27. 320

Question whether the Prince should go away with Mr V: M. wants him to suggest going [330] away with her – which he doesn't, waiting for her to suggest it.

28. 337

Maggie gives a party as part of her scheme; & the 2 couples swap in a delightful quartette. drags a little. Why did V. marry? to give M. greater freedom, when, in truth it gave her less.

29. 349

Vague & difficult – What has M. to say to her father? All the harm unselfish people can do each other by their unselfishness. 'We do it all (live) so beautifully' Nothing to do, nothing to want, so they sit & analyse their happiness.

30. 361

Rather drags. Prince & Ch. again stay away. M. asks Mrs A. her opinion is there anything between them? Ms. extraordinary innocence prevented people really from knowing her. Ch & Prince actually now afraid to give up flirting with each other lest it should disturb M! Can Mrs A. denounce M? Mrs A: says its impossible to accuse the Pr & Ch. M: agrees.

31. 376

Mrs As: subtleties. Interest flags. The summer at Fawns the critical point when the lovers will have to take care. Not a book to which one will return unless one wants intellectual exercise – no scenes stand out in ones memory: the whole effect is that of uniform cleverness & closeness of thought.

32. 385

More elaboration. A touch of genius would lighten the whole, but it dont come. M. sends for Mrs A: the crisis has come.

33. 399

'He knew her before I had seen him' too well for M to have been told. The bowl says M. has a crack in it. Then your story has a crack too: Mrs A. lifts it & lets it fall, so that it breaks into three pieces. M. left with the Pr.

34. 418

There have been 2 relationships between P. & Ch. M. had only known of one. 'the coincidence was the sort of thing that happens mainly in novels & plays' HJs little contempt for his own artifice, because it is a little obvious. The shopkeeper came round & told M. that the bowl had a crack & how the Pr a year ago had inspected it. How the Pr & Ch had wished to make it each other presents. The only object M. gains by this scene is that now the Pr knows that she has learnt *not* to know.

35. 434

The P. recognises the change by telling M. & Ch. alone. M. wants the bowl with all happiness in it; 'the too bowl without the crack'. Ch. begins to wish to communicate with M. through her cage door. Ch. hasn't been told.

36. 451

'to feel about them in any of the immediate, inevitable, assuaging ways wd. have been to give them up' M & Ch meet together 'out of the cage' alone, on the terrace in the evening. Ch 'Is there any wrong you consider I've done you?' 'You've received a false impression.' M. denies on her honour that there is anything wrong.

37. 467

M. had lost her first interest, & place, in her fathers heart, her possession of her husband too was challenged. HJ puts in too much. There are muscles which exist, but which we cant see: to draw them in therefore is wrong. a display of his knowledge of anatomy. Show us, rather, the result, & let us trace causes for ourselves. The book might be called a study in unselfishness: how much harm supremely well bred, & finely tempered people may do it [sic] each other; all in fear of hurting each other's feelings.

38. 484

All the characters distinguished ghosts. Prince finds the situation at Fawns too great a strain. Mrs A says that M. has done it: that her Father & Ch. will go: Ch. realises this, & can't stop it. M. goes out to meet Ch. alone again. Ch. I'm tired. Our real life isn't here. Take him home immediately. 'I'm your difficulty'. 'Its always with you that I've had to see him. How I see that you've worked against me!' M. pretends she's failed. Yes she had done all.

40. 514

Ch. & Mr V prepare to leave for America. M. wants Ch. & the Pr. to meet for the last time.

41. 526

Ch. & Mr V on the verge of going come to say good bye. M. tells the Pr. that they are coming. He explains what, during all these months, he has understood 'Only wait till we're alone.' Maggie had saved herself. Ch: never understood her.

42. 538

Last chapter. Mr V. & Ch. come to say good bye. Say it, & go, leaving M & the Pr. at last alone. Now, has it been worth while? What is her reward? Prince comes in. 'I see nothing but *you*' – & the reward is sufficient.

APPENDIX IV

Notes on the Journals

Virginia Woolf's relations with the editors of the journals for which she wrote during the period 1904–12 are variously discussed and documented in the introduction and in the notes to the essays. This appendix provides further background to the journals and their editors, taken as available from the *Newspaper Press Directory* (*NPD*) and other miscellaneous sources, including the *DNB* and John Gross's *The Rise and Fall of the Man of Letters* (Weidenfeld and Nicolson, 1969). Against each periodical are also given details of VW's contributions.

Academy & Literature

Founded as *The Academy* in 1869 and also known as such in the period 11 March 1905 to December 1910. The journal was owned and controlled from 1896 by Pearl Craigie (the novelist John Oliver Hobbes, b. 1867), and acquired on her death in August 1906 by Lord Alfred Douglas. The *NPD* for 1905 describes it as: 'an illustrated review of weekly literature and life' containing 'reviews of books, literary news, and articles on subjects of interest to all readers and writers'. To which was added for 1906: 'its favourable criticism is one of the prizes the author of a book values most, all work being taken strictly on its own merits . . . Specialists in every branch of thought are included among its contributors, and one may feel that its views on any subject are based on a thorough acquaintance with the facts.' VW's contributions: *1905*: 'The Decay of Essay-writing' (25 February); 'Their Passing Hour' (26

August); *1906*: 'The Sister of Frederic the Great' (13 January); 'Sweetness – Long Drawn Out' (28 July).

Cornhill Magazine

Founded in 1860 by George Smith, with W. M. Thackeray as its first editor (it was edited during the period 1871–82 by Leslie Stephen, among whose contributors were Matthew Arnold, R. L. Stevenson, Thomas Hardy and Henry James). The editor in VW's day was the barrister and principal of the publishers Smith, Elder & Co., Reginald John Smith (1857–1916), an Etonian and graduate of King's College, Cambridge, where he took a first in Classics. The *Cornhill* published 'fiction and general literature', each number containing 'in addition to instalments of serial stories by Popular Authors, short stories and articles by the best writers' (*NPD*, 1908). VW's contributions: *1908*: 'The Memoirs of Sarah Bernhardt' (February); 'The Memoirs of Lady Dorothy Nevill' (April); 'John Delane' (June); '*A Week in the White House*' (August); 'Louise de La Vallière' (October); '*The Journal of Elizabeth Lady Holland*' (December).

Guardian

Founded in 1846, and incorporating from 1903 the *Churchwoman*; published by James Bailey. Virginia Woolf's relations with this Anglo-Catholic newspaper are discussed in some detail in the introduction, as are the paper's general policy and contents. With the exception of her obituary of her aunt Caroline Emilia Stephen, all VW's articles in this paper were published in those pages 'under the supervision of the Hon. Mrs Arthur Lyttelton'. VW's contributions: *1904*: '*The Son of Royal Langbrith*' (14 December); 'Haworth, November, 1904' (21 December); *1905*: '*Next-Door Neighbours*' (4 January); 'On a Faithful Friend' (18 January); '*The Feminine Note in Fiction*' (25 January); '*A Belle of the Fifties*' (8 February); 'Mr Henry James's Latest Novel' (22 February); '*Nancy Stair*' (10 May); '*Arrows of Fortune*' (17 May); '*A Dark Lantern*' (24 May); 'The American Woman' (31 May); '*Rose of Lone

Farm' (19 July); 'An Andalusian Inn' (19 July); 'A Priory Church' (26 July); 'The Letters of Jane Welsh Carlyle' (2 August); 'The Value of Laughter' (16 August); *'Lone Marie'* (1 November); *'The Devil's Due'* (1 November); *'The House of Mirth'* (15 November); 'A Description of the Desert' (6 December); *'The Brown House and Cordelia'* (6 December); ' "Delta" ' (13 December); *'The Tower of Siloam'* (20 December); 'A Walk By Night' (28 December); *1906: 'After His Kind'* (10 January); 'The Poetic Drama' (18 April); 'The Bluest of the Blue' (11 July); *'The Author's Progress'* (25 July); 'Portraits of Places' (3 October); *1907:* *'The Private Papers of Henry Ryecroft'* (13 February); *1909:* 'Caroline Emelia Stephen' (21 April). See also Appendix I.

National Review

Founded in 1883, under the editorship of Alfred Austin, assistant editor W. J. Courthorpe. From 1893 it was owned and edited by Leopold Maxse (1864–1932), whose marriage in 1890 to Kitty Lushington (the original for Mrs Dalloway) had been, to some extent, engineered by Julia Stephen. Under Maxse the review became stridently right-wing and almost exclusively political. Politics notwithstanding, Maxse published in 1903 a series of autobiographical articles by VW's father (collected as *Some Early Impressions*, Hogarth Press, 1924). Stephen was no stranger to the review's pages: the greater part of his *Hours in a Library* had appeared there in Austin's day.

Maxse's enthusiastic acceptance of VW's 'Street Music' (March 1905) led her to hope that she had now secured another outlet for her work; but this was not to be and it remained her only contribution to the review.

Speaker

A Liberal weekly founded in 1890. Edited from 1899 to 1906/7 (when it was converted into the *Nation*) by the historian and journalist J. L. Hammond (1872–1949), it was a journal 'of politics, literature, science, art and finance . . . in the front rank of English journalism', advocating 'the great principles . . . common to all sections of the Liberal Party' (*NPD*, 1906). Desmond MacCarthy, one of the older generation in Bloomsbury, began contributing reviews to the *Speaker* in 1903 and became its dramatic critic; he describes it in his memoir 'Apprenticeship' (in *Humanities*, 1953) as 'vigorously anti-Imperialistic'. VW's contributions: *1906*: 'A Nineteenth-Century Critic' (6 January); 'Poets' Letters' (21 April); 'Trafficks and Discoveries' (11 August).

Times Literary Supplement

Founded in 1902, the *TLS* was edited from 1902 to 1938 by Bruce Lyttelton Richmond (1871–1964) whose relations with VW are discussed in the introduction. Richmond was educated at Winchester and at New College, Oxford, where he read classics; he was called to the bar by the Inner Temple in 1897, and appointed an assistant editor of *The Times* in 1899. In the autumn of 1902, he succeeded James Thursfield as editor of the newly founded supplement. VW's contributions: *1905*: 'Literary Geography' (10 March); '*Barham of Beltana*' (17 March); '*The Fortunes of Farthings*' (31 March); 'Journeys in Spain' (26 May); '*The Letter Killeth*' (27 October); '*The Debtor*' (17 November); '*A Flood Tide*' (17 November); '*The Making of Michael*' (17 November); 'Two Irish Novels' (15 December); *1906*: '*The Scholar's Daughter*' (16 February); '*A Supreme Moment*' (16 February); '*The House of Shadows*' (9 March); '*Blanche Esmead*' (23 March); '*The Face of Clay*' (13 April); 'Wordsworth and the Lakes' (15 June); '*The Compromise*' (15 June); '*Mrs Grundy's Crucifix*' (22 June); '*Coniston*' (13 July); *1907*: '*Temptation*' (22 February); '*Fräulein Schmidt and Mr Anstruther*' (10 May); '*The Glen o' Weeping*' (24 May); 'Philip Sidney' (31 May); 'Lady Fanshawe's Memoirs' (26 July); '*The New Religion*'

(6 September); '*A Swan and her Friends*' (14 November); 'William Allingham' (19 December); *1908*: '*The Sentimental Traveller*' (9 January); 'Thomas Hood' (30 January); '*The Inward Light*' (27 February); 'Shelley and Elizabeth Hitchener' (5 March); 'Wordsworth Letters' (2 April); '*The Diary of a Lady in Waiting*' (23 July); 'The Stranger in London' (30 July); 'Scottish Women' (3 September); '*A Room With a View*' (22 October); '*Château and Country Life*' (29 October); 'Letters of Christina Rossetti' (12 November); '*Blackstick Papers*' (19 November); 'A Vanished Generation' (3 December); *1909*: '*Venice*' (7 January); 'The Genius of Boswell' (21 January); '*One Immortality*' (4 February); 'More Carlyle Letters' (1 April); '*Gentlemen Errant*' (15 April); 'A Friend of Johnson' (29 July); 'Art and Life' (5 August); 'Sterne' (12 August); '*Oliver Wendell Holmes*' (26 August); 'A Cookery Book' (25 November); '*Sheridan*' (2 December); '*Maria Edgeworth and her Circle*' (9 December); '*The Girlhood of Queen Elizabeth*' (30 December); *1910*: '*Lady Hester Stanhope*' (20 January); '*Modes and Manners of the Nineteenth Century*' (24 February); 'Emerson's Journals' (3 March); '*Mrs Gaskell*' (29 September); *1911*: 'The Duke and Duchess of Newcastle-upon-Tyne' (2 February); '*Rachel*' (20 April); *1912*: 'The Novels of George Gissing' (11 January).

The article 'Frances Willard' (28 November 1912), published after VW's marriage, is reprinted at the start of *II VW Essays*.

VW also contributed two articles to *The Times* itself: *1909*: 'The Opera' (24 April); 'Impressions at Bayreuth' (21 August).

Bibliography

This list does not include information about the several collections of Virginia Woolf's writings to which reference is made in the annotations. For this information, and for certain other bibliographical references, the reader should consult the list of Abbreviations at p. xxvii.

ESSAYS

The Death of the Moth and Other Essays, ed. Leonard Woolf (Hogarth Press, London, and Harcourt Brace & Co., New York, 1942)

The Moment and Other Essays, ed. Leonard Woolf (Hogarth Press, New York, London, 1947; Harcourt Brace & Co., New York, 1948)

The Captain's Death Bed and Other Essays, ed. Leonard Woolf (Hogarth Press, London, and Harcourt Brace & Co., New York, 1950)

The London Scene (Frank Hallman, New York, 1975; Hogarth Press, London, and Random House, New York, 1982)

OTHER WORKS

Moments of Being. Unpublished Autobiographical Writings, ed. Jeanne Schulkind (Hogarth Press, London, 1976; Harcourt Brace Jovanovich, New York, 1977; revised 1985)

The Complete Shorter Fiction of Virginia Woolf, ed. Susan Dick (Hogarth Press, London, and Harcourt Brace Jovanovich, New York, 1985)

WORKS OF REFERENCE

Virginia Woolf's Reading Notebooks (Princeton University Press, Princeton, New York, 1983) by Brenda R. Silver

Virginia Woolf's Literary Sources and Allusions. A Guide to the Essays (Garland, New York, 1983) by Elizabeth Steele

INDEX

This index is not exhaustive: references to fictional characters in the ephemeral, popular novels which VW reviewed are not entered; fictional characters are otherwise identified in this way: 'Bartlett, Charlotte, E. M. Forster's character . . .' Place names are indexed on a selective basis, according to the frequency of reference and also to their significance to VW. Works are indexed under their author and in the case of biographies, their subject. The notes are indexed selectively, generally only in relation to references in the text. A number of single references to phenomena of interest to readers of VW are also incorporated, e.g. 'Lighthouse, flashes golden pathway, 80'; and the index further includes references under the following heads: Aristocracy; Art; Biography; Criticism; Essay, the; Human Finery; Humour; Letters; Literary Pilgrimages; Music; Novel, the; Poetry; Prose and Women. General references under a given subject are cited last, unless written works are involved, in which case these conclude the entry concerned.

Acres, Bob, Sheridan's character, 307, 313n29

Adams, Mrs (or Miss), E. Hitchener's mentor, 174, 177n4

Addison, Joseph, xviin5, 201

Aeschylus, 26

Agnes, Black, 212, 214n6

Ainger, Alfred: typical 19th-century product, 83; ethical critic, 84, 85; *Lectures and Essays*, review, 83–5, 85n1

Aird, Thomas: friend of 'Delta', 76; ed. *The Poetical Works of David MacBeth Moir*, 77n2

Aldine Press, 245, 248n11

Allen, Dr John, Lady Holland's dependant, 236, 239n25

Allingham, Helen, 156 & n7

Allingham, William: his first impressions, 155; among the great, 155–6; true in the best sense, 156; *William Allingham. A Diary*, review, 154–6, 156n1

America: culpable ignorance of, 17; its unrestrained citizens, 19; and Thackeray, 33; and *Mansie Wauch*, 76; and early English voyagers, 121; and Roosevelt, 204–9; undergraduate life in, Emerson's cause, 336

American Civil War: outbreak of, 19, conclusion of, 20; *The Rivals* during, 20; and Leslie Stephen, 21n1

Andalusia *see under* Spain

Andersen, Hans, 60

Angelico, Fra, 291

Ann, De Quincey's friend, 159, 163n2

Anstey, Christopher: *New Bath Guide*, 160, 152, 154n18

Argyll, 5th Duke of, 195

Aristocracy: and the modern novelist, 79; Lady Dorothy Nevill on, 178–82; and England's future, 179; virtues of, lack of natural gifts among, 180; and the tenantry, 181; and insolent disrespect for art, 182

Aristotle, 288

Foscari, Francesco, Doge, 243, 247n2
Foster, Lady Elizabeth: and Sheridan, 311, 314n51
Fox, Archibald Douglas: *Sir Thomas More*, review, 97–100, 100n1
Fox, Charles James: and Sheridan, 310
France: women in, 211; an image of, 224; and Italy, 273; and the stage, 351, 263
Francis, Sir Philip, 249, 253n4
Frederic, Prince of Wales, 88
Frederick II, Elector Palatine, 266
Frederick III, Emperor, 265
Frederick II of Prussia (Frederick the Great): proposed entrance examination on, 51; essay on his sister, 87–91
French Revolution, 309, 331, 332
Frere, Catherine Frances: ed. *The Cookery Book of Lady Clark of Tillypronie*, review, 301–2, 302n1
Froude, James Anthony: on Jane Welsh Carlyle, 55; *History of England*, and Elizabeth I, 319, 321, 322, 323n1; *My Relations With Carlyle*, 257, 261n2; *Thomas Carlyle: A History of His Life in London*, 57n1.
Ed. *Letters and Memorials of Jane Welsh Carlyle*, 56, 57n1, 261n2
Fry, Mrs: and Lady Hester, 327
Fry, Roger, xii, xvii
Fyvie, John: *Some Famous Women of Wit and Beauty*, review, 61–3, 63n1

Galsworthy, John: *Strife*, and Mrs Gaskell, 341, 344n7
Gaskell, Elizabeth: on the Brontës, 5; surprising that she should be read, and Galsworthy, 341; and the mid-19th century novel, and Charlotte Brontë's world, 342, 343; what a pleasure to read, 344; and Gissing, 357; *Cranford*, 343; *The Life of Charlotte Brontë*, 5, 6, 7, 9n3, n4, 344n13; *Mary Barton*, 342, 344n8; *North and South*, 341, 342, 344n9; *Wives and Daughters*, 344n11.
Mrs Gaskell. Haunts, Homes, and Stories, by Mrs Ellis H. Chadwick, review, 341–4, 344n1
Gaussen, Alice C. C.: *A Woman of Wit and Wisdom*, review, 112–14, 114n1
Gay, John, 212, 214n8
Gell, Sir William: and the Princess of Wales, 197, 200n16
George I, 87
George III, 310
George IV: and Princess Caroline, 198; and Sheridan, 304, 310, 312n11

Gerard, Dorothea: *The Compromise*, review, 110, 110n1
Geryon, mythical character, 158
Gibson, Molly, Mrs Gaskell's character, 343
Giggleswick, Yorkshire, xii
Gilbert, Sir Humphrey: his dying moments, 123, 124n11
Gissing, Algernon: *Arrows of Fortune*, review, 31–2, 42n1
Gissing, George: as Ryecroft, his austerity, 132; scrupulous refinement of, 133; and delightful freedom 134; new edition of his novels, review, 355–61; the fruit of his life, respected, 355; a born writer, with one great theme, 356; and the terrible importance of money, 357; never popular, severe, 358; his characters, and the English method, 359; a world of his own, 360; a true writer, life and completeness, 361, 361n1; *Born in Exile*, 355, 361n2; *Demos*, 357, 360, 361n6, 362n8; *Denzil Quarrier*, 355; *Eve's Ransom*, 361n1; *Human Odds and Ends*, 361n1; *In the Year of the Jubilee*, 361n1; *The Odd Women*, 361n1; *The Nether World*, 361n4; *New Grub Street*, 355, 358, 361n5, n7; *The Whirlpool*, 361n1. *The Private Papers of Henry Ryecroft*, review, xii, 131–4, 131n1
Gluck, C. W.: v. Wagner, 270; *Armide*, 269, 272n2
Goethe, Johann Wolfgang von, 129, 137, 158
Goldsmith, Oliver: and Baretti, 274, 275
Goldoni, Carlo: denounced by Baretti, 273, 275, 247, 248n23
Gordon-Cumming, Miss, 180
Gore House, Kensington, 63, 64n15
Graham, Harry: *A Group of Scottish Women*, review, 211–13, 213n1
Graham, Mrs Henry: *The Tower of Siloam*, review, 79–80, 80n1
Grammont, Count, 349, 351n27
Grand Opera Syndicate, 269, 272n1
Grant, of Laggan, Mrs, Lytton Strachey's relation, 213, 213n1
Grävenitz, Wilhelmine von: could she have existed?, 118; dismissed courtesan, 120. *A German Pompadour* by Marie Hay, review, 117–20, 120n1
Greek: and the woman novelist, 16; and 18th-century women, 113; taught by Leslie Stephen, and read by, 129; Sappho 'quoted' in, 179; and Elizabeth I, 321; and the Duchess of Newcastle, 348, 245
Greeks, the, 332

Waddington, Mary King: *Château and Country Life in France*, review, 222–4, 224n1

Wagner, R.: Gluck, 270; Wagnerians, primitive and scholarly, 271; and Vernon Lee, 277; his overwhelming unity, 289; like Shakespeare 290, 291; VW's taste for, 292n3; *Die Gotterdämmerung*, 292; *Lohengrin*, 291; *Parsifal*, 289, 290, 292; *Die Walküre*, 269, 272n2

Wales, 124, 327

Wales, Princes of *see* Caroline, Queen

Walpole, Horace: Wordsworth on, 185; and Lady Ritchie, 229, 229n7

Walter, John, proprietor of *The Times*, 188, 194n2

Walton, Octavia, 18, 21n8

Ward, Mrs Humphry: and the essentially feminine, 15; peoples the Palace, 179, 183n2, 315; *Fenwick's Career*, App. II, 374–6 & n1; *Lady Rose's Daughter*, 16n3

Warwick, Diana, Meredith's character: and Caroline Norton, 61–3; 64n2–4, 64 n13, n18

Washington, D.C., 18

Watson, Gilbert: *The Voice of the South*, review, 72–3, 74n1

Watson, William: 'Word-Strangeness', quoted, 255, 256n2

Webster, Sir Godfrey: and Lady Holland, 230, 231, 238n12; a monster, 232; restive and impatient, 233; divorced, 234; 238n4

Webster, Lady *see* Holland, Elizabeth, Lady

Wellington, Duke of: and Maria Edgeworth, 317; and Rachel, 352

Welsh, Jane *see* Carlyle, Jane Welsh

Wendell, Sarah *see* Holmes, Sarah

Westbrook, Harriet *see* Shelley, Harriet

Westminster Abbey, 198, 200n26, 349

Whalley, Rev. Thomas Sedgewick, 152, 154n18

Wharton, Edith: *The House of Mirth*, review, 67–8, 68n1

Whistler, James McNeill, 156

Whitbread, Samuel, 196, 199n9

White House, Washington D.C., 204–9

Whitman, Walt, 137, 156

Wilhelmina, Margravine of Baireuth (*sic*): precocious child, 88; enjoyed few happy years, 89; brilliant and volatile 89,

intimacy with Voltaire, affection for Frederick, 90.

Wilhelmina Margravine of Baireuth by Edith Cuthell, review, 87–91, 91n1

Wilkins, Mary E.: *The Debtor: a novel*, review, 16n3, 68–9, 69n1

Wilkinson, Rev. Joseph: *Months at the Lakes*, review, 105–9, 109n1

William the Conqueror, 97

Wirtemberg, Eberhard Ludwig, Duke of, 118, 119

Women: and the 'feminine note', 15–16; are seldom artists, write for women, 16; the American woman, 46–8, as opposed to the English, 48; humour denied to, 58, and to girls, 308; women and children, and humour, 60; famous women, 61–3; E. Barrett's monstrous story, 102; Scottish women, 211–13; slave with thick legs, 212, 214n4; Venetian women, secluded voluptuaries, 246; strikingly modest writers, 316, 317; detested by Lady Hester, 326

Woodham, Dr Henry Annesley: and *The Times*, 190, 194n11

Woods, Margaret Louisa, 16n3

Woodville, Queen Elizabeth, 264, 267n8

Woolf, Leonard: and Henry James, xiii, ix, x, xvii

Wordsworth, Dorothy, 184, 185

Wordsworth, William: Ainger on, 84; on the Lakes, candid and conscientious, 106; and what's seriously important, 107; solemn enthusiast, 108; and Leslie Stephen, 128, 129; as a letter-writer, loathed penmanship, 184; and Coleridge, 184, 185, 186; relationship with Dorothy, 185; upholds sanctity of genius, and immeasurable virtue of poetry, 186; his perfect sincerity, 187; and Lady Holland, 237; and Cambridge, 336; *Essay upon Epitaphs*, 187n9; *Lyrical Ballads*, 184; 'Ode on Intimations of Immortality', 84, 86n8; *Wordsworth's Guide to the Lakes*, review, 105–9, 109n1; *Letters of the Wordsworth Family*, review, 183–7, 187n1

Wordsworth, Mary, 186

Wotton, Sir Henry, 346, 350n7

Wrangham, Francis, friend of Wordsworth, 185, 187n12